Ey Up Adolf

Ey Up Adolf

Neil Whyke

Ey Up Adolf

All Rights Reserved. Copyright © 2011 Neil Whyke

No part of this book may be reproduced or transmitted in any form or by any means, graphic, electronic, or mechanical, including photocopying, recording, taping or by any information storage or retrieval system, without the permission in writing from the copyright holder.

The right of Neil Whyke to be identified as the author of this work has been asserted in accordance with the Copyright, Designs and Patents Act 1988 sections 77 and 78.

Spiderwize
Office 404, 4th Floor
Albany House
324/326 Regent Street
London
W1B 3HH
UK

www.spiderwize.com

The views expressed in this work are solely those of the author and do not necessarily reflect the views of the publisher, and the publisher hereby disclaims any responsibility for them.

ISBN: 978-1-907294-99-0

Author's note

This book is based on a true story as told to me by Edgar and Ann, my mother. On one occasion I commented to Edgar that he was a spy.

"No I wasn't I was just a soldier in the Signals," was his reply.

"You were in civilian clothes with forged documents and behind enemy lines. What would you call it?"

He paused for a moment then said, "I could have been shot, couldn't I?"

This was very typical of his attitude, he did not consider he was doing anything special, just his job as a Signalman.

Ann was a teenager when she first met Edgar while walking her dog on the Herringthorpe Playingfields, a large expanse of grass covered with football pitches in winter and cricket matches in summer. Ann was a secretary/bookkeeper at a furniture shop in Sheffield while her father was a miner at the local pit. She had three brothers, two older, Arthur, who she did not get along with, and Norman then Douglas who was younger by several years.

Edgar was a couple of years older and worked at the Post Office as a messenger. Although only educated at the local secondary school he was always determined to succeed in life.

Ann and Edgar lived in Rotherham, a small town close to Sheffield and mainly dependent on mining and the steel industry for jobs. The centre of the town was dominated by the magnificent church, which could be seen from the surrounding hills, and an open square where the buses used to pick up their passengers. The river Don meandered its way through the centre of the town, crossed by the historical bridge complete with its own chapel. Before the war Rotherham was a bustling, vibrant place with several cinemas, a theatre and its own cattle market although It was quite normal for none of this to be visible in winter when a thick fog descended, fuelled by the thousands of open fires in the terraced houses.

John came from Chapletown, a small village about six miles away, and was employed in the local iron foundry, one of two in the centre of the village. His father worked as a deputy at the local pit and lived in a miner's house. Although John passed the examination his parents would not pay the fees to allow him to go to the nearest Grammar School.

Both Edgar and Ann struggled at times to remember details like names and dates, (they are both around ninety years old after all) so I have used my imagination to fill in while keeping true to the story-line.

Some of the information is based on supposition as I have found it impossible to obtain confirmation either from Edgar's war record or other sources. According to Edgar's war record he never left this country and requests for further information have either been ignored or been replied with 'no further information is available'. My MP even made enquiries on my behalf with no better success.

From the research that I have been able to do I believe Edgar was conscripted into the SOE as they appear to be the only group operating in the area at the time. Unfortunately the SOE headquarters suffered a fire shortly after the war and the records were destroyed. Believe that if you want!

The meetings with the Civil Service are imaginary but included as a useful tool to give the reader necessary information.

When I first heard this story I found it interesting but during the course of researching this book, and talking to Ann and Edgar further, I found it fascinating and I hope you agree.

Neil Whyke

Chapter 1

*T*he specks of dust reflected in the bright sunlight as they swirled on the slight draughts then gradually sank to the floor. Slowly the pale, almost violet light cast by the magnifying glass moved down the page of the local rag, word by word, letter by letter. Even reading the obituary page was a strain and hardly worth the effort because, at eighty four, the number of people Ann knew became less with each passing year.

Exhausted, she was about to give up when the magnifying glass passed over a name. With a jolt she sat up. The light moved back and passed over the words again, 'the beloved wife of Edgar Stanton.' Slowly Ann lowered the paper onto the seat next to her and considered for a moment. Then she made a decision, sixty years was long enough. Ann picked up the telephone. It was a very long time, perhaps Edgar wouldn't remember her. Even in her eighties Ann did not like the idea of being forgotten and her nerve almost failed.

She could hear the phone ringing then a well remembered voice answered, sounding no different to sixty years earlier.

"I have just read about your wife dying and having lost my husband a few years ago I know what it is like." She paused then realised that she had not announced herself. "This is Ann Whyke, I'm not certain if you remember me." She stopped and all she could hear was her own breathing.

At the other end of the line Edgar sat down on the edge of his bed, totally shocked by the voice from his past. "Of course I *remember you, how could I ever forget?" There was a long pause then he continued," Do you still live in the same place?"*

"My mother's old house, yes."

"Would it be alright if I came and visited?"

"Of course. When would you like to come?"

"Straight away, I'll ring for a taxi."

Ten minutes later a white Toyota pulled up outside Ann's house, the driver stepped out and opened the rear door for a frail, slim man with a stick.

Edgar pressed the bell and waited, hearing the ringing inside. He looked around, it had changed very little since the last time he was there.

The door opened and Ann smiled, instantly recognising Edgar. "Come in and I'll make a cup of tea." He turned right and entered the 'front parlour,' the one only used on special occasions.

A few minutes later Ann entered, carrying a tray with two mugs and a plate of biscuits. They sat facing each other, sipping their tea, neither knowing what to say, there was so much. "I was sorry to hear about Rosa," started Ann. "It must have been a shock."

With the ice broken they both started talking, polite nothings at first but gradually the conversation turned to the past. Suddenly Ann stated, "Why did you stop writing? Did you have someone else?"

Edgar jumped, choking on his chocolate biscuit. "What! No! I thought you did when you returned the ring."

"That was because you didn't write, not one letter after your leave. I thought you were too busy chasing around the countryside on your motorbike chatting up all the local floozies." Ann's voice took on a more insistent note. "I was writing every week to Salisbury asking what was the problem but you never once replied."

"I never received them, I, er..." Edgar paused. *"It was a bit complicated but I wasn't in Salisbury at the time, in fact I wasn't even in the country. But I was writing, regularly, lots of them and I was assured that they would get to you."* He stopped and nibbled another bit of his biscuit. Considering what he now knew about Captain Leigh and his shady organisation the letters probably went straight in the bin. They both lapsed into another silence, each studying the surface of their tea.

"I even had a dream," continued Ann, *"you were with a blonde woman and then people kept telling me that you were up to no good, that you'd been.....distracted."*

Edgar sat perfectly still, conflicting thoughts racing around inside his head, a sense of duty, now considered out of date, or setting the record straight with the woman he loved. He made a decision, he had done his duty to the country, now it was his time. He sat back, made himself comfortable and started, *"Look I'll tell you the full story, something I've never told anyone until now, not even Rosa."*

* *

It was one of those hot summer days, blue skies, fluffy white clouds and the sun warm on your back. Ann walked across the wide, grassy expanse of the municipal playing fields, her dog, Daisy, running in front of her.

She sauntered on, only vaguely aware of the group of lads, dressed in their cricket whites, playing nearby. She did not see the bowler charge down, slip, and send the easiest of dolly drops, a ball just waiting to be thumped. The batsman, a slightly built youth with short, light brown hair and an easy smile, took half a stride forward, connected with a resounding 'thunk' and in a blur the ball shot across the grass.

The batsman shouted a warning but it was too late. The ball shot straight towards Ann then hit a tuft and bounced in the air, catching her above the ankle. With a shriek of pain she dropped to the grass.

"Well, done, Edgar lad," said the wicket keeper, "tha's just made cricketing history, the first batsman to bowl a maiden over."

Concerned, Edgar dropped his bat and ran across. Ann looked up with tears streaking down her face and Edgar thought she was the prettiest girl he had ever met.

"I'm really sorry, I didn't mean to hit it at you."

"I sincerely hope not," was the tearful reply.

Edgar held out his hand. "Do you need a help up," desperately hoping the answer would be yes, at that moment there was nothing he wanted more than to hold the dainty hand of this pretty young girl.

After what seemed an eternity Ann smiled, reached up and took his hand. He breathed a sigh of relief. "I'm Edgar Stanton," then in a rush continued, "how's your leg can you walk?"

Ann gingerly tried her weight on the bruised ankle then nodded. "Yes, if you let go of me."

Edgar realised he was still holding her hand so reluctantly let go. "Perhaps I should take you home, just to make sure you are alright." He gallantly took her arm to offer support. From behind he heard chuckles and hoots from his friends.

"Edgar the charmer strikes again."

"What do you mean again? That's the first female hand he's held since his mother used to take him to school."

"You're just jealous. She's very pretty."

Despite his slight tan Edgar could feel his face redden with embarrassment.

Ann announced that she only lived round the corner and that her father would know how to treat the large, red mark that had appeared on her leg. Edgar had not considered having to explain to an irate father how he had come to injure a precious daughter. Suddenly taking Ann home did not seem such a good idea.

"Will your father be in when we arrive?"

"Yes, he'll have had his bath now."

Things were rapidly going downhill. The only job where you had to have a bath immediately you came home was a miner, a tough, hardy and often short tempered breed.

Ann turned off the main road and down a narrow cul de sac, lined with new, red-brick, semi-detached houses, each fronted by a small, neat garden surrounded by a low fence. Edgar was taken aback, subconsciously he had not expected her home to be as nice and middle class, not with her father being a miner.

Half way down Ann opened a gate but Edgar stopped. "Well, you're safely home so I'll get off back."

Ann winced and said in a small, helpless voice, "It's still painful, perhaps you should take me inside."

Edgar's stomach churned at the notion of confronting an angry, red eyed, muscled miner but the idea of being thought a coward was too much to consider.

Immediately the door opened Edgar was aware of the delicious smell of steak and kidney, overlaid with the sweet aroma of warm jam, as a steamed pudding bubbled. Ann marched straight through the small scullery and into the large kitchen, no sign of a limp in her step.

"I'm back and I've brought someone with me."

Edgar sensed, rather than saw, a movement then Ann's father appeared from the large armchair in front of the fire. His smile of welcome froze on his face as he realised the 'someone' was male.

"I've come to apologise," announced Edgar. "I was playing cricket with my work team and I accidentally hit your daughter on the leg with the ball. Naturally I made sure she arrived home

Ey Up Adolf

safely." This little speech was made in the voice he was trained to use when addressing customers, rather than the one he employed with his mates on the cricket field.

Suddenly a small, dark-haired woman wearing a flour-covered apron popped round the door, a welcoming smile on her face, and strategically positioned herself between Edgar and her husband. "Which firm is that?"

"The post office, I deliver telegrams."

"A very respectable and responsible job that," she replied in a very pronounced Geordie twang. Edgar realised that Ann also had the same lilting accent, but not so distinct.

"Since Ann is home safe and sound, I'd better be going," Edgar said and turned to leave.

"Wait a minute," Ann's mother disappeared behind the door, only to return a moment later with a warm, freshly baked scone. "For your trouble."

Edgar mumbled his thanks and retreated, but as he closed the door he heard her say, "What a nice young man and so well spoken." Ann's father's reply was lost as the door shut tight.

Chapter 2

As Edgar entered the imposing swing door that led into the cavernous hall of the Victorian building that was the post office one of the counter staff called, "The Postmaster wants to see you right away ......and I don't think it's about your cricketing skill," he added with a wink.

"Strewth," Edgar thought, "gossip spreads faster than cholera around this place," then his mind started to whirl. "Why does the Postmaster want to see me, what have I done wrong?" Then it struck him, had his little scheme come to the manager's attention. Many of the telegram boys were ex-grammar school and didn't like working at weekends so Edgar would take their shift for the paltry sum of half a crown. Although there was nothing wrong in this it was definitely a very unofficial arrangement.

With some trepidation he walked up to the office and knocked. A stern voice called, "Enter" and he stepped inside. The Postmaster was sitting behind a large, polished oak desk peering at a very important looking document. Edgar's heart sank, was it an official complaint, was he about to be sacked and join the long queue at the dole office?

"Mr Stanton, I have received a report from your superior about your work...."

"Here it comes," thought Edgar.

"...and he is very pleased. As a result he has recommended that you are to be promoted to telegrapher. I understand you

Ey Up Adolf

already have some knowledge of Morse code." At this point he peered enquiringly over his wire framed glasses.

"Er, yes Sir," stammered a relieved Edgar, "I've been interested since I was a small boy so I taught myself from a book."

"Excellent! That should help you overcome the disadvantage of not having a grammar education," replied the manager.

Edgar felt his blood start to boil, how many times was that going to be thrown at him? Had his parents been able to afford it he would have gone to the Grammar School, he was clever enough.

"You start next Monday at Sheffield Head Post Office, nine o'clock sharp and remember that the reputation of this office rides on your shoulders, so I will be watching your progress."

"Thank you and I won't let you down," said Edgar eagerly. He left the office. "No, I certainly won't," the extra wages would mean he didn't have to work weekends.

That evening as he was walking home through the park the person in his thoughts was just stepping down from the bus. Ann was irritable after a long and frustrating journey home from the furniture shop in Sheffield where she worked as a secretary and book keeper. Because the tram was full she had to stand until Attercliffe, usually a smile was enough to persuade a gentleman to relinquish his seat but not today.

Then she had missed her bus from town. As she waited for the next one a telegram boy whizzed past giving her a wolf whistle.

"Cheeky thing," she exclaimed, but secretly enjoying the compliment. This made her think about Edgar. He had seemed polite with a warm and genuine smile and he did speak nicely.

The next bus arrived, she climbed aboard and sat down. Ann was staring in Hastings window when a voice said, "Do you mind if I sit here?" Looking up she saw it was Michael, the boy she sat next to at junior school, the one who had called her a foreigner because of her Geordie accent. She edged along, making room on the hard, worn seat and soon they were deep in conversation.

As the bus passed the chip shop then the row of terraced houses Ann stood up and so did Michael. "I'm meeting some friends for a game of footy. You'll know most of them, they're from the old school." He stood on the platform at the rear of the bus, held onto the bar and leaned out, the wind making his clothes flap around him, squinting into the slipstream.

When the bus stopped they stepped down and saw the group of lads who were all looking at her with obvious appreciation.

"You remember Ann from junior school?" Michael said.

As recognition dawned one of them, David, said in an excruciatingly bad attempt at a north eastern accent, "Whey ay hinnie."

"Ey, up Dave," replied Ann in broad Yorkshire. She started to cross the road heading home. Dave and Michael scowled at each other then both scurried over the road after her. "I thought you were going to play football," she called over her shoulder.

"They'll wait, we'll see you home first," said Dave, hurrying to catch up. "There's some rum folks around these days now they've built that big council estate."

"Ay like you for instance," replied Michael, jostling him out of the way so he could walk next to Ann.

"Mebe, but at least I'm not a snob, going to become a solicitor." Dave tried unsuccessfully to regain his place, failing because of a judiciously placed elbow in his side.

"You two never change do you," answered Ann.

By now they had reached the end of the street where Ann lived. They stood chatting and laughing for several minutes, oblivious to their surroundings especially the burly figure making his way up the slight incline towards them. Suddenly Ann felt a light slap around her head. Turning she gazed up into the angry face of her father, one of his gloves held in his calloused fist.

"Get inside at once," he growled, then rounding on the boys, "and you two can clear off." Without a word or backwards glance they retreated down the hill.

"In!" he repeated.

Tears welling in her eyes, Ann scuttled down the road and into her house. As she burst through the door her mother looked up from the pan she was stirring. "What's the matter, have you had an accident?"

"No, It's him," she sobbed pointing backwards. "I've never been so embarrassed."

Her father followed her into the kitchen, a scowl on his face. "I'll not have you hanging about on street corners like a trollop."

"We were only talking, we weren't doing anything wrong." Ann shouted back.

Realising that this was getting out of control Ann's mother gently shooed her upstairs. "Go and wash your face," then she muttered quietly to herself, "what you need is nice, respectable boyfriend."

Chapter 3

The following Monday Edgar was sitting on the train, his shoes brightly polished, his trousers pressed to a knife-like crease and his shirt freshly starched so that it was as stiff as a board.

Edgar peered out of the window watching the terraced houses and shops give way to the massive, dark canyons formed by the steel works and their attendant offices, with shadows so deep that sunlight never reached the pavement level. The whole area seemed perpetually covered by a fine layer of grit from the smoke belching out of the massive chimneys, a grit that wore away clothes and ingrained itself in the skin of the workers giving them an unhealthy grey colour as if they had a terminal illness.

Eventually the train rattled and clanked its way through the cutting and into Sheffield station, a final blast of steam spreading over the platform like a cloud. Slowly the passengers inched their way out and stepped down from the train.

Edgar made his way up the hill towards the shops and the imposing portals of the post office. Once inside he was met by an old caretaker holding his brush like a soldier on guard duty.

"I'm here for the …"

"Telegraphy course," interrupted the grizzled guardian. "I can tell you know."

"Where do I…."

Ey Up Adolf

"End of the corridor then turn left and, before you ask, toilets are second door down but be careful I've just mopped 'floor."

Shaking his head in wonder Edgar set off but behind him he heard a hesitant voice say, "I'm here…"

"End of the corridor then turn left."

Edgar entered a long room filled with individual desks each containing a telegraph key, a blackboard and a chart showing Morse. Standing at the front of the room was the hairiest man Edgar had ever seen, he had a thatch of coarse black hair on his head, a bushy black moustache and his sleeves were rolled up to reveal arms covered in a mat of black hairs. Intense blue eyes peered out from under thick, overhanging eyebrows. He glared round the room and Edgar thought he was the most intimidating person he had ever met, except Ann's father he added as an afterthought.

"I'm Mr Barry, your instructor. I suppose this is a daft question but have any of you any idea what this is," he asked pointing to a series of dots and dashes on the board.

Edgar waited a few seconds to see if anyone else was going to respond then in a confident voice he replied, "It's the letter 'c'."

He received a nod of approval. "I'm glad one of you has made an effort before coming here."

A feeling of pleasure swelled up inside Edgar, for once not having a grammar education was not a problem, amongst this lot he was king.

*   *

The next morning Edgar arrived at the station then with much clanking the train pulled in. Over the top of the waiting passengers he saw Ann, the slight figure, light brown hair, smiling face and warm eyes. Immediately he felt his heart skip a beat and, ignoring the disapproving frown of the other travellers he called out, "Ann, over here!"

She hesitated at first then, with a clicking of heels on the hard paving stones, she made her way to join him. "Good morning, Edgar, what are you doing here? Not on your way to cripple another unsuspecting young lady I hope?"

With a face that burned hotter than the morning sun and rivalled a poppy for colour Edgar stammered, "No, I'm on a course in Sheffield." Always the gentleman he took Ann's arm and helped her up the step. "Wasn't life wonderful," he thought to himself.

With a jolt they set off and Edgar was sitting next to the girl of his dreams. All he had to do was think of something to say but his mind had gone a complete blank, his mouth had become as dry as the Gobi desert, his tongue was stuck to the top of his palate and his throat had shrunk to the size of a drinking straw. He tried to produce some saliva to lubricate his vocal cords but he might just have well tried to wring wine from a stone. "Erg," was all he managed to say.

"Pardon?" said Ann giving him a quizzical look.

Edgar knew it was no use trying to reply, his vocal cords were paralysed.

"Tickets please," came the conductor's voice as he entered the compartment.

Edgar realised his was in his pocket and started to fumble for it.

"Hurry up," demanded the grumpy conductor. "We'll be in Sheffield before you're ready."

Edgar located the offending ticket and handed it across with a mumbled, "Sorry!" Thankful that he been able to utter these few syllables he smiled, the spell had been broken and now he could talk. "How's your leg?"

Ey Up Adolf

"It's fine now, look." She turned slightly sideways so that Edgar could have a better view of her ankle and the fading yellow bruise and he felt his face start to blush all over again as he gazed at the shapely calf. "The bruise is going. I'm glad because you could see it through my stocking. Talking of which you owe me a new pair."

The rest of the journey flew by and all too soon the train was making its way under the tunnel, with its water soaked brickwork glistening in the early sun, and into Sheffield station.

Carried along by the sea of departing commuters they quickly arrived at the exit where Edgar took his courage in both hands and blurted out hopefully, "Perhaps I could take you to the pictures sometime?"

"How about Saturday? I'll meet you on the corner above the Odeon cinema." She smiled and walked off.

Edgar stood on the pavement, mesmerised, admiring her trim figure as she walked away towards the Moor.

*   *

On Saturday the banks of grey cloud were sweeping over the distant hills of the Pennines like ravaging hordes bursting over a castle wall and a fine, sopping drizzle was descending, soaking everyone and anything in its path. Rivulets of grimy water trickled down the sooty stone walls of the buildings and joined together to stream down the gutters. Even the pigeons sitting on the ledges looked miserable. In fact it was just another typical summer day.

Edgar was standing on the corner of Corporation Street waiting, water was dripping off the peak of his cloth cap and adding to the large wet patch on his gabardine. What he would really like was a trench coat, they looked classy but tough at the same time, the sort of thing that private eyes in the movies wore.

As he gazed around at the greyness, sky, buildings, clothes and people's expressions his mind wandered back to something he had read in the paper about Germany expanding their army and stockpiling weapons ready for an invasion. "Not here," he thought, "who in their right mind would want to invade this sodden, damp, miserable place." Then the sound of clicking heels on the pavement caught his attention, he turned round and all his dismal thoughts disappeared as Ann walked towards him.

She was wearing a long, pale blue skirt which ended just below her calves with a tight waist that emphasised her slimness, a white blouse and it was all covered with a light coat with slightly padded shoulders. To ward off the inclement weather she was holding a small umbrella, to Edgar she was the ultimate in loveliness.

"Hello," he said tugging at something in his pocket that refused to come out into the wet. Eventually he managed to extricate the bar of Cadbury's chocolate and present it. "I hope you like milk chocolate," handing over his offering.

"Thank you," replied Ann with a smile. "The bus was delayed and I was afraid we'd be late meeting the others."

"Others!" blurted Edgar. "What others? I thought this was just us."

"Don't be silly, the rest of the gang are going as well, it's much more fun." Edgar felt crushed. All week he had been imagining this evening, three hours of Ann's undivided attention and now his dream was shattered.

When they reached the front of the queue Edgar asked, "Where do you want to sit?"

"We usually go in the rear circle but if that's too expensive we can go in the stalls."

"No that's fine," he said, mentally working out his resources. If he walked into town each day next week he would be alright, just. He needed to get back to work soon and start making his extra money, between fares to Sheffield and going out his eight shillings a week wages were not going to stretch very far.

At the top of the steps was an usherette with a torch who showed them to their seats.

Edgar sat down, a slight cloud of steam rising from his wet trousers and smiled. This was his idea of perfection. Well almost, he could have been sitting several rows back, right at the rear and the rest of Ann's friends wouldn't be there but he'd make do with this for now.

The lights dimmed and the curtains covering the screen swept back. A large cockerel appeared, crowed and the words PATHE NEWS leapt on the screen. German troops marched past their leader, Hitler, but the voice said that the government had announced that there was no danger to this country. Looking at that army Edgar was not so sure, suddenly a cloud passed across the sunshine of his evening out.

After the film Edgar saw Ann home. As they made their way down the narrow road that led to Ann's house Edgar suddenly had a moment's panic. What was he expected to do at her gate, shake her hand and thank her for a wonderful evening, a gentle peck on the cheek or a proper kiss. Would the effects of his decision be disastrous if he got it wrong? Would she storm off in a paddy because he was not romantic enough or, worse, slap his face for being too forward? Footsteps approaching behind them solved the problem as a voice said, "Watcha Edgar." Turning he discovered Ann's older brother, Norman, following them in. "Come on little sis," he said, opening the gate and leading Ann inside. Half way up the path she turned and called back, "Come round tomorrow afternoon and we can go for a walk," then she disappeared round the corner of the house.

Whistling to himself Edgar strolled back down the road, he could hardly wait for tomorrow to arrive, if he could have speeded up the Earth's spin he would have done so.

*   *

The next months followed the expected pattern, dates at the pictures, walks holding hands, a first kiss then the dreaded tea with the family. Edgar arrived in his best, and only, suit to be met with a warm and welcoming smile from Ann's mother and a forced politeness from her father, who had received a severe warning about his behaviour beforehand.

The growth and pleasure of their relationship was the direct opposite to the feeling in the nation. Every week the news from Germany deteriorated, Hitler was gaining in strength, his armed forces were increasing in might and his speeches were becoming more vociferous. War seemed more and more likely.

By now Edgar was a fully-fledged telegrapher working on the new high speed senders, at one of only four places in the country doing so, earning the princely sum of thirty five shillings a week and was hoping for a further promotion that would enable him to be able to afford the deposit on a house.

When the following year Hitler occupied Czechoslovakia and Britain promised support to Poland if it was invaded Edgar made up his mind. War seemed to be inevitable and if that happened he would join the air force and become a pilot but before that there was a something more important to settle.

He suggested they go out into Derbyshire for the day and so they sat side by side on the hard seats as the train chugged its way into the rolling hills and sheer sided valleys of Derbyshire.

As they walked along the bank of a small stream Ann commented on how quiet Edgar had been all morning and he decided this was the moment. He sat Ann down on a small, grey

Ey Up Adolf

boulder, bent down on one knee and solemnly asked her to marry him.

"Of course I will, I was beginning to think you'd never ask." Edgar climbed to his feet and they huddled together kissing and earning disapproving glares from a passing group of middle-aged ramblers.

When this momentous news was announced both families gave their consent, even though there were some misgivings, but with war being imminent conditions were not normal.

The next day Ann was lying in the bath, enjoying a good soak, when she heard footsteps on the stairs and excited voices, snatches of conversation, "On the radio…" "Poland….." "Hitler's tanks….." "Mr Chamberlain said……"

"What's happened?" Ann shouted.

"It's just been announced on the radio, Mr Chamberlain…." started her mother.

"He's the Prime Minister," interrupted Douglas, her younger brother.

"I know who he is," retorted Ann haughtily.

"Do you?" replied Douglas, "I'm surprised. I thought you only knew about film stars and soppy stuff."

"Shut up! What's been announced?"

"We've declared war on Germany."

"What should I do?"

"Get out of that bath for a start," replied her mother.

Ann stepped out, wrapped herself in a towel then sat on the toilet seat. It wasn't fair, she had just become engaged now this.

*   *

Two weeks later Ann arrived home to find Edgar waiting, a letter clutched in one hand, a brown envelope in the other and a worried expression on his face. She sat down next to him just as Douglas entered.

"Hiya Edgar, do you want to see my new comic?"

"No he doesn't."

"But it's the Hotspur."

"I don't care, why don't you go outside and play football."

"Don't feel like it."

Edgar could sense that Ann was about to lose her temper so intervened. "Douglas, would you do me a favour?"

"What?"

"Nip round to the ironmongers, I need a left handed screwdriver for work." He fished in his pocket and found a shilling. "You can keep the change."

Douglas took the money and disappeared.

"I didn't know they made special screwdrivers for keggies," Ann said.

"They don't. There's no such thing as a left handed screwdriver but it'll keep him out of the way for a bit."

"Just don't expect to see your money again when he finds out."

"It'll be worth every penny for the peace and quiet." He paused, took a deep breath then continued in a serious tone, "I've been called up."

"When?"

"Straight away, Thursday. I have to report for initial training and allocation to a regiment. I'm not allowed to join the air force either."

"Why not?"

"Because I'm a trained telegrapher, I'm going to the Royal Corps of Signals instead."

"It's not fair, I hate that Hitler," she sobbed.

On Thursday Ann stood on the platform at the station watching the train pull out in a cloud of steam and smoke accompanied by the high pitch squeal as the wheels spun on the wet and greasy rails. Edgar was leaning out of the window waving madly as the train disappeared round the bend and Ann wondered if that would be the last time she ever saw him.

She took a deep breath, wiped her eyes, held her head high and set off down the hill towards the town centre. "He'll be home soon," she said to herself, twisting the diamond engagement ring on her finger as she did so. "And the war won't last long, he might never even leave the country. By the time he's finished his initial training Hitler will have realised he has bitten off more than he can chew and surrendered."

Chapter 4

After initial training Edgar found himself on an overcrowded train pulling into the station at Liverpool. Edgar stepped down onto the busy platform, squared his cap, now bearing the badge of the Royal Corps of Signals, and formed up with the rest of his unit. A sergeant came and marched them out of the station and onto a battered, open truck for the short ride to their new home, an abandoned girls' school near Sefton Park.

They had just made their way up the steep, carpetless stairs to a large empty room when a corporal came in and dropped a number of material bags in a heap in the middle of the floor.

"What's this, corp?" someone asked.

"Your beds."

Edgar looked at the thin material then down at the hard, bare floorboards. This was going to be a very uncomfortable night he thought to himself.

"Right, grab one each and fall in."

They all stepped forwards, took one of the bags then shuffled into a line down the middle of the room.

"Follow me."

They all strode from the room and down the stairs, boots clattering on the bare boards. Outside, in the yard, was a large pile of dry straw and a fork.

"Fill your bag, tie it with that string then return to your room."

Understanding dawned, this was to be his mattress, a slight improvement on bare boards but not a lot. As the first soldier drove the fork into the straw there was a scrabbling, a wave flowed across the pile then a large, brown rat shot out. Pursued by the corporal it fled across the yard then disappeared through a hole in the wall. Gingerly the rest of them filled their 'beds,' giving them a good shake to make sure there were no unwanted guests, before tying the ends. Slowly they heaved and tugged their ungainly parcels up the stairs, accompanied by many and varied oaths. Eventually the beds were all in place and they could relax. Edgar 'bagged' his space, sorted his gear then sat down to write to Ann.

"Coming for a jar?" asked the soldier in the next 'bed', a good-looking blond lad called Jimmy Parr.

Along with several others they made their way along the almost deserted streets. "People are reet put off by all this talk of air raids," Edgar said. "Gas bombs tha' knows."

"You don't really believe all that clap-trap do you?" answered Jimmy. "Mind, these gas mask cases are pretty useful." He opened his to reveal a packet of cigarettes and a box of matches but no gas mask. "Stops 'em getting crumpled. Now where's this pub?" Chatting like old friends they continued down the terrace-lined road towards a swinging sign that announced the Nag's Head.

*   *

Ann had just arrived home from work with a dejected look on her face. On Monday she had been transferred by her boss to a new shop they had opened in Rotherham but, today, when she opened her pay packet it was ten shillings short. Her wages were reduced as she no longer had to pay train fares.

"Wey aye, lass what the matter," asked her mother.

Ann collapsed in the arm chair and explained about the cut in wages.

Neil Whyke

"The chiselling skinflints! Typical of Jews." her mother exclaimed, her strict Methodist upbringing preventing her from saying anything stronger. "Right, first thing Monday you hand in your notice."

The next day Ann handed in her notice, much to the annoyance of the manager. On the way home from work that evening Ann bought the local paper. There were plenty of jobs going for shop assistants but very little for a qualified shorthand typist. She was just about to give up when a large advert caught her eye. It was for a private secretary at the ICI offices in Tinsley, half way between Rotherham and Sheffield. She hesitated, surely it would require far more experience than she had, but what the heck, nothing ventured nothing gained. When she arrived home she immediately sat at the table and composed her application which she dropped in the letter box on her way to work the next day.

When she arrived back she found a serious looking mother waiting for her. "I hope you get the job or it's back to college for you. I'm not having you in the house all day, your brothers will just treat you like an unpaid skivvy."

Ann grinned at that and knew it was true. Only the other night her eldest brother, Arthur, had thrown a pair of trousers at her and demanded that she iron them for him as he was going out on a date. Infuriated by his attitude, the assumption that she had nothing else to do and that she would happily agree to his demands, she had left it until the very last second then pressed them with the seam down the side instead of down the front. When he had stormed in asking where his trousers were she had thrown them at him in the same manner that he had done earlier. Seconds later she heard a bellow of rage and Arthur had burst back into the room, his face a beetroot red with anger. Pointing at the offending trousers he shouted, "You've done that on purpose, you'll have to do them again."

Ey Up Adolf

She looked at him with a bemused expression, as if she could not understand why he was annoyed, and in a sweet voice replied, "I thought that was where the crease went these days. Isn't that the latest fashion? I'm certain I read it somewhere."

"You know very well it isn't. I can't go out like this, I'll look stupid."

"We can't have that can we? I'll do them as soon as the iron warms up again."

"What! How long will that take?"

"Ten to fifteen minutes….. then another five to actually iron them."

"Bl….," he stopped, remembering his mother's strict adherence to no swearing. "I can't wait that long, I'll be late, Gladys will be furious." He turned on his heel and stormed out of the door. "I'll remember this," he growled ominously as the door closed behind him.

"So will I," Ann whispered with a satisfied grin. "We might be the weaker sex but we are sneakier and don't forget it." Arthur might be older and stronger but she was quite capable of sticking up for herself.

A week later Ann heard a clatter as a letter fell onto the hard, linoleum floor.

Quickly she scanned the few lines, it was from ICI about the job. She burst through the door into the sitting room and shouted excitedly, "Mum, I've got an interview."

"Of course, lassie, I never expected anything else, they'd be daft lummoxes not to."

Chapter 5

The following morning Edgar woke to the strident voice of a sergeant bellowing, "Wake up you useless imitations of soldiers. You have exactly thirty minutes before I want you assembled outside ready for inspection, so move your miserable carcasses."

Gradually the squad crawled from their mattresses, stretching numerous kinks from their spines as they did so, and began to dress.

Stuart, a squaddie, started scratching at various areas scattered around his torso then peered at the blotchy, red marks. "Look, I think I've got measles."

"Let me have a look," said Tom, a short, dark-haired soldier wearing wire rimmed spectacles. "I used to work in a chemist's before the war; I've seen lots of cases of measles." He leant close to Stuart's stomach, adjusted his glasses for a better look then stood up. "Not measles."

"Chicken pox?" enquired Jimmy helpfully.

"Not that either."

"Well what is it then," asked Stuart irritably.

"Flea bites. Probably from that rat we saw in the straw."

"Fleas, from a rat," spluttered Stuart.

"I remember my teacher at junior school talking about that," said Edgar. "It was how the plague started in London. It killed thousands."

Stuart's face lost its colour. "You mean I'll get the plague."

Ey Up Adolf

"Definitely," added Jimmy, catching on and just managing to suppress a grin. "You'll go all blotchy then burn up."

"Your eyes will pop out and finally you'll turn into a quivering mass of jelly. Horrible it'll be." added Edgar.

"Ignore them," said Tom, taking off his glasses and wiping them on the tail of his shirt. "They're winding you up. There hasn't been a case of the plague in this country for hundreds of years. Just report to the MO and he'll give you some tincture of iodine to dab on. You'll be covered in purple splodges for a week but that's all. You won't even be excused duties."

"I'll get you two for this," threatened Stuart at the retreating backs of Edgar and Jimmy, both convulsed with the giggles.

After a quick wash and gobbled bowl of porridge the squad assembled outside. An officer approached and addressed them.

"Have any of you had any experience with messaging equipment and morse code?" Edgar and Jimmy stepped forwards. "Right you two, report to the main post office in the centre of the city. The rest will accompany the sergeant for basic instruction."

Edgar and Jimmy headed for the street. The bus ride into town was short but occasionally they caught sight of a large ship through gaps in the buildings then they heard the conductor shout, "Oy you two, post office."

They stood looking at the magnificent building in front of them. It was four stories high topped by several long chimneys. On the first and second floors large, square-cut bays butted out proudly from the rest of the wall and some were surrounded by small, railed balconies and protruding from the roof were several box-like gables. Edgar had thought the post office in Rotherham was in a grand building but this knocked its socks off.

They crossed the road, entered the imposing doors and marched up to a corporal. "We've been instructed…" started Edgar.

"Ordered," whispered Jimmy who was more worldly-wise, "we're in the army now, we always obey orders then if it goes wrong it's someone else's fault."

"Ordered," continued Edgar, "to report here."

"Follow me and I'll show you how to send a message."

Edgar opened his mouth to say he had been doing that for years but Jimmy put a restraining hand on his arm and whispered, "Rule two and three, never argue with someone who has stripes and never volunteer."

They were shown into a room that contained several telegraphy sets. Edgar idly tapped at the keys for a few minutes then he heard the door open. Edgar turned and looked up. "Harry!" he exclaimed.

"Edgar lad, what's tha' doin' 'ere?"

"Reporting for instruction."

"Cobblers, there's nowt this lot can learn thee. Tell you what tho' we're short handed and I need somebody that's accurate and quick." As he led Edgar out of the room Barry said, "I'm reet glad to have someone who can speak proper, these scousers all talk queer."

*   *

ICI, a huge chemical and steel conglomerate, were occupying a suite of offices at the headquarters of British Steel and it was through the imposing portals of this building that Ann made her way. She negotiated reception and was shown into an office lined with seats occupied by neatly dressed women, all of whom were much older and more experienced than she was.

She perched on the edge of her seat, her handbag resting on her freshly washed and pressed dark-grey skirt. A door opened, a mature woman stepped out and walked down the office. As she passed Ann tried to smile at her but she marched straight on with an air of confidence that Ann neither felt nor showed, in fact she was ready to get up and leave. Slowly the line moved down as, one after the other, prospective interviewees went in.

Eventually it was Ann's turn and she entered. Seated behind a wooden desk was a small, thin man in a dark grey suit. Despite his stature he gave off an aura of determination and authority, definitely not someone to trifle with. "Good morning, I'm Mr Munroe and I'll be your boss if you get the job," he said, his Scottish accent very prominent, then indicated for Ann to sit on the seat opposite while he re-read her letter of application. "And why do want this job? It's very different to your last one."

Having had a long and tiring day waiting for an interview that she considered was a waste of time Ann saw no reason to be diplomatic. "Because I'm tired of working for skintflint Jews."

Mr Munroe looked at her for a few seconds in silence then burst out laughing, while Ann stared at him in confusion. "You do know that Lord Melchit, the chairman of ICI is, in fact, Jewish." Ann felt her jaw drop in shock and hastily covered her mouth, for once in her life she did not have a ready answer. "Well thank you for your time," he continued. "You will be informed in a few days of my decision."

Ann rose and left, mentally kicking herself for letting her mouth run away with her and spoiling any little chance she may have had. As she closed the door she took a last look at the magnificent office she might have been working in and caught a glimpse of Mr Munroe smiling. What was he thinking, probably 'what an idiot'.

After the door closed Mr Munroe sat back and laughed, that had brightened up a boring and tedious day. He glanced at the pile of letters of application, briefly considered the strengths of the candidates and quickly made a decision. He knew who his new secretary would be.

Chapter 6

The next day Edgar and Jimmy reported to Harry at the post office expecting to be assigned to a station but he shook his head. "We're fully staffed today so we don't need you. Take the day off, look around the city or take the boat across the river Mersey to New Brighton."

Side by side they made their way down to the ferry and bought tickets for the short journey. As the ancient boat chugged away from the pier they looked back and saw the towering warehouses, cranes lining the banks and further up an armed merchantman unloading its cargo, its guns a reminder of the danger sailors faced every convoy.

The ferry pulled up at the New Brighton Pier and they disembarked. Unlike the others, who immediately hurried off towards the town centre, Edgar and Jimmy stood where they were then leant on the pier rail. Edgar had only been to the seaside a few times before and enjoyed watching the waves roll across the small beach. After a few minutes Jimmy heaved himself up straight, adjusted his uniform and said, "Right, enough of the view, what now?"

"I'm parched, it must all this salty air. Let's get a cuppa."

"Good idea."

Further down the pier an old man in a worn, grimy coat was holding a fishing rod, the float bobbing gently in the water below. "Let's ask that old codger where to go."

The man turned and stared at them with piercing grey eyes and a scowl on his face. "I might be old but I'm neither senile

Ey Up Adolf

nor deaf." Then he saw their uniforms and relaxed. "You want a cup of tea?"

"Yes, but somewhere not too expensive," responded Edgar.

The grizzled veteran indicated for them to move closer. "The best two are at the baths café and Woolworths, up in the town, but mind on, both of them charge a deposit on the cups and saucers. At the baths it's five shillings and at Woolies it's five and sixpence, but they both use the same crockery. Now I'm sure a smart couple of lads like you can do something with that information." He turned back to the water and continued watching his float.

Edgar and Jimmy wandered off the pier and headed in the direction of the tallest buildings. "Did you get what he was saying?" asked Jimmy who was quick on the uptake.

"Yes," replied Edgar eagerly, "looks like it's the café at the baths then."

Several minutes later they arrived at the small café, ordered two cups of steaming tea and paid, including the five shillings deposit. For the next half an hour they sipped and chatted about life at home before the war, with Edgar revealing that he was engaged. Jimmy explained that he had contemplated a career as a pianist but this Hitler chap had put an end to that.

Eventually the last dregs of tea had gone and it was time to move. Quickly they stood up, slipped the crockery inside their uniform jackets, scurried through the open door and sprinted down the road.

Five minutes later, hearts still pounding, they were inside Woolworths. When the staff were busy Jimmy picked a tray off the pile. They surreptitiously slipped the cups and saucers from their jackets onto it.

As they reached the head of the queue the matronly lady by the till looked up then asked, "Did you enjoy your tea?"

"Yes, thank you," replied Edgar.

Without another word she pressed a key on the tall, metal till and the drawer shot out. She reached inside and took out a collection of coins. "Enjoy your leave."

"Thank you we will."

Further down the street was a chip shop and they spent their ill-gotten gains on a bag of chips and some scraps, which they devoured eagerly as they walked towards the river.

*   *

Back in Rotherham Ann was reading a letter that had just arrived. With a yell she rushed into the small scullery at the back of the house where her mother was up to her elbows in sudsy water. She turned and raised one eyebrow in enquiry.

"I've got that job, I start on Monday," Ann cried excitedly.

"Never doubted it for a moment," her mother replied.

*   *

On Monday morning Mr Munroe was sitting at his desk wearing a dark, double breasted suit made of expensive worsted and making notes with a gold fountain pen when Mr Turner, a colleague, poked his head round the door. "Your new secretary starting today?"

"You know bloody well she is," the little Scotsman replied. He carefully placed his pen on the blotter, laced his fingers and looked up

"Well that's something you'll have to cut out. You've always had male secretaries before and they didn't mind your foul language but a delicate, well brought up young lady is a different matter. So I've got something to help you." From behind his back he produced a large cocoa tin with a slot cut in the top. "A swear box, a shilling for every obscenity. It'll help you remember."

Ey Up Adolf

"Not bloody likely," Mr Monroe replied, only to have the tin thrust under his nose. Reluctantly he reached in his pocket and removed a silver coin, then on second thoughts he pulled out a selection and placed them in his drawer, near at hand.

*   *

Ann stepped down from the tram, took a deep breath and pushed open the heavy, glass and metal door. The receptionist looked up with a supercilious sneer. "The staff entrance is further down the street."

"I'm sorry, I didn't know, it's my first day," replied Ann. "I'm here to work for Mr Monroe."

"Oh," replied the receptionist. "Upstairs turn left, directors corridor, his name is on the door."

For the first time Ann realised just how far up the pecking order was her new boss. She made her way to the room and timidly knocked on the door. "Don't just stand there, come in," called a voice with a strong Scottish accent. "I don't have all day to wait while you dither aboot. That's your desk over there," he waved his hand across the office. "Now take your coat off then get me a cup of coffee." Ann looked round the room, the glossy wood panelling, the heavy, soundproofed door and the double glazed windows, but she could not see a kettle or any cups. Her boss glanced up. "It comes from the directors' canteen, top floor, just tell them it's for me. And since you look ready for one, get two cups."

Ann took off her coat then made her way to the door. Just before she got there the phone rang, Mr Munroe picked it up then exploded, "Bloody hell!" He glanced in Ann's direction, reached into his drawer, took a coin out, dropped it into a tin on his desk and grumbled under his breath

Ann timidly entered the canteen. "Can I help you, love?" came a voice from her left as a cook appeared.

"I'm Mr Monroe's new secretary and he'd like two cups of coffee."

"I'll have them sent down with some biscuits."

"Biscuits." Ann turned and left, this definitely was another world.

Half way through the afternoon Ann was busy when the door opened and a head popped round. "How's it going?"

Mr Munroe picked up the cocoa tin and threw it across to him. "Take that thing away. She'll just have to get used to it. Either that tin has to go or she does, so the tin is fired."

With a grin Mr Turner closed the door behind him, he had just won ten bob, he had bet that the tin wouldn't last the day.

Chapter 7

In a small office overlooking Whitehall three men sat around a wooden table that was scarred by long usage, one was a typical civil servant, pin-striped suit black, polished shoes and impassive face, and two serving officers.

"Thank you for coming, Colonel," said Mr Baker. "The Prime Minister has asked for an update on our project. He is very keen that the new unit is up and running as soon as possible, it still needs to be kept secret and not only from the enemy. There will be opposition from the service chiefs and the regular intelligence departments." Mr Baker continued in a silky, dry tone, the voice of a political Machiavelli, "Yours will be a dirty little army fighting a very dirty war, but secrecy will still be one of your best weapons. Your actions may be extremely visible but you and your men will not be, in fact you will be completely deniable if anything goes wrong."

The officers nodded in agreement. "Quite. If we are successful we will be a real pain in the enemy's backside. Our proposal is to use irregulars in civilian clothes and dissatisfied locals to lead raids on vital points behind enemy lines."

"How is your plan to identify useful personnel coming along?"

"Very well. In fact we are in the process of trawling through the regular army units for specialised personnel at this moment; Colonel Miller is going to Liverpool this week to inspect the latest communication recruits to see if there are any suitable candidates."

"Excellent. Well keep me informed of your progress. I think that concludes this meeting."

*   *

Two days later Edgar and Jimmy presented themselves at the post office and reported to Harry. "Do you need us today?" asked Edgar, hoping the answer would be no, the sun was shining outside.

"Sorry, you will have to stay, you have visitors," Harry replied with a worried frown that caused deep creases across his brow. Edgar wondered who it could be to cause Harry so much agitation.

"What do you reckon this is all about?" asked Jimmy taking out his ever-present Woodbine. But before it reached his mouth the door opened and Harry appeared followed by three army officers, all with red bands round their caps indicating staff officers. Immediately Edgar and Jimmy snapped to attention and saluted, the cigarette dropping to the floor at their feet.

"This is Mr Stanton," stammered Harry then as Colonel Miller stared at Edgar, "we knew each other before the war."

"Well, Mr Stanton," Colonel Miller said in a high-pitched voice, laced with a strong helping of sarcasm, "I understand you are quite proficient at Morse code?"

"Yes Sir."

"Well we'll see." Colonel Miller sat at a telegraphy set and indicated for Edgar to take the other. "I will send a message and you tell me what it says," and he proceeded to tap at the keys.

At his own set Edgar winced at the poor technique but instantly recognised the content, it was a standard test communication that he had sent and received hundreds of times. Without really bothering to listen he sat as the butchered Morse was sent over a closed loop to his set.

Ey Up Adolf

> "Mary had a metal cow
> She bought it for a tanner
> When she wanted milk
> She had to use a spanner."

Colonel Miller turned and looked at Edgar. "Right, read me the message."

Without hesitation Edgar repeated the transmission. The colonel nodded in approval, impressed that Edgar could remember the message from memory. Jimmy then took Edgar's place and the process was repeated.

When he had finished Colonel Miller turned to one of his entourage and nodded, two names were then jotted in a small, black book and they all departed without another word.

As the door closed everyone heaved a sigh of relief. Jimmy bent down, retrieved his cigarette from the floor, straightened it, blew the dust away then placed it in his mouth.

"What was all that about?" asked Edgar.

"No idea," replied Harry. "They just turned up this morning and said they wanted to see the best operators we had, and that was you two. I'll tell you what though, they were important, the one who spoke was a colonel and the others were captains. And did you notice the red cap band?"

"Yes," they both replied in unison.

"That says they are staff officers, attached to the War Office, very high muckety mucks."

Edgar and Jimmy looked at each other with worried expressions. What did high ranking officers want with them? Whatever it was it did not bode well.

*   *

Ann settled into her job at ICI but two things concerned her. She had to sign the Official Secret Act meaning she could not talk about her job and, being naturally talkative, she found this irksome. Also Mr Munroe would often say, "Ann, go and take a walk for five minutes."

Mr Munroe answered his phone, listened, then his face changed, darkened, and his eyes started to blaze. He took the receiver from his mouth, covered it with his hand and glanced in Ann's direction so she rose and left the office. Looking out of the corridor window she could see a casting was in progress, bright sparks from drops of molten steel splashed into the air through the rising cloud of steam. At the sound of footsteps she turned and saw Mr Turner from the next office approaching.

"Sent out of the classroom again," he said with a smile.

"Yes, I don't understand, what is it that I can't hear."

"It's no great secret. Mr Munroe has a very vivid turn of phrase at times." Ann continued to look puzzled. "He swears like a trooper. Every time something goes wrong and he knows he's going to explode he sends you away first." He walked off down the corridor.

"Ann, you can come back in now."

She returned to her desk. "I'll bet someone's ears are burning," she said knowingly as she wound a fresh piece of paper into her typewriter.

"Burning, they should be molten blobs by the now, the raving idiots!" Then calming slightly, "Have you heard from Edgar?"

"Yes he wrote yesterday. He's still at training in Liverpool but thinks that something is about to happen but he doesn't know what. I hope he's not going to be sent abroad or on a ship, too many are being sunk by submarines and we don't seem to be able to do anything about them."

Mr Munroe glanced down at a secret report on his desk. "No, but that will change, take my word for it."

Chapter 8

"Stanton and Parr, CO's office straight away," barked the sergeant, "and look lively."

Edgar and Jimmy stared at each other, they were about to leave for the Post Office. 'What now?' they both thought.

Briskly they strode along the corridor to the Commanding Officer's office, ensuring that all buttons were fastened and caps on straight. They polished their boots on the backs of their trousers then Edgar knocked.

"Come in," commanded the CO. "I have received this," he waved a paper in their vague direction, "and I am surprised." Edgar and Jimmy wondered which of their many escapades was finally coming home to roost and just how long they would be spending in the glasshouse.

"It is a transfer order." They heaved a sigh of relief. "You are to report to a top secret signals base on Salisbury Plain, starting tomorrow, so you'd better get a move on. Collect your travel warrants, pack your gear and clear off."

"Yes Sir," they answered and saluted. Once outside the office they relaxed and Jimmy said, "A top secret base, I wonder what it will be like?"

"I don't know," answered Edgar. "Do you think it will be underground with the entrance covered with camouflage netting and the aerials disguised as trees or something?"

"Or perhaps it's an old country house with rooms for code breakers and top secret messages being taken by dispatch riders.

Whatever it is it will be an improvement on this dump. But why us?"

"Because there are only a handful of people in the country who know how to use the new equipment and only us in the army, the rest are too old,"

"I never thought of that."

So far they had not really felt that they were involved in the war, after initial training they had been transferred here to Liverpool and spent most of their time at the Post Office helping out.

"We'd better call in and tell Harry we won't be around any more."

"Do you think that's wise, this being a top secret base. What if it gets out?"

"It's Harry you are talking about, not a German spy, and besides we'll only tell him we're being transferred away from Liverpool, not where we're going."

An hour later they were on a train heading south, making the long and laborious journey to Newbury and wondering what the new base would be like and whether it would make a major change to their lives. Leaving the station they caught a bus to Andover.

As they descended in the middle of the town the sun was setting, casting long shadows across the road. Clutching their kit bags they prepared to walk to their destination. Edgar was fishing in his pocket for the directions when a green army truck ground by with a crashing of gears and a cloud of smoke then it stopped and a head stuck out of the window.

"Watcha' mates," a cockney voice shouted. "Signals?"

"Yes," replied Edgar, "just transferred from Liverpool."

"You'll be going to the secret base then," the driver replied with a grin. "I'm going past there, got a load of tank shells to deliver. Hop in."

Ey Up Adolf

Edgar and Jimmy squeezed on the hard bench-seat, the driver forced the protesting vehicle into gear and they hopped down the road.

"Problems with the gear-box," inquired Edgar.

"Naw, not really, it's more me. I was only learned last week."

"And you've got a load of tank shells in the back?" Edgar paused as the truck swerved violently to avoid a bicycle. "I take it they are just dummies, for practice."

"Naw, they're the real thing. Them tanks go blasting them all over the Plain, it's got more holes in it than a pincushion."

At that moment the truck hit a pothole and bounced. Edgar heard a crunching noise from the back, as if a wooden crate had just splintered. "Is it far to our base?"

"Only a couple of miles,"

Edgar fervently hoped they would last that long.

*   *

Ann was just putting the cover on her typewriter at the end of a long day. As she was reaching for her coat the door opened and Mr Munroe entered.

"Still here, I would have thought you'd be gone by now."

Ann started, her thoughts returning to the present. "Those letters needed to be finished, you said they were important." Ann could see he was impressed.

"Well done. I'll tell you what, have you anything to do after work tonight?"

"No, not really."

"Right then, I've got to meet a colleague for a drink at my hotel." Mr Munroe stayed at the Victoria in the centre of Sheffield during the week and travelled home to his family in Teesside at weekends. "Why don't you join us then I'll drop you at the station afterwards. Call it a thank you for being so conscientious." Ann was undecided, she didn't really like being out after dark because of the blackout.

As if reading her thoughts Mr Munroe added, "I'll make sure you are back before nine, even if I have to take you home myself."

That settled it. She had never been inside a real, posh hotel. "That would be nice, thank you."

They made their way to the director's car park and Mr Munroe guided her across to a big, blue-black Rover 14 saloon with a wide running board and huge chrome lights. He opened the door and Ann slid in, enjoying the smell of polished leather and mahogany then he climbed, literally, into the driver's seat and peered out, his head only just reaching over the dashboard. He started the engine and the car swept along the almost deserted road.

*   *

Edgar and Jimmy descended from the truck and walked down the track, lit by the last rays of the sun. Jimmy, who was in the lead, stopped suddenly, causing Edgar to run into the back of him.

"What's the matter," Edgar muttered grumpily, his back ached, his boots rubbed, his shoulder was sore from his kitbag and he was hungry.

"It's the secret base!"

Edgar stared in disbelief. In front of him was a collection of corrugated iron huts and a forest of tall masts, all surrounded by an eight foot high, barbed wire fence with stout gates manned by two, armed soldiers. On a mud splattered sign they could just make out the word 'Signals', the rest was completely obliterated by the sticky soil.

Ey Up Adolf

So much for being a 'secret base', it was the least secretive looking place they could imagine, it stuck out like an elephant on a beach.

"Welcome to your new home," muttered Jimmy as he trudged forwards, released the buttoned-down flap on his pocket and reached inside for his orders.

*   *

The sun had just sunk behind the surrounding hills as the Rover swung into the car park of the Victoria Hotel, a tall redbrick Georgian building with high chimneys and a covered entrance, where a uniformed doorman waited. "Good evening, Mr Munroe."

"Good evening, George," he replied, while, following behind, Ann tipped the doorman a small, shy smile. They turned left into the bar, "He's not here yet, not that I'm surprised. What would you like to drink?"

Ann realised she did not have a clue what to order. With her parents being strict, Methodist teetotallers, she had never had a drink before. Suddenly this did not seem such a good idea. "Oh whatever you're having."

Mr Munroe looked at her quizzically then ordered. "Two pink gins please."

The bar keeper placed the drinks on the counter. "I'm sorry, Sir, we have no lemons, the war you know."

Mr Munroe signed the tab while Ann looked at the drinks with suspicion. The delicate colour was like her mother's rosehip syrup that she was given every winter. She lifted the glass to her mouth, noticed the strange aroma of the gin then took a tentative sip. As soon as the fiery liquid hit the back of her throat she started to splutter, it felt on fire and her eyes simultaneously started to water. She gasped for air, unable to utter a word while Mr Munroe watched with amusement.

"Not your usual, is it?"

Between gasps Ann shook her head then whispered, "No, in fact I've never had a drink before, it's against my parents' beliefs."

"Perhaps you'd better have something else then." He signalled the barkeeper for attention and ordered a sweet sherry. When it arrived he added, "And take it slowly, despite its sweet taste it is still alcoholic, I don't want you turning up for work tomorrow with a hangover, there's far too much to do."

Chapter 9

After his shift had finished Edgar sat down to write a letter to Ann then Jimmy tapped him on the shoulder. "I'm off down the pub for a pint, are you coming?"

"I want to finish this first so I'll meet you there."

"A word of warning," came a voice from further down the long room. "On the edge of the village there's a small labourer's cottage, you can't miss it. The old guy who lives there is a regular nuisance. He has this wireless his son bought for him and it won't work, probably came off the black market, so he keeps stopping us to have a look at it. Take my advice, nip past there as fast as you can."

"Thanks," answered Jimmy. "See you later, Edgar."

"Yes, won't be long," Edgar returned to his letter but found it hard going. Half an hour later, and only four lines written, he gave up. Perhaps a few pints would help his literary flow?

He grabbed his cap, set off to the village and as he marched through the country lanes, he let his mind wander so didn't realise until it was too late that he was walking past a rustic-brick cottage with undersized windows and a yellowing wooden fence, on which a grizzled, weather beaten labourer was leaning. His grey hair poked out from his faded, sweat-stained cap and a hand-rolled cigarette dangled from his lips. He stuck a calloused thumb inside his braces and gave them a tug as he watched Edgar approach. "Watcha, mate, you from that secret wireless base?"

"Did everyone and their grandmother know about the base, some secret this was turning out to be?" Without remembering the warning Edgar stammered, "Er yes."

"Good, I've got this wireless but it won't work, have a butchers at it for me, will you."

"Alright, but I don't know much about civilian sets." The truth was he knew nothing about repairs.

The labourer stuck out his hand, "Tom Flippance," he said with a smile, revealing a set of stained false teeth.

"Edgar."

Tom winked at him. "Can't say more, I understand, what with you working at the secret base. Careless talk costs lives."

With trepidation Edgar followed Tom inside, bending to avoid banging his head on the low door frame, and he allowed his eyes time to accustom to the dark. It was a typical labourer's cottage, one room that doubled up as kitchen, dining and sitting room with a big, open fireplace. From an ancient sideboard Tom lifted a wireless, placed it reverently on the battered table in the middle of the room then produced a screwdriver from a drawer. "The last soldier left that behind."

Edgar took it, turned the set round and warily removed the back, carefully placing the screws in a line on the table. He peered intently for a few minutes then came to a conclusion; he hadn't the faintest clue what was wrong. The best thing he could do was prod about for a bit with the screwdriver, admit defeat and leave as quickly as possible. He handed the plug to Tom and told him to fit it into the socket on the wall. Gingerly he poked the screwdriver inside.

"What do think is the problem?"

Edgar had been concentrating so hard he hadn't heard Tom come behind him and peer over his shoulder. He jumped, the flat blade moved a fraction of an inch, there was a sudden

Ey Up Adolf

bright-blue flash followed by a pungent smell of hot metal as one of the wires melted.

Edgar waited for the torrent of abuse coming his way. "My giddy aunt," exclaimed Tom, "thar's cured it!"

Peering inside Edgar could see the valves lighting up as the current flowed through them. Carefully he turned the set round as the strident brass of a dance band blared out.

"Well done, lad, thar's cleverer than them others, they couldn't fix it but you have." Tom reached up to a large enamel jug, lifted it off the wall and strode to the open door. Sticking his head out he yelled, "Dan, Dan come here." A few minutes later a smaller, eleven year old version of himself, minus the cap and cigarette stub, arrived. "Take this to the pub and get them to fill it," he ordered.

The boy disappeared. Edgar noticed no money had been proffered. Tom caught his look, "I have an arrangement with the land-lord, I get beer and he gets eggs from the farm." He sat down on a wooden stool and listened to the music for a minute, muttering, "Well I never thought it would ever work, thar's a genius, but then I suppose you have to be to work at the secret base, they wouldn't let just any old idiot operate all that special hush-hush equipment, would they?"

Edgar thought about the Spartan accommodation, the battered furniture and old worn equipment and nodded but he was saved from answering by the return of Dan, staggering under the weight of the brimming jug. Tom took down three glasses from a shelf, filled two and poured a drop in the bottom of the third then added water from the pump over the pot sink before handing it to his son. Pushing another to Edgar he lifted the third, "To the cleverest soldier in the army," he stated then took a deep drink

An hour, and several glasses, later Edgar weaved his way back to camp, now he had something to write in his letter, not that he was in any fit state to put pen to paper.

*   *

When Ann arrived home Pat, her best friend, was waiting for her. "It takes you some time, I've been here ages."

"Busy day. What's that?"

"Chocolates, I swapped some cheese for them." Pat had a good system going with various local shops in the centre of town, cheese, eggs and butter were exchanged for a variety of goods from other shops. When she came to visit she always arrived with goodies. "I've been thinking."

Ann took a chocolate, popped it into her mouth then gave her friend a piercing stare. When Pat had been thinking it usually meant trouble. "Go on."

"Well, with the war on, all the men have gone to the forces so there's none left for us."

"You, you mean, I'm engaged to Edgar remember."

"Well alright, if you're being picky, so I wondered where will there still be some men?"

"You're not thinking of going down the pit are you? I know there's a war on but I don't think that's been allowed for a hundred years."

"Not the mines, dozy, it's far too damp and dirty, it would ruin my perm. No, I was thinking of the Fire Service. We could volunteer."

Ann thought about this for a few seconds. They could get out and meet people, do something worthwhile for the war effort and her dad couldn't object about her being out late. "Ok, where do we go?"

"That's the good thing, they've set up a station down Wellgate."

"You don't mean in the funeral parlour?"

Ey Up Adolf

"They've moved into the back and the fire service is using the front office."

"But, dead bodies?"

"I don't think they'll object."

"You know what I mean."

"It'll be alright." Pat made her eyes go wide and pulled a frightened face, "You're not scared of ghosts are you?"

"Course not."

"That's settled then, we can go this evening." Then she raised her voice and shouted into the scullery, "Aunt Marge, can I stay for tea?"

"Wey, aye, pet, of course you can."

Chapter 10

When Edgar woke a little man with a large hammer was sitting inside his head, banging on his skull. Gingerly he made his way to the wash room and stuck his head in a bowl of icy water which improved matters slightly.

In the mess tent the cook, Fagin, was stirring a large pot of stew and muttering darkly to himself. Edgar wondered if it was a secret spell to improve the quality of the meat, then he remembered the last stew and decided that was not the answer. The cook picked up a bucket of waste and disappeared, making his way to the pit outside where all the kitchen rubbish was deposited.

Edgar took a slice of bread, spread it with jam, which was mostly turnip, then slowly started to munch, wishing the man with the hammer would give it a rest. As he washed the last mouthful down with a swig of strong, lukewarm tea he saw the cook return, the bucket now empty.

On his way back to his hut Edgar held his breath as he passed the foul-smelling pit. He collapsed on his bunk, stared at the plain, corrugated metal walls, then took out the letter he had started yesterday and commenced writing, this time with more success as he related the tale of Tom Flippance and his wireless set. Once he had finished he picked up a piece of discarded wood, took out his penknife and started to slice off the rough edges while letting his mind wander.

Edgar became aware of a low drone, like a powerful motor bike. He stood up and wandered to the window, set in the

Ey Up Adolf

corrugated iron wall, which had a good view over the flat sea of grass. In the distance a small dot in the sky rapidly approached and this was the source of the noise.

A trail of black smoke followed the course of the plane as it traversed the clear sky. "That doesn't look too good, I hope it makes it back to base in one piece." Edgar stared, wondering what sort of plane it was. He knew it was neither a Spitfire nor a Hurricane but he thought he should recognise it. Then, as the plane jinked to avoid a small puff-ball of white smoke, he saw the black cross on its side. It was a German Messerschmitt and it was coming straight towards him. He could hear shouts and the sound of small arms fire. Finding cover seemed an excellent course of action, the thin walls of his hut would offer no protection from a hail of bullets.

He opened the door and started to sprint, arms and legs pumping madly. Ahead soldiers were heading for the trenches that had been installed for such an emergency. He had only gone a few strides when he saw the line of spurts in the ground, the soil and small stones flying in all directions, and they were coming directly towards him. He was being shot at and there was no possible way he could reach the safety of the trenches in time.

Edgar frantically looked around, he was trapped out in the open and death was only seconds away. An image flashed into his brain, Fagin carrying a pail of rubbish out to the refuse pit. Without hesitation, he swerved sideways and dove headlong towards the foul-smelling hole. He flew through the air and came to rest on a deep, slimy, rancid layer of rotting organic matter.

Cursing and trying to burrow deeper into the heap of refuse Edgar held his breath, sensible considering the range of repulsive odours around him, and waited for the hail of hot lead.

Neil Whyke

With a roar the Messerschmitt hurtled above, its guns still blazing.

Second after second ticked by then he heard the growl of engines and a pair of Spitfires roared by in hot pursuit. Gingerly Edgar crawled over the lip of the hole, covered in squashed pulp and gunk like a creature from the Black Lagoon. He started to make his way back to the hut, leaving a trail of carrot peelings, tea leaves and brown, slimy assorted vegetables in his wake but thankful to be alive.

* *

Ann had finished her tea and was sitting in front of the huge, Yorkshire range listening to Cab Calloway on the wireless and thinking about her interview at the fire station the previous night. They were both accepted and instructed to report as soon as the sirens sounded.

The voice on the wireless announced the next tune and a peculiar wailing started. She listened then realised the noise was not coming from the radio but from the air raid siren on top of the Girls High School a few streets away.

A clatter of feet on the stairs announced her brothers' arrival, followed by her mother who had been cleaning in the front room. "Why are you still sitting there, move it?" ordered Arthur, her oldest brother.

"Aye pet," added her mother, "and don't forget your coat, it'll be cold out there."

Together they made their way down the shadowy, garden path to the hump of the Anderson shelter sitting, squat and ugly, by the far wall. Quickly they hurried through the darkness, all the while listening for the dull crump of anti aircraft fire or the louder explosion of a detonating bomb, but nothing could be heard above the banshee howl of the siren.

Ey Up Adolf

Douglas, as befitted the youngest, pulled open the door and held it for the others to enter but Ann stopped. From the blackness strange noises were emitting, a cross between wheezing and blowing a raspberry. Startled, she looked at her mother, who squeezed past, then switched on a hooded torch with its feeble pinprick of light. Huddled shapes perched on the bench seats with gas masks firmly jammed in place, the goggle-like lens failing to hide the fear in their eyes.

"Your husband said it would be alright for us to come in your shelter until we get our own," came the muffled voice of their neighbour from behind the mask.

"Wey aye, pet," came her mother's reply, "course you can, but I don't think you need to wear yon mask though, I doubt that them Germans have got round to using gas yet. And besides how can we have a good gossip with that on." She gave a cheerful smile and sat down next to them. "Have you heard about Mrs Fernleigh on the main road, her husband has only just been called up and already she's got a lodger, if you know what I mean."

"I was told about that in the butcher's," replied her neighbour, leaning across her husband, "a Pole I heard, escaped before the Germans invaded, a good looking lad, by all accounts." Within seconds the danger of being blown to bits was forgotten in the latest going-ons of the local, scarlet woman. Ann's mother turned back and winked, she knew her neighbour liked nothing better than a good gossip and that took precedence over all else. Ann sat back and closed her eyes, letting the voices wash over her like a warm sea.

*   *

The all-clear sounded to everyone's relief, especially Douglas who had been bored after the first five minutes then they made their way back inside. "I'll put the kettle on," announced her mother, stirring the ashes in the grate.

Ann settled back in the chair then shot bolt upright again.

"Now what's the matter?" grumbled Arthur.

"I shouldn't be here."

"Why? Were you going out with Pat? She'll understand."

"No, when the siren went I should have reported to the fire station."

"Well, no matter," announced her mother, pushing past. "No bombs were dropped so no harm done."

Chapter 11

Salisbury Plain was covered with a grey, clinging, wet blanket of cloud when Edgar crossed to the mess tent. As they were a small unit everyone took turns at helping the cook prepare food for the day and today was Edgar's stint. Yesterday, Jimmy had warned, "That cook is scary."

"You mean Fagin, the inventor of Fagin's Folly, the worst porridge in the world."

"Yes him, all the time I was there he was muttering to himself and stabbing at the meat with a sharp knife as if he hated it. If he reaches for a cleaver, I suggest you beat a hasty retreat."

"I'll keep a beady eye on him."

Edgar entered and called out a cheery, "Morning cook." All he received in reply was a grunt and a hard stare. Edgar noticed Fagin had developed a definite tick at the corner of his eye as if he was permanently winking. "What do you want doing?"

Without a word a sack of carrots, a bucket and a peeling knife were passed across then the cook went back to hacking lumps of beef ready to go in the oven. Edgar picked up the first carrot and whispered to it, "Looks like you are going to be the best source of conversation today." At least he could listen to the wireless that was playing quietly in the corner.

Edgar started to pare the outside off the carrot, his foot tapping to the music. By the time the recording had changed to Artie Shaw the bottom of the bucket was covered in peeled carrots and Edgar had mentally switched off, his mind reeling back through yesterday's shift in the wireless room where he had been listening in to a series of coded messages, noting the time, duration and direction of the transmissions. Although his knowledge of geography was fairly basic he was pretty certain they were coming from somewhere near Birmingham and, as far as he knew, there was no signals station based near there. If you continued the line onwards it would pass over Germany. The conclusion was fairly obvious, he was tracking a spy.

Edgar looked down at the bucket by his feet which was now a quarter full. He picked it up and carried it over to Fagin, "Is that enough?"

The cook turned and gave the bucket a baleful glare. "More!"

Edgar returned to his stool, picked up the next carrot and started again. Soon the bucket was over half full and Edgar was convinced that should be enough. Again he carried his bucket across and presented it for the cook's inspection.

"Need more," he grumped accompanied by a huge twitch, which made the entire left side of his face contort. Hastily Edgar retired, seriously worried about the state of Fagin's mental health.

Unhappy about having his back to the cleaver-wielding cook he moved his stool so that he faced Fagin, sat down and continued peeling until his bucket was almost full. "There's enough there for every soldier on Salisbury Plain," he grumbled, "and I've got a blister on my finger." He half carried, half dragged the heavy, vegetable filled bucket across the duck-boards to the cook. "There, it's full."

The cook stopped stirring a gooey mixture in a bowl, wiped his hands on his grubby apron and grunted satisfaction. Bending slightly he picked up the heavy bucket easily and, without a word, carried it outside, a puzzled Edgar tagged along behind. They were heading towards the same pit he dove into yesterday, the one containing the rotting refuse. Fagin stood precariously on the crumbling edge, looked down at the mouldering remains then upended the bucket, pouring the fruits of Edgar's labours on top of the other decomposing rubbish.

Edgar's mouth opened in shock, he had a numb bum from the hard stool, a blister on his finger and he had spent ages peeling those carrots now the cook had thrown them away. "What? Why?" then in a voice brimming with rage he shouted, "You raving lunatic, you've just thrown away perfectly good carrots. There's a food shortage you know, what's your problem?"

"Had carrots yesterday," came the gruff answer. Fagin turned and stomped to the tent leaving a flabbergasted Edgar staring at his retreating back.

*   *

Ann opened the door to find Mr Munroe placing the phone back on its receiver with a frown on his face.

"That was a complaint about you." Ann looked shocked and worried. "The girls who work for English Steel have grumbled about the way you dress." Ann looked at her smart grey skirt, pale blue blouse, black shoes and failed to see a problem.

"They are annoyed they have to wear dark-blue to work which is eating into their clothing coupons, while you can wear the same clothes for work and outside."

"Right, they have a point," Ann conceded. "I'll buy some dark-blue ones this weekend." She was disappointed, she had seen a bright, orange corded-velvet skirt but she wouldn't have enough coupons for both.

"Don't you dare!" exploded Mr Munroe. "You work for me at ICI not English Steel and I like you dressed just the way you are, it brightens this dull and grimy place. If I ever see you wearing dark blue I'll fire you on the spot and you can tell that lot downstairs that I said so."

Neil Whyke

Ann smiled to herself. She would definitely buy that skirt on Saturday and wear it on Monday.

*   *

Jimmy met up with Edgar as he walked across to the wireless room. "Have you heard about Fagin?"

"Don't talk to me about that man, I'm certain he's going mad."

"You're probably right and this will confirm your opinion. He's getting married."

"What! That lunatic Irishman, getting married, she must be as mad as he is………wait a minute, I thought Fagin was married already, his wife's still in Ireland."

"You thought right."

"So when did he get divorced?"

"He hasn't."

Edgar stopped walking and stared at his friend. "Did I hear you correctly, Fagin is still married but he's getting married again."

"Spot on!"

"Then he'll be…"

"A bigamist."

"Wow! I've never known a bigamist before, he must really be balmy."

"I know what you mean, imagine two mothers-in-law. The man must be stark, staring bonkers. Anyway we are all invited."

"Are you seriously thinking about going?"

"Of course, it'll be free beer."

"Well in that case…"

They entered the wireless room, Edgar sat down at his set and put on his headphones. "Now you dirty, little spy," he muttered, "I wonder what you are up to tonight."

Chapter 12

Two days after the wedding Edgar was still suffering from the celebrations to mark Fagin's nuptials. He hated Mondays normally but this one in particular, as he was still feeling green about the gills and definitely not running on all four cylinders. He stared up at the dingy ceiling and smiled at the memory of the tiny, full church, most of the base had turned out and not just for the celebration afterwards. When the vicar came to the part about 'any just reason why these two should not marry' an intense silence enveloped the entire congregation, everyone held their breath expecting the door to surge open and Fagin's first wife to burst in, followed by a brace of shotgun-toting brothers. After a few seconds the vicar continued and there was an enormous sigh from the assembled masses.

Afterwards everyone retired to the local pub, numerous pints were drunk, Jimmy entertained on the piano and at some point Fagin and his wife disappeared. When closing time arrived the doors were locked, the local policeman came and joined them, and the party continued until the early hours of the morning.

Jimmy entered, parked himself besides Edgar and blurted, "Guess what's happened?"

Edgar turned slightly, forced his eyes to focus and his brain to work, "The Martians have landed and joined up with Hitler."

"No, be serious." Jimmy sat there with a satisfied smirk on his face, "Fagin's done a runner."

"What! Gone AWOL"

"Yep, deserted. He had two days leave and should have report back for duty this morning. When he failed to turn up the CO sent a couple of Military Policemen round to the hotel in Salisbury where he was supposed to be staying, only to find he scarpered the day before."

"So now he's not only a bigamist but a deserter as well." Then the full extent of the calamity struck home, "Who's going to do the cooking?"

"Sorted! We are going to take turns. We drew straws earlier and since you were still fast asleep I took your go for you. Congratulations you are today's cook."

Edgar gave a suspicious look, it was far too much of a coincidence that he was the only one not present and he was the first to cook. "What about food?"

"Organized, today's has already been delivered."

"So what is on the menu?"

"Beef, there's a huge piece in the cookhouse just waiting for you to practice your skills on. Come on, it can't be that hard, all you have to do is shove it in the oven and boil some vegetables."

Edgar rolled his eyes in disbelief, eating he could do, but how it got from raw to edible was a mystery to him. But Jimmy was right, if Fagin could do it so could he.

An hour later Edgar was ready, the fire under the oven was burning well and he fortified himself with a couple of brews. Now he was looking at the massive piece of beef. Edgar's culinary skills were meagre but of one thing he was certain, a piece of meat this large would take until next month to cook, no way would it be ready for the evening meal. The only answer was to cut it into smaller, easier to cook chunks. He took out a large knife and was sharpening it when Jimmy entered. "How's the chef doing?"

"Push off! I haven't forgiven you for stitching me up."

Ey Up Adolf

"What me, your best friend?" asked Jimmy, with a tone of injured innocence.

"Yes, you Brutus," but before he could expand on this the flap was lifted and the local farmer, a stocky bad-tempered man entered.

"Where's Fagin?"

"Gone."

"Transferred," added Jimmy.

"Here's your milk." The farmer lifted two large canisters onto the table next to the meat. "And since Fagin's gone it'll be the last, it's not worth my effort to traipse out here just for that."

Edgar and Jimmy stared then realisation dawned, Fagin had an arrangement with the farmer.

"Well you wouldn't have been delivering much longer anyway," replied Jimmy quickly.

"What do you mean?"

"You won't have enough land to keep cows." Edgar looked at his friend, he hadn't the faintest idea what he was on about. "Haven't you been told, we are taking over your field for more masts?"

"You can't! I need those fields."

"Tough, there's a war on and besides if you're not delivering to us there won't be a problem."

A look of panic crossed the farmer's face, "Perhaps I was a bit hasty. Who is making the decision?"

Jimmy jerked a thumb in Edgar's direction, "Him! The CO will have the final say but he's the expert on where the masts need to go. That's what he did before the war, site masts."

A sly look crossed the farmer's face and his voice took on a wheedling tone, "Look mate, I'm sure we can come to an agreement."

Catching on to Jimmy's scam Edgar shook his head solemnly, "Perhaps, but that's the best site, it'd take a very convincing argument for me to change my mind."

The farmer thought for a moment then offered, "How about a couple of free pints each?" It would cost him several eggs and possibly some sausages but it would be worth it to keep his fields.

Edgar looked at Jimmy and received a nod. "Ok, I suppose we could site them somewhere else if I really think about it. But we will need the milk to continue being delivered as well."

"Of course, every day," agreed the relieved farmer. "Right, I'll be off," and he hastily backed out of the tent, letting the flap drop behind him.

Once they heard the farmer's cart leave they both burst out laughing. "If you'd been negotiating with Hitler instead of that weed Chamberlain we'd not be at war now," Edgar said to Jimmy.

"Yes, Hitler and that farmer are both nasty, greedy, grabbing swine. Let's hope it's as easy to get one over on Adolf."

Edgar returned his attention to the beef, inexpertly cutting it into more manageable pieces then placing them in the bulky oven. "Right, now the vegetables." He peeled several large potatoes, turnips and parsnips, he could not face carrots, and left them in billies full of water while he retreated to his hut for a well earned snooze.

A couple of hours later he woke up, checked his watch and hurried across to the cook tent, to be met with a strong, meaty smell. He was going to check the oven when his eyes fell on the cans of vegetables. With considerable effort he lifted the full pans onto the stove. then opened the door to the oven. The pieces of meat were a deep brown with a dried, crusty coat.

"They'll be alright inside, it's only the outer surface that's a bit dry." He ladled some of the juices over them, satisfied that

Ey Up Adolf

would cure the problem, then returned to the pans which he stirred with a wooden spoon. He trudged back to his hut, picked up yesterday's paper from the table and went to sit on the step. When he had read it from cover to cover he rose, stretched and returned to the cook tent.

As soon as he opened the flap he saw the bluish haze in the air and an acrid, smell, something was burning. Immediately he rushed to the pans but they were only just starting to boil so that was not the problem. Then he saw the slight wisps of smoke escaping from the oven door. Grabbing a cloth he opened it and was immediately engulfed in a cloud of greasy, pungent fumes that burst from the hot oven. Reaching inside he pulled out the roasting dish and examined the shrunken, hard, coal-like objects. What had once been nice, succulent pieces of beef were now blocks of charcoal. He removed one and attempted to cut it but it merely shattered and small pieces shot around the tent like shrapnel.

Horror struck he placed them on a plate and turned to the vegetables. Taking a knife he poked at them, only to see them roll away, still rock hard and raw. Looking again at his watch he realised that it was almost time for the change of shift and soon his fellow soldiers would be arriving.

After dinner it was unanimously agreed that Edgar had produced the worst, most inedible meal in the history of army catering and that he was never, ever to be allowed in the cook tent again, a decision that Edgar agreed with whole heartedly.

*   *

A few days later Ann sat holding her tea, reading Edgar's account of the day's proceedings, tears of laughter rolling down her cheeks. When her mother came in, she asked, "What on earth's the matter pet?" Ann handed across the letter. "Just like a man to be totally useless in the kitchen."

Neil Whyke

Ann leaned back in her chair with a contented sigh, Edgar's letter had finished a good few days. She gently brushed a crease out of the bright, orange skirt she had worn to work and remembered the jealous looks of the other girls at the offices. "Served them right for being so spiteful," she thought with satisfaction.

Chapter 13

Edgar was being addressed by his CO. "Next week you will be transferred for a short time to London. As you will have realised the conditions and equipment here are primitive so a new operational base is being prepared deep under the War Office. I want you to go there and test the new equipment, make sure there are no glitches." Edgar's face fell and the CO noticed. "Is that a problem?"

"I was going on leave this weekend, starting today, my first one since I was called up, and I was looking forwards to seeing my fiancée."

"I don't see why that should cause a problem. How are you getting there?"

"Train, but it'll take forever and I'll have to set off back early Sunday to get to London."

"Can you ride a motorbike?"

Edgar had ridden on one and knew the rudiments of operation. "Yes Sir."

"Well there are plenty floating around the base, the despatch riders use them," replied the CO.

"What about petrol?"

"I can't give you permission for that but I'm sure a capable and resourceful soldier could find a way round that problem," replied the CO, raising one eyebrow. "Just one other thing. I know this place is jokingly referred to as the 'secret base', I'm surprised there aren't signs up pointing here, but the new place will be very different, security will be at the top level and lives really will depend on the people working there keeping their traps shut, so not a word to anyone, not even your fiancée."

"Yes Sir."

"Dismissed."

Edgar scoured the base for a motorbike that wasn't being used and wasn't tied down. Eventually he came across a BSA M20, propped against a fence post, with a bored looking private standing nearby, smoking a cigarette.

"Who does this belong to?" asked Edgar.

"No idea, mate. It's been there for days and no-one's been near it, why?"

"I've something to do for the CO," replied Edgar, warping the truth slightly, "so I'll borrow it."

"Fine by me, it ain't mine, and the army won't miss one, especially for a good cook."

Edgar groaned, were his culinary escapades known to the entire army? He opened the petrol cap but the tank was empty, which explained why it had been abandoned. Not a problem. All he needed was an unattended lorry and a length of tubing.

He pushed the BSA across to the mess tent. During his disastrous day as a cook he had noticed a pile of junk in a corner and amongst it was a length of old hosepipe. He sneaked round the back and lifted the side of the tent. Carefully he reached through and cut off a long-enough piece with his pen-knife. Pleased with himself he stood up then jumped a mile in the air when a voice said, "Excuse me mate, can you tell me where I can leave my lorry for a few minutes while I visit the lav."

"Where is it now?" Edgar asked, not believing his good luck.

"Behind that hut."

"It should be alright but just to make sure I'll keep an eye on it for you."

"That's great and where are the toilets."

Ey Up Adolf

"The nearest is the other side of that building," Edgar replied, pointing to a hut a hundred yards away.

"Ta, mate, I won't be long."

As soon as the driver had turned the corner Edgar wheeled his motorbike across to the lorry. Looking around to make sure no-one was watching he carefully siphoned petrol from one vehicle to the other. Once the tank was full he trundled his bike round the corner, out of sight.

A few minutes later the driver returned, climbed into his cab and, with a cheery wave, drove off.

Immediately Edgar sat on the M20, turned on the fuel tap and stomped down on the kick-start. The engine coughed a couple of times then exploded with a roar. Keeping the revs to a minimum, and the noise to a deep grumble, he unsteadily rode back to his hut, loaded his gear on the carrier, settled on the broad seat and grinned. Pulling on a pair of goggles he wobbled down the track to the camp gates. In a few hours he would be back home in Rotherham and for the next two days the war, the army and Hitler did not exist.

Chapter 14

"Why, Edgar lad, come in, we didn't know you were arriving this weekend." Ann's mother opened the door wide enough for him to slip through then quickly closed it, making sure the blackout curtain was firmly back in place. "I'll just put the kettle on and then give Ann a shout, she's not long since come home." She called up the stairs, "Ann pet, come on down you've got a visitor." Turning to Edgar she continued, "Sit down, hinnie, you must be exhausted with that long journey." Edgar thankfully sank into the armchair. "Have you had anything to eat?"

Edgar shook his head, realising that he was starving.

"Well you'll have dinner with us, it's only corned beef stew and dumplings but it's hot and filling."

The door opened and Ann entered. Edgar stood up, turned and gave her a big hug. "You look wonderful."

"This is a marvellous surprise, I wasn't expecting you."

Ann's mother squeezed past them with a large, brown teapot in her hand which she filled with boiling water before placing a garish, knitted cosy over it and putting it on the hearth to keep warm. "Set the table, pet, Edgar is eating with us."

"What about Arthur?"

"No, he's out with Gladys, they've gone to the pictures."

"Isn't Arthur in the army?" inquired Edgar. "I thought he had been called up."

"Turned him down, flat feet," replied Ann's mum.

Ey Up Adolf

When they were all seated with plates of steaming stew in front of them, the fluffy, white dumplings sticking up like rounded, snow capped hills in a brown sea she said, "Now, what have you been up to?"

For the first time Edgar realised he had a problem. Although they laughingly referred to the camp as the 'secret base' the truth was that much of what he dealt with was indeed secret. He found himself having to be evasive which led to embarrassing silences. To avoid this he turned the conversation to Ann's job. She happily chattered about mundane, office gossip but when he tried to press her about further details she blushed and changed the subject. He was confused, after all she was just a secretary in the works.

Ann's mother realised there was a problem so prattled on about queuing for rations, the films at the Odeon and of course the latest on Mrs Fernleigh and her succession of 'lodgers'. "I don't really understand, she's not exactly attractive with that thin, weaselly face, pot belly and skinny legs; and she has the most awful temper. What they see in her is a mystery."

"Some men just aren't choosy," Ann replied.

When the meal was over Edgar left, saying that he'd had a long journey and been on duty the night before so needed an early night.

Ann's mother listened to the roar of the exhaust as the BSA drove off into the night then sat next to her daughter. "What's the matter, pet?"

"I don't know, there's something different about Edgar, it's like he's holding back, keeping a secret."

"Well, there is a war on, perhaps he can't talk. You weren't exactly forthcoming about your job, a bit guarded like."

"That's different, we deal with hush-hush stuff, I signed the Official Secrets Act."

Ann's mother shook her head slowly, she did not really understand what her daughter did, but she did know it must be important otherwise her boss would not have a petrol ration or stay in the Victoria, a very posh hotel. "Perhaps Edgar has a secret job in the army."

"Secret! You saw what he came on, a motorbike, he's a despatch rider! How important is that? No, there's something else and I intend to find out what it is."

The next day was no better with both of them being very guarded about what they said. Things went downhill until, by the evening, they were barely speaking. Sitting in the darkness at the pictures Edgar took little notice of the film but spent most of the time wondering why the weekend had gone wrong.

When Ann arrived home her mother asked, "Have a nice time, pet?"

Ann sank into the other chair. "Not really."

"What do you think is the matter?" asked her mother, dreading the answer.

"I don't know. I thought he was being transferred to somewhere dangerous. Then I wondered if he had met someone else, but that doesn't sit right. I just don't know." She took out a small handkerchief and dabbed at the corner of her eye.

Her mother came across and put an arm round her shoulders. "Don't fret, hinnie, it's the war, it'll sort itself out when it is all over and hopefully that won't be long now."

Edgar lay on his bed staring at the ceiling. He had so looked forward to this weekend and now it was all going wrong. Both of them were keeping secrets and that was contrary to their natures so the strain was showing. They were still very young, not used to being apart and having to be guarded, forming the perfect breeding ground for distrust.

The next day, as he was leaving the house, Edgar noticed a letter addressed to him. He shoved it his pocket to read later,

Ey Up Adolf

packed his bag onto the carrier of the M20 then drove round to Ann's to say goodbye. He wanted to clear the air and put things straight but he did not know what was causing the problem.

Ann's mother came out, wearing her best hat and coat, hurrying off to chapel. "Go straight in, Edgar lad."

Ann was standing at the sink, washing her stockings ready for work the next day. On seeing Edgar she wiped her hands on her pinny and turned, revealing a blob of suds on the end of her nose.

Edgar took out his handkerchief and gently wiped it away, smiling at what he considered was the prettiest face in Yorkshire. Everyone knew that was where the best looking girls in the world were to be found, along with the best beer and the best cricketers. "I just called in to say I'm off."

"Back to camp?"

Edgar hesitated.

"Edgar, tell me the truth," demanded Ann, her cheeks flushed. "Have you got another girl-friend?"

Edgar stood in the doorway, mouth open, mind a blank, not believing what he had just heard.

"Watcha, Edgar." Arthur came out of the sitting room and squeezed past. "Like your bike," then he was gone.

"Another girlfriend!" Edgar managed to exclaim. "You think I've found someone else. Why would I want to, I've already got the best girl the world?"

"Well you've been so funny and secretive all weekend, I didn't know what to think."

Edgar smiled with relief, at last he knew the cause. "I'm sorry. I assure you that is not the reason, it's all to do with my job in the army."

"What, a despatch rider, how secret is that?" interrupted Ann.

Totally bewildered Edgar stammered, "I'm not a despatch rider."

"But the motor bike, it's like the ones they have on the films."

"There's thousands like that, lots of people ride them. I just borrowed it for the weekend."

"But the petrol!"

Edgar was at a loss, he couldn't say he pinched it. "War department, special allowance," he replied, making it up on the spur of the moment. "I'm doing more or less the same as I was in the post office, but for the army instead and with a lot more important messages than 'uncle Joe has died'. They are top secret so I can't talk about it that's all."

Ann felt an enormous sense of relief. "I know what you mean. My boss works on all sorts of experimental stuff that I can't talk about. I wish you'd said that earlier."

"You too," thought Edgar, but he realised that this was not an opportune moment to mention it. They gave each other a big hug then Edgar said, "I've got to go, my pass runs out at five."

"Write as soon as you get back, let me know you're safe."

"Yes I will. You'll hear from me often."

"Unless your other girl friend won't let you," Ann joked.

With a lighter step Edgar walked down the path, started his bike and drove off.

In the scullery Ann turned back to her washing just as the door opened. She thought Edgar had forgotten something but was disappointed when Arthur entered. "Ey up, sis. Finished with him then?"

"What?"

"You and Edgar, have you dumped him?"

"Why should I?"

"Because you've been rowing all weekend, what's up, has he got someone else?"

Ey Up Adolf

"Of course not! What makes you say that?"

"Well you know what girls are like, even the ugliest guy can get one if he's in uniform, even Edgar."

"You can talk utter rubbish at times," retorted Ann. "I don't know what Gladys sees in you, you're grumpy, mean and you've got flat feet. I know, it's because you're the only fella' left and she's desperate." Arthur reached past, picked up some suds and flicked them in her face.

"Good answer, very intelligent and grown up," she called at his retreating back. Then, as she wiped her face, she thought about his words.

Despite Edgar's reassurances, what if…..

Chapter 15

Edgar arrived in central London during a torrential downpour. Soaked to the skin, cold and generally dejected he showed his papers to an equally wet and miserable-looking policeman and asked for directions.

"Come far?" the constable asked in a suspicious voice.

"Blinking 'eck," Edgar thought, "does he think I'm a flipping spy or summat?" then he answered, "From up North, Roth'rum."

"Sorry mate, can't be too careful these days, but only a Tyke could speak like that. Now, where are you going?"

"Eaton Square."

"Belgravia, toff country. Impressive."

His billet was a large, imposing, four storied house with Georgian windows and a majestic entrance, complete with white painted columns. After climbing the threadbare stairs he found a bunk then thankfully undressed, crawled between the scratchy sheets and fell into a deep sleep.

The next morning he was awoken by the sound of boots on the landing. Grumbling he rose from the creaky bed and poked his head out of the door, just in time to catch a ginger-haired soldier in the uniform of the Welsh Guards.

"Morning, mate," called Edgar. "Where can I get breakfast round here?"

"Well there's Lyons Corner Café or there's a decent greasy spoon just down the road that does good fried bread."

"Thanks, I'll try that first."

Ey Up Adolf

He had finished his breakfast and was reaching into his pocket for some money when he felt the envelope. Taking it out he slit it open, read it then crumbled it up in disgust. It was an anonymous message informing him that Ann was seeing other men while he was away. "Jealous little swine, haven't you anything better to do with your time rather than spread malicious lies." He ran down a list of who could have sent it and finally settled on a portly youth who lived near Ann and always fancied her but she had refused to go out with him. "Just wait until next time I'm home," he muttered darkly under his breath.

Fortified, Edgar arrived in Whitehall and stared around at the tall, imposing buildings, even bigger and grander than the town hall in Sheffield. He climbed the wide steps, showed his orders to the guard then stood and gazed round in awe.

"I felt like that the first time but you get used to it. Those steps that you are thinking are so grand become tiring when you have to go up and down them forty times a day." Edgar turned to see a matronly, dark haired WAAF standing beside him. "First day?"

"Yes. I'm here to help with the new wireless room. Do you know where I report?"

"Down that corridor, they'll issue you with a pass and living expenses, then I'm afraid it's down to the sub basement, that's where the new communications room is housed."

*   *

At the same time a small and very select meeting had just started on an upper floor. Colonel Hudson, Captain Lister and Mr Baker were sitting round a table. "How are things progressing with your mission to Lisbon?" inquired the civil servant.

"Most things are in place, the operational staff are ready and we will be recruiting specialists this week. In fact that is a second reason for us being here today, our records show the right man is setting up the new communication equipment. When we have finished we will go and have a word."

"Excellent, now to the next item."

*   *

Edgar quickly completed administration and made his way down the tunnels until he arrived in a long, low room, the only illumination being provided by a series of lights slung from the ceiling. The nearest daylight was several floors above his head.

Around the walls ran pipes and ducts, giving the whole place a very austere and temporary feel. Across the room were numerous long desks, some covered with wireless and teleprinter equipment, while others had long lines of pigeon holes ready to take written messages. Dangling from the roof were signs indicating where the individual sections were linked, France, Cairo, Italy and Melbourne.

At one of the radios was a sergeant from the Signals Corps, headphones clamped to his ears and a frown on his brow.

"Signalman…" was as far as Edgar got.

"I know who you are and it's about time they sent us someone who knows what he's doing. We are supposed to be up and running by the end of the month but at the moment that seems very unlikely." He turned back to his set, swearing under his breath at the malfunctioning piece of equipment. Soon Edgar was busy trying to persuade a recalcitrant teleprinter to work and did not notice the two officers with the red hat bands silently slide into the room, nor hear one approach until he was next to him. He glanced sideways, ready to curse if it was a technician bothering him again, then jumped to his feet, trying to button his tunic and salute at the same time.

"At ease. How is the work progressing?"

"Slow Sir, but we will get there."

Ey Up Adolf

The captain turned on his heels and strode off without another word and rejoined Colonel Hudson. "He'll do."

The sergeant came across to Edgar, "What did the brass want?"

"Nothing much, they just asked how things were going."

The knowledgeable sergeant looked puzzled then wandered back to his station wondering what trouble was brewing.

For the next week Edgar was kept very busy. He had just received a test message from Melbourne when he felt a tap on his shoulder. Turning he saw the sergeant accompanied by a slim, blonde woman in army uniform. "Get someone to take over then accompany the young lady."

Edgar followed his guide from the room, not seeing the worried shake of the head from the sergeant as he left. They made their way down a tunnel that eventually exited through a thick door, manned by a tough-looking soldier with a holstered sidearm.

Edgar's trouble sensor was screaming loudly. The young lady approached another door, knocked, opened it and stood aside to allow Edgar to enter, feeling like a naughty schoolboy being summoned to the Headmaster.

He stepped in and saw two officers seated at a regulation army desk. "Sit down."

Edgar perched nervously on the hard wooden chair and waited expectantly. "Well, Mr Stanton, we've met before."

Edgar was so tense he did not notice the use of his civilian title. "Yes Sir, I remember, I was stationed in Liverpool."

The colonel smiled and continued, "We would like to give you the opportunity to go abroad." He paused then continued, "It would, however, mean you volunteering to join the Diplomatic Corps for a while." Jimmy's advice 'never volunteer' rang loudly in Edgar's brain but he was like a rabbit trapped in a car's headlights, he knew it spelt danger but couldn't move.

The colonel leant across, offering a cigarette from a silver case. "You would be manning a wireless station at one of our embassies but, because it is in a neutral country, we are not allowed to use service personnel. You will of course still receive your army pay plus a generous living allowance. What do you say?"

Again the nagging voice appeared in his brain saying, "if it's too good to be true then it is" but he silenced it.

"Of course Sir, anything to help the war effort."

"Good, well done."

Then Colonel Hudson leant forwards and, looking at the hard, ruthless face staring at him, Edgar suddenly wondered if he made the correct decision. "This is a top secret mission. You will not tell anyone about it and I mean anyone. I promise you this, if I find out that you have done so, I will shoot you myself. Do I make myself clear?"

Edgar nodded, unable to speak as his vocal cords were paralysed with fear. This was no idle threat.

"Excellent. Now I understand you have a fiancée?"

Again Edgar nodded.

"You will continue writing to her but do not say where you are, make her think you are still in this country, at Salisbury. The letters will be brought back in the diplomatic bag and posted over here. No one can know what you are doing, is that clear? Many lives depend on this, including yours."

Despite a throat that felt as dry as the Sahara Edgar managed to croak, "Yes, Sir."

"Good. Now do you know where Goodge Street tube station is?"

"No but I'm sure I can find out."

"Report there at ten o'clock tomorrow morning." He leant back to show that the interview was over. Edgar rose unsteadily to his feet, saluted and left the room. Outside his escort was waiting and was that a look of pity he noticed on her pretty face?

Ey Up Adolf

As he made his way back to the War Office he wondered what he had done and if he would ever see Ann again? Despite what had been said he questioned if a neutral country was his real destination, that colonel was far too intimidating to be involved with the diplomatic corps.

*   *

Back in the office the two colonels were talking in hushed tones. "Just how are we going to get those letters back to this country, we don't have access to the diplomatic bag, we don't exist?"

"What letters?"

"But if the letters stop I should imagine the young lady will not be pleased."

"Sometimes sacrifices have to be made in war time," came the cold answer.

*   *

Edgar returned from his interview and gave the sergeant a description of the colonel. "I think I've come across him, slightly tubby with a high, pitched voice, sounds a bit like a school teacher, you expect him to call you sonny."

"That's him," replied Edgar, "who is he?"

"Sounds like 'soapy' Miller. Don't let that act deceive you, he's as sharp as a razor blade, not someone you can fool easily. Mind like a filing cabinet, never forgets a thing and an organisational genius."

"What unit is he with?"

"The rumour is he has been transferred to some hush-hush lot. Whatever they wanted you to do I hope you said no." The sergeant turned back to his teleprinter, leaving Edgar to consider his future, or possible lack of it.

Chapter 16

The day was overcast and miserable, echoing Edgar's mood. He wondered if he had made the biggest mistake in his life. It had seemed a good idea, get away from the army, the bombing and food shortages, visit a foreign country, something he had never done, but when Colonel Hudson spoke suddenly it had all changed.

The bus arrived, Edgar boarded then sank back into his dark thoughts. What had he got himself involved with, who were these colonels, why was it so secretive and why on earth was he reporting to a tube station?

The bus made its way through the streets and Edgar stared out of the window until, with a start, he saw 'Tottenham Court Road' and the familiar sign of the tube flashed past. He wearily pulled himself to his feet and rang the bell for the bus to stop. Feeling much like the condemned man on his way to the gallows he descended the stairs and stepped from the platform. Across the road was Goodge St station so he approached the entrance set in the red brick wall.

Inside was cool and very quiet, as if normal noises were afraid to enter. Edgar had expected passengers scurrying along but the only person present was a big, tough-looking man in a long, woollen overcoat, leaning indifferently on the wall, one hand in his large pocket clutching a bulky object.

"Can I help you mate, you look lost?" he asked in a deep, gruff voice from smoking too many Park Drive cigarettes.

Ey Up Adolf

"I was told to report here, but I am beginning to think I must have mis-heard."

"Name?" questioned the man, suddenly becoming far more alert, approaching Edgar and towering over him. Edgar noticed he had not removed his hand from his pocket and whatever he was holding was now pointing at Edgar's stomach.

"Stanton, signalman."

"Take the first lift down to the lowest level and someone will meet you."

Edgar slipped inside and immediately started to sink into the bowels of the earth. He felt the lift would never stop then it shuddered to a halt and he opened the door, to be faced with a long tunnel lit by weak electric bulbs slung from the ceiling. Suddenly a skinny private in army uniform appeared from a side branch and asked, "Stanton?"

"Yes."

"Follow me." He disappeared back through the archway. Inside was a desk and, disappearing down the tunnel, racks of clothes and other assorted items and equipment. After consulting a sheet of paper he demanded, "Paybook and identity card!" Edgar fumbled in his pocket and produced both, these were the army passport to anything. Satisfied Edgar was genuine he again consulted his list. "Right, suits, civil servant, two, shirts same grade, shoes…….."

To Edgar the list seemed endless and with each item a short, bald man would appear from somewhere down the tunnel, carrying the correct article, until finally a suitcase appeared.

"Here are your papers, travel warrant and some local currency. You will be paid the correct expenses for your grade, for meals and such like, plus your army pay will be accrued over here for your return."

Edgar's eyes bulged. He had assumed he would either eat in a mess or have to use his own money to live on. It had not occurred to him that living in a foreign country pound notes would not be any use. There was a lot he was going to have to learn.

"You have everything you need here, do not take anything else with you. Your personal things will be collected and stored. You leave from Netheravon at 09:00 tomorrow. Well, get a move on."

In a daze Edgar packed the clothes into the suitcase, returned to the lift and ascended to the surface where he found the minder in the coat had gone and the sun was starting to peek from behind the clouds. For the first time in twenty four hours Edgar felt he could breathe freely.

*   *

Ann was busy rattling away at her typewriter when Mr Munroe came in and sat down at his desk. He cleared his throat to attract her attention, "Ann, how much do we pay you?"

"Thirty five shillings a week," she replied, smiling inwardly because that was a big increase from her previous employment. Even so, she still managed to spend it fairly easily.

"I think we should do something about that." For a moment her heart quaked, had Mr Munroe decided she was being overpaid. He picked up the phone. "Munro here," he barked. "How much do we pay secretaries in London? Well, the cost of living in Sheffield is nearly as high, it's making me a pauper staying here, I want to raise my secretary's wages." There was a pause then he exploded, "No, I bloody well do not agree!" Then, "Effective immediately," and banged down the phone. "That's settled, you are getting a raise."

"How much?" Ann asked timidly, hoping it might be as much as five shillings, two pounds a week was a good wage for a girl.

Ey Up Adolf

Mr Munroe sat twirling his pen around, enjoying stretching out the moment then he announced, "Your new remuneration will be…….." Ann held her breath. "…… five pounds a week."

At first she could not believe her ears then she exclaimed, "Bloody hell!"

Mr Munroe looked at her sternly. "I think you have been working with me for too long, you are picking up my bad habits."

*   *

Ready to travel Edgar made his way to the train station wearing one of his new suits and bought a ticket to Salisbury where he would have to change for the next leg of his journey to Netheravon, the RAF base in Wiltshire. He had never been able to afford clothes like this and now he had been given them. Just wait until he came home and showed them to Ann, boy would she be envious of the quality.

When Edgar arrived at the airfield he presented his pass to the guard at the gate. Instantly a klaxon sounded and a fire engine screamed across the square, its bell ringing imperiously, followed a moment later by a sputtering roar from above as a Spitfire hurtled overhead, dense black smoke streaming from the engine. It was so close that Edgar could see the line of bullet holes down the side. The pilot held up a thumb, whether to signify he was alright or that the enemy was in a far worse state Edgar was not certain.

A few seconds later the bell stopped. "He's down safely," announced the guard.

"Not quiet round here, is it?"

"Not often. If you report to the office they'll allocate you a bunk for the night."

It was dark when the sirens sounded, filling the night sky with their banshee wail and people's hearts with dread. Ann headed for the door and picked up her bag as she passed the sideboard. "Will you be alright pet?" asked her mother. "I don't like you going out in the dark like this, there's no-one to walk down with you."

"I'll be fine, even the bogy men are in the shelters." They went out of the back door then parted company, Ann down the path to the street, while her mother and Douglas made their way to the air-raid shelter.

She hurried alongside the dark mass of the playing fields looking into the sky where she could see the searchlights moving questioningly around, probing the skies for enemy bombers. Occasionally they would reflect back off the silent, hanging shape of a barrage balloon, soundlessly standing guard over the massive complex of steel works.

Walking briskly Ann quickly covered the half mile to the fire station and signed in for duty. One by one the others arrived, until they had enough for a full crew then she picked up the telephone and announced they were operational. She had just replaced the receiver when it rang. "They can't want us already?"

"I bet it's Dave, wanting us to sign him in," replied Pat sitting alongside. Dave worked in the Clifton pub and was always late, his regulars weren't going to leave their pints until they had drunk the last drop. They were Yorkshiremen after all. Ann or Pat, depending who answered the phone, would sign him in then when he arrived he would always present them with a small, miniature bottle of something, brandy or rum usually, to put in their drink later.

"Right Dave, two minutes," said Ann then she put down the phone. Another long, sleepless night had just begun.

Chapter 17

The next morning Edgar made his way to the mess hall. He was both looking forwards and dreading the next few hours. He had never flown and was uncertain what to expect. He looked at his breakfast and wondered if this was a good idea.

"First time up?" asked a flight lieutenant at the next table. Edgar nodded a reply. "Don't worry, if the worst happens you'll have a brown bag."

"What for?"

"To be sick in," chuckled the flier then departed, leaving Edgar feeling even more apprehensive.

Eventually a WAAF approached him. "Mr Stanton, your flight is ready."

At first Edgar did not react, he was unaccustomed to being addressed by his civilian title. He rose to his feet, picked up his suitcase and followed the guide across the grass to the waiting aeroplane. Edgar recognised the plane that stood on the tarmac, he had seen it on countless news reels, a two-engined Dakota. Edgar looked in awe, how was something that large going to get into the air, and more importantly, stay there?

Gingerly he made his way round the tall tail and climbed the steps. The interior appeared cramped, with rows of uncomfortable canvas seats fastened to the sides and a curved roof that arched over his head. For once in his life Edgar was glad that he was not six foot tall.

Suspiciously he sat down on the flimsy seat and tried to look casual, as if he did this every day, then glanced sideways trying to see if there were any brown bags about.

A few minutes later the door was closed and the propellers started to move slowly. As he stared they spun faster and faster, until they were a blur, then he felt a slight jolt as they taxied to the end of the runway. "I don't know what the fuss is about, this isn't too bad, it's like being in a car." He felt the plane swing round then stop. "What now?" he wondered. Seconds later the engines revved, the whole plane shook violently and Edgar was convinced that the wings would fall off with the vibration. Suddenly they were off, speeding down the runway. The bumpy ride smoothed out, they were airborne. He felt the pressure build up in his ears, becoming painful, suddenly they both popped. He peered out of the window at the clinging whiteness as they passed through the blanket of clouds. As they burst through into the brilliant sunshine Edgar relaxed. He was on his way to Lisbon.

*   *

Ann dismounted from the tram outside her offices, yawning and having difficulty keeping her eyes open. Twice on the short journey from Rotherham she had felt her head nodding and her eyes closing.

Two men in front of her were discussing the previous night. A bomb had landed where they lived in Sheffield. It destroyed a row of terraced houses, fortunately killing no-one, only the neighbour's cat. "Not that it was any loss, always leaving its calling card on my path." She realised they had been lucky, not a single bomb had dropped on Rotherham but she knew it was only a matter of time. At least Edgar would be safe, it was unlikely the Germans would drop a bomb on Salisbury Plain.

Thinking about Edgar made her remember his last visit and how strained their relationship had been, but at least they had sorted it before he left. "Perhaps there will be a letter from him

Ey Up Adolf

when I get home," she wondered as she made her way down the corridor to her office. He had promised to write regularly.

*   *

The sun was high in a cloudless sky as the Dakota started its descent towards Lisbon, the city spread out alongside the deep blue ocean. Edgar stared out of the window, his nose flattened against the glass for a better view. As they sank lower he made out the waves breaking on the beaches then individual white buildings and green parks until finally the wide, grey runway flashed beneath them. The wheels touched with a screech and puff of burning rubber, the plane bumped, bounced slightly then returned to earth to continue down the straight ribbon of tarmac. For the first time in his life Edgar was on foreign soil.

He cleared through the official checks, aided by his diplomatic papers, and stood on the pavement outside wondering what to do next. As his knowledge of Portuguese was not even sufficient to order a glass of beer he could have a problem. Then an English voice called, "Mr Stanton. I've been sent to collect you, throw your bag in the boot then climb in."

Edgar did as he was instructed then settled onto the hot seat, already he could feel the sweat forming under his armpits. "A bit warmer than England?" asked the driver as he swung the car into the fast moving traffic, ignoring the honking horns.

"Just a bit. Are we going to the embassy?"

Swerving round a slow moving tram the driver replied, "Sort of. We are actually situated round the corner in a separate building, security you know."

Edgar nodded sagely even though he didn't understand why they could not be in the same building as the rest of the embassy staff. He sat back, wound down his window and, as the breeze helped to cool him down, realised there was a problem with the traffic. They were all driving on the wrong side of the road.

Chapter 18

The driver turned down a wide avenue lined with large buildings set back behind wrought iron gates and Edgar noticed a union jack hanging in front of one of them. "That's the embassy, we are just round the corner." The car slid to a halt outside a tall, three storey, Georgian-looking building complete with small balconies on the first floor. "That's us, hop out and announce yourself while I park the car."

Edgar climbed out, squinted in the strong sunlight, removed his suitcase, crossed the pavement to the heavy, wooden door, tapped and waited. It opened and he was ushered inside. He stepped into the cool interior where two armed guards were on duty in the corridor with a third behind a barred grille at the far end.

"Welcome," announced a wiry, fit-looking man in a light-coloured, linen suit who appeared from a side office. "You must be Edgar Stanton, our new wireless expert. How was the flight, boring as usual?"

Edgar was about respond that, as it was his first time in an aeroplane it was not boring at all, but refrained.

"I'll show you to your quarters then where you will be working." He led the way up a flight of stairs that had an ornate, gold painted rail running along the open side then up a second flight that was not so impressive. At the end of the corridor he opened a door and indicated for Edgar to enter. "I'm afraid the rooms are not that big but the compactness is compensated by the view." He opened the wooden shutters to reveal

Ey Up Adolf

a panorama of the city and river mouth beyond, with a multitude of small boats flitting about. After his cramped barracks this was palatial and the view breathtaking. Edgar was duly impressed.

They went downstairs and along the corridor to a heavy, varnished door. "This is your domain." Edgar entered a small room with the wireless, teleprinter and other assorted bits and pieces that were familiar to him. On the table was a pile of messages waiting to be sent. "There's a small kitchen downstairs, grab a sandwich or something then start on that lot will you."

A few minutes later Edgar was back, with a sandwich containing soft cheese and tomato, which he'd almost forgotten existed, and, wonder of wonders, an orange. He removed his jacket, unfastened his collar, picked up the first message, glanced at the jumble of letters, obviously in cipher, then started.

The sun began to lose its burning heat and the shadows lengthened by the time Edgar finished the last message. He rose, stretched his back and stepped into the corridor. There was no-one about but he could hear voices so he proceeded in that direction. Another, larger room with the door open allowed him to see a couple of desks, a map of the city and the man who he had met earlier, but no-one else.

"Hello, come in. I realised I didn't introduced myself, I'm Captain James Leigh." Although he was dressed as a civilian Edgar sensed a vitality about him, a feeling of energy mixed with something else that he couldn't put his finger on. Edgar started to salute but was stopped by a shake of the head. "Like you I'm unattached at the moment so there are no ranks here."

"No," thought Edgar, "but you made sure I knew you were a captain and I'm just a signalman. No ranks, my elbow."

"How far have you got with those messages?"

"Finished," replied Edgar, taking a small pleasure from the startled expression on the officer's face. "I don't mess about."

"We were told you knew your stuff but I'm still surprised. Well, there won't be anything else today, it's a well know fact civil servants don't work after five o'clock so the evening's your own. Might I suggest you try one of the cafes down by the harbour, the meat's nothing special but the fish is first class. I'd join you but I've a report to finish and at the rate I'm going it'll take me all night. Unlike real civil servants I have to keep going until the job is finished."

Edgar left the building and wandered down the narrow road opposite, taking in the sights and smells. He passed narrow, enclosed alleyways, certain he would not venture down one of those after dark, especially near the waterfront.

At the bottom of the hill he came to a wide thoroughfare lined with lofty, white buildings that seemed to go all the way to the clear blue sky, at least five stories high, with tall, narrow windows on each floor. Edgar stopped to admire the view, he had never seen anything like this before, he would bet that even Leeds had nothing as grand.

Having had his fill of architecture, and feeling his stomach rumble, Edgar continued down the wide street, the salt in the air telling him he was close to his destination. He came out on the edge of the harbour, the wide expanse of clear blue water extending in front of him with a multitude of different craft bobbing on the slight waves. He wandered along the quayside, stepping over the wet mooring ropes, until he found a tiny café with tables outside. This represented everything foreign, the sort of place he had only seen in films. He crossed the road and sat down on one of the small chairs at a wobbly, cane table. Immediately a waiter appeared and spoke in Portuguese. Edgar had not given the language barrier a second thought, "Er, I want a drink," he said, pantomiming lifting a glass to his lips.

Ey Up Adolf

"You are English, I can speak a little of your language as I have a cousin working in London. What do you want to drink?"

"Do you have beer?"

"Certainly." He disappeared leaving Edgar to fish in his pocket for money. The waiter reappeared with a bottle, a glass and a small slip of paper, all of which he placed on the table.

"How much?" asked Edgar, holding out a brightly coloured note.

The waiter shook his head, "No, pay at the bar when you are finished."

Edgar was amazed, beer on tick, that certainly wouldn't happen at home. He poured the pale liquid into his glass, looked at it suspiciously, lifted it to his nose and sniffed. "It smells like beer," he muttered to himself, "but it's a funny colour, perhaps they water it down." He placed the glass to his lips and took a small sip. It actually tasted like beer, a bit sweeter than he was used to, more like that mild stuff, but definitely drinkable. He picked up the menu and started to read but it might have been written in Chinese for all the sense it made. He glanced round, saw the same waiter so attracted his attention. "Can you explain what it says?"

The waiter took it from him and read down the list, pronouncing each one slowly then describing it. Many were fish dishes with contents that Edgar had never heard of before, let alone eaten, like tuna, or even more exotically swordfish. "What happened to battered cod," he wondered. Then his ears heard something he knew, 'Sausage.' "I'll have that. Even in a foreign country they'll know how to cook a banger."

Chapter 19

Ann was returning from work, the bus chugging up Clifton Lane past the park.

"I didn't really want to finish," said a stout woman in a grey, woollen coat with a floral full-length apron showing underneath, "but my old man doesn't like me being out late. Well that's what he says but I think it's because of all the young men there, he's jealous."

Ann looked at the woman's ample figure, large false teeth and small, bald patch and just managed to hold back a chuckle.

"What exactly do you do?" enquired her friend.

"Help with the food. Quite a lot of the lads pop in for a quick bite and play snooker."

Ann almost stopped listening, snooker halls, dens of iniquity her mother called them, full of spivs and ne'r-do-wells.

"Of course there's other things, a reading room with the daily papers and a wireless to listen to. The vicar pops in occasionally so they can talk to him if they have a problem."

"That doesn't sound like a snooker hall," thought Ann.

"Well, the YMCA is going to have to manage without you in future."

"Yes, until they find a replacement."

Ann stood up to leave. "The YMCA. There'll be lots of people my age there and I've always liked cooking, perhaps I'll look into it." She was still considering as she entered her house. "Hello mum, is there a letter from Edgar today?"

"No, pet."

Ey Up Adolf

"That's strange, he's never missed so many days. In fact I've not heard from him since….." Suddenly it struck her, she had not received a letter since his leave when she accused him of having another woman. The claws of nagging doubt started their work, sowing the seeds of distrust. "I'll write after tea and make sure he's alright."

She plonked down in the chair, flicked off her shoes and sat back. Her father had finished his dinner and picked up his cup of tea. He took a sip then placed it back down on the table, next to the sugar bowl. Very deliberately he picked up the spoon, tapped it against his cup then sat back and waited. After a few seconds he repeated it but louder this time.

"What's wrong hen?" asked her mother, appearing from the back.

"There's no sugar in my tea."

"Oh, sorry." She took the spoon from his hand, carefully ladled two heaps into the cup, stirred it and handed it back. Without a word of thanks her father raised it to his lips and drank.

Ann sat and watched the performance, one she had seen many times. "If Edgar believes he will behave like that when we are married he has another think coming. If I'm out working he can jolly well help me around the house when he comes home. I'm not going to be a slave in my own house."

*   *

Edgar completed his work for the day. "Civil service hours! Baloney!" He switched off his equipment and closed the door, bumping into Captain Leigh in the process.

"Evening, Edgar, just finished?"

"Yes, I'm off for something to eat."

"Still going to that café down by the harbour?"

"Yes but I'm taking your advice and sticking to the fish. Those sausages were terrible, full of pepper and garlic. It is a good job I'm here on my own, if there had been anyone else in the room they would have had to wear a gas mask."

Captain Leigh smiled, "Typical Englishman abroad," he thought. "If you want to try somewhere else for a change I can recommend a nice café near the square."

"Thanks," replied Edgar, "and I am learning a few words of the local lingo, I can say please, thank you and a beer."

"Very good but don't forget my suggestion. Why don't you try it tonight? It's called 'café do alimento de mar'"

"Sounds a bit of a mouthful and very expensive," replied Edgar.

"You can afford it, treat yourself. The food is very good and the place is renowned throughout Lisbon," said Captain Leigh, "and not just for the food," he thought to himself.

"Reight, I'll give it a go then."

Captain Leigh returned to his office, sat down and heaved a sigh of relief. He thought Edgar was never going to leave his nice, little, safe café but now he would be out in the open, a tasty worm dangling on the end of the hook and all he could hope was that a shark took the bait.

Unaware of the machinations that were going on around him Edgar strolled to the large square surrounded on three sides by shops and cafes. The evening was warm, people sitting outside having a drink, so different to home with its constant threat of bombing, blackouts and shortages. Here the shops were bursting with goods, both legal and smuggled. Edgar decided to take Ann a nice present back, something she would not be able to get at home. Thinking of Ann he wondered if she had received the letter he had sent three days ago. Captain Leigh had taken it from him, promising it would go in the diplomatic bag.

Had he not been so engaged with his own thoughts and more observant Edgar might have noticed, a hundred yards behind, the young couple walking in the same direction.

Ey Up Adolf

Crossing the square Edgar saw a three-storied, white building with the typical Lisbon orange, terracotta tiled roof and several tables outside which were all taken. He opened the door and found himself in a low-ceilinged, smoky room with crumbling ornate coving. "Not unlike the tap room at the Angel back in Rotherham," he thought. At the far end a small band, guitar, accordion and some sort of lute, were playing quietly. Although it was early evening only a few tables were still vacant, Edgar sat down at one of them. Suddenly a waiter appeared to take his order.

"Uma cerveja por favour," stated Edgar totally exhausting his entire knowledge of Portuguese. While he waited for his drink to arrive he surveyed the menu and wondered if he had made a mistake. There was nothing he recognised and now the waiter would think he spoke the language.

"Excuse me," came a pleasant, slightly accented voice from just behind him. "The café is very full tonight and all the tables seem to be taken so would you mind if I sat with you."

The young couple watched the scene unfold from the back of the room. The man leant close to his companion so that no-one else could hear and whispered, "Bingo, the bait is taken."

Edgar turned to see a smartly dressed lady, probably in her thirties, though he would be the first to admit he was not very good at judging women's ages. "Er, yes, I mean no, please do."

She smiled, sat down and straightened her calf length dress and as she did Edgar caught the faint scent of expensive perfume.

"Are you new to Lisbon?" the lady asked.

"Yes," replied Edgar nervously. She was slightly older than him, attractive and obviously sophisticated. "I work at the embassy."

"A diplomat, how glamorous," she replied with a smile.

"No, I'm just a wireless operator, I send messages back to England."

"You must be very clever and so young." A waiter appeared. "What are you having?"

"I don't know. I haven't a clue what the menu says."

"You could try the lamb."

"Good idea, I've eaten so much fish I think I'll be developing fins."

The lady chuckled. "I know what you mean. When I first arrived my husband advised me not to touch the meat."

"Is he joining you," asked Edgar. "I can move to another table if you want."

"No, he won't," she replied with a touch of sadness in her voice, "he's in England, a fighter pilot with the Free French squadron but I haven't heard from him for several weeks." Edgar saw a small tear appear in the corner of her eye which she dabbed delicately with the tip of her handkerchief.

Across the room the young couple strained to try and hear the conversation above the clatter of plates and buzz of people talking. "She's very good," murmured the young woman, "just the right touch, that dabbing at a crocodile tear."

"I'm Claire Loussier," the lady said, presenting her slim hand.

Edgar hesitated, was he supposed to shake it or kiss it. Uncertainly he took it and gave it a gentle shake, "Edgar Stanton," he announced.

While they waited for their meals to arrive Claire kept Edgar amused with stories about France.

At the end of their meal she rose, shook his hand, letting it linger a fraction longer than necessary, and left. As she walked across the room, with a casual, elegant stride, Edgar's gaze, along with those of all the other men in the room, followed her.

Ey Up Adolf

"That was a master class in how to hook a fish," muttered his female watcher with admiration. "She really must be French, no other nation has the same savoir faire as they do."

"Never mind that," ordered her companion, "we need to find out where she's going." He threw a handful of currency onto the table and they departed.

*   *

After they had finished eating Ann said, "When I was coming home on the bus a woman was saying that the YMCA was looking for a cook. It's volunteer work, for the war effort you know, helping out." Ann realised she was starting to babble so shut up and waited.

"I think it's a good idea. You have made Sunday lunch since you were only a bairn. Are you going to call in tomorrow?"

"I thought I'd collect Pat and go down tonight."

Her mother gave a suspicious look but agreed, so an hour later they were both making their way through the door into the YMCA, receiving appraising looks from the group of soldiers in the snooker room and a mistrustful glare from a middle aged lady behind the food counter.

"Girls aren't allowed in here!"

"We heard you are looking for a cook," Ann announced.

"What both of you?"

Pat's face took on an expression of shock. "Not me, I can burn water, I only came to keep her company."

"Very sensible. You should never go anywhere on your own after dark, especially if you have to pass close to a public house, terrible places."

"She sounds just like my dad," whispered Ann out of the corner of her mouth.

"Pardon."

"That's what my dad says, not to go out alone."

"Sensible man. Now did you say you can cook?"

"She was the best in school," replied Pat before Ann had time to speak, "her mum used to work as the cook in a big mansion."

"It wasn't a mansion just a large house up north, near Durham. But I do know how to cook."

"Right, I'll give you a week's trial, starting Monday."

Ann's face fell. "I won't be able to work every night, I'm a fire-woman as well, we both are."

The woman smiled. "Well, you're doing your bit aren't you. I'm certain we can work round that. Now how about your friend, we could do with a washer-up as well."

Pat spluttered, "Thank you but I have enough on, with a job and the fire service, but it was kind of you to consider me," then dragging Ann by the arm she retreated. "We need to go, don't like being out late. Bye!"

Chapter 20

Ann found her mother standing at the end of the street. "What are you doing here, I told you I'd be back early?"

"It's not you, pet, it's that stupid dog." After their original dog, Daisy, had died they had replaced it with a new one called Peter, a mongrel, with a large dollop of bulldog, short legs, barrel chest and obstinate nature. Recently he had taken to running with a pack of strays. "He ran off earlier and I haven't seen him since." Together they walked back to their house. "It would serve him right if the Germans dropped a bomb on him," grumbled Ann's mother, who had never really taken to the dog.

They settled in front of the fire, a cup of Camp coffee clutched in their hands when they heard a scratching at the back door. "That'll be the brainless hound," her mother said, "now he's had his fun he's come back for food."

"Stay where you are," said Ann, standing up. She made her way to the back door and opened it. A low, bulky shape sloped inside, emitting an awful smell. "What on earth?" She looked at the bedraggled, mud splattered animal that stood, dripping dirty water on the lino. "Don't you dare move!" she shouted at the smelly animal. "Sit!"

With a doleful expression the dog did as it was ordered, squatting on the hard, shiny floor, a puddle of rank-smelling water forming round it.

"Where's he been to get in that state?" asked Ann.

"On the allotments. There's an open sewer at the bottom end, near the houses, and he's been chasing about in it. You naughty dog," her mother added, wagging a finger at the cowering animal. "Put some warm water in the sink, get some old cloths and the carbolic soap, he'll have to have a good bath to remove all that filth."

The dog let out a whimper and hung his head, whether in shame or in fear of what was to come was uncertain.

*   *

Edgar arrived back, climbed the stairs and was surprised to see a light on in Captain Leigh's office and voices, then a floorboard squeaked as he put his weight on it. From the office there was a shuffling movement, the sound of a door closing then Captain Leigh emerged.

"Evening Edgar, did you take my advice?"

"Yes, I did."

"Good, so how was it?"

"Fine, very busy, full of interesting people."

"Excellent! Glad you had a decent time."

"Did you have a visitor?"

"No, just finishing a report," he replied unconvincingly.

Edgar turned to go to his room. There were things happening that he didn't know about but he was determined to make it his business to find out.

*   *

Ann rinsed the last suds off the dog and was drying him with an old towel when her mother came back in. "There, finished." Ann lifted the dog out of the sink and placed him on the floor. Immediately Peter padded through into the kitchen, his rear waddling from side to side, then he settled down in front of the fire. Ann and her mother followed. "Glad to see you managed to clean him up," then, leaning forwards, she wagged a finger and said, "Bad dog!"

Peter lifted his head, growled and bared his teeth as if to state, "You can say what you like when I'm dirty but don't criticise me when I'm clean."

*   *

The next morning Edgar considered his options for gathering information. He made his way to the ground floor, ostensibly to locate some breakfast, but in fact to start operation 'Edgar investigates.'

At the bottom of the stairs he paused, nodding to the sergeant in the booth, "I'm just going to the kitchen, can I get you a cuppa?"

"No thanks," came the gruff answer.

Ten minutes later he emerged clutching a cup of coffee, paused in the corridor long enough for the aroma to percolate to every corner of the hall then made his way up the stairs to his tiny office. Once inside he found there was a pile of messages so he picked up the first one, turned on his teleprinter and started to transmit.

When he had worked his way through the stack he stopped. "Right, coffee time."

Again he made his way to the ground floor. "Ey up," he called cheerfully. "Starting to get warm out there. I'm just making a brew, anyone want one." A shake of the head from the booth then, from down the hall, "Love one mate. We are not supposed to, so just slip it on that ledge and I'll sup it when no-one's about."

"Right-oh, tea or coffee?"

"Tea, milk, three sugars."

Five minutes later Edgar was back with two mugs in his hand, one of which he slipped onto the shelf, tucking it behind a vase, partly out of sight.

"Cheers, mate," whispered the guard gratefully.

Edgar made his way back to his room, stage one of his plan complete, he'd made a friend.

*   *

Ann entered her office and was surprised to find Mr Munroe was not there. She contemplated going to the canteen for a drink when the door opened.

"Good morning, Mr Mon…" then realised it wasn't her boss but the receptionist.

"I'm sorry to intrude. I've a message for you from Mr Munroe." She paused and consulted a note in her hand. "He wants you to order a car and come to his house straight away. Here is the address." She placed the paper on the desk and scuttled out, closing the door behind her.

"Mr Munroe tends to have that effect, his bite is definitely worse than his bark. Mind he's always polite to me so I can't complain." She looked at the address and remembered that, a week earlier, he had taken a house on the outskirts of Sheffield so that his family could join him.

Ten minutes later she was sitting in the back of a long, black Ford as it sped down the road towards the centre of Sheffield and beyond that the rising mass of the Derbyshire hills and the home of Mr Munroe.

*   *

Normally Edgar didn't bother with lunch time but today he made his way downstairs at one o'clock. On a previous occasion he had noticed that the guards took it in turns to nip into

Ey Up Adolf

the kitchen between one and two to eat. He entered the room and saw the friendly guard sitting at the small table, a slice of bread and cheese in his ample fist.

"Ey up," said Edgar. "That looks good, I think I'll have one."

"Not seen you down here before."

"Usually too busy, I just grab a bite when I can. I don't get to see much stuck up in the wireless room, unlike you lot who see everything, no-one gets in or out without you knowing."

"That's true, unless they use the back entrance."

Edgar's ears pricked up at this. "What back entrance?"

"There's another way in, at the rear, only a very few people use it and they have their own key." He leant forwards and whispered, "I think they're spies. I saw one once, a muscular young guy, he slipped in and nipped up the back stairs a bit sharpish."

Edgar tucked this piece of information away then returned upstairs with a puzzled frown on his face. What was going on? He had a lot of questions and as of yet no real answers.

*   *

The Ford turned onto Ringinglow Road, now they were in the country, climbing up the backbone of England. They turned off, the tyres crunching on the loose gravel, an impressive, stone detached house appeared, at least six bedrooms and with the traditional, chunky slates on the roof. As soon as the car stopped Mr Munroe emerged, wearing his coat and hat.

"Thank you for coming straight away. My wife has had an accident and I need to get to the hospital at once. As there is no-one to look after the children I wondered if you'd mind." Without waiting for an answer he leapt into the car and it roared away.

With trepidation Ann climbed the steps and entered the house. She took off her coat, hung it on the stand then walked the length of the hall to where a door was slightly ajar, allowing the sunshine to stream through and reflect off the patterned tiles on the floor. Pushing it open she found herself in a large kitchen with a wood fire burning in the Yorkshire range. At either side were tall, wooden cupboards that stretched from the floor to the ceiling.

She was so engrossed that she failed to hear tiny footsteps approaching down the hall so she jumped a mile in the air when a small voice said, "Hello! Have you come to look after us?"

Chapter 21

Ann felt exhausted. For three hours she had played hide and seek, raced around the garden trying to 'tig' the squealing children, Mary and Stuart, and helped build a den from branches and fern leaves. The two siblings thought it was hilarious when an earwig dropped onto Ann's shoulder and she frantically tried to brush it off. Now it was lunch time.

"What would you like to eat?"

"Eggs!" came the instant reply.

Ann's face fell, eggs were firmly rationed "You might not have any."

"Yes we have," replied Mary, "lots."

"They are in a bucket," continued Stuart. He pointed to a door in the corner. "In there."

Apprehensively Ann approached. Was this a trick? Would she open it and walk into a huge spider's web, complete with massive, ugly, long-legged occupant. Very carefully she unlatched the door only to find a large, clean pantry with a marble slab to keep food cool and a bucket filled to the brim with eggs, at least four dozen, all resting in water-glass to preserve them. Ann was dumbfounded, there must have been about six months ration lying there.

"It's alright to use them," stated Mary, as if she was reading Ann's thoughts. "We'll have some more tomorrow."

"Where do you get them from?"

"Chickens, don't you know anything?" asked Stuart.

"I know they come from chickens," replied Ann, but was interrupted by Mary.

"Or ducks."

"Pardon."

"You can get eggs from ducks."

"And geese and pigeons and sparrows."

"You can't eat sparrow's eggs, silly, they're too small," replied his sister.

"You could if you had enough."

"Stop!" said Ann firmly. "Where are the chickens these eggs came from?"

"The bottom of the garden," answered Mary.

"Where at the bottom of the garden?"

"In our hen house. Do you want to see it?"

Now the conversation started to make sense. Together they went out of the kitchen and, hand in hand, they trooped down the path until they came to a thick, laurel hedge. Letting go, the two children squeezed through a narrow gap in the foliage and disappeared. Ann followed and emerged by wire fencing, with a wooden hut in the middle and, scratching around, ten hens.

"Right, how do want your eggs?"

"Fried."

"Sunny side up."

"With soldiers."

*   *

Edgar finished sending a routine message as Captain Leigh entered, a worried frown on his brow and a sheet of paper in his hand. Edgar recognised the decoding pad used to make sense of the ciphers. "I'm sorry, Edgar, but I'm going to have to ask you work late tonight. We will be receiving an important signal. I don't know when, but I must have it as soon as it arrives."

Ey Up Adolf

*   *

Ann had finished drying the plates and was relieved to hear the crunch of tyres on the gravel. She hurried through the hall and opened the door in time to see Mr Monroe get out of the car.

"How is your wife?"

"Much better. I don't suppose there's a cup of tea going?" At the sound of his voice Mary and Stuart raced down the hall with excited squeals of joy. Picking one up in each arm he gave them a hug. "You are getting as big and heavy as giants."

"How's mummy?" Mary asked, a look of concern on her face.

"Why isn't she here?" demanded Stuart.

"Take them in the sitting room and I'll bring your drink," said Ann.

"That would be good."

"Would you like something to eat as well?"

"Marvellous. I knew I was right when I set you on, fast typing and can cook, what more could you ask from a secretary?"

After she had served Mr Munroe his meal he told her the car was waiting to take her home and she could have the rest of the day off.

Climbing from the posh car outside her house she wondered what the neighbours would make of it, as she had noticed several curtains twitch.

"You're home early."

"I'll tell you all about it in a minute," she replied, looking on the sideboard, disappointed that there was no letter. "Did the postman come today?"

"Yes, there was one from Norman but nothing for you. Is there a problem?"

"No, I don't know what's wrong. I'll write again and see if I can find out." She disappeared upstairs, partly to write the letter and also to avoid any more questions to which she had no answers.

*   *

Dusk had descended when Edgar finished his routine work, now all he could do was wait. "This is going to be a long evening." Knowing that the message would arrive via the teleprinter he idly twirled the knob on his wireless set, perhaps he could find some music or even a news report from home. Nothing. He kept revolving the knob, more to have something to do than expecting to find anything. Suddenly the chatter of Morse broke the silence. Instinctively he picked up his pencil, jotted down the letters and the frequency on which they were being transmitted. When it finished he glanced at what he had written but it made no sense, not that it was in a foreign language but in the randomness of the letters. It was obviously in code.

Just at that moment the door opened and Captain Leigh entered. "No joy yet?"

" 'fraid not but I just picked this up. It's not on any of our frequencies."

"German?" questioned Captain Leigh.

"Quite probably."

"Hmm, interesting. Any idea where it came from?"

"Sorry, possibly about three hundred miles from the strength of the signal but I could be way out."

"Send it to the code-breakers at Bletchley and see if they can make any sense from it. And keep a note of the frequency in case you've stumbled on something important. As a reward I'll send you up a cup of cocoa and a buttie."

"Great," replied Edgar, but a glass of beer would have been more to his liking.

*   *

Ann made her way to the post box, letter firmly grasped in her hand. She gave it a little kiss then dropped it through the

Ey Up Adolf

slot. Then she crossed the road and proceeded to Pat's house, she needed someone to talk to for reassurance, someone who inevitably had chocolate.

Ten minutes later she was sitting at the table in the kitchen, dipping into a bag of Thornton's Mis-shapes, when Pat's parents returned from the whist-drive at the church.

"Hello, Ann love, your mum alright?" asked Pat's mother.

"Yes, thank you."

"And how's that young man of yours?"

"Alright as far as I know."

"She's not heard from him for a few weeks," added Pat teasingly.

Her mother pulled up a chair and sat down. If there was a gold medal for gossip Pat's mother was a certainty to win. "Is that right? Do you think he's had an accident or summat?"

Ann shook her head, "No, Jimmy would have told me. I don't know what the problem is."

"It's always the quiet ones you have to watch out for," said Pat's father from the back of the room in a voice like the bell of doom. "Still waters run slow you know."

"Deep, dad, still waters run deep," corrected Pat.

"Well you know what I mean. He's away from home and hanging about with all them other young fella's, you never can tell what he's up to."

"Edgar's not like that."

"Well if it was me I'd write and tell him to pull his socks up and get in touch pretty sharpish, that I would," stated Pat's mother in a voice that dared you to argue.

Ann felt even more uncertain about her future than she had when she arrived. She just hoped that tomorrow would see a letter arrive.

Chapter 22

Edgar gazed out of the window, a cup of tea in one hand and a biscuit in the other. It had been a quiet morning but he knew that could easily change and a rush of messages arrive.

The door opened and Captain Leigh entered, followed by a soldier who was a stranger to Edgar, carrying a new wireless set which he plonked on the only available space in the room then departed.

"I have received an order from London concerning that message you intercepted. You were right, it was German, in fact it was from an agent in Spain, and he was reporting that he had found a suitable site for Operation Oversight. If they come on the air again you're to contact Gibraltar and Cairo at once and they'll help you triangulate the sender."

"Great," thought Edgar, "I'll be stuck in here night and day until it's all done."

"Private Jones will help you, he's not in your class but he can use a wireless." He paused as the door opened and the Private reappeared carrying a direction finder. "Hopefully our friend will resurface soon and we can get this dealt with." With a brief smile he turned and left.

"Right," said Private Jones in the deep burr of Somerset, "I'll be back to relieve you at six o'clock," then he too was gone, closing the door behind him. Edgar sat down at his desk wondering what sort of hornets nest he had disturbed this time.

Ey Up Adolf

* *

Ann arrived at work to find Mr Monroe already at his desk. "Morning Ann, I didn't really have time to thank you properly yesterday for your help."

"It was no problem and your children are wonderful, in fact I quite enjoyed it. How is your wife?"

"She's fine, she was pruning the roses in the garden and stabbed her finger on a thorn. Unfortunately they had been treated with insecticide a few days earlier and she had a bad reaction." He did not reveal that it was a new product from ICI and had now been withdrawn for further tests. It might not be suitable as an insecticide but it could have other uses, especially in wartime. "Have you heard from Edgar yet?"

"No. I wrote to him a few days ago but I have not received a reply."

"Don't worry, you know what the army is like, combine them with the postal service and his letter could easily have ended up at the North Pole with Father Christmas, though it's a bit early to ask for presents. Talking of which," he produced a bottle wrapped in tissue paper, "this is a thank you." Ann took it from him, opened it and found a bottle of sweet sherry inside. "Just don't drink it all once."

She thanked him and made her way to her desk, wondering what she was going to do with her present, she couldn't take it home, not with her parents being, strict, teetotal.

* *

Bang on the stroke of six the door opened and Private Jones appeared, his face looking flushed.

"You needn't have rushed," Edgar said, "I haven't got a date to go to or anything."

"It's not from hurrying. I was tired after arriving out here and fell asleep in the park. When I woke I had sunburn. It feels as if my face is on fire."

"Well this is the best place to be, it's like being in a dungeon."

Edgar made his way outside and strolled to the harbour, whistling 'In the Mood', the thin notes bouncing off the white walls of the narrow street. He arrived at his little, uncomplicated café, sat down at his rickety table, and Ronaldo, the waiter, appeared greeting him like a long, lost friend.

"Good evening, Mr Stanton, it is good to see you again."

"Watcha, I'll have beer while I decide what to eat."

"Certainly!" As he departed Edgar wondered if he had been too generous with his tips previously or whether he was genuinely pleased to see him. A few minutes later his beer arrived, Edgar put the glass to his lips and took a long, relaxing swig.

*   *

Ann solved the problem of the sherry by giving it to Pat for safe keeping. Now she was on her way round for a private chat and, perhaps, a small drink before they went on duty at the fire station. As she walked into the kitchen Pat was helping her mother with the pots and the bottle was standing on the small table, along with three, short-stemmed glasses. The two women put down their tea-towels. "I hope you don't mind but I offered mum a glass of your sherry, it's almost impossible to get hold of these days, especially good stuff like this."

Pat opened the bottle and poured the dark, sweet liquid into the glasses. They all took a small sip then Pat's mum launched her opening barrage, "How's Edgar, have you heard from him?"

Ann had been dreading this, she had secretly hoped that Pat's mum would not be in. "No, not yet."

Ey Up Adolf

"I think you are being too soft with him, you should put your foot down, tell him what's what."

Ann was saved from answering by the door opening and Pat's father appeared, but the respite was short lived. "Hello Ann, have you heard from Edgar yet?"

"No, she hasn't, the poor girl. I've just told her, he needs an ear-bashing."

"Like I said the other day, when the cat's away the mice will run about." Pat rolled her eyes, if her dad couldn't get the sayings right he shouldn't use them at all. "I reckon he's got a bit on the side."

"Jack, language!"

"Well, you know what I mean," he continued meekly. "He's only a young lad, away from home, down south, you don't know what temptations he has met. A well brought up Yorkshire lad, he'd be a good catch for one of them southern lasses."

"Where would he find anyone as pretty as Ann?" stated Pat, jumping to her friend's assistance. "Even Edgar's not that daft, you're talking bunkum."

"Well, I'm only saying what I think," mumbled Jack, retreating from the room under the baleful glare of his daughter.

Pat finished her drink and stood up. "We need to get off or we'll be late for duty."

"You two take care, and you, lass, think on what I said. Make sure that young fella' of yours knows where he stands, that you'll not put up with any nonsense."

As they walked through the deserted streets Ann was quiet, she had a lot on her mind.

Chapter 23

"What's up, love?" asked Pat.

"What if your dad is right, what if Edgar has found someone else?"

"How much of that sherry did you drink? You are talking rot. Edgar wouldn't dream of even looking at another woman and besides he didn't have much of a chat up line when he met you, did he? Come on, where is he going to find a cricket bat and ball down south somewhere?"

As Pat and Ann continued down the gentle slope towards the fire-station Ann watched the sun sink behind the spire of the parish church, as it had done for five hundred years.

"It has been there during the civil war, seen the industrial revolution come and go and will still be there after this little skirmish has finished, it's a symbol of permanence," Ann thought then she rubbed the ring on her finger with its small precious stones, "just like a diamond."

* *

Edgar made his way back to his base and decided to pop into the radio room. Quietly opening the door he saw Private Jones sitting in the chair, leaning backwards with his feet on the desk, his eyes closed and his breathing slow and rhythmical. Unable to resist the temptation Edgar firmly grasped the back of the chair and gave it a sharp yank. With a start the unfortunate man waved his arms about, frantically trying to regain his

Ey Up Adolf

balance. Edgar quickly righted the chair, setting all four legs on the floor again.

Private Jones turned and saw Edgar standing there with a wide grin on his face. "You daft…"

Before he could continue Edgar interrupted, "Has there been anything from our friend?"

"No, it's as quiet as a mouse. We have received a couple of other messages but I have left them for you to deal with. They are…"

He did not have time to finish the sentence as the wireless set spluttered into life. Instinctively Edgar grabbed a pad and pencil and started writing, while nodding towards the direction finder. Understanding what he meant Private Jones started transmitting to Cairo and Gibraltar to alert them as well as grabbing the wheel on the direction finder. Slowly the loop aerial revolved until the dial showed the strongest signal strength, just in time as the transmission ended.

"Did you get it?" asked Edgar eagerly.

"Yes." Now they had to wait and see if the other two listeners were quick enough to plot from their end.

*   *

Ann and Pat had just entered the yard when the siren started. As they hurried inside the phone rang.

"Dave?" queried Pat.

"Yes, he's on his way."

"That's quick, they must have been quiet at the pub tonight."

"Or he's run out of beer."

"The Clifton, not on your life."

A few minutes later the door burst open and Dave entered. "Can't chat, I'm desperate for the toilet, I'll use the one out back." He threw his jacket over the chair and raced out.

"Don't switch the light on, there's no blackout curtains in there." The 'one out back' was an outside toilet, situated in the yard behind the building and accessed through the mortuary.

"And watch out for the ghosts and bogy men." added Pat with a grin.

Now that Dave had arrived they had a full crew so Ann reported in. She picked up the pen, noticed that the sirens had stopped, and started to make a note in the report book.

Startled by a loud crash they both jumped. "What was that?" asked Pat, her eyes wide with fright.

"Well it wasn't a bomb or neither of us would be still alive. Do you think Dave's tripped over something in the dark? We'd better make sure he's alright."

Just then Alan, a grizzled veteran of the first war, ran in.

"I heard the crash, what was it?"

"We don't know but it came from the back," responded Pat, pointing through the adjoining door, "and Dave's out there."

"We'd better go and see." Alan picked up a hooded torch, turned it on and passed through the doorway, followed by the two women close on his heels. He shone the beam around. At first nothing was obvious then as he passed the light across the floor they saw the unconscious form of Dave, lying between the two rows of sheet-covered bodies. They rushed up to him just as his eyes flickered open, wide and staring.

"Are you alright?" Pat asked, as they helped him to his feet and back into the light.

"What happened?" asked Ann.

"Jacket pocket," muttered Dave, pointing to his coat. Pat tentatively felt around and found a small bottle of brandy, usually their reward for signing him in. She passed it across, he screwed the top off and took a drink. As colour reappeared on his pasty-white complexion he took a deep breath, "It was horrible. I was just coming back from the loo, there was plenty of

Ey Up Adolf

light as the moon was shining through the window when I heard this awful noise, a groaning but really deep."

The two women took a step closer to each other.

"I looked round to see what it was and a movement at the far end of the room caught my eye." He stopped and took another sip from the bottle. "I'll replace this next time," he said apologetically.

"That's fine, Dave don't worry," said Ann.

"Then what," asked Pat, by now she was holding Ann's arm.

"I turned to get a better view and saw one of the sheets start to rise up, then it slipped down to reveal the body of an old man with a bald head, staring eyes and a gaping hole where his mouth should be."

Both women's eyes shot wide, their mouths dropped open and they gasped with shock.

"That was the last I remember, I must have fainted."

Alan picked up the torch again and started towards the door.

"Where are you going?" asked Ann incredulously.

"To sort out a ghost. This station is for authorised personnel only, it has no permission to be here." He picked up a brush that was standing in the corner and held it in front of him like a rifle and bayonet. "Don't open this door for anything after I enter." Before anyone could say a word he dived through the doorway and pulled the door closed with a resounding thump.

All three gazed at the door then each other. "Should we go after him?" asked Dave.

"Not blooming likely, you heard what he said," answered Pat in a timid voice.

They stood holding their breath wondering what was going to happen next. Three sharp taps on the door. They jumped. A brief silence followed when all that could be heard was the ticking of the old clock on the wall. Again three knocks, but this time louder and with longer spaces in-between.

"Do we answer it?"

"You can," replied Pat, diving behind Dave, "personally I'm going no-where near that door. Whatever is on the other side can jolly well stay there."

They heard a low moan, a long howl and a creepy voice. "Dave, come baaaack."

"Hang on a minute," said Ann. "I know that voice. Alan stop messing about and come in here at once."

There was a titter of nervous laughter as the door opened and Alan stuck his head round with a grin from ear to ear. "Got you all going, didn't I?"

"Not at all," answered Pat turning away, "knew it was you all the time."

"But what about that corpse?" asked Dave.

"Oh, that, it's quite normal but I must admit it's a bit off-putting the first time you see it. Used to happen a lot in the trenches, gas builds up in the stomach causing the body to fold in the middle then it's forced out making the moaning sound."

"But what about the gaping mouth?"

"His false teeth are missing."

Fortunately at that moment the sirens started again so Dave's reply was drowned out.

*   *

When Edgar received confirmation from Cairo and Gibraltar he went through to Captain Leigh and handed him the figures. The officer quickly drew three straight lines which intersected at a point near the southern Spanish coast, "San Roque," he stated, "that's where he is."

"What now?" asked Edgar.

"I code a message to London, you send it and someone else makes a decision. Our job is done."

Chapter 24

A couple of days later Captain Leigh popped his head out of his office. "Now that you've got a helper why don't you take the day off? It'll give you a chance to see some of the sights and get some sun."

"Thank you, it is some time since I had any leave." As soon as he said the words he flinched, remembering the awkward time he spent with Ann.

"Are you alright?"

"Yes, fine. Wind, that spicy sausage, it doesn't agree with me. I miss a good, honest English banger."

"Don't we all, that's why we are fighting this war, to preserve the banger from the Frankfurter. Enjoy your day off," then he disappeared inside, closing the door behind him. Edgar could have kicked himself, he had wanted to have a word with the Captain but the closed door meant he did not want to be disturbed. Edgar was beginning to worry about not receiving any letters from Ann, he was concerned for her safety with all the bombing.

Edgar left the building, he was not certain what he was going to do but he was leaving before the Captain changed his mind.

*   *

Ann took the cover off her typewriter and fed in a sheet of paper, ready to start. While she waited for Mr Munroe to arrive

Neil Whyke

she considered the decision she had made last night, wondering if she had she been too hasty. When she had arrived home and discovered that there was still no letter from Edgar she had been annoyed. Straight away she wrote a short, sharp letter, demanding that he explain why he wasn't writing. She was very curt, almost bossy, and now was having second thoughts but it was too late, the letter was already in the post and making its way to Salisbury.

* *

Edgar started to relax, the sun was shining and the wine was pleasant. He suddenly jerked forwards as two men pushed past, jostling his chair, then they sat at the next table, summoning a waiter. "Zwei Lager, schnell!" one demanded arrogantly.

Edgar's feeling of well being was instantly shattered. He knew there were many Germans in Lisbon but it was still a shock. Here were his country's enemies, sitting next to him and ordering beer.

He started to his feet, his northern pugnacity rising ready to give vent to his feelings, but changed his mind. He dropped some notes onto the table and left. It was not until he was a hundred metres down the road before he started to unwind and breathe steadily again.

* *

Ann arrived home feeling tired. She glanced at the sideboard but, as every other day, there was no letter waiting. She glanced at the empty armchair. "Where's dad?"

"He had to go in early,"

As she turned, Ann saw the dried traces of tears. "What's the matter?"

Ey Up Adolf

"There has been an accident, part of the roof collapsed, and there are men trapped on the other side. Your dad has gone in to help with the rescue." She paused to wipe her nose on the corner of her pinny. "Sorry, it's just that dangerous job he has, one day he might go out and never return. At least I should be thankful that he won't be called up and killed." Suddenly the realisation of what she had just said occurred to her. "Oh!"

"It's alright. Edgar is fine, he's stuck in the middle of Salisbury Plain, well out of danger. The worst that could happen is getting a blister from too much sending on his morse key. Now do you need any help with tea, I'm starving."

"No thanks, it's all ready. I managed to get a pig's head from the butcher so I've made us some nice thick soup and the bread's fresh from the oven."

Later they were finishing the pots when Arthur bounded down the stairs noisily, his hair plastered down with Brylcreme and a clean shirt on. "Going out with Gladys?" Ann asked.

"Yes, not that it's any of your business," he replied gruffly, then stopped as the siren started to wail.

"Looks like the Luftwaffe have other plans, not unless you feel she's worth getting blown up for." Arthur glared at her then shot back upstairs as her mother gave a quizzical look. "He's going to get changed, he doesn't want to sit in the shelter in his best clothes." She picked up her coat and headed for the door. "See you later."

As Ann left her mother wondered what the world was coming to, her daughter was going out in the middle of an air raid while her son was hiding in the shelter, it just didn't seem right somehow.

Ann arrived at the fire station safely, reported them ready for duty then relaxed. There was nothing to do now but wait and see if they would be needed.

Neil Whyke

* *

After lunch Edgar caught the tram to the beach, walked along the sand, decided to have a paddle, rolled up his trousers and ventured into the rippling waves. As the cold water flowed over his bare feet he yelped with surprise. Because the sun was warm he had expected the sea to be the same, forgetting that it was the Atlantic Ocean and as cold as the North Sea at Bridlington.

* *

A clock somewhere at the back of the building struck twice and Ann yawned. They had not been needed and it had been a very long night. In an effort to keep awake she stood up and walked round the desk but the slight feeling of queasiness had now multiplied. She was certain that if she looked in a mirror the face staring back would have a green tinge.

"Are you alright? You look a bit off colour."

She turned and saw Alan standing there, a cigarette dangling from his mouth. "I'm just tired, it's making me feel a bit sick, that's all."

Alan nodded and held a packet of Benson and Hedges towards her. "Try one of these, they'll stop it."

She looked at the cigarettes with suspicion. She had never smoked, nor did any of her family. Then another wave of nausea hit her, stronger than before. "Anything must be better than this," she thought, carefully taking one of the proffered cigarettes and delicately placed it between her lips. As Alan flicked his lighter and held it up she saw a trace of a smile on his lips. Just before she touched the cigarette to the flame he withdrew it.

"You've not smoked before have you?"

"Never. How do you know?"

Ey Up Adolf

"Because that's a filtered cigarette and you are about to light the tipped end. Turn it round and try again."

Feeling her cheeks redden she did. Immediately the end glowed she took a deep breath, inhaling the smoke like she had seen Lauren Bacall do on the cinema screen. But, instead of a controlled stream of smoke issuing, seductively, from her mouth, she burst into a fit of lung-wrenching coughing.

"You're not supposed to inhale the first time you try it."

"Now you tell me," Ann spluttered, as tears rolled down her cheeks. "It's disgusting, I don't know how you can do that. Mark my words one day they will be banned."

"Never, too many people enjoy them." He turned and left.

Ann got herself a drink of water and sipped it carefully. "Well at least the sickness has gone," she thought as another bout of coughing wracked her body.

Chapter 25

The next morning Ann woke up for work after having only three hours sleep. "I can't do this for much longer," she thought as she swung her legs out of bed. "At least tonight I'm only going to the YM, so I'll be finished at nine." As she came downstairs she bumped into her father who had just arrived home, still covered in a layer of coal-dust.

"Morning hinnie," he said. "Just off to work?"

"In a few minutes."

He hesitated. "I know you get paid monthly and you are not very canny with money so here, take this." He handed across a grubby pound note. "Just don't tell your mother, she'll think I'm going soft." He gave her a smile that showed his teeth, white against his blackened face, before disappearing for a bath then some sleep. Ann slipped the note into her pocket, just in time as the door opened, and her mother came in. She fussed around for a few minutes putting out a bowl of porridge that had been slow-cooking all night. As Ann started eating, her mother looked at her with a worried expression. "You're working too hard, pet."

"I'm alright. There is a war on you know, we all have to do our bit." She swallowed a spoonful of porridge.

"I know it's the end of the month," whispered her mother, sitting down next to her, "how are you off for money?"

Ann shrugged her shoulders. "I'll manage"

Looking behind to make sure her husband had not returned her mother reached into her pinny pocket and produced a ten

Ey Up Adolf

shilling note, which she handed across. "Here take this but don't tell your father, he'll only worry about you."

Ann slipped the money into her pocket, wondering why they went through this pantomime every month, surely by now they had both realised what was happening.

After breakfast she made the slow journey to work, only to find that there was a message from Mr Munroe saying he had gone to Cardiff but could she type up the report on his desk. She crossed the room and picked up the folder, noting the red writing that said 'TOP SECRET'. Nothing new there then.

Just before lunch time the door opened and Mr Turner stuck his head round, "I'm popping into Rotherham and, since it's pay day, do you want me to go to the bank for you?"

"Yes, please." Ann smiled, armed with her wages, the money from her parents and her clothing coupons she could go shopping at the weekend.

*   *

Edgar sat back and stretched, it had been busy the last week since the fuss with the intercepted messages. Captain Leigh stuck his head round the door, "I need a word."

Edgar started to complain he had a pile of work to do but the expression on the captain's face stopped him. Wordlessly he followed him down the corridor and into the office. Gesturing to a spare chair Captain Leigh started speaking. "First let me congratulate you on a job well done but I have been pestered by the army, so it has been decided, reluctantly, to send you back to Salisbury. You leave tomorrow." Edgar's jaw dropped but he knew he would have to return at some point. "I suggest you take the rest of the day off."

Edgar rose to his feet, without thinking saluted, then turned, quietly closed the door, made his way upstairs and quickly packed his few possessions.

Neil Whyke

Ready, Edgar looked at his watch, he had time to nip out and get Ann a present. He crossed the road and waited in the shade for the tram. "This sunshine is something I'll miss when I get back to England," he thought to himself, "but there will be compensations, I'll be able to see Ann instead of sending letters all the time."

*   *

Ann sat at her typewriter but for once her fingers were not flying over the keys, she was thinking back to the night before. She had visited Pat and had received the customary grilling from her mum. Had Edgar written? What was the problem? Did he have someone else? All she could do was shake her head in reply but deep down she felt she knew the answer. He must have received her letters and was ignoring them. It was over. All their plans and dreams, gone.

Convinced that her friends were right and Edgar had found someone else she decided to end it rather than be made a fool of. She wrote a very short, cryptic letter, took the ring from her finger, slipped it into a registered envelope and marched resolutely to the post-box.

Now she wondered if she should have waited, but she knew the decision would have to be made at some point. It might as well be now then she could get on with her life.

*   *

Later that night Edgar was looking out of the bedroom window, watching the lights on the boats in the harbour sway on the night tide. The sky was an intense black and the stars shone brightly, tiny, sharp pinpricks. Suddenly a flickering, orange glow appeared down in the old town, flames, and now he could make out a dense cloud of black smoke.

Ey Up Adolf

"That doesn't look too good," he muttered then jumped as a sudden flare of intense light followed by a burst of sparks lit the air. "Wow!" he exclaimed, involuntarily taking a pace backwards. "That was gas exploding." Lulled into a sense of safety here in Lisbon he realised such sights would have become commonplace in England, bombs dropping and buildings exploding, and his thoughts returned to the missing letters and the possible answer.

After a disturbed night Edgar rose and prepared to leave. He had finished a meagre breakfast, caused by the memory of the brown bags, when Captain Leigh appeared. "The car's here." He reached out his hand and shook Edgar's. "Glad to have known you, you did a good job, and perhaps we'll meet again before this lot's over."

Mumbling something suitable Edgar returned the handshake then left. Outside was a long, grey estate car with flared wheel arches and running boards. "Very snazzy," he thought as he opened the door and climbed in. While the car drove through the streets Edgar contemplated home and the girl he had left behind. Soon things would be back to normal.

Chapter 26

Edgar stood on the tarmac, a light drizzle descending from the grey blanket of clouds. "It is good to be back to some real weather," he thought then made his way to the canteen for his first cup of proper tea in weeks. As he lifted the cracked cup, allowing the steam to drift upwards, a beam appeared on his face.

"Back from leave?"

"Sort of."

"Thought so, didn't take you for one of them civil service types. Where you stationed?"

"Signals on Salisbury Plain."

"Oh, the secret base. I've got to deliver some supplies near there, I can give you a lift if you like?"

"Thanks, that would be great."

An hour later he climbed, stiffly, from the cab and watched the lorry drive away. Carrying his suitcase in one hand and a brace of canvas bags in the other he walked through the gate.

"Halt! Where do you think you are going?" A soldier appeared, his rifle pointing at Edgar's middle.

"To my bunk, I'm tired, fed up and cold." By now the light but persistent rain had soaked through his suit jacket.

"No civilians allowed in here without authorisation. This is….."

"A secret base, I know, I was here when it started. And I'm not a civilian, I'm in the Signals."

"Where's your uniform and papers?"

Ey Up Adolf

"In London," snapped Edgar. "Now stop messing about and let me in." His temper was not being helped by the relentless drip of water down the back of his neck.

"You just stay there, you could be a spy for all I know."

"For heaven's sake! Just how many spies talk like this, sithee. Now shift and let me in, you big lummox."

"I'd shoot him now and save everyone a lot of trouble," came a voice from behind the guard. "Whatcha' Edgar!" Jimmy came into view, now with the two stripes of a corporal on his arm. "Put that rifle down before you shoot yourself and let him in. You don't know him but he's the best wireless operator in this army, after me of course."

Reluctantly the guard moved to one side, Edgar entered and shook his friend's hand.

"Where have you been?" Jimmy asked. "You went home and disappeared. We thought you'd dropped off the edge of the world."

"You're not far wrong." Then he handed across a canvas bag. "A present."

Jimmy opened the holdall, peered inside and gave a yelp of surprise. He delved in and produced a fresh orange, one of more than a dozen that nestled in the bottom, along with other goodies like chocolate and a bottle of whisky, all freely available in Lisbon.

"Where did you get this? I haven't seen an orange for months."

"The local market. Look, Jimmy, don't ask me where I've been, let's just say it was a special assignment and leave it at that."

Jimmy gave his friend a curious look then nodded. "OK, as long as you return with goodies like this every time. Now let's get you dry on the outside and wet on the inside." He led the way, opening the bottle of whisky as they went.

Later they were sitting on Jimmy's bunk, Edgar wearing a spare jumper borrowed from his mate, glasses of amber Scottish nectar firmly grasped in their hands. Jimmy brought Edgar up to date with everything that had happened on the base, including the latest on the missing cook and the news that they were about to leave for a proper, secret base in London.

"I know all about it, I was helping set it up before I was sent to…. somewhere else," he finished lamely.

"So that's where you went after leave. That reminds me," he paused, stood up and went to a shelf at the end of the room, returning with a pile of letters. "These came for you. I've been keeping them safe until you returned."

Edgar took the pile from him and stared. The mystery of the missing letters was solved. All the time he had been waiting they were sitting here, collecting dust. It was just a good job the same had not happened with his, he had been assured that they had got away in the diplomatic bag and that was as safe as it comes.

He returned to his own bunk to have some privacy, took the top letter from the pile, glanced at the postmark and realised that it was only a couple of days old. They must be in chronological order with the newest on top and the oldest at the bottom. That would make sense, Jimmy would have just added them to the pile as they arrived. Then he realised that it was a registered letter and his heart sank.

With trepidation Edgar ripped it open and was surprised when something dropped out, fell to the floor and rolled under the bunk. He bent down and felt about until his fingers met something cold, round and metallic. Carefully he grasped it, closing his fingers around the small object. He sat down on his mattress, his fingers still tightly closed then slowly he uncurled them. Sitting there in the palm of his hand was a shiny band with three diamonds mounted on it.

Ey Up Adolf

He stared in disbelief then turned his eyes to the letter, reading the few cryptic words. "I've returned your ring. You know why."

He hadn't a clue what the message meant but he did know his world had just collapsed.

Across the room Jimmy glanced at his friend and immediately knew something was seriously wrong. The expression on Edgar's face was one of sheer, mind-numbing shock. He walked across and sat down. "What's wrong mate?" he asked, fearing the worst. Everyday the news reported bombing of the cities and he knew that Sheffield had received its share. Had something terrible happened to Ann or Edgar's family? In reply Edgar simply passed across the letter for Jimmy to read.

When he had finished Jimmy placed it on the rough blanket, "I don't understand?"

"Neither do I but I've an idea."

"Perhaps if you read the rest it'll explain."

Edgar pushed the pile away, causing several to fall on the floor. "No point, she's met someone, probably an officer. I'm not surprised, she's very pretty, everyone fancied her. And last time I saw Ann things didn't go very well, in fact she accused me of having somebody else."

"Rubbish. Even if you wanted you couldn't, stuck miles from civilisation like we are." Then he continued, "If there was a problem why didn't you go back and sort things out? It's not that far from London, I'm certain your CO would have let you if you'd explained to him."

"It wasn't that easy but I couldn't go. Sorry, I can't say more."

"But you have been writing?"

"Regularly."

"And you didn't sense anything was wrong?"

Edgar waved to the letters. "I don't know, this is the first post since then."

"You could write to her, demand to know what's happening."

"No, there's no point, it's over." Edgar gathered together the letters and dropped them into his drawer. "Let's go for a beer, in fact lots of beer. I've not had a decent pint for weeks."

"Right. Tell you what, there's a new barmaid at the local that I've been trying to chat up but she's got this mate, inseparable, like Siamese twins."

"Count me out, I'm off girls."

"That's alright, she's so ugly she doesn't qualify. I think they used her ancestors as models when they built Salisbury Cathedral."

"Still not interested, do your own dirty work. Let me check I've got enough money." He put his hand in his pocket and pulled out a handful of cash, coins and notes, one of which fell on the floor. Jimmy bent down and picked it up then stared. Instead of a ten shilling note he was gazing at something very different. A puzzled frown appeared on his face. 'Why did Edgar have Portuguese currency in his possession? Had he been abroad and that was why he hadn't been able to go back to Rotherham?'

Edgar suddenly realised what Jimmy was looking at, snatched it back and hid it in his drawer, along with the rest of his money. "Come on, let's go have a pint and meet this gargoyle of yours, but you'll have to pay, I'm a bit strapped at the moment." Still puzzled Jimmy followed, what exactly had Edgar been up to for the last few weeks and why all the secrecy. For no apparent reason the memory of the visit by the colonels in Liverpool popped into his brain. Was there a connection?

Ey Up Adolf

*   *

Ann arrived at the YMCA in a rush. As seemed to be happening more frequently these days, the tram was late then Arthur had hogged the bathroom, getting ready for his date with Gladys. "This is getting serious," thought Ann, "he's been dating her for ages." Eventually she managed to get in, only to find he had used all the hot water. Now she was late.

Diving into the small kitchen she asked what there was to cook. "Not much I'm afraid. There's plenty of potatoes, some stale bread and two tins of salmon. I suggest we cook chips and the lucky ones will get some fish."

Ann did not like the idea of anyone going hungry. She looked at the meagre rations. "I know how to make it go further. Help me peel the potatoes then put them on to cook."

Twenty minutes later she mashed a huge pan of potatoes, opened the salmon and mixed it in. Taking a blob in her hand she moulded it into shape and rolled it in bread crumbs grated from the stale bread. Now she had a pile of fish cakes, hopefully enough for all their needs.

"What have you got tonight?" asked a freckled faced lad in an ARP uniform.

"Fish cakes."

He crinkled his nose. "I've never had them before. Do they have icing on the top?"

"No silly, they're savoury." She dropped one in a sizzling pan and watched carefully as it warmed through and the breadcrumbs turned a golden brown. Scooping the fishcake out, she passed it across. The suspicious young man carefully cut a bit off, speared it on his fork and popped it into his mouth. A smile split his face, "Great." Then he turned to his mates, "Try these, they're brilliant." Ann grinned; she had a success on her hands.

Chapter 27

The next morning Edgar woke with a splitting headache. Slowly vague memories of the previous night crept back, the pub, lots of beer, Jimmy playing the piano and strangely a church gargoyle. He sat up carefully, aware that any sudden movement could cause his head to fall off. Outside he could hear the growl of lorry engines as three army trucks crawled past in convoy, heading for the main hut. "What are they doing?" he muttered.

"Where have you been for the last week?" Then the speaker noticed his crumpled suit jacket draped over the end of his bed. "What are you doing here, this is a …"

"Secret base, yes I know all about that. And I'm not a civilian."

"It's Edgar you twit," came a grumpy voice from under a pile of blankets. "Don't you recognise that ugly mush."

"Sorry, Edgar, it was that sun tan that threw me. Where have you been, I've not seen you for weeks."

"On holiday, Blackpool. You still haven't answered my question, what are those lorries doing?"

"We are transferring everything to London, very hush-hush."

"Oh, the new centre at the War Office," Edgar groaned. "I thought it would be something interesting." He lay back and closed his eyes, ignoring the astonished looks.

"He has only just arrived and already he knows more than anyone else, how does he do it?"

Ey Up Adolf

Edgar was starting to doze off again when he heard the sound of boots. He partially opened one eye and saw the sergeant looking down at him. "Stanton, you're wanted by the CO. Now!" Wearily Edgar started to put on his trousers. "Where's your uniform?"

"Somewhere in London, as far as I'm aware!" As the sergeant's face started to turn purple with rage he added for good measure. "If you really want to know I suggest you ask Colonel Miller, that's who I've been working for." Edgar knew he shouldn't have revealed that last bit of information but it was worth being shot to see the expression on the sergeant's face. And besides, he couldn't feel any worse than he did at this precise moment.

Confused, the sergeant turned and left. What was that little oik, signalman Stanton, doing with Colonel Miller?

Once outside, the cool, morning air had an invigorating effect, so by the time he arrived at the CO's office Edgar was almost functioning like a human being.

"Morning Edgar, I understand that you had a good time last night, celebrating your return to the fold."

"Yes, Sir, or at least what I can remember of it."

"Well don't get too comfortable, you are off to London."

"Right, Sir, back to…"

"The War Office, yes. There have been problems so I want you and Jimmy to sort things out." He reached into his drawer, removed a small object and threw it across. "Apparently someone at HQ seems to think you did something right while you were away from us, as I've been instructed to award you these." Edgar stretched out and picked up the set of corporal's stripes "Now go and see if you can rouse that Jimmy Parr, I just hope London is big enough for the two of you."

Edgar saluted then made his way back to his friend who was still curled up in bed. Edgar kept prodding him until a tousled head appeared from the blanket. "Morning, fellow corporal," he said, dangling his stripes in front of his mate's astonished face. "Time to get up, we've got our marching orders."

"Where to?"

"London."

Immediately the blankets were thrown back and a fully dressed Jimmy leapt from the bed.

"London. Why didn't you say so? That's the place for a couple of bright young chaps like us, we can make a fortune down there."

*   *

In a small room at the War Office a meeting was taking place. Sitting round the table were three people, two in army uniform and one in a smart pinstripe suit. Mr Baker stated, "Your operations have stepped on too many sensitive toes with your masters in the Foreign Office, so from now on your section will be the responsibility of the Department for Economic Warfare."

"And which poor, unknown politician has been handed the poisoned chalice of running that department. Someone totally dispensable I assume," replied Captain Lister.

A slight smile slipped briefly across the face of Mr Baker but instantly disappeared. "Someone even you may have heard of, a certain Winston Churchill."

"The Prime Minister!"

"I'm glad you are not totally, politically illiterate."

"Well there goes my promotion when he reads the minutes of this meeting."

Mr Baker gave him a look of disbelief. "He will not see the minutes of this meeting as there are none, in fact this meeting never happened. Now the Lisbon matter, I understand it was successful."

Ey Up Adolf

"Better than anticipated. We have eliminated a major Nazi espionage cell," stated Colonel Hudson.

"I hope it will not be attributed to His Majesty's government, that could prove quite embarrassing."

"Not at all," replied Captain Lister. "Some of those buildings in the old town are highly flammable and the Germans were using one for their base. A fire broke out, there was an explosion and unfortunately there were no survivors."

"Also we had another success, thanks to our wireless operator. He stumbled on a German transmission, outside the normal frequencies, in code of course which we were able to break. It turned out the Germans wanted to set up a listening post in Spain to intercept our messages in and out of Gibraltar. Again, once we were aware of their presence they suffered a serious setback."

"Fatal in fact," added the Captain.

"Might I suggest political pressure be applied to the Spanish Government to persuade them it would not be in their best interests to allow the Germans to mount this sort of operation in the future."

Mr Baker considered this for a moment "Yes I will propose that. If they seem hesitant we could suggest that the alternative would be your people become more active in their country, something they would not want, you are already gathering quite a reputation for, shall we say, direct action."

"Also, we want to organise a section to monitor for unauthorised transmissions from this country, we might get lucky again and catch a spy."

"That could easily be arranged. I will speak to the PM immediately after this meeting. Now anything else?"

Neil Whyke

* *

Ann was just about to leave for work when she heard the clip-clop of hooves and the jangle of harness outside. "Dad, the man from the Co-op is in the road."

Heavy footsteps descended and her father appeared, "Has he been there long?"

"No, just arrived this second."

"Then it might not be too late."

He dashed out of the back door, picked up a bucket and hand shovel and disappeared. Hiding behind the corner of the house he watched the horse and cart make its way down the road. Outside number twelve the horse stopped, the driver collected some stores and disappeared up the path. Her father held his breath, then let out a snort of approval as the horse decided that this would be a suitable place to empty its bowels.

He rushed out just as another figure appeared further up the road, bucket in hand. "Hard luck, Sid," then scooping up the dung, "this will help the rhubarb grow a treat." As he returned to his house he gave a cheery wave to his disappointed rival.

When Ann left to catch the bus she passed her father and noticed the smirk of success on his face.

Chapter 28

Edgar was reading the paper when Brian, a friend and fellow Signalman, approached, "Edgar mate, can you do me a favour?"

"Will it cost me money?"

"No, just some time. My dad's come down to visit so I want to go and see him but I'm supposed to be on duty today. Will you swap and I'll do yours tomorrow?"

"Alright, but it'll cost you a pint."

"Done."

Edgar picked up his jacket then heard his name called.

"Where are you going?"

"On duty, I swapped."

"No, you're not. Orders from the CO, you are leaving tomorrow."

"What! How about some notice? What about our work here?"

"All done from London, most of the gear is already there. Some new unit is moving in here, a listening post." He departed leaving Edgar shrugging his shoulders; what the army wants, the army gets.

*   *

When Ann arrived home from work the first thing she heard was her father's voice raised in anger. The door opened and her mother entered, her face flushed and her eyes shining, trying to hold back tears.

"What on earth's happening, why's dad so angry?"

"It's Arthur."

"Is he hurt?"

"Not yet, it depends if your dad manages to keep his temper."

"Why?"

"It's Gladys, he's got her pregnant."

Ann gasped. She knew things like that happened but not in her family.

The door burst open and her father appeared with a face like thunder. "Well that's settled. He's getting married as soon as possible and, considering the circumstances, I'll offer to pay part of the expenses."

"Is that a good idea?" asked mother. "Perhaps her parents don't know, she might not have told them."

"It'll be pretty obvious soon," thought Ann.

"Perhaps you're right. I'll wait a bit and see what happens. Arthur's going to the council tomorrow to see if they can get a house, we haven't room here and besides I don't want that trollop under my roof."

Outside the sirens started to howl so that cut an end to the conversation.

"I'd better get off," said Ann, thankful for an excuse to leave. "Perhaps the Germans will drop a bomb on Gladys and save us all a lot of trouble."

*   *

"Here, this is for you," said Brian carrying a newspaper-wrapped parcel.

Edgar carefully unfastened it to reveal two large trout. "Where are these from?"

Ey Up Adolf

"My dad's a keen fisherman ...."

"I didn't know you fished," interrupted Jimmy.

"I don't, can't stand the cold, smelly things. Anyway we were down by the river, my father was happily fishing away, when this bloke started ranting at us in his posh accent. Apparent he owns the fishing rights and was taking exception. Well my father also has a cut glass accent, he went to some private school near Warwick, and when he started to apologise the guy changed his tune. The next thing I knew we were invited back for lunch, a real spread too, my dad and him chatted like old, lost friends. We left with those trout he had caught, a pheasant and a couple of rabbits as well. I think dad only gave them to me because he knows that I hate fish. Can you do anything with them?"

Jimmy gave Edgar a sideways look then replied, "Possibly." He knew very well that he could swap them at the pub for beer.

"Right, we're off now and by the way you owe me a couple of pints for doing your duty."

"A couple?"

"That's what you said, I'm certain." He waited while Brian dug into his pocket and counted out the required amount then, as they went out of the door, he said, "By the way we're leaving tomorrow, you need to make sure you are all packed ready."

"What about my bike?"

"Take it with you, there's plenty of room on the lorry." They were out of the door before Brian realised that, if they had been packing all day, Edgar had not done his duty for him but then it was too late as the pair had disappeared down the track.

The next morning Edgar and Jimmy were loading a battered truck. "Is that everything?" asked Jimmy.

"Yes, unless you want to take the kitchen sink as well."

"No thanks. Right, let's go."

"Hang on, put this on as well," shouted Brian. He wheeled his motorbike down the track towards them.

"Can't you ride it?"

"No petrol."

"Nick some. There's usually a bit floating about if you look hard enough."

"Tried everywhere. The only place on the entire camp is here in your lorry and the CO's staff car, and he's put an armed guard on that."

"Ok. Use those planks as a ramp to get it onboard."

After a lot of huffing and puffing the bike was installed and the lorry set off, with Edgar and Jimmy squashed into the cab with the driver, as befitted their rank as corporals, and Brian perched precariously in the rear on top of all the gear.

"Will he be alright back there?" asked the driver.

"Yes, no problem," answered Jimmy then the lorry ran over a huge pothole. The front dropped sharply jarring the suspension, the vehicle swayed from side-to-side and they were thrown around the cab. Then there was a crash and loud swearing. "As long as we don't hit any holes that is."

Several hours later they drove through the outskirts of London, passing collapsed and burnt out houses on both sides of the road. "Looks like they have had it pretty rough," said Edgar.

"Not as bad as the East End," their driver replied. "I was at the docks last week and whole streets have gone." They drove on in silence for several minutes.

Eventually they arrived in the centre of the city and the driver asked, "Where do we go?"

"War Office first then Eaton Square," replied Edgar.

The driver whistled in appreciation. "That's a pretty posh area."

"Gone down a lot now," replied Jimmy jerking a thumb in Edgar's direction, "must have to let him live there."

Ey Up Adolf

The lorry made its way down Whitehall and pulled up outside the War Office where Edgar jumped down. Approaching the armed guard outside he said, "Ey up, I've got a load of signals gear for the communication room."

"Next door, they've opened a new entrance now."

The driver drove slowly then stopped alongside a wall of wooden sheets, the sort you find round building sites. "Are you sure this is where he said, this place doesn't look finished to me?"

"Yes, this is the only next door. Drive to the end and see if there is a way in."

Ignoring the honking horns behind the lorry crawled along until the driver spied a narrow opening. "What about that?"

"Try it."

Carefully the lorry turned off the main road, swaying perilously on the uneven surface. At the end was a squat, concrete structure with two military policemen, rifles in their hands and suspicious looks on their faces.

"You shouldn't be here, authorised personnel only."

"Secret base all over again," murmured Jimmy.

"Yes, except this time I think they take security seriously. That guard hasn't taken his finger off the trigger the whole time," replied Edgar. He leant out of the cab, offering his orders. "We're here to deliver some gear for the new wireless office. We're starting work tomorrow."

The guard examined the orders carefully then passed them back. "You'll have to leave it with us, we'll see it's taken inside. Before you come tomorrow get a pass from the War Office, no one's allowed in without one."

"We'll see about that," Jimmy muttered, a mischievous look on his face.

They clambered down, and with Brian's help unloaded the wireless equipment. "Are you sure it'll be safe? We don't want it nicked."

Jimmy gestured towards the military police. "Would you fancy your chances with that pair about?"

Brian looked at the stern expressions and the loaded guns. "Perhaps not."

Chapter 29

Having unloaded the equipment the lorry backed out onto Whitehall. As they passed the Houses of Parliament Jimmy commented, "You would have thought that would be a prime target for the bombers."

"Well either they are rotten shots or there's a gentleman's agreement, you don't bomb our house and we won't bomb yours," replied Edgar.

"Somehow I don't think I'd trust Adolf to keep to it, would you?"

The lorry chugged its way past Buckingham Palace with Edgar and Jimmy staring through the windshield like a couple of tourists. After a few more turns they stopped at a main road, alongside were large, white, stucco houses with bay windows and iron railings.

"Pretty posh," said Jimmy. "This must be where the toffs live. How much further is it to our billet?"

Edgar and the driver exchanged glances. "Not far."

The lorry turned the corner and stopped.

"What's the matter, lost?"

"No, we've arrived." They climbed down and Jimmy stared around him, taking in the grandeur of the area.

"You had nobility, millionaires, film stars and prime ministers living here before the war," informed the driver. "Now the army has taken over."

A door opened, a sergeant appeared and marched down the steps.

"What's all this lot?" he asked, staring disapprovingly at golf clubs, tennis racquets, a record player, an over-stuffed armchair and of course Brian's motor bike. "You emptied a junk yard."

"No, it's all ours," replied Jimmy.

"Are you allowed to 'ave this lot?"

"Allowed!" said Edgar indignantly. "Allowed, we're not only allowed but positively encouraged. You could say it's standing orders in our corps."

The sergeant stood on the pavement, staring in disbelief. "There's a coach house at the back, leave it there."

As they climbed into the cab Jimmy whispered, "I think I'm going to like it here. I can already see my room, huge bay window, double bed with duck down pillows, thick pile carpet and space for a piano once I can find one."

Edgar smiled to himself, plenty of time to spoil the dream later.

With all their gear stored away Edgar, Brian and Jimmy entered the house through the basement and climbed the stairs. Jimmy noticed the bare floorboards and scratched paintwork. "I'm not impressed but it is the servant's quarters so I suppose they didn't spend money down here. Upstairs will be more sumptuous." Edgar just nodded, he had been here before.

Jimmy led the way up to the first floor bedrooms. "Let's try in here."

"Fine," agreed Edgar and waited while Jimmy opened the door.

"Nooooo….." Instead of the luxurious and spacious bedroom that Jimmy had expected there were bunks filling every wall, standard army issue cupboards and nails hammered into the wooden panelling to hang coats on. In most respects it was even worse than the 'secret base' they had left.

Ey Up Adolf

"Welcome to Millionaires Row," Edgar said. "Top or bottom bunk?" Jimmy was too dumbfounded to answer and merely pointed to the top one.

The following morning they made their way down Whitehall, Jimmy was still complaining but now he had finished with their spartan accommodation and had moved on to the long walk. "It's miles, we've been marching for hours," he moaned.

"It's not that far, probably a mile or so," replied Edgar. "And we'll find a short cut when we know our way around."

"No, we need a better solution, something that doesn't involve walking."

"What about a cab?" replied Brian.

"And doesn't cost money."

They arrived at the imposing entrance to the War Office, produced their papers and showed them to the guard. Once inside they were issued with passes, subsistence allowance and ration books, as there were no cooking facilities at their billet. Edgar was about to make his way down the stairs to the communication room.

"Where do you think you are going?"

"Wireless room."

"Not that way, VIP's only now. The entrance for you lot is next door."

"What, that building site?" exclaimed Jimmy.

"That's it, good camouflage what, no one will suspect."

"Just how many people are going to be working there when it's fully operational?" Jimmy asked Edgar.

"Not sure, at least a hundred."

"About a hundred people, men and women entering a building site then disappearing down a hole in the ground.... and that won't arouse suspicion! What planet do these people live on? It's the secret base all over again."

"At least we'll be fifty feet underground this time," answered Edgar, remembering the attack by the fighter plane.

Jimmy thought for a moment, "Yes, but doesn't that mean we will also be under the level of the river Thames. Won't we leak?"

"Only if the water can get through two layers of steel and three feet of reinforced concrete. This is probably the most secure place in England. I'd have thought they would have taken leaks into consideration when they designed it."

"Maybe, but it was the army who built the place." On that sobering thought they left the War Office and made their way next door. As they approached the guards Jimmy was pleased to see they were the same ones as yesterday.

"Back again," Jimmy said cheerfully. "We're like bad pennies."

"Passes," demanded the military policeman but a little less officiously than the day before. They presented them for inspection.

"Careful they are still wet," joked Jimmy, "made them myself." This time he almost raised a smile from the guard.

"Ok, in you go." He opened the door and allowed them inside. Directly in front were a set of bare concrete steps leading down into the bowels of the earth, lit by a string of electric bulbs dangling from wires fastened to the roof.

"Reminds me of the Ritz," said Edgar, "the Ritz chip shop in Mexborough that is."

At the bottom of several flights of stairs they found their room, most of the equipment had been set up and checked, it only needed Edgar and Jimmy to test the new high speed senders, their speciality.

By mid-morning the equipment was ready, so they set off to find the canteen when the sergeant approached Edgar, a serious

Ey Up Adolf

look on his face. "The captain wants to see you," then seeing the questioning look he continued, "sorry I don't know why."

Edgar made his way across to the officer who looked up from a paper in his hand. "Oh, Stanton, can you make sure you are available this afternoon, someone is coming to see you."

"Who?"

"I don't know, but the orders are very specific, you are needed for a special mission."

"Who for?"

"Again it is not clear, but it has originated from the Department for Economic Warfare. Never heard of them before." He squinted at the sheet. "The writing is very scrawly but it might be a Colonel Millet."

Edgar's heart sank. "Could that be Colonel Miller?"

"Well done, that'll be it. Why have you heard of him?"

"Possibly," replied Edgar. "What am I getting involved in this time?" he speculated as he wandered off to catch up with his mates. Then a second question entered his head, "I wonder if this canteen serves whisky, I think I'll need one."

Chapter 30

Edgar worked steadily all afternoon and eventually everything was operating to his satisfaction. He had forgotten about the officer's message until he felt a tap on his shoulder and a voice behind him spoke. Turning round he found himself looking into the smiling face of Captain Leigh.

"Hello Edgar, keeping busy." Edgar saw Jimmy's ears prick up. "We will need your expertise in the near future, just a listening job mainly, like the one in Lisbon." By now Jimmy's jaw was in danger of getting friction burns from the floor. "I'll be in touch."

Immediately Jimmy shot across to Edgar but was stopped by a raised hand. "Not a word. You could be shot for what you have just heard." For the first time since he had known him, Jimmy was speechless.

By the time they emerged above ground it was dark. They made their way through the park, disturbing a flock of ducks that were snuggled down on the path, enjoying the slight warmth trapped in the tarmac. "What now?" asked Brian.

"Something to eat then a pint?" suggested Edgar.

"Sounds good to me," replied Jimmy. "There's probably somewhere down Victoria Road still open."

They trudged through the dark streets and found a café with a chink of light showing through the blackout curtains. Quickly they slipped inside, finding themselves in a large split-level area with stairs leading up to the higher floor. Several customers were seated at small tables, some of them smoking after their meal while others were drinking cups of tea.

"What about that table over there?" Then Jimmy's face lit up as he spied a piano nestling in the back corner. They gave their order from the very limited menu then Jimmy asked if he could play the piano.

"Of course, ducky, something happy to cheer everybody up."

He walked across, played a couple of scales to test that the piano was in good working order then launched into 'In the Mood'. The conversation petered out, everyone turned and listened. This was followed by 'Alexander's Ragtime Band'. At the finish he received an enthusiastic round of applause.

"That's done it, we'll never get him off," moaned Brian.

"Yes we will, there are only two, no three things that rival playing the piano as far as Jimmy's concerned, food, beer and pretty girls." Cupping his hands round his mouth he yelled, "Jimmy, nosh!"

Jimmy nodded in return, held up a finger to say just one more tune, then launched into 'Boogie Woogie Bugle Boy'. At the end he stood up, gave a slight bow and returned to his bangers and mash.

When they asked for three teas they were told they were on the house, for the entertainment. "Well done, Jimmy," said Edgar. "Perhaps we should have let you play some more then we might have got the whole meal for free. We'll have to think about that next time."

*   *

Ann helped herself to a portion of fish pie and looked at the greyish flesh. "Yes it is fish but I'm not certain what." Since the start of the war there seemed more and more varieties appearing in the shops.

Her mother produced a letter from under her pinnie. "Norman's coming home on leave this weekend." Ann's older brother was stationed outside Manchester, where his skills as a joiner were being put to good use building gliders. "Do you remember Vera?" Ann nodded in reply, carefully removing a fish bone from her mouth and adding it to the considerable pile on the side of her plate. "Well apparently he's been writing to her while he's been away and wants to bring her round for tea on Sunday."

"That will be good," replied Ann. "Does that mean they are courting?"

"Wey, aye, lass, it seems that way." She stood up. "You'll never guess what else I've got for us?" She disappeared into the pantry so the next few words were muffled. A few seconds later she reappeared holding something behind her back. "And I only had to queue for half an hour, I don't think word had gone round yet." With a flourish she proudly produced two bananas. She passed one across, enjoying the beam on her daughter's face. Slowly, prolonging the moment, they both peeled back the skin then took a small bite. Something this good needed to be savoured and made to last as long as possible.

*   *

As they wandered through the almost deserted streets Brian suggested "What about a drink?" and the other two nodded in agreement. They turned down a side street and found a small pub, The Victoria. A long bar took up one end of the room, battered, dark, varnished tables lined up down the side with a long bench seat behind. A small fire burnt in a black, iron grate, with a mirror above, its silvered surface pitted by many brown, rust-spots. Brian groaned as his gaze fell on an old, battered upright piano. "That's torn it," he muttered. "Guess where we'll be drinking from now on?"

Ey Up Adolf

Before Edgar could answer Jimmy was on his way down the room. One or two of the regulars frowned, this was their pub, so what did this soldier think he was doing, but as Jimmy's fingers darted over the ivories their frowns quickly disappeared. When he started on 'Roll Out The Barrel' he received his first applause.

"I wish he'd waited a few minutes," whispered Edgar, "then I'd have had time to make a deal with the landlord. Quick, nip across and tell him to stop." As Brian darted across the room Edgar approached the bar and put on his most winning smile. "Evening, mate. As you can see my friend is pretty good on that piano, so how about an arrangement, he keeps your customers entertained and we get free beer?"

The landlord considered then replied, "Two pints each?"

"Three."

He thought about it for a moment, undecided, so Edgar nodded to Jimmy. Instantly he started to play Tuxedo Junction and everyone clapped along with the music. The burly landlord smiled and thrust out his hand, "Since it's for the army, agreed."

Edgar returned the handshake and watched as the pints were pulled. Perhaps Jimmy was right, coming to London seemed to be working out alright so far, apart from the reappearance of Captain Leigh who was looming like a dark, thundercloud on the horizon.

The next morning they all set off for the 'building site' in a fine, freezing drizzle. Edgar did not fancy the walk but there didn't seem to be any alternative apart from spending money on bus fares which he was loathed to do.

Jimmy piped up, "I've had an idea." Edgar was concerned, some of Jimmy's schemes were verging on the manic at times. "No, this is a good one, just follow my lead." A few minutes later a bus pulled up and they climbed on board. Jimmy looked downstairs and saw the conductor near the front. "Ideal," then charged upstairs, followed by his two mates. He sat down and indicated for the other two to sit in front of him. The minutes passed by with Whitehall getting nearer. Edgar thought the idea was to try and sneak off before the conductor arrived then walk the rest of the way but Jimmy stayed seated.

Eventually they heard footsteps on the stairs and the conductor's voice saying 'fares please'. When he arrived Jimmy held out a half crown. "Sloane Square."

"You're going in the wrong direction, mate."

"But we were told to catch this number," complained Jimmy as another stop flashed past outside.

"Right number, wrong direction. Get off at the next stop, cross the road and go the other way." Ignoring the proffered fare he continued down the rest of the bus collecting money.

When the three of them descended to the pavement they found they were only a hundred yards from the entrance to the building site. "Well, done Jimmy lad," said Edgar slapping his mate on the back.

"Yes and if we are careful we can do it often. I asked at the billet and there are several different routes we can use, all coming in this direction. By the time we get back to the first one either it will be a different conductor or he'll have forgotten us, especially if we take it in turns to ask for the fare."

"They say the pavements in London are paved with gold, it seems it might turn out to be true," said Edgar. "All we need is to be left in peace to get on with it." He had already forgotten about Captain Leigh but unfortunately the captain had not forgotten about him.

Chapter 31

Life, as far as Edgar was concerned, had resumed some sort of normality. During the day they were kept busy handling the huge volume of traffic from various theatres of war and in the evening Jimmy played the piano in return for free beer, which Edgar, as his manager, negotiated.

"Hi Edgar, I require you for a minute."

He did not need to turn round, Edgar had heard those dulcet tones enough in Lisbon to recognise Captain Leigh and his heart lurched. Trouble had raised its ugly head again.

They moved to a quiet corner. "We want you to come and monitor a signal, study the sender, any mannerisms or anything out of the ordinary."

"Where do I have to go this time, Timbuktu?"

"Not that far, a little place called Englefield Green near Windsor."

"If it's that close why can't I just do it from here and save a lot of trouble."

"I can't explain at the moment, but if I tell you we are working with MI5 on this one perhaps that will give you a clue." Edgar considered this. If MI5 were involved then it meant espionage, a German spy, working in England. "Go and pack enough gear for a couple of weeks. I'll collect you in an hour."

"But what about…"

"It's already been cleared with your officer. He wasn't happy but the orders came from high up."

Neil Whyke

Edgar had a feeling Colonel Miller, or even his boss, was probably the 'high up' but that wasn't what he was going to say. He had lined Jimmy up to play that night and he wanted his share of the beer.

An hour later an Austin pickup pulled up in Eaton Square and Edgar climbed in, several spare sets of underwear, jumpers and blankets stuffed into bags were loaded into the back and they were off, with Captain Leigh ignoring any speed restrictions.

Within the hour the small vehicle pulled up outside a derelict stone-built lodge on the outskirts of Windsor Great Park. The door was askew, straining on the hinges, and some of the windows were boarded up. The place looked as if it had been uninhabited for years. "Welcome to your new home."

Edgar just looked with disgust. "So what's so special about this place?"

"Its location and the spectacular views."

Edgar glared at the high stone wall and copse of trees, which were the only things visible from the lodge. "So much for the views, what's special about the location?"

They forced the door open and went inside. The interior was as bad and unloved as the outside. There was no furniture or carpets and what little wallpaper remained was dangling off in strips, revealing patches of black mould. Glancing out of the broken panes in the window Edgar realised that the frames were leaning to one side and, on close inspection, so was the floor. That explained the sticking door, the entire place was affected by subsidence and was slanting perilously

Edgar was surprised that there was electricity powering the single bulb but then he saw the modern wireless set and direction finder and he realised that, of course, there had to be electricity. In the corner of the room was a cot and through an open

Ey Up Adolf

door he could make out a toilet. A log fire burnt in the grate and spare chunks of wood were piled by the fender.

"What about food?"

"Your guard will bring it when he comes on duty."

"Guard!" exploded Edgar.

"You don't think we'd leave you here on your own, do you? There will be an armed guard outside all night."

Edgar wasn't sure whether this was to protect him from harm or stop him sneaking out to the local pub, but he suspected it was the latter. He looked at a slip of paper the captain handed him and realised straight away that it was a wireless frequency.

"Now that you are secure I can tell you what this is about. We have picked up an unauthorised transmission, same as you did in Lisbon."

"A spy," interrupted Edgar and received a nod in return.

"We have pinpointed it near to Liverpool and we believe it is going to Paris, reporting the convoy departures. We want you to listen in and get the feel of this guy. When you are confident let me know and we'll move to stage two. Enjoy the peace and quiet," then he was gone.

Edgar picked up the headphones, noticing the long lead and sat down in the chair next to the wireless set.

"Forgot to say," said Captain Leigh sticking his head back round the door. "He seems to keep irregular hours, so you need to have the headphones on all the time, that's why the lead is so long." He gave a long stare at the toilet. "And I mean all the time," then he was gone.

*   *

Ann returned from work, thankful that it was Friday, she was in need of a rest. As she entered the house she could hear her mother chatting away excitedly, her Geordie accent more pronounced than usual and she realised what the commotion was, her brother Norman was sitting there. He stood up and gave his little sister a hug. "Mum's been bringing me up to date on all the news, I'm sorry about you and Edgar, it seems so out of character for him. He always struck me as a solid, dependable type. Are you sure there's not a mistake?"

She shook her head, "No, I gave him plenty of chances, he just didn't want to reply. It's not like he was at the North Pole, he was only in Salisbury for heaven's sake." She received a severe frown from her Methodist mother but ploughed on. "He could easily have written, or even come back home."

"Or you could have gone and visited him?"

"What, go down south on my own! Not likely!"

That exhausted that topic of conversation so her mother asked, "A cup of tea?"

While she was busy Ann leant closer to her brother, "What's this about Vera?"

"We're friends, that's all." He received a disbelieving scowl. "Alright, we have been out once or twice."

"And you've been writing a lot."

"So, what's the matter with that?"

"Nothing, in fact I'm quite in favour, I like Vera, she's alright, unlike someone else I could mention."

Norman heaved a sigh of relief; he had gained an ally.

*   *

Edgar peered through the crooked window. Outside the sun was beginning to set behind the trees, turning the sky a vivid orange. He sighed, this was only the first day and already it was tedious. Then a soldier wearing an army uniform crossed in front of the glass.

"Watcha mate," came a cheery voice and the next instant a small, dark haired squaddy entered, carrying a wicker basket.

Ey Up Adolf

"Here's your dinner, breakfast and tomorrow's lunch." He placed it close to Edgar's foot. "I'll be outside."

"You could guard as easily in here, it'll be much warmer. I bet the temperature drops below freezing tonight so I wouldn't fancy pacing about out there."

"I'm not supposed to. Take up position outside the door and make regular perimeter sweeps, them were my orders."

"Suit yourself, but the offer stands." He opened a can of steaming hot corn beef stew. "That'll do nicely."

He had just finished when the earphones crackled and instantly a flood of morse filled the air. He dropped the can and grabbed his pencil, immediately realising it was code, but he had not expected anything else.

When the airwaves went silent he went over the message in his mind, noting anything unusual in the style of the sender as every telegrapher had their own idiosyncrasies Edgar gave a few taps on the table with his fingers. "Give me a couple of days and you'll never know the difference."

Chapter 32

Ann's mother looked at the food on the table. Despite the severe rationing she considered she had put on a reasonable spread, tinned salmon, potatoes, a green salad, homemade bread, elderberry jelly made from the summer's crop and scones fresh from the oven. She knew it was slightly excessive but she wanted to make a good impression. Besides, anything that was left over could go in dad's snap the rest of the week.

At the sound of the door opening she removed her pinny. Vera entered, looking shyly around then Ann rushed across and gave her a hug. "Nice to see you, come and tell me all the gossip." Leaving Norman with his mouth open, she led Vera to the armchairs. "Don't just stand there like a dummy, take her coat." Numbly Norman did as he was told, with Ann taking charge so firmly he felt like a spare part.

"Well, pet, how long have you two been courting? Norman has never told us anything."

Vera blushed slightly, "I wouldn't know if I'd call it courting, we've only been out a couple of times and then written to each other while he's been away."

"Well in these hard times I'd say that's enough. From now on just call this your second home."

Vera and Norman smiled, but for different reasons, Vera because she felt made welcome and Norman because he realised that his mother had spoken to his father and everything was alright. Now he wouldn't have to do it, something he was not looking forward to after the Arthur debacle.

Ey Up Adolf

*   *

Edgar removed the headphones and stretched. Now he felt confident that he would be able to pass himself off as the mysterious spy, he could not only replicate the speed but also the little pause he made every time the letters 'F' and 'L' occurred, obviously the sender had a problem remembering which way round the dots and dashes went in those two letters.

The door opened and his guard entered. "Watcha Edgar. It's real brass monkey weather outside tonight, wouldn't be at all surprised if it snows." He rubbed his hands together vigorously to return the circulation. "Does that offer to guard in here still stand?"

"Of course, mate, I could do with the company. I only wish I could offer you something stronger than tea but I was rushed down here so fast I didn't have time to stock up."

Reaching inside his coat the guard produced a half bottle of rum and put it down on the table. "Thought that might be the case so I brought this, you might like a drop in your tea."

"Good man." Edgar took the lid off one of the containers. "Treacle sponge I think, with congealed custard, want some?"

"No thanks, I ate before I came on duty, but a cuppa would be nice."

"Would you mind making it," he held up the lead to the earphones, "this is a bit short to reach the tap, if I take them off I have to dash round like a maniac, hoping nothing comes through before I get them on again."

Even as he spoke the set burst into life. He quickly jotted down the message.

"I don't know how you do that," his guard stated. "I would have trouble writing down words at that speed, let alone change it from those dots and dashes."

"Practice mainly," Edgar replied. Then he read the message and flinched.

"Problems?"

"No, my boss is coming down tomorrow and his appearance always means trouble."

The next morning broke clear and bright, the sunlight reflecting off a fine layer of snow that had fallen during the night. Edgar heard the crunch of tyres as the car turned from the road.

"Morning Edgar," Captain Leigh announced cheerfully as he entered the room, knocking the slight layer of snow from his shoes. He glanced at the fire burning brightly in the grate, went and stood in front of it, warming the back of his trousers. "It's freezing out there and I don't think the heater's working properly in the car. Don't suppose you have a cup of tea?"

Edgar removed the headphones and handed them across. "You'll have to listen for me though. Give me a shout if our friend puts in an appearance." He disappeared into the back and returned a moment later with the kettle. Captain Leigh picked up a cup then placed it near his nose and sniffed. "If there's any of that left I'll have some as well, it'll warm my bones better than this fire." Edgar perched the kettle on the front of the fire then washed out the cups, returning with the remains of the rum. "On second thoughts I'll not bother with the tea." He held out his cup for some of the Jamaican rum, took a sip then continued, "At two o'clock tonight the signals from our friend will abruptly cease then you will take over. We have established that there is no set pattern to the times he operates, it must just be when he feels it is safe. We want you to send these," he passed over a folder he had brought in, "he usually reports two or three times a day so keep to that pattern. The messages are coded, all you have to do is send. If you are good enough the enemy will never realise what has happened."

Ey Up Adolf

"I'm more than good enough," replied Edgar, stung by the insinuation.

"That's what I told the Colonel. Remember, anytime after two a.m. and you're on." He finished the last few drops of rum and handed Edgar the empty cup.

As two o'clock came Edgar wondered if the spy had been arrested but deep down he doubted it. They would not want any mention of his detention to be made public, alerting the enemy, which a court appearance would create. Also Captain Leigh was involved, somehow Edgar could not see him standing there, reading the spy his rights. A more direct and permanent approach seemed more his style.

Edgar took the top message off the pile. For the first time since his call up Edgar felt he was doing something definite for the war effort, the messages he was sending would be saving the lives of the merchant seamen on the convoys. Raising his voice he called, "Sam, have you got that rum?" His guard appeared from the kitchen, bottle in hand. When he had poured two small measures Edgar held up his cup and announced, "To the confusion of our enemies."

Although he hadn't a clue what Edgar was on about Sam raised his cup and drank.

Chapter 33

The snow drifted down in lazy flakes so that the ground had a considerable covering as Edgar drank tea, nattered to Sam the guard and, at random intervals, transmitted the phoney messages. Now he didn't have to listen in all the time he had more freedom. He explored the back garden, which took five minutes, and even strolled up the road to a point where he could see over Windsor Great Park.

He was on his second cup of tea when he heard wheels crunching the snow outside. He peered through the window then went to open the door for Captain Leigh.

"Morning Edgar. How's things going, not too bored I hope?"

"Getting that way, it's not exactly bustling with activity round here. The most exciting thing is watching the fox go past."

"Perhaps these will help." He produced a couple of magazines and the day's paper. "Besides you won't be here much longer. How are the messages going?"

"Finished, have you brought me some more?"

"No, just make some up from now on."

Edgar looked aghast. "I can't! I wouldn't know what to say! Besides I haven't got the code book."

"You don't need it, just make up random sets of letters. The Germans will be as puzzled as you look, they'll think there is a foul-up with the coding, you know what the Teutonic mind is like. If we are really lucky they might send an agent round to

Ey Up Adolf

check up." He finished talking, walked to the window and looked out. "I went to school just up the road from here. Right, I must be off. Toodle pip." He fastened his coat and walked out of the room.

"Toodle pip," thought Edgar. "Who in his right mind says toodle pip?" Images of toffs in top hats mixed with pictures of Fred Astaire, then a name from the map of the area. "Well, the Little Lord Fauntleroy, he went to Eton. No wonder he's so devious."

* *

Ann was sitting at her desk sipping a cup of tea. Mr Munroe was out at a meeting and she was up to date with her work so she felt entitled to a break. It was a shock finding out that Norman had a steady girlfriend, even more so when he confided in her and said that he was going to propose the next time he came on leave. "I'm glad for Norman, Vera seems nice and I'm sure we will be friends."

She put down the empty cup just as the door opened and Mr Munroe entered, his customary scowl on his face, he really hated meetings. "A bloody farce presided over by idiots," was his usual comment.

* *

Edgar sent his invented messages. No matter how hard he tried he found he was using proper words, something that rarely happened with real codes. Eventually he hit on the method of closing his eyes and stabbing at the paper with his pencil. This gave him suitable random letters, except once, when by sheer coincidence, not only did the letters spell a real word but a very rude one. Edgar was tempted to leave it, as he considered it quite suitable for Hitler, but decided not to. He settled for second best by using the same letters but in a different order.

Captain Leigh stepped from the pickup then, seconds later, walked through the door. "Hi, Edgar, how are your messages going?"

"They're not any more, the Germans have finally caught on and are not acknowledging."

"I'm not really surprised, in fact I expected it. Whatever you were sending must have had them really mystified."

"So what now?"

"Your job here is finished, what would you like as a reward?"

"Some leave?"

Captain Leigh reached into his pocket and pulled out the required papers. "A week do you?"

"Fine, but how...." then Edgar stopped. A silly question, it was the obvious answer. "It's a pity you didn't turn up half an hour ago then I would have had chance to get back to London and catch the connection to Sheffield. Now I haven't time to walk to the village and get a bus to Windsor."

"What about if you took the pickup? You could leave it in Windsor, I can easily walk there to collect it."

Edgar was not surprised that the captain would lightly talk about a six mile walk through the snow in the gathering gloom of a winter's evening. He probably trekked across the Arctic, living on polar bears which he wrestled with his bare hands. "Thanks that would be great." He took the papers, gathered up his things and started to leave.

"Forgotten something?" asked Captain Leigh.

"Oh, yes, thanks again."

"No, I was thinking more like these," holding up the keys to the van. He threw them across to Edgar. "Take care, I have a feeling we might have need of your services again."

Ey Up Adolf

At that Edgar scurried out of the door as quickly as he could and climbed into the small vehicle. The warm engine caught and he gingerly pulled out into the road. He found it light to steer, especially on the snow covering, but after a few minutes he became more confident and increased speed.

He was on a narrow country lane with a line of telegraph poles to his right. He switched on the hooded headlights, not that they made a great deal of difference. Ahead he could see the snow-covered road bending to the left so steered in that direction but the pickup continued straight on. Edgar pulled harder on the wheel. Instantly the vehicle spun round in a flurry of snow, completely out of control. Edgar stared, wide-eyed, out of the window at the world flashed past until, with a mighty crash, the pickup collided with a telegraph pole. He was thrown forwards, his head smashed into the windscreen and everything went black.

When he came too he gazed out of the cracked windscreen at faint lights moving backwards and forwards. Confused he stared until, as his vision cleared, he realised the lights were from wires reflecting the full moon as they slowly swung to and fro directly in front of the glass. "Why are they so low?" He turned his head painfully to the side. The telegraph pole, its shattered base clearly visible, was resting on the top of his van, buckling the roof.

"I'm in trouble," then the blackness closed in again.

When he awoke he was being lifted out by a passing lorry driver. "You alright mate? That looks a nasty cut."

Edgar put his hand to his head, feeling a lump the size of a chicken's egg and the warm stickiness of congealed blood. "I've felt better."

"Can you walk?"

Edgar took a step and his legs buckled. "I might need a bit of help."

Supported by the burly driver he made it to the lorry. "I'll get you to hospital in Windsor, they'll take good care of you."

"Marvellous," thought Edgar, "what a way to spend your leave." Then he realised he had another problem, how was he going to let Captain Leigh know his pickup was a crumpled heap, with a telegraph pole draped across its roof.

Chapter 34

The three officers sat with their heads bowed towards each other in whispered conversation. A white haired colonel in the middle stared straight at Edgar through his wire-rimmed glasses.

"Corporal Stanton," Edgar shuffled from one foot to the other, "this Board of Enquiry has been convened to look into the circumstances of the accident in which an army vehicle and an article of public property, namely a telegraph post, were destroyed by you. It is agreed that the road conditions were extreme but we do not consider that an excuse for dangerous and reckless driving." Edgar thought this was a bit unsympathetic. "Normally this would be a serious matter, to be dealt with harshly…."

"Bang goes my stripes," contemplated Edgar, "Jimmy will have a good laugh then try to boss me about."

"…however we have received a commendation on your behalf, stating that you were engaged in work of vital importance and speed was of the utmost necessity. The officer…." he glanced at the paper in front of him, "…a Captain Leigh, requests we take this into consideration." He paused dramatically. "As a result we have decided that you will be forbidden to drive any army vehicle in the future. Dismissed."

Edgar saluted and left the room, breathing a sigh of relief. "Fancy Captain Leigh coming up trumps like that," he muttered.

Later that morning he walked into the signals room to be greeted by Jimmy. "I'm surprised to see you today, I thought you'd be locked up in the glass-house at the least."

"Me, no chance, I've friends in high places." He gave a smug smile then strolled to his station.

Later he saw Jimmy approaching. "Ready for a break?"

When they were in the canteen Jimmy leaned forwards and whispered, "Have you seen the new chap yet?"

"What new chap?"

"He came this morning and no-one seems to know anything about him. He's a funny little guy, foreign, Balkan at a guess. Wears a tight-fitting belt round his tunic which makes it stick out at the back.

"Sounds a bit ridiculous. What's his name?"

"Nicholas."

"I see, Nicholas is Ridiculous," added Edgar and Jimmy's face cracked into a broad grin. Nicholas Ridiculous it was from then on.

"What's he doing here?"

"No-one knows. He came in with some brass earlier, they set him up in his office and disappeared. Even the sergeant doesn't have a clue. And," continued Jimmy with a self-satisfied expression on his face, "just before they left one of the brass, a captain, fit-looking, asked if you were back from the inquiry."

Edgar sat there, if Captain Leigh was involved then the new man was up to his knees in murky business. "Let's go and take a peek at this stranger."

*   *

When Ann returned from work she found Pat sitting in front of the fire. "I just popped in to see you and your mum invited me to stay for dinner."

"Pat brought a block of butter with her," answered her mum. "She's been saving her coupons."

Ann gave her friend a questioning look, she knew it had 'walked' from the shop.

"You know what your mum's like, she wouldn't have taken it if she had been aware of the truth. It's the least I can do, a little white lie doesn't harm anyone."

"That's a whopping great big one."

"Anyway," continued Pat, "I came to make a suggestion. How about a weekend away at Scarborough? A break and some fresh air will do us both good. What do you reckon?"

"Sounds an excellent idea to me."

Saturday arrived with a fresh breeze blowing off the sea. Ann and Pat had found a guest house for the night then walked down to the harbour. A fishing boat arrived, with a flock of noisy gulls wheeling overhead then diving into the freezing, grey water. Ann pulled her coat tightly around her slender body and complained, "It's bitter here."

"If you weren't so skinny perhaps you wouldn't feel the cold so much."

"We don't all get loads of chocolates you know, not like you."

"What do you want to do?" asked Pat, changing the subject.

"Let's go up through the Italian Gardens, there'll be some protection from the wind."

Laboriously they made their way through the winding paths that snaked up the steep cliff-side until they emerged onto the wide grassy expanse with magnificent views over the bay, the castle standing proud on the headland, undefeated by the vicious storms that battered it from the North Sea. It mirrored the mood of the nation, no matter what was thrown at it, it would stand firm.

"Squad, 'tenshun!" They saw a group of young soldiers, rifles over their shoulders, staring fixedly ahead at an officer who did not appear that much older. Pat's eyes shone with malicious humour. "Come on this could be entertaining."

They stepped smartly across the road and stood directly behind the group of squaddies. Pat noticed a couple of the soldiers glancing in their direction and smiled encouragingly but a glare from the officer soon brought their eyes to the front.

"Squad, from the right, number."

"One," came a gruff Yorkshire voice followed by "Two" in the same accent.

"They're local," whispered Pat.

"Three."

"Four."

"Five."

"Sounds like it."

"Six."

"Seven."

"Let's have some fun. Just do the same as me."

"Eight."

"Nine."

Pat took a deep breath.

"Ten."

Before the next soldier had time to speak she shouted out, "Jack, queen, king."

There was a moment's shocked silence then several sniggers. The officer glared at the two young ladies smiling sweetly at him then coloured up, there was nothing in the regulations to cover this situation. The nearest was, "When opposed by a superior force, retreat." "Squad right turn, quick march."

Quickly they progressed fifty yards up the road then stopped. Once again he gave the command but to his horror he could see Ann and Pat making their way up the pavement, smiles on their faces. With dread all he could do was wait.

"Eight, Nine."

He held his breath, hoping his worse fear was not going to happen.

"Ten."

The world stood still for an instant then two sweet voices sang out in perfect unison. "Jack, queen, king."

This time the sniggers were more pronounced and lasted longer.

Again the squad marched up the road but as the officer glanced out of the corner of his eye he could see the swirl of skirts accompanied by the sharp, staccato clicking of heels on the pavement. He halted the squad, prepared himself for yet another humiliation then shot a despairing, pleading look at the two young ladies. They glanced at each other, grinned, turned to the officer, winked and Pat blew him a kiss. With a whirl they turned and disappeared down a side street, their laughter carrying clearly despite the wind.

They wandered down to the deserted promenade for a bag of chips and ate them as they walked round the headland. To their right the waves of the North Sea rolled in, heavy, grey and sullen while to their left, across the road, gulls flew through the air, gliding gracefully on the up-draughts then settling on one of the thousands of ledges that dotted the white-streaked cliff face.

Suddenly there was a roar and a huge wave crashed against the sea wall in front of them. A shower of icy water rose twenty feet into the air, towering over them. Blown by the wind it spread forwards then smashed down to the road, forming a swirling puddle, several inches deep.

"I'm not going through that," stated Ann firmly. "We'll have to go back." Then she looked across the road at the towering cliffs, ignoring the faded sign that leant, drunkenly to one side. Further along a narrow path wound its way up from the promenade to the top of the cliffs, their boarding house and warmth. "If we cross over and climb the wall we could scramble up and meet the path halfway. I know it's steep but it's better than being soaked."

"I have a bad feeling about this," mumbled Pat.

"Stop whinging."

"It's vertical! Only a mountaineer could get up there."

"Oh come on. It's either this or get drenched."

Fifteen minutes later, tired and out of breath, they slipped under the handrail and stood on the tarmac surface that wound its way in a series of u-turns to the top of the cliff.

"Hello dears," said Mrs Turner, the owner of the guest house as they returned. "What have you been up to?"

"We went for a walk along the front," replied Ann.

"Until we were nearly drowned by the huge waves," added Pat. "Then my friend decided we were mountain goats and climbed the cliff."

"You didn't clamber over the wall did you?"

"Yes."

"But didn't you see the notices."

"What notices?"

"The ones put there by the army, 'Danger Minefield'."

Ann's eyes opened wide with shock and she clutched Pat's arm tightly

"I'm surprised you weren't both blown to bits." Taking a look at their shocked faces she went on, "I think you need a good, strong cup of tea."

Chapter 35

Arthur's wedding was a strained affair, made worse for Ann by Gladys's confidence that she was not pregnant and never had been, she just wanted to get married. Ann was furious. Although there was no love lost between herself and her oldest brother, she considered this a despicable trick.

A few days later Ann arrived in from work and sensed her mother's excitement. She fished a letter from the pocket of her pinnie and brandished it like a royal proclamation. "It's from Norman, he's coming home this weekend."

"That's nice, it'll be good to see him again."

"Yes, pet, but there's more, I think he's going to propose to Vera."

"That's good, his wedding will be more enjoyable than the last one. It will be a real celebration," then under her breath she added, "instead of a wake."

*   *

"Evening Alf, do you reckon we will manage without any interruptions tonight?" The Victoria was now their local but the last time they were in the sirens had sounded and everyone had to make their way to the shelters.

"Who knows? By the way I've a business proposition for you. My brother runs a big pub, the King Henry, in the East End. I've told him about Jimmy and he wants to hire him for an evening, what do you think?"

"How much?"

"Five pounds plus beer."

"I'll speak to Jimmy but I should imagine it'll be alright." He lifted his pint but Alf continued, "That guy in corner was asking if Jimmy was playing tonight. He seemed really interested."

Edgar looked across with curiosity. He was small and well dressed, in a flashy way, he wore a grey, trilby hat and an overcoat with a fur-lined collar.

"Cheers Alf, I'll find out what he wants." He walked across."Ey up, I understand you have been asking about my mate, Jimmy."

The man put down his glass. "Yes, I have been informed he's quite good."

"Quite good, he's brilliant. He's should be on the radio or playing with one of the big dance bands, Benny Goodman or someone like that, but he's too important to the war effort."

"Well that's why I'm here. I'm from the BBC, looking for new talent for Worker's Playtime and we may be able to use him. I am sure we could arrange something with the army to fit in with his duties. The people's morale is important you know."

Edgar was flabbergasted. This could be a big break. He excused himself and wandered across to Jimmy to give him the news. Two lucrative proposals in one night, things were looking up.

The next morning they joined the steady stream of people entering the building site all showing their passes. "I bet I win this time," said Jimmy as they approached the guard. He had devised a competition and they all chipped in five bob a week. Instead of showing their security passes they would produce a variety of other papers and see if they would be accepted. Last week Edgar had won with a chunk cut from the paper and stuck onto a piece of cardboard from a cereal packet.

"Morning Bert," Jimmy said cheerfully. The guard nodded and allowed them in, hardly bothering to glance at their passes.

"Alright," said Edgar, "What was it this time?"

It did look official until you examined it carefully then you realised it was a soap coupon. "Top that!"

Edgar nodded in appreciation but said nothing, he had plans for tomorrow, two bus tickets stuck one above the other. They were about the right size and colour so he reckoned he would get away with it but would it be enough to trump Jimmy's soap coupon?

When they arrived they found a bustle of activity, a new section was being created. Two soldiers were finishing hanging a sign from the ceiling, joining the likes of Cairo, Melbourne and Delhi. Unlike the others this one merely said 'SECTION X'.

"What's this then?"

"New section. Spy stuff, ultra top secret signals, going directly to Bletchley," whispered the sergeant arriving at their sides. "And guess who is being put on there?"

Edgar and Jimmy looked at each other. Of course the answer was obvious, as the two most experienced operators it would be them.

Everything was checked and working before the finish of their watch, so they were able to leave on time. As they made their way across London, the bomb damage become more evident the nearer they came to the dock area.

"They've taken quite a pasting," observed Brian. In some streets whole rows of terraces were gone, only one or two houses standing, resembling lonely defiant outposts.

"It's like the rows of grimy terraces down Attercliffe," thought Edgar. He pictured the streets with the steelworks behind, the chimneys, furnaces and offices, the same ones at which Ann would be working. He shook his head and the images disappeared, instead he could see a group of children swinging on a rope fastened to a bent lamp-post, surrounded by rubble, while behind them a clothes line weighed down with washing flapped dejectedly in the slight breeze. "Life goes on."

Five minutes later they arrived at their destination, the King Henry. One of the windows was boarded up, the glass blown out by a nearby explosion, and the inevitable word, 'VICTORY' daubed in whitewash on the wall.

They pushed open the door and entered. The room was long, wide and dark, faded wallpaper hung on the wall, along with the usual notices exhorting the patrons to dig for victory or watch against careless words. A bar ran the full length of the room, with a brass foot rail and a couple of battered wooden stools in front. The mahogany handles on the pumps and the inlaid ivory decoration sparkled and shone in the faint light, whether from loving polishing or long use was uncertain. At the far end stood a baby-grand piano. Jimmy's eyes opened wide in astonishment, he had expected a battered upright, most of the keys still in place if he was lucky, not this beauty.

Behind the bar an elderly man with white hair and wire rimmed spectacles was polishing a glass and looking at them expectantly. His sleeves were rolled up, revealing the bottom of a tattoo, a black waistcoat stretched tight across his ample stomach and a gold watch and chain snaked across the front.

"Evening lads, what do you want?" he asked, starting to set up three glasses.

"Ey up, I'm Edgar, these are my mates Brian and Jimmy Parr. Alf told us you wanted a pianist."

"Good to meet you," the landlord replied. "My brother said your mate was brilliant, a real crowd pleaser. We could do with a bit of entertainment round here, usually it's our friend Adolf who provides the excitement."

Edgar faced south, towards Germany. "Ey up Adolf!" he said cheerfully then, pulling a face, made a rude gesture.

Ey Up Adolf

"I'll pull you pint each then your mate can start when he's ready." Seconds later the glasses were full, the froth dripping down the side.

"It's a great piano, not what I expected," commented Jimmy.

"It was shipped in then the owner died, so it sat in a crate down on the docks, unclaimed. A mate told me and it ended up here." Edgar and Brian carried their pints across to a table while Jimmy went to the piano and sat down. After stretching his fingers for a few seconds he started playing, a selection of dance favourites. The landlord looked across and raised his thumb in acknowledgement.

Within half an hour the place was full. Edgar made his way through the crowd at the bar and put their glasses down. A barmaid came up and Edgar said, "Ey up love, a couple of pints of best, please."

She looked at him curiously. "Best what?"

Her buxom colleague finished serving her customer and walked down the bar. "I'll serve the soldier. Wheer tha' from, love?"

Edgar was taken aback. "Roth'rum."

"I'm from Middlesbrough originally, nice to hear a northern accent again. What do you want?"

"Two pints of best."

The barmaid went down the bar and started pulling the beer. The thin man next to him turned. "Are you foreign?"

"Ey, I'm from Roth'rum, up north sithee," replied Edgar, thickening his accent. "What was it with these southerners, didn't they understand simple English?"

"What's up?" asked Brian.

"That weasly bloke at the bar, he thought I was a foreigner!"

"He's just southern, they don't know anywhere north of Watford."

The meeting was coming to a close when Mr Baker announced, "Last item, the Balkan question. When Germany invaded Yugoslavia the royal family escaped and fled to Britain, leaving a nasty little power struggle between their forces, the Cheknics, and the communist Partisans. We have been supporting the troops loyal to the King, but recently we received disturbing information."

"Yes, the Cheknics have made an unofficial arrangement with the Germans to aid them destroy the Partisans. We consider it might be better if we changed sides."

Mr Baker contemplated this statement. "This would be quite contentious, many in the government regard the communists as nearly as big a threat as the Germans." The military sat in silence, waiting his next statement. "However the PM agrees with you. Take the necessary steps but keep it very, very secret. Do we have a way to contact the Partisans?"

The Colonel smiled. "As it happens we have. We can arrange to have a presence out there straight away.

Chapter 36

Norman was sitting in the chair, a cup of steaming tea in his hands. "I thought you were coming tomorrow," Ann cried, giving him a hug.

"I was but I managed to wangle an extra day's leave. It seems there's a rumour going around the camp that this is an important weekend for me."

"And is it?"

"Wait and see. What are you up to tonight?"

"Working at the YM, do you want to come?"

"Sorry, I'm otherwise engaged," then he blushed when he realised what he had just said.

"Not yet, you're not," Ann giggled.

"What has someone said?"

"Nothing, nothing at all," answered Ann then she set off upstairs. "Must rush or I'll be late."

Norman was still sitting in the same place talking animatedly to his mother as she disappeared out of the door. Twenty minutes later she arrived at the YMCA, the warm, smoky air striking her the second she entered. Already it was quite full, with a lot of servicemen present. She disappeared into the kitchen and soon the hatch opened, signalling that food was ready. The small queue was served then two quiet young men in Polish airforce uniforms approached.

"Ey up, lads," greeted Pat, now conscripted and on serving duty that night.

The airman at the front looked up, his face wearing a puzzled frown. "I'm sorry, what is up?" he asked in a strong, foreign accent.

"That's alreet," answered Pat. "What's tha'want?"

Again she received the puzzled look. Ann gently barged her to one side. "He can't understand your accent."

"And he'll do better with your Geordie? I've known you for years and I still can't understand when you and your mum start."

"Yes but that's when I don't want you know what we're talking about."

"I always suspected as much."

"Now gentlemen," continued Ann in her telephone voice, "what would you like, we have chips in a breadcake."

"A chip buttie," interrupted Pat.

Ignoring her Ann continued, "or shin beef stew."

"The stew would be nice, two please," answered the airman with a relieved smile.

Ann smiled back and went to get the order.

*   *

"Guess what happened yesterday?"

Edgar, who was suffering from lack of sleep which made him feel grumpy, replied, "Hitler surrendered?"

"No, much more unlikely, Nicholas Ridiculous had visitors."

"Never! Nicholas never comes out of his office let alone has company."

"Well he did yesterday, two of them, a full staff colonel and a civvy in a pin-stripe suit. They were with him for nearly an hour and Marge swears she heard him cheer at one point." Marge was a young Scots girl who operated one of the stations near Nicholas's office.

Ey Up Adolf

"What did the Colonel look like?" Jimmy gave an accurate description of Colonel Hudson, especially his stern expression. What was he doing with Nicholas Ridiculous and more importantly, would it involve him?

*   *

The next day Ann made her way to the YMCA thinking about the news at home. Norman had indeed proposed to Vera and they were to be married at the Talbot Lane Methodist Church, whose imposing spire dominated the skyline above Rotherham. It was only a few minutes walk from Vera's house which was convenient. They were going to have the banns read as soon as possible then get married.

When Ann arrived she found the two Polish airmen waiting. "Sorry lads, it'll be a bit yet."

"That is alright we do not mind," replied the tall one then continued, "My name is Pawel and my friend is Henryk."

"Watcha, I'm Ann," then she disappeared into the kitchen.

At the end of the shift she found Pawel and Henryk standing there. "Would it be correct if we escorted you home? It is not right for a young lady to be out alone in the dark."

"That would be nice." It was normal for one of the lads to accompany home whoever was on duty so she had a succession of different escorts, one more would make no difference.

*   *

Edgar, Jimmy and Brian arrived at Eaton Square tired and hungry. Jimmy glanced at the small table inside the front door and saw a long brown envelope with his name on it. Quickly he tore it open. "Guess what?"

"Unless it's an invite to dinner I couldn't care less."

"Ignore him," Brian stated. "What is it?"

"They want me to play on Workers' Playtime, Corporal Parr Entertains."

"That's great Jimmy," responded Edgar, his hunger momentarily forgotten, being famous meant they would be able to charge more beer for his concerts. "This needs a celebration. Let's go to that posh place in Chelsea for a meal then back to the Horse and Groom for a pint afterwards."

As they finished their meal Edgar reached into his pocket for some money. "This is one of the few good things about the war."

"What is?"

"That all meals have a maximum price of five shillings. I hate to think how much it would cost to eat in a posh place like this normally."

"True, but fish and chips is still fried potatoes and something that swims in the sea no matter how opulent the place is," answered Jimmy. "Now what about that drink?"

The bar at the Horse and Groom was crowded, with a thick fog of tobacco smoke hanging from the ceiling. After pushing their way to the bar they stood in a tight group discussing life in general when Edgar felt a light touch on his arm. Turning, he found a small man standing there. He had a bald patch, a hangdog expression and alert eyes.

"Evening squire, I see you're in the Signals, do you work at the place in Whitehall by any chance?"

Like a magician the stranger produced a card from his pocket and presented it for inspection. Peering at it, like a shortsighted owl because of the poor lighting, Edgar could make out the word 'PRESS'.

"I'm a reporter for the Telegraph," the man continued. "I'd like to talk to you about a little business proposition." Pointing to a small table in the corner that had become free he continued, "Let's sit over there, it's a bit more private."

Ey Up Adolf

When they were all seated he said in a low voice, "I know it is supposed to be a secret but all the journalist know about it. Is there any time when you are not busy? It's just that sometimes we need to get a message to our people covering the war, and vice versa, and normal channels are too slow. Now, if we could find a quicker way we would be prepared to pay for the privilege."

"How much?" asked Edgar, his northern bluntness coming to the fore.

Taken slightly aback the reporter thought for a minute. "Depends on the importance of the news, say from five upwards."

"Five, that's not very much. Up to what?"

"Twenty if it was really good, front page stuff."

"Twenty shillings," considered Edgar, "that's better." Then he realised what the reporter had said, twenty shillings, why hadn't he said a pound. "Let's get this clear, you are willing to pay from five to twenty depending."

"That's what I said, five pounds for anything normal and twenty pounds for something special."

Jimmy, who had been following the conversation closely, grabbed Edgar's arm and squeezed hard, signalling his acceptance. "And how would we get paid?"

"Cash. I'll meet you here, swap the money for the message and everyone is happy."

Edgar looked at his mates who both nodded. "You've got a deal. Your round."

Chapter 37

Ann was walking through the town square, avoiding workers huddled up in hats and scarves to escape the icy wind. As she passed the door to Davy's cafe she could still smell the fragrant aroma of fresh coffee. Although none had been available since the start of the war the smell seemed to have permeated the very fabric of the building

"Hello Ann." Startled she looked up and saw Vera, her collar turned up against the weather. "You're late from work"

"Yes, there was a report that needed doing. I haven't got time to go home so I thought I'd get a bite here."

"Don't waste your money, come to my house, its only five minutes walk?"

"Thanks, that would be good and you can tell me all the gory details of my brother's proposal."

Arm in arm they strolled up Wellgate to Vera's home, a small cottage. They opened the creaking gate, skirted the outside toilet and crossed to the door. Inside they found Vera's mother and father pegging a rug from scraps of old clothes.

"Hello, love."

"I bumped into Ann and invited her for tea."

"You're welcome, but it's nothing special, tinned pilchards and potatoes."

"That will be fine, better than a plate of chips and my own company," Ann answered.

Vera's mother fussed about setting plates then produced some home-made chutney. When everything was ready Vera's

Ey Up Adolf

father put down the rug and joined them, a scowl on his face. "I'll be glad when this war's over," he complained, "then perhaps we will be able to get some decent food."

Ann felt uncomfortable, as if the comments were directed at her. Throughout the meal she tried to make cheerful conversation but it all seemed to no avail, Vera's father kept a permanent scowl on his face and his eyes followed every forkful that Ann took to her mouth. As soon as the meal finished she made her excuses to leave, saying she was needed at the YMCA early that night, thanked Vera and left, glad to disappear into the darkness. She knew, with rationing, things were tight but, even so, she was surprised by Vera's father's attitude. "Perhaps he's just a natural, bad-tempered scrooge and that's all."

As soon as Ann entered the YMCA she saw Pawel and Henryk so gave them a friendly wave before disappearing into the kitchen. For the rest of the evening she was kept busy so she was thankful when, at last, they closed up and she made her way towards the exit.

"Please, wait a moment." She turned to see Pawel, his dark eyes glowing with excitement, hurrying towards her. "Is it permitted for me to escort you again?"

"If you would like."

"Yes, very much, it would give me great pleasure."

Ann was amused by the way he spoke, so old fashioned in its courtesy. "Where's Henryk tonight?"

"He is busy," Pawel replied awkwardly. Ann felt that Pawel was uncomfortable, as if there was something he wanted to say but could not find the right words. Finally he plucked up courage. "Would it be acceptable for me to take you to the pictures on Saturday."

Ann was at a loose end, Pat had a date with a soldier she had met and Vera was working. "That would be very nice. I'll meet you on Davy's corner at seven o'clock."

Neil Whyke

*   *

Edgar and his friends decided to return to the Horse and Groom to see if their new-found friend was in but they were disappointed. They were sitting at a table, quietly discussing Jimmy's new role as radio star and pulling his leg, when they became aware of a stranger standing next to them.

"Can I sit for a moment?" Edgar looked him over, middle aged, worn mackintosh over a sports jacket with pencils poking from the top pocket and sturdy, brown, leather shoes, suitable for long days on his feet. "I noticed you talking to a ….. colleague of mine the other night."

"You are from the press," interrupted Edgar. "Do you have identification?"

The man fished in his jacket pocket and produced a worn and dog-eared pass, which he handed across for inspection. Edgar noticed he worked for the Times, a rival to the Telegraph, then passed it back. "From your uniforms I assume you work at that building site ….."

"Some secret this is," considered Edgar, "everyone and their granny seems to know about it."

"….and I wondered if you would be interested in..."

"A business proposition."

"Yes, precisely."

"You want us to deal with messages for you when there is spare time?"

"Yes."

"And you will pay for doing that?"

The man nodded.

"Ten pounds for routine and twenty five for anything special or rushed."

The man gulped, it was more than he was expecting, but he was sure he could get his editor to agree. "Fine."

Edgar reached across and shook his hand. "You have a deal, now what about some drinks." When neither Edgar nor his friends moved the reporter took the hint and made his way to the bar.

While he was away Edgar leant across the table and whispered to his friends, "We could have hit on a gold mine, if these two are prepared to pay us I'll bet others will as well."

"But how do we get to find out," added Brian. "We can't put an advert in the local shop, 'wireless operators, willing to take payments for messages,' can we?"

"We won't need to, if these two characters were able find us, I'll bet others will, all we have to do is wait."

*   *

"Good evening Ann," Pawel said then he produced a block of chocolate. "I hope this is acceptable."

"Very. How did you get it?"

"I have been saving my coupons and Henryk gave me some of his as well as I still did not have enough." Ann made a mental note to make sure that there was some left at the end of the evening for Henryk. "Shall we go so that we are not late?" Together they walked across the square towards the Odeon.

After the performance Ann and Pawel walked back to Ann's house "What's the problem, you're very quiet all of a sudden?"

"I have something to say but I do not have the words in English. We have been given orders to report to a Polish squadron in the south, near Oxford."

"That will be nice, you must be lonely at times."

"Yes I was but then I met you." Quickly he took hold of her hand making her jump but, before she had an opportunity to say anything, "When the war is over I will come back for you and we can go to Poland and get married."

At first she could not believe what she had just heard, then hastily removed her hand and stared him in the eyes. "Hold your horses! One visit to the pictures does not mean I have any intention of getting married to you and definitely not in Poland. I've been engaged once and that was enough, thank you." She paused, breathing quickly, her face flushed with anger. "I think you had better go, I can make my own way home from here."

Pawel stood at the edge of the pavement, a look of disbelief on his face. "But I thought…."

"I don't care what you thought, I am not in love with you and have no intention of marrying you, and that is final!" She turned and stalked off up the road, her voice trailing off into the distance. "The arrogance of the man! And I thought he was sweet"

Chapter 38

For days Ann had spent all her spare time helping to organize Norman's wedding; cooking then borrowing chairs, plates and cutlery. Their friends and neighbours had been amazing, donating coupons for food, bringing round anything they thought could be useful and offering their services. Now their special day had finally arrived.

Everyone was at the church, Norman and his best man were at the front, looking very nervous. Ann could not help wondering if Edgar would have been in the same state had they made it to the altar and she felt a pang of jealousy.

There was a ripple of unease among the congregation. Vera's mother spoke to the man behind who immediately made his way down the side of the church then disappeared out of the door.

"What's the matter?" Douglas asked, digging her in the ribs to attract her attention. "Why aren't we starting?"

"I don't know, everyone's here except the bride." She had a spasm of panic, surely Vera hadn't changed her mind. Then she realised someone else was missing, the vicar.

Abruptly the door at the side of the altar was flung back and a very flustered vicar rushed in, his tie askew and his jacket unbuttoned. Red faced and embarrassed he smiled at the assembled congregation, opened his bible and nodded. Immediately the organ started its bellow, announcing the arrival of the bride.

Vera entered, dressed in white with a matching veil, accompanied by her father. As they made their way to the front a wave of muttering followed, the vicar had fallen asleep in front of the fire and had to be woken up by one of Vera's relatives.

"I bet that gave Norman a few palpitations," Ann thought.

The reception went off without a hitch but Ann never quite understood how twenty people managed to squash into their kitchen, seated round an extended table, with two of their friends acting as waitresses.

Finally it was over and everyone took their leave, after thanking her mother for an excellent time. Exhausted Ann's mum collapsed into her chair. "Put the kettle on pet."

"Never changes," Ann thought, "a cup of tea, the universal panacea."

*   *

Edgar stepped off the bus and made his way to the 'building site'. With the extra money from their private arrangements plus the going rate in beer had increased since Jimmy had started appearing on the radio he was almost enjoying the war, especially since Captain Leigh had vanished. He entered the signals room and was collared by Brian.

"Nicholas Ridiculous has disappeared."

"What do you mean disappeared?"

"Gone, not here, possibly AWOL."

"Perhaps he's ill or something." The something could be more serious, there had been severe bombing last night. Edgar had been on duty and could feel the tremors through the walls.

"No, it's more than that. A couple of staffers came in earlier and removed everything from his office."

Edgar wandered off, puzzled, but it didn't concern him and wasn't going to upset his life. Just as he was about to don his headphones Marge came across, bent over and whispered, "Have you heard about Nicholas?"

"You mean that he hasn't come in?"

Ey Up Adolf

"No, he's been locked up for being drunk and disorderly, he attacked a policeman, knocked his helmet off and everything."

"How do you know this?"

"It's common knowledge, everyone is talking about it."

"Right, ta, it's good to know these things." Edgar went back to his set only to be interrupted a few minutes later by Wendy.

"Have you heard about Nicholas?"

Edgar turned, intrigued to know what the tale would be this time. One thing was certain, it would not be the truth. "What?"

"He's been arrested by MI5, he's a spy," she said with wide eyed innocence.

"A spy, arrested?" replied Edgar, trying his best to sound as if he believed her.

"Yes. They shoot spies you know, after the trial, that is. Don't tell anyone, it's a secret," then she moved on to tell someone else.

"Curiouser and curiouser, I wonder what the real story is?" His thoughts went no further as the sergeant tapped him on the back to attract his attention. "The CO wants you."

Puzzled, Edgar made his way to the small office.

"Sit down." Edgar moved a pile of papers from the chair. "I've some good news, you are being promoted."

"Thank you Sir."

"Nothing to do with me, not that I don't think you deserve it," he added too quickly. "The promotion has come from the War Office, for special services it says, must be for that business in Windsor. You never did say exactly what you did there."

"No Sir, I didn't." He received an icy glare but the Captain knew better than to pursue it, not if you wanted to stay in London rather than be out in the desert with a tank regiment.

Edgar smiled, a sergeant, it gave him superiority over Jimmy, something he was going to enjoy.

Neil Whyke

*   *

Ann hoped she would be able to relax but Hitler had other plans so she set off for the fire station. The heavy drone of enemy aircraft engines was clearly audible and passing directly overhead. She hugged the hedge as if it would make her invisible to the bombers then heard a strange sound, a whistle, as something heavy dropped through the air. Bombs! She held her breath, expecting the blinding flash, the tremendous roar and the shock wave of detonating explosive. Nothing. She breathed again. Relieved, she started on her way but the inky blackness of the Playingfield was now dotted with small but intense lights.

The grass was littered with incendiaries, markers for the following bombers. They were aiming for the steelworks and missed, but now the houses nearby, including hers, were in great danger. Suddenly indistinct shapes moved in the darkness. One by one the lights went out.

"They didn't last long. Hopefully the bombers haven't seen them." Relieved, she continued down the road, walking next to the grass. Out to her left she saw a hump, with the faintest ray of light escaping from it, an eerie green as it reflected off the turf beneath. Intrigued, she made her way across the damp ground then burst out laughing. "Typical and effective," a metal dustbin lid neatly enclosed the incendiary. "Not only does it prevent the light being seen but it says a lot about we think about Hitler, what a load of rubbish!"

Arriving at the fire station she reported in, saying what she had seen.

"This could be a busy night, probably a big attack."

People had become a bit blasé about the raids, very few bombs had actually dropped on Rotherham and even Sheffield had escaped the major damage of places like Coventry. Ann hoped the officer was wrong.

She heard the drone of aircraft engines, lower and louder this time, then the crump of anti aircraft fire, a raid was in progress.

She felt a series of dull thumps and tremors that shook the building.

"Was that bombs?"

"Yes, and nearby but they didn't explode."

"Probably landed in Boston Park, the deep, soft soil would have absorbed the impact, but it's close enough for us to feel the shock," added Dave. "We'd better report it so that someone can go and check in the morning. We don't want some old biddy, walking her dog, to find them first."

"Right. She might get hurt."

"More likely she might try and flog them for scrap."

Chapter 39

Calls came in all night reporting bombs, one landed in Clifton Park, causing a massive crater and shattering windows. A second in the Holmes area, destroying offices, but luckily no-one was killed.

The following morning Ann stepped off the tram and saw a pall of smoke rising from behind the offices. The air held a sooty, pungent smell and every flat surface was covered in a layer of dust. As she walked across the pavement slivers of glass crunched under her shoes and, glancing up, she could see cracked and broken panes in the windows. Entering the building Ann caught a glimpse of the receptionist, the tell-tale streaks of tears on her cheeks. Then she hurried along to her own office.

The room was devastated. Windows were shattered, the magnificent panelled walls were scored with deep scratches from flying glass and the whole office was covered in a layer of grey, gritty dust. Mr Munroe stood by his desk talking earnestly into the phone. When he finished he hung up. "A stick of bombs landed on the works. I know it looks bad, but it could have been worse. We'll be up and running in a week." He stared at her stricken face. "Take the time off, there's nothing you can do here at the moment."

Ey Up Adolf

*   *

Using part of a railway timetable as a pass Edgar descended the stairs. Coming in the opposite direction was an unmistakable, squat figure with a large cigar clenched between his teeth and a bulldog expression on his face. Edgar stepped to one side then saluted. "Morning Sir."

As Winston Churchill passed he let out a grunt of acknowledgement then, like a destroyer with an Atlantic convoy, continued on his way, single-minded and unstoppable. "And a well done to you too," muttered Edgar under his breath, "but to be fair I suppose you do have things on your mind."

He finished dealing with the messages, sat back and stretched, glancing up at the sign above. Section X. After his time in Lisbon he now knew it handled messages for the clandestine services, mostly passed on to Bletchley. How many people were out there, agents operating abroad, many behind enemy lines, spies and saboteurs, risking their lives daily? He was glad his short spell abroad was somewhere safe and now safely behind him.

The officer-in-charge never came out of his room so when he approached Edgar was instantly suspicious.

"Sergeant Stanton, you're wanted. Get someone to man your post."

Edgar attracted Jimmy's attention. "I'm needed, keep an eye on things."

"What have you been up to now?"

"Nothing new, but that still leaves plenty."

Edgar knocked and a voice he remembered with dread answered, Colonel Hudson.

"Morning sergeant." Edgar's stomach lurched. "I hope you enjoyed your time in Lisbon, a very pleasant city I always think."

"Yes Sir," stuttered Edgar hoping the colonel would come to the point.

"I received a glowing report from Captain Leigh, he was quite impressed." Edgar stared ahead, dreading what might be coming next. "As a result we wondered if you might like to volunteer again."

He had enjoyed having the good food, sunshine and an expensive suit, instead of his scratchy uniform, so Edgar replied, "Yes, Sir, I would."

"Of course this is top secret. You remember what I said last time."

Edgar certainly had not forgotten, he still had nightmares about it. "Yes Sir, if I told anyone you'd shoot me personally."

"Good man, I'm glad to see your memory is still functioning. Now go about your duties and we will be in touch before long."

Edgar saluted and left. "What have I just done?" he said to himself.

"What was all that about?" asked Jimmy then he saw the troubled expression. "Not again! Tell me you've not got involved with anymore of that silly spy nonsense."

"Whatever you do, never, ever mention a word of this to anyone, for both our sakes," blurted out Edgar, the memory of the scary colonel still too fresh in his memory.

The following morning Edgar was decidedly worse for wear, after his interview with Colonel Hudson he had felt in need of considerable refreshment. No sooner had he carefully lowered himself into his seat when the sergeant approached. "New orders, you are transferred."

"What? Where to?"

The sergeant peered at the sheet myopically. "Typical, can't do a simple job right, some clown has forgotten to fill that part in." Edgar's heart sank. "It just says to report to Goodge St. I didn't know we had a base there, the only place I know of is the tube station."

"It's alright, I know the place, I've been there before. When does it say to report?"

"Today, another snafu, you'd better get a move on. Jimmy will have to take over."

Reluctantly Edgar stood up and made his way to the door, where he stopped and looked back, wondering when he would see the place again. Or even if!

As he dismounted from the bus he still did not believe he was here again. After negotiating the plain-clothes guard he made his way down the tunnels to the counter. After proving his identity he waited for his expensive clothes to arrive, but this time it seemed to be taking longer than he remembered.

Eventually the little man arrived back at his counter clutching an armful of rags.

"Typical," Edgar thought, "I'm hanging around while he tidies out the rubbish. I wonder when he'll get round to finding my suit."

A pile of grubby papers was produced and dumped on top of the rags. "Right," started the clerk, "jacket, trousers, shirts, underclothes, socks and cap, all genuine Croatian."

"Croatia, that's part of Yugoslavia!" exclaimed Edgar. "What do I want those for, I'm going to Lisbon."

The man behind the counter consulted a list, "Stanton, Royal Corps of Signals, clothes, genuine, and papers, forged, Yugoslavian. That's what it says here."

"There's a mistake, I'm supposed to be going to Lisbon."

"Not possible, we have no base in Portugal, never had."

"But I worked there," replied Edgar, his voice rising several decibels.

"Sorry mate, you must be mistaken. Anyway those are the clothes and stuff you've been allocated."

"He's right," came a voice that Edgar recognised. "You were asked to volunteer for service abroad, you just assumed that it was Lisbon."

"He said I'd not been to Lisbon," answered Edgar pointing at the clerk.

"He's technically correct," continued Captain Leigh, "officially you were never there, you never left this country, and neither did I. This time you are going to Yugoslavia."

"But I thought the Germans had invaded there."

"They have, that's why we need you and your bag of tricks."

"But," Edgar started then closed his mouth, he knew when he was beaten.

"Good. When you change make sure you do not take anything from this country, coins, bus tickets, nothing at all, your life will depend on it."

Finally the seriousness of the situation sank home, his chances of survival had just plummeted. Edgar's face took on a very forlorn look.

Chapter 40

Three days later Edgar walked across the tarmac of an airfield in North Africa, the stars shining in the sky were far brighter than they did back at home in Yorkshire. He could still feel the heat beneath his feet although the air, striking through his threadbare jacket, had a chill feel. Scattered around the perimeter of the base lay shattered hulks of lorries and tanks, the remnants of Rommel's Africa Corps. Ahead was a DB7, otherwise known as a Havoc, a light bomber with a top speed of over three hundred miles an hour, now in the allies' hands and a very suitable plane for their purposes.

As soon as Edgar and the other members of his party had strapped themselves in, the twin Cyclone engines fired up and the plane rolled forwards. With a roar it left the ground and leapt skywards, swinging in a leisurely curve until it was pointing north towards the Adriatic and their destination in Croatia.

*   *

Ann climbed from the tram as it ground to a halt on Corporation Street and straightened her uniform. She was going to grab a quick bite then report for duty but the question was, where to eat? The choices were Davy's, the Whitehall or the Odeon. She didn't really like the Whitehall that much but it was on the way to the fire-station, as was Davy's, but she had eaten there last time and felt like a change. That left the Odeon. It was in the wrong direction, but always had a pleasant atmosphere.

Having made her decision she set off down the hill. As Ann pushed open the door she immediately realised it was even busier than usual, but spotted an unoccupied table for two.

She was staring out of the window when she became aware of a slim, young man in RAF uniform, with the three stripes of a sergeant on his arm, standing next to her.

"Do you mind if I sit here? All the tables are occupied and I don't feel comfortable with civilians then I saw the uniform."

Ann smiled and his grey eyes twinkled with pleasure as he sat down. "What do you recommend?"

Ann laughed. "It's not exactly a big choice or gourmet food?"

"As long as it's not bacon and eggs I don't care." Ann's eyes opened wide in astonishment, that would have been a treat for her, both bacon and eggs were rationed, always assuming they were available. "I'm in bomber command and they always give us that before we fly. Sometimes take-off is postponed so we can end up having it two or three times in a night."

"What a hardship!"

"Also we're issued with these." He produced a chocolate bar from his top pocket. Handing it across, he continued, "Please accept it for interrupting your meal."

"Thank you." She reached across the table. "Are you on leave?"

"Yes. My family live in Chapletown but there's only my sisters left, everyone else is in the forces, there's no-one I know there."

"Well now you know me," offering her hand. "I'm Ann."

"John, navigator, Lancasters."

Ann was impressed, she had seen the pictures on the newsreels, the searchlights, the fighters with the trails of incendiary shells, the anti-aircraft fire and the brave crews battling to drop their bombs on German factories.

Ey Up Adolf

"What's your uniform?" John asked.

"Auxiliary fire service. I'm on duty tonight, as soon as I've finished eating."

"Are you on duty every night?"

"No but on others I work at the YMCA as a cook."

"So you are busy every evening?"

"No, I do have some free time."

"Good. When you're free would you like to go to the pictures?"

"What about Saturday?" she answered quickly.

"Fantastic! I'll see you outside here then."

*   *

The twin engines droned on as the light bomber skipped over the waves. Edgar could see the coast, with a line of breaking surf and occasionally a fishing boat on its way to harbour. Around him were tough looking men cradling the new sten gun, a cheap, efficient way of dispensing a large number of bullets very quickly. As none of them seemed inclined to chat Edgar sat in silence, wondering why he ever agreed to come.

He felt the plane heel as they changed direction, he could see they were passing over the narrow coastal plain where the Germans were strongest and had control. By twisting his neck he managed to look beyond the high-set wings, and made out the rocky tops of the mountains, the wild country where the Partisans were fighting on two fronts, against the Germans and the rival Cheknics.

Edgar felt the men round him stir with expectancy, they were going to land in occupied territory, dressed in civilian clothes. Spies. And Edgar knew all too well what happened to spies.

His stomach lurched as the plane dropped from the sky, hurtled straight for a wall of rock then turned violently, the wing tip missing by inches. Levelling, it followed a narrow, tree-sided valley. The engines throttled back and the undercarriage dropped into place. Outside the window tall fir trees rushed past in a blur. A bounce, followed by a second, and they were down. Instantly dark shadows emerged from the gloom of the pines and rushed towards the Havoc, all heavily armed and wearing a sort of uniform. Edgar hoped the natives were friendly.

A blast of cold air announced the hatch was open and instantly his companions leapt out, their guns cocked and ready. Edgar sat still, ears straining, trying to make out what was happening. Suddenly a stranger, a stocky man in a tattered, Italian uniform jacket, cap and strong trousers tucked into leather boots climbed into the cabin. Dark, penetrating eyes peered out from under bushy eyebrows that perfectly matched his luxurious moustache. He looked Edgar up and down then stuck out a grimy hand, "Welcome to my country," he said in perfect English. Edgar took it and returned the handshake. "Please hurry, there is a German patrol nearby and they will have heard your arrival. We need to be well away before they get here."

They jumped to the ground and Edgar saw a score of figures, all carrying heavy loads. They scurried from the aircraft and disappeared into the tree line. The Havoc spun round, the engines roared and it leapt down the grass runway marked out with oil lamps. Within seconds it was airborne, rapidly becoming a dot in the sky.

Edgar looked round at the dark trees, the rugged mountains and the motley crew of tough and battle-hardened Partisans. "I wonder what Jimmy would say if he could see me now. Probably 'You idiot'."

Chapter 41

Raised voices were coming from Ann's living room, her brother's and Mr Birch, who lived further down the road. Red-faced and angry he shouted and furiously wagged his finger but Douglas was defiant.

"It wasn't him, Peter wouldn't do such a thing."

"And I'm telling you I saw it with my own eyes. There were a pack of dogs, terrifying my chickens, and yours were among' 'em. By the time I managed to scare the brutes away I doubt if any of my birds had more than two feathers remaining. I'll be surprised if they lay an egg for weeks, they're traumatised. If they die I'll be round here for compensation."

"That's not exactly fair," said Ann's mother, speaking for the first time. "Even if our dog was involved, and you could have been mistaken, it wasn't the only one. You can't hold us responsible for all the damage."

"Ey, but yours is the only one I could recognise so there's only you to get money from." He turned, rudely pushed past Ann and stormed off.

"I hate him," stated Douglas. "Peter wouldn't do anything like that."

"Go upstairs and wash for dinner," said Ann's mother, propelling him in the direction of the door.

As soon as he was gone Ann said, "What do you think?"

"It is quite likely Peter, he's been running off more and more recently, and that pack on the fields are like wolves rather than dogs, they're completely wild."

"Talking of which, where is the pest?"

Ann's mother shrugged her shoulders. "I tried tying him up but he chewed through the rope and I've not seen him for two days."

"So he could have been responsible." She received a nod in answer. Just then there was a scratching at the back door. Ann opened it and in walked the offending animal, its tail wagging, causing a shower of short brown feathers to fall onto the carpet.

*   *

For two hours Edgar toiled up the valley, pack on his back, struggling to keep up with the Partisans. Several of them split off, accompanied by the soldiers from the plane, carrying a number of sacks.

"Where are they going?" asked Edgar.

"The railyard."

"And what's in the sacks?"

"Exploding rats."

Feeling they were taking the Mickey Edgar stopped asking questions and concentrated on plodding up the steep, slippery track. As a light, icy drizzle started to fall they emerged into a hollow, hidden by overhanging boughs. The leader called a halt and Edgar thankfully sank to the ground. His Partisan companion sat next to him, rummaged inside his jacket and produced a bottle, which he opened and offered to Edgar.

"Try this, it will help against the cold."

Edgar eyed the coloured liquid suspiciously then placed the bottle to his lips and took a small sip. He spluttered and coughed, feeling his mouth was on fire, then asked. "What is that stuff?"

"Plum brandy, we make it ourselves."

"Tastes like it." Gingerly he took another sip. "Mind, I reckon I could get used to it." He handed the bottle back to its

Ey Up Adolf

owner, who raised it to his lips and took a long swallow, much to Edgar's admiration. "You must have a gullet like a coal grate."

"Yes, it is pleasantly warming."

"What was that crack earlier about rats, were you taking the mick?"

His host smiled. "Your people stuff explosive inside dead rat skins. We toss them into the coal tenders of the trains. It is very common to find dead rats in the coal, the engineers ignore them and throw them into the boiler with everything else. When they explode one disabled train. Eventually they will realise what is causing the problem but then they will have to examine every dead carcass, which will slow up the job. Anything that causes a problem is a success for us."

"I'll drink to that," replied Edgar holding out his hand for the bottle. "By the way, I'm Edgar."

"Javor."

"You speak excellent English, where did you learn it."

"I was a lecturer in English before the war, at the University. When it closed I took to the hills."

"A bit drastic."

"Well, the fact I blew up the German garrison first was a contributory factor to my leaving."

"Nice one!"

*   *

When the sirens started Ann wearily rose to her feet.

"Must you go, pet, you look exhausted."

Ann nodded, gave a wan smile then left.

The first person she saw when she entered was Dave then the phone rang. "Answer that for me as you're nearer."

Dave picked up the receiver, listened, and Ann saw his face turn a deathly white. "Right, that's understood. We can cope."

Neil Whyke

As he replaced the handset Ann stared at him. "What's happened?"

"There's a bomb exploded in the centre of Sheffield, one of the pubs in the square."

Ann knew where he was referring, they were always busy, especially this early in the evening, with people popping in on their way home from work. Even with an air raid it would have been packed. "Is there much damage?"

Dave looked devastated, "A total write off. The walls have collapsed."

"What about the people inside?"

Dave cleared his throat and in a voice breaking with emotion, "No survivors. In fact the whole place is so dangerous they'll have to topple what's left, with the bodies inside." This was the worst disaster that had happened while they were on duty. "Anyway, Rotherham has sent crews to help so they want us to take over as main duty station. I'd better go and inform everyone."

Ann sat down. For the first time the real hideousness of the war struck home. The death and destruction had seemed distant and illusory, something on the newsreels, but now it was happening just down the road. Real people were being killed, you didn't know who would be next, and for the first time Ann felt afraid.

*   *

Edgar came out of the forest into a broad clearing, in the middle stood an old farmhouse with a dilapidated barn alongside. Just over a slight hillock, he could make out the top of another building, with a faint wisp of smoke coming from the chimney.

As they approached, the leader of their group called out a password, the door opened and a figure emerged, wearing

Ey Up Adolf

motley bits of uniform and heavily armed, ammunition belts, rifle and a vicious-looking dagger stuck in a belt.

Edgar was amazed. It was a girl, slightly built with long, unkempt, dark hair which fell across her face in ringlets, partly obscuring her deep, brown eyes. The hands that held the rifle were long and slender with ragged nails from hard, manual work and she was obviously used to handling the weapon. When she saw Edgar she gave a welcoming smile. Despite his exhaustion from the long, gruelling hike up the mountain Edgar found himself smiling back.

She led him inside, while his escorts disappeared back into the forest. Edgar found himself in a large room, with a wood-burning stove, table and plain pine chairs set up in the middle. In one corner was his wireless equipment, very basic, not the same as he had in London.

The girl indicated for Edgar to sit down then went to a large pan that was simmering on the stove, ladled out a plate of steaming stew, cut off a chunk of dark bread with her dagger, and handed both to Edgar. As he accepted the meal he stared at the gleaming, sharp knife making a mental note always to be polite and respectful to his host. This assignment was not like his last one, smart cafes, wine, sunshine and smiling people. Here it was a dilapidated farmhouse, thick, greasy stew and a grubby, heavily-armed, dark-haired girl who hadn't spoken yet. A movement at his side, a bottle of coloured liquid and a glass appeared. Pulling the cork he recognised the strong, fruity scent. "At least they had plum brandy."

Chapter 42

Edgar was concentrating on his stew so was only vaguely aware someone had entered. He glanced up and saw a man standing in the doorway. There was something familiar about him, whether it was his voice or the way he stood, but he knew that, somewhere or other, they had met before. With a curt nod the man left.

The girl approached and pointed to his empty plate. "Would you like some more?"

Surprised, Edgar stared at her, realising that beneath the layer of grime she was quite young, probably in her early twenties, and pretty in a fresh, country-girl way. "Er, no thanks."

"It would be alright, I know you have food shortages but here we are surrounded by farms and the people are very adept at hiding things from the Germans, and not just food."

"No, seriously, I am full. Does everyone round here speak excellent English?"

"No, just a few of us. I was a student before the invasion, when my tutor left to join the Partisans I went with him."

"Was that Javor?"

"Yes, he was very angry with me, he said hiding in the mountains was no place for a girl but it turned out I was a natural shot, much better than him, so he had to accept it. Then there is Nicholas of course, but he's very important, a colonel no less and a friend of our leader, General Tito."

Edgar was shocked. Nicholas Ridiculous, a high-up in the Partisan army. "So this is where he disappeared to."

Ey Up Adolf

"Sorry, what do you mean?"

"No, it's me who should apologise. When he entered just now I couldn't place him. We worked at the same office in London."

"That is possible. He came back a few days ago with some people from London, very good warriors I am told. They are here to train us to fight the Germans."

"Since we are to be working together I'd better introduce myself, I'm …"

"Edgar, one of the men from England told me, an officer, he said you were …." she paused trying to remember the strange phrase, "…a whiz with radios."

Edgar felt embarrassed. "I wouldn't exactly say that."

"He also said you were quite shy and we weren't to scare you too much."

"Thanks. Since you know my name, what's yours?"

"Call me Nada, it's not my real name but if I'm caught the Germans can not take reprisals on my family." Edgar did not like this talk about being captured, he felt far too vulnerable. "But do not worry about that, we will have plenty of warning if anyone comes, the local people hate the Germans nearly as much as the accursed Cheknics." She picked up the bottle and poured Edgar a substantial measure.

"Won't you have one?"

"No thank you, I never touch the stuff. I need a clear head, I'm going on a raid tonight."

Despite her weapons it had never occurred to Edgar that she would actually shoot someone. He would have to alter his thinking if he was going to survive this mission.

*   *

Saturday arrived and Ann made her way towards the Odeon cinema and saw John waiting, wearing his blue RAF uniform.

She had not realised at their first meeting how smart he looked, standing out among the drab clothes of the other people waiting to go in. His hair was light brown and swept back, his jacket and trousers were pressed and his shoes gleamed from layers of polish. She felt a buzz of expectancy as she walked down the road. This was the first proper date she had been on since….. Suddenly she felt uncertain but life had to go on.

When she was only a few yards away John produced a bar of chocolate from behind his back.

"Courtesy of the RAF?" she asked,

Smiling, "Yes, the last of my stash. I'll need to go flying again to build up a new stock."

"How come you have so much?"

"We are all given stuff when we fly. I'm the only one on the plane who has a bag, for the maps and bits and pieces, so the others ask me carry it for them. Sometimes when we return they're too tired and don't want it back, so it becomes mine. Besides, the crew is from all over, Canadians, Australians, New Zealanders, they have no-one to give it to, whereas I have two sisters," he paused briefly then added, "and now you."

"And now me," she repeated to herself as they went into the cinema.

When they came out two hours later John asked if he could see her home. Ann readily accepted but then paused. "Won't you miss your last bus?"

"Probably."

"Well how will you get home?"

"Walk."

"But it's six miles, it'll take you forever?" Ann answered, appalled.

"Not that long. I've always enjoyed walking and the RAF taught me how to march."

"Of course, I never thought of that." She linked her arm through his and together they made their way through the square to wait for her bus, two, young people, both with grins on their faces.

*   *

Edgar had settled into his new posting, every day he laboriously tapped the morse code into a machine that produced a strip of perforated paper that could be fed into a sender at the required time. This way the message that had taken him hours to compose could be sent in a matter of seconds to an aircraft that flew overhead then on to London. There were problems of course, he kept getting blisters on his finger, from the crude morse key, and the batteries for the wireless had to be replaced with new ones every few days, as there was no method of recharging them. When he had asked where they came from all he got was 'the Germans'.

While he was tapping out his messages he listened to the German frequencies, noting any messages between Berlin and their commanders on the Russian Front, more work for the code-breakers at Bletchley.

He stopped, stretched his back and glanced out of the window. A group emerged from the tree-line and made their way across the open grass. Edgar returned to his task and took no notice when the door opened, until he heard Nada give a cry of joy. Turning he saw Javor standing there, but it wasn't him who gave Edgar the biggest shock of his life, it was his companion.

Chapter 43

"Hello Edgar, got here safely then," said Captain Leigh.

"Er," was all a shocked Edgar could manage.

"Is there any of that plum brandy about, it's been a long and eventful night."

Edgar pointed to a shelf, he did not dare wonder what they had been up to if the captain considered it eventful. Once two glasses had been filled they sat down at the table while Nada poured steaming bowls of stew. He had quickly discovered that there was always a pan bubbling on the stove as people came and went twenty four hours a day. Edgar kept a respectful distance from the others, as if they had an infectious disease. Whatever they were up to he didn't want to know.

After several spoonfuls of stew Captain Leigh took a drink of the brandy. "Bet you're glad I recommended you for this job, much more interesting than sitting round that subterranean office in London."

"What! I'm out here because of you."

"Yes, but you don't need to thank me."

"Thanks is not exactly what I had in mind."

"Anyway, we have a little task to do and we need your help."

"Typical! Blow things up or shoot people and you are in your element but do a simple thing like transmit and you're stuck. What do you want sending?"

"Just a short message."

"Can't you do that yourself? Everything is set up," waving a hand in the direction of his domain.

Ey Up Adolf

"It's not that simple and I will be otherwise engaged," added Captain Leigh between mouthfuls of stew.

Now Edgar was becoming concerned. "There's more to this than just sending a message isn't there?"

"A little. The Germans are storing a large amount of explosives and fuel in a cave system, not far from here, and we've been instructed to destroy it."

"Isn't it heavily defended?" asked Edgar, worriedly.

"Yes, but we have an advantage. Apparently a group of speleologists found another way in."

"Who?"

"Cavers. They discovered a back door, but it was never made public knowledge as war broke out shortly afterwards. That is how we are going in."

"But why now?"

"The allies have landed in Italy and are fighting their way north. It would be a great help if those supplies never left here. If we fail then London needs to know and they will try to bomb them instead."

"Why not just do that in the first place?"

"Because they don't know if it will work, the caves are very extensive. Our going in has a better chance, as long as we are not discovered. That is where your services are required."

"I see, if you're not back here within a certain time I have to send a message."

"Not quite. The message will need sending straight away. If we are discovered before we blow the place up the Germans will move the stuff immediately. So that means," concluded Captain Leigh, "you have to come with us."

*   *

Ann was sitting by the fire reading the letter from John for the third time. After their visit to the pictures he had come for tea the next day. Both her parents took to him immediately, her mother because he looked dashing and her father because John's dad was a deputy at Thorpe Hesley pit. Since he returned to his squadron they had been writing to each other regularly.

She looked across at her mother, who was knitting, a worried expression on her face and grumbling to herself.

"What's wrong Mum?"

"Nothing."

"Don't lie to me, it's a sin you know."

"So's black marketeering."

Ann looked at her mother with astonishment. "What are you on about?"

Her mother glared, her face a battleground of conflicting emotions. "It's your dad."

"Dad, a black marketeer, selling hooky stuff! You are pulling my leg."

"He's not selling, he's bought something." She made her way upstairs, an intrigued Ann following. They squashed into the box room, her mother opened the wardrobe and stood back. Hanging from the rail was a full, cured ham.

"He brought it in this morning. Someone at the pit has a brother who keeps pigs, and had this for sale. I don't know what came over the daft loon. Then, to make matters worse, I was talking to Mrs Green……" Mrs Green was the next-door neighbour and her husband was the local bobby "….she was talking about the black market and how she was never offered anything."

"Well, it's not surprising, considering her husband's job," Ann answered. "But then," she thought, "from what Pat says, there are plenty of bobbies in town who regularly visit the pubs after hours for a free drink."

"So there I was, saying how awful that some people could get stuff off the ration, and all the time I had this hanging in the wardrobe. What shall I do?"

Ey Up Adolf

"I know it's only powdered eggs, but what about ham and eggs for tea? I'm starving."

*   *

The others disappeared for a few hours sleep and Edgar was left alone. He knew his services were necessary for the mission, but he wished they weren't, he wasn't the gung-ho commando type. He hadn't even played rugby at school, the most dangerous thing he had done was face a fast bowler, then usually for not more than a few balls.

Across the room Nada saw his troubled expression. "Don't worry, it will be alright, you aren't going inside the cave, only to the rear entrance. And you'll have a bodyguard with you, the best shot in the group."

"Who?"

"Me, of course."

As soon as the sun sank behind the mountains the little band set off, quickly disappearing into the Stygian gloom of overhanging trees. Javor was scout, checking the way was clear of danger, then Captain Leigh, accompanied by a local caver who would help guide them, using a map smuggled from England. Behind came Edgar and Nada, carrying her rifle. Edgar felt sorry for any poacher out that night, but then he felt sorry for himself, he spent most of his time tripping over hidden tree roots. "Why do they only get me," he wondered, as he stumbled for the fiftieth time. "Never mind, only another six hours then we can rest, in a wet, cold forest, surrounded by Germans, and using packs filled with high explosives as pillows. Just what I always wanted to do."

Chapter 44

For two days Edgar trudged through damp forests, waded across small rivers, climbed mountainous passes and was generally miserable. Carrying the field transmitter was awkward and painful, the sharp edges constantly dug into his back, the straps chaffed his shoulders and there was the continuous danger they could be spotted by the Germans. Now they were scrabbling up a steep gulley lined with limestone crags.

"This track is not meant to be used by humans," Edgar moaned, as his boots slipped on the wet rock. "It's only suitable for mountain goats."

Nada was used to his good natured grumbles. "Never mind, Edgar, we'll soon be at the top. Of course you will be out in the open, an easy target for any passing fighter plane, but you will always be able to run for cover, carrying that heavy wireless set." She gave him a big grin then continued scrambling upwards.

Soon they emerged onto a flat, grassy plateau. "Not far now," stated Captain Leigh. "We'll hide in the forest until night-time then go into the cave. It will take three hours to make our way through the system, half an hour to set the explosives then out again. We will be back before dawn."

* *

John left the briefing decidedly worried, they were scheduled to fly that night, a big raid on an armaments factory and railway yard deep in the heart of Germany. There were going to be a lot of planes involved, all Lancasters, from other bases as well as his own. Recently Bomber Command had been running into more and more resistance, searchlights, anti-aircraft fire and night fighters. As a result they had been taking heavy losses, far greater than was being admitted by the government.

So far he had been lucky, his plane had only once suffered damage on a raid, and that was only superficial, but he knew one night their luck would run out. The heavy droning became louder and louder, then a Lancaster took off from the runway in front of him. It was so big and heavy it looked impossible for it to leave the ground, despite the four massive Rolls Royce engines. It was an ugly aircraft, the pilot's cabin looked like a greenhouse stuck on as an afterthought, the gunners turrets were like carbuncles and the huge double tail looked ungainly, but to John it was the best plane in the RAF. The fighter pilots could keep their Spitfires and Hurricanes, for sheer destructive power there was no plane to match the Lancaster, whether it was its huge four thousand pound bombs or the eight machine guns for defence. He continued to his barrack room, time to write to Ann, get a few hours rest then the fun would begin.

*   *

Edgar stood on the edge, looking down at the sheer drop as a limestone cliff fell away in front of him. "You are joking!"

"Don't worry, there are plenty of trees to break your fall if you lose your footing," joked Javor.

"Take no notice," said Nada. "We brought some ropes so we can lower you down, along with all the gear."

"I'm being let down there on a thin rope, along with tons of high explosives."

"It'll be quite safe," added Captain Leigh. "We'll be very careful, we can't afford to lose the explosive."

"And what about me!"

"Well I suppose you are quite useful as well."

"Thank you, at least I know where I stand."

"Ignore them, they are only teasing," said Nada. "Here, I'll tie you on myself to just make sure."

When the rope was fastened Edgar made his way nervously to the edge.

"Just one thing," Nada added, "Don't look down."

As the rope slowly paid out Edgar leant further and further backwards, then looked down, his nerve gave out and he jerked upright. Immediately his feet slipped, he felt himself dropping as the rope was allowed to run in a controlled descent. Before he had time to yell his boots touched the ground and stopped.

Above him Captain Leigh peered over the edge. "Stop admiring the view and get the rope unfastened. We haven't got all day you know."

Fortunately Edgar's reply was blown away by the wind.

Very quickly all the supplies were lowered then the other members of the party.

"What about Captain Leigh, how will he get down?" asked Edgar. He appeared at the edge, the rope wrapped round his body, quickly slid down, landing lightly on his feet.

"Typical," thought Edgar. "And I bet he can cook as well."

*   *

Ann was in the Whitehall cafe with Pat, nibbling a toasted tea cake and relating the latest news from John. "Of course he can't say too much about the flying, the censor would only cut it out anyway, but he hopes to be home soon and wants me to meet his parents."

"What! I didn't realize it was that serious," exclaimed Pat. "I mean, you've not known him that long."

"Longer than your romances usually last!"

Ey Up Adolf

"That's because I actually see my boyfriends, unlike you, so I get a chance to find out what's wrong with them. Wait until you meet him again, I bet he's not what you remember, or he has a horrible habit, perhaps he picks his nose."

"Like your last."

"Don't remind me." Pat gave an exaggerated shudder. "So are you going?"

"Going where?"

"To meet his parents, silly."

Ann finished the last of her breadcake and delicately wiped the crumbs from round her mouth. "Of course."

*   *

The Lancaster stood at the end of the runway, its engines warmed up, the crew in place, the upper gunner perched on his canvas seat and John in his little, blacked out space. He needed light to navigate but any stray chinks would give away their position in the inky sky. The pilot revved the engines, the metal body rattled and shook, then he released the brake. Immediately the massive plane surged forwards, racing down the tarmac. With a jerk it freed itself from the cling of the runway and soared upwards to join the scores of others on their way through the dark, cloudy sky to deliver another load of destruction to the heart of Germany.

*   *

Edgar crouched beside the trunk of a huge, fir tree watching the dark figures as they ran across the intervening space, aiming for a small, black shadow set in the base of a rocky outcrop. Captain Leigh gave a brief wave then entered the cave mouth.

"Now all we have to do is wait," whispered Edgar.

He had finally made himself vaguely comfortable when Nada tensed.

"What?"

She silenced him by putting a finger over his mouth then noiselessly raised her rifle. There was the tiniest, metallic click as she removed the safety catch. Edgar stared into the blackness but could see nothing. He heard rustling and the snap of a twig.

"Wild animal?" he whispered, picturing a slavering wolf.

Nada shook her head. "Far worse and more dangerous. It's a German patrol. We'd better cross to the cave for better cover."

Edgar gathered up his precious wireless and ran the short distance to the entrance. Once inside Nada sighted down the barrel of her rifle. The sounds of the patrol were definitely coming nearer. Were they aware of Edgar's little band and, if so, what were they going to do about them?

Chapter 45

The incendiaries dropped by the Pathfinders were clearly visible. John checked with his own calculations, they were spot on. "Time to ....."

"Enemy fighter right behind!" This cry was followed by the intense chatter of the rear machine guns. The night sky was lit by lines of tracers, a second later the upper gunner joined in. John tried desperately to disregard the mid-air battle between the big, heavily-armed bomber and the faster, nimble fighter. Glancing up he saw the compass mounted on the airframe veer wildly as the plane lurched from side to side.

"Lost him," he heard Bob shout. "He's decided to look for an easier target."

"Well keep your eyes peeled, there are probably more enemy aircraft about," replied Tom, the pilot. "Alright John bring us back on course and let's get this show on the road. The sooner we complete this run the sooner we can all go home."

John read out the changes and felt the huge aircraft swing slowly through the sky. "Time to bomb-drop one minute and thirty, ...now."

In the nose of the plane Jack, the bomb-aimer, squinted out of the Perspex window, concentrating on the lights ahead, ignoring mushrooming detonations of high explosive as the planes in front dropped their deadly cargos. "Steady, steady, steady, bombs gone!"

The crew felt the plane jerk upwards, relieved of thousands of pounds of weight as the massive bombs hurtled earthwards.

"Right lads," the captain's Australian twang more pronounced because of the tension, "let's go home!"

*   *

Edgar and Nada took it in turns during the night to watch for the German patrol. When it was her time she crept next to him. "Any sign?"

"Not a peep, perhaps they've gone home, as any self-respecting person would." The temperature had dropped dramatically and Edgar could feel the cold steal into his bones. He glanced at his watch, using the faint moonlight to see the fingers. "How much longer do you think they will be?"

"Anytime now I would imagine but it will depend how difficult is the passage through the cave."

Edgar nodded wisely, even though his only experience of caves were the small ones near Flamborough Head. "Suppose so." He returned his gaze to the forest then tensed as a faint noise came from deep inside the cave.

Instantly Nada swung the muzzle of her rifle in that direction. Was this their friends or a squad of highly armed German troops? The next few seconds would provide the answer.

*   *

The Lancaster accelerated towards England. The entire sky was criss-crossed with searchlights, highlighting a Lancaster or Messerschmitt ME109. The heavens were filled with aeroplanes, lights and exploding anti-aircraft shells.

Abruptly Bob's voice burst onto the intercom, "Our friend is back." All the Lancaster's armament opened up, hosing the sky with instant death. The upper gunner suddenly saw the sleek shape of the Messerschmitt as it flashed above them and immediately opened fire, raking the fuselage with high velocity shells noting a burst of smoke appear directly behind the propeller. Instantly Tom dipped the nose of the bomber.

"Good idea" said John calmly. "Go as low as you dare then turn eighty degrees right."

"That isn't the route we were given?"

"No but if you want to arrive home in one piece I suggest you take my advice."

"You've always been right so far, who am I to argue?" The pilot pushed hard on the yoke that steered the bomber and the big plane responded, falling from the sky until it brushed the tops of trees and rattled slates on the roofs of the houses. Lancaster D-Dog was on its way home.

*   *

Edgar peered into the shadows at the back of the cave. The sounds became louder, heavy breathing, rustling of clothes, the clink of metal on rock and, occasionally, a subdued voice. He was no wiser, was it friend or foe coming through the passageway.

A faint light could be seen, flickering off the glistening, wet rock. Then a shadow. Edgar feared the worse, this was a squad of Germans coming to mop up the remainder of the attack force, namely him and Nada. She obviously had the same thought as her finger tensed on the trigger. Edgar looked frantically for a weapon, but the cave was bare, there wasn't even a handy sized rock that he could throw.

The shadow on the wall loomed ever larger then it stopped, scratched its head and called out softly, "Take your finger off the trigger, Nada, it's us," in the unmistakable drawl of Captain Leigh. A few seconds later he crawled out of the passage and stood up.

"Well, were you successful?"

Captain Leigh did not answer but looked at his watch instead. Immediately there was a slight tremor, a layer of fine rock-dust fell and several large spiders scurried to their holes.

Edgar switched on his wireless, "I suppose you want me to send the signal."

"Too right. We don't want them dropping great big bombs on our heads after we have done the job."

Edgar looked at Captain Leigh and waited.

"Send 'ignite' that will tell them we were successful then it's back to camp"

Nada, in lookout position, quietly replied, "We might have a problem, the patrol is back."

Edgar replaced his headphones and quickly scanned all the frequencies. "It appears we have stirred up a hornets' nest, there's a lot of angry voices and all speaking German."

"Looks like we'll have to wait." Captain Leigh sat down with his back to the cold rock, closed his eyes and appeared to go to sleep.

*   *

The Lancaster thundered on through the night sky, now all alone. Faintly, away to their left, the darkness was punctured by a series of flashes. "Looks like the ack-ack gunners are busy."

"Yes and it would be us if we had stayed on course," John replied. "Now keep an eye open for a river."

"It's pitch black out there."

"Maybe, but the river will still show, just look for a long, silver ribbon, moonlight reflects off the water."

The minutes ticked by. "Got it, straight ahead."

"Jack, can you see a break in it where a bridge crosses?"

"Yes."

Ey Up Adolf

"Shout as we pass over. This next bit is crucial and I need an accurate fix. There are two searchlight batteries ahead, we need to go slap bang between them and hope we get lucky."

At Jack's shout John made a mark on his map then set his stop-watch. "Tom, in ten seconds swing round to 40 degrees North, five, four, three, two, one, now." He felt the big plane bank round then level off again. Now all he could do was hope he was right.

*   *

Nada strained her eyes, peering into the blackness. Earlier she had spotted shadowy shapes moving through the trees but it had been quiet for some time.

"Captain," was as far as she got before he was at her side, peering out. "Right, let's go."

Edgar was the first to move, he had been waiting for just this moment. The sooner he left this damp, cold, German in-fested region the better as far as he was concerned.

Chapter 46

The pilot of D-Dog stared through the windscreen. Ahead two sets of searchlights, with accompanying guns, waited for them. The four Rolls Royce engines were fantastically reliable and packed a real punch, but they were also very noisy. The unmistakable sound travelled for miles, announcing their arrival to sharp-eared gunners.

Suddenly the sky to his left was lit by four beams of intense light that swung back and forth across the black sky, searching for the intruder, seeking revenge. Easing the stick to the right Tom edged away from the questing lights, until John's voice ordered, "Don't! You'll turn us directly into the path of the second set. Keep to the course and pray."

The pilot edged the plane back onto its original heading. "I just hope you know what you are doing."

*   *

Ann woke with a start and stared around the blacked out room. Lying there, listening to the faint noises in the house, she wondered what John was doing at this very moment. "He's probably fast asleep, like I should be."

She rolled over and closed her eyes, not that it made any difference, the blackness in her bedroom was so complete. The image of a huge Lancaster ploughing through the night kept creeping into her mind, forcing sleep away.

Ey Up Adolf

*   *

As the seconds ticked by they almost dared to believe they were going to pass undetected.

"Looks like we might get through," came Tom's voice. Immediately a searchlight, directly in front and unavoidable, blasted into view. "Sorry, spoke too soon." The Lancaster was thrown into a tight turn, banking sharply. A collection of expletives sounded all over the plane as the crew were thrown about, first one way and then the other as a second light joined in the hunt. The pilot tried every trick to avoid detection but when two more joined in the options ran out, all they could do was run the gauntlet. He pushed the throttles to the stops and dipped the nose, sending the plane into a shallow dive to coax a few more miles per hour onto their speed.

The lights continued to weave bright patterns across the sky, until finally one caught a brief glimpse of the bomber. That was enough. Other beams quickly joined it, skewering D-Dog.

The anti-aircraft guns opened fire, filling the sky around the plane with fiery bursts, explosions and hurtling fragments of red-hot, sharp metal. The mighty engines strained to their limit as the pilot urged them onwards. The second hand on John's watch slowly ticked round, counting off the seconds to safety. Suddenly the aeroplane shuddered, knocked sideways.

"Everyone alright?" One by one the crew answered, except Bob, sitting in his rear turret.

"Bob, Bob, respond!"

Silence.

"I'll go back and see if he's hurt," said John, turning off his light and opening the curtain. Eyes readjusting to the darkness he made his way to the back of the plane. It was far colder out here than in his 'office' and there was a strong wind blowing. "Not good, not good at all."

Carefully he inched his way along the plane, mindful of the strut that crossed the fuselage, just waiting to claim the head of the unwary. He could still hear the bursting shells, less frequent and fainter, they were almost clear. He rested one hand on the outer skin for support then staggered as he failed to meet any resistance and was immediately blasted by a freezing cold gale. Carefully John drew it back through the jagged, gaping hole and gazed out at the stars then noticed a further three gaps with serrated edges. "That must have been close." Apart from the holes in the fuselage he could not see any obvious damage, but in the darkness it was impossible to be certain. Ahead the faint glimmer of moonlight shone through the rear turret and he could make out a shadowy shape, crouched over the gun, not moving.

"Bob." No reply. Fearing his friend was dead or seriously injured he reached out a gloved hand and lightly touched his crewmate on the shoulder.

Bob jumped six inches in the air and spun round. "I suppose you think that is funny, creeping up on me. You might have given me a heart attack. Why didn't you say you were on your way back?"

John held up the severed end of the intercom wire.

"How did that happen?" asked Bob, incredulously.

"That last shell."

"You mean we were hit! I knew it was close but…"

"More than close, we have several large holes with the wind whistling through them. I suggest you put on your spare long-coms, it's going to get cold before we arrive back at base." John plugged into the intercom system, "Tom, this is John."

"How is he?"

"Fine but I passed several large holes on my way here."

"That's why the steering is sluggish. Alright, return to your magic cave and get us home as quickly as possible."

"That might not be the best answer in the circumstances. I suggest the scenic route, over the North Sea and land at an emergency base in East Anglia instead."

"Whatever you say. Plot us a route and let's get going."

Gingerly John made his way past the damage and settled down in his cubbyhole. The sooner this plane was on the ground the happier he would feel.

*   *

The sky showed the first signs of dawn as Edgar's little band crossed the ridge and he glanced back at the plume of smoke that reflected the raging fires deep in the cave. They entered a copse of trees and settled down to sleep. Edgar looked at the motley crew and wondered, not for the first time, what he was doing here. All the others, even Nada, seemed at home amongst danger and mayhem, but he was different. All he wanted to do was survive this war and return to normal, but that was not going to happen, too much had changed, Ann for one thing.

*   *

As the sun crept over the horizon, illuminating the grey waves and the line of yellow sand ahead, the crew breathed a sigh of relief. All they had to do now was land this damaged bomber and they were safe.

"Sorry to be the bearer of bad tidings," shouted Bob "but there's a nasty black dot coming straight at us and I don't think he's going to play nice."

Instantly the crew were alert, all the guns trained backwards, ready to fend off this new threat. "Where are we?" asked Tom.

"Nearing Great Yarmouth."

"D-Dog approaching the coast at Yarmouth, and we have an enemy fighter following us."

"Roger," came the tower in reply. "Remain on course."

Whatever response Tom was going to make was interrupted by the chatter of the machine guns, as a deadly hail of bullets streamed from the bomber, causing the fighter to suddenly bank away, climbing for height.

"Why is everyone picking on us tonight?" moaned Bob, as he stared up into the pale blue sky, vainly trying to catch a glimpse of the enemy.

"Port side, eleven o'clock," came the frantic voice of the upper gunner, "and he's coming in fast."

The fighter pilot had planned his attack well, only one gun was in position to fend him off. Twinkling lights on the front of the wings signalled his guns starting to fire then suddenly he veered away.

"What?" exclaimed Tom. With a roar two Spitfires flashed overhead, streaking in pursuit of the German, who had rapidly changed from the predator to the prey. "Go get him lads, teach him to pick on someone his own size."

Chapter 47

All night the rain had fallen from masses of cloud that drifted overhead. After a fitful sleep Edgar woke with water dripping from the branches and straight down his neck. A hand on his shoulder attracted his attention. "Very quietly," Captain Leigh whispered. "We have visitors."

Edgar sat up and saw the others were awake and alert, Nada and Javor had their rifles at the ready. Captain Leigh reached into his pack and produced a revolver which he handed to Edgar. "I assume you have used one before." Edgar nodded, even if it was only once, during his basic training.

The metallic butt of the gun felt very cold and uncomfortable in Edgar's grip and his hand was shaking. "Why didn't I listen to Jimmy when he said never volunteer? Then I would not be sitting here freezing, wet and scared silly." He peered into the surrounding undergrowth, wondering what would happen in the next few minutes and whether he would emerge alive.

*　　*

The Lancaster continued towards the coastline, now clearly visible. "John, shout down to Bob and ask if he can see the tail on the starboard side, there seems to be a problem with the aileron, it's not responding."

Bob craned round in his cramped turret then called back. "I'm not surprised, half of the tail is missing."

"Great ! John how long to the nearest field?"

"About fifteen minutes."

"Right. Tower this is D-Dog, I am making an emergency landing, my aircraft is severely damaged and request crash trucks." In the plane everyone went quiet, landing one of these huge planes was tricky enough at the best of times, unable to steer it was a hundred times worse. Alone, in semi-darkness, John thought of Ann's pretty, young face, wondering if he would ever see it again.

*   *

As water dripped from the trees, plopping quietly on the sodden ground the little group tensed, clutching their guns, then a voice called out from the approaching strangers.

"Relax," announced Javor, "they are Partisans."

A few minutes later a group of warriors entered the camp, dark, dirty and with the obligatory large moustaches. They each wore some sort of uniform and carried an assortment of weaponry, from new bren guns to ancient rifles.

Javor went to meet them. "Captain Leigh, I would like to introduce our leader."

"General Tito," acknowledged Captain Leigh.

"I know of your mission," stated Tito. "I am happy you are on our side."

"And we are glad your Partisans are with us," replied Captain Leigh then he continued, "I don't suppose you have any of that plum brandy, this damp gets right into your bones."

Tito stretched out his hand and received a full bottle from one of his men.

"That's the best sight I've seen for days," thought Edgar.

When the Partisans heard about the raid on the cave they had gone round everyone, shaking hands and slapping backs. When the men saw Edgar with the revolver stuck down his trousers they all chuckled and made coarse comments what might happen if it went off by accident, then one of them, a big,

Ey Up Adolf

muscular chap, handed over a holster. Edgar strapped it around his waist and Nada smiled. "All you need is a big moustache and you'll be a real Partisan."

*   *

Shakily the Lancaster flew over the outer marker and the assembled crash trucks. Sweat appeared on Tom's forehead and his muscles ached with the effort as he fought to keep the bomber on course. The crew tensed, expecting to lurch off the runway any second and end up in a tangle of burnt metal. With a squeal of protesting rubber the tyres touched down and skidded, throwing the plane sideways. Expertly Tom corrected, using the little control he had and they pulled straight. Followed by their attendant emergency vehicles they majestically moved down the tarmac, their speed slowly dwindling, until they finally taxied to a halt.

Joking to hide their real feelings the crew climbed down the ladder, gathered in a tight group and inspected the damage, the gaping holes in the fuselage and the big chunk missing from the tail.

"Guess we won't be flying again tonight," stated Tom.

"Or for a few more," added Bob.

"So that means," stated John.

"Leave!" they chorused together.

John picked up his bag and set off for the cluster of huts nearby. The sooner he debriefed the sooner he could cadge a lift to the nearest station and a train back to Rotherham. After his near-death experience he had made a decision, he had someone special to see and something very important to buy.

*   *

When Ann arrived home she heard voices coming from the sitting room. She rushed in and saw John sitting there. When she had finished hugging him she said, "I didn't know you were coming on leave."

"Neither did I until this morning. We had slight problem with the plane so can't fly for a few days."

She knew he wouldn't say anymore at this point, he wouldn't reveal anything that would worry her parents, but she would wring the full tale from him later. "When did you arrive?"

"Only an hour ago, I came straight here. I wanted to know if you were free tomorrow, to come to Chapletown."

Ann could sense an undercurrent, there was something that the others knew but she didn't. "Yes, tomorrow's fine." She wasn't working at the YM, or on duty at the fire station, so she was available to go.

John left early to catch the bus as he had his heavy bag with him, even though it was lighter by several chocolate bars. After seeing him on his way Ann came back inside and found her parents sitting by the fire, satisfied smirks on their faces. There was something going on and she was peeved she didn't know what it was.

"I'd better be getting off," her father said, rising from his chair. Then he winked at her mother. Now this really was becoming annoying.

*   *

Throughout the day the enlarged group trudged through the dripping forest. Edgar felt a glow of pleasure, which wasn't only caused by the fiery plum spirit, he had been introduced to Tito himself as their wireless expert. Now he felt he belonged, not just a spare part, excess baggage. He had the revolver that Captain Leigh had given him, proudly tucked into his holster, even if Nada did have to remind him to put on the safety before he shot himself in the leg.

Chapter 48

The visit to Chapletown had gone quickly, John's sister had called round and they all sat talking, accompanied by the noise of the gas lights which cast their pale, yellow glow on the room. Ann was amazed that didn't have electricity, in fact the whole house seemed from a bygone age, with its zinc bath hanging on the kitchen wall and dolly-tub for the clothes, corrugated washing-board and cast iron wringer.

Now they were waiting for the bus back to Rotherham. Ann had said that she was alright on her own, it seemed silly for John to go all that way then walk home afterwards, but he was adamant. Ann noticed he was nervous, constantly fiddling with something in his jacket pocket. She knew that he had already been approached about going to a Pathfinder squadron but had declined. Had he been asked again and was considering accepting?

The bus arrived and they sat on the back seat. John looked round the near-deserted top deck and visibly relaxed. Then he turned to Ann and took her hand.

"I know we haven't know each other very long and the future is very uncertain, especially mine, but I want to ask….." he paused and cleared his throat, "will you marry me?"

Ann sat there stunned. Now she understood the smiles and winks, John had spoken to her parents first. She sat there silently, while these thoughts raced around inside her head, as John waited patiently, his expression gradually become more worried as the seconds ticked by. Suddenly Ann realised that she had not replied and blurted out, "Of course."

John fished in his pocket and produced a small blue box. "Is this alright? I bought it today in the hope that you'd say yes." On the top of the lid were written the words, 'Masons Jewellers.'

Ann stared, it was identical to the one from Edgar. Carefully she opened the lid, inside was a shiny, three stone engagement ring, very similar to the one she had before but then Masons was a small, local shop and would only have a limited stock, especially with the war.

John removed it from the little cushion and slipped it on her finger, where it waggled about, several sizes too big. "I can have it made to fit, the man in the shop said so, or swap it for another if you don't like it."

"No it's wonderful, just what I would have chosen, but it is a bit too big. Perhaps we can go in at the weekend and have it made smaller."

John put his arm round her and they snuggled together gazing out of the window as the dark countryside flashed past. The war was forgotten as they planned their future together.

When she arrived home she rushed inside and, without either removing her coat or saying a word, she stretched out her hand and displayed the ring to her mother.

"Wey ay pet," her mother said, "he's a smart young fella', you'll be happy together." Then ever the practical one, "We'd better start planning for the wedding, it'll take a lot of coupons you know."

*   *

Edgar woke up late, they had all arrived back in the early hours of the morning and he had retired to his bed immediately, totally exhausted, leaving the others to open the ever-present bottle. He dressed, made his way down the sturdy wooden stairs and bumped into Nada. "It's very quiet, everyone else still in bed?"

"No, they were up at dawn and have gone."

"What!" exclaimed Edgar, nothing short of a bombing raid would have woken him. "They must have constitutions like oxen."

"No, an important message arrived so they went to check it out."

Edgar realised that he had been off the air for several days so went to switch on his set but it was dead, the batteries were flat. "Have the new ones arrived yet?"

"No, there's a problem. The Germans have tightened security everywhere with patrols roving the roads, so it is difficult getting replacements. We will just have to wait."

Now Edgar was at a loose end. "I think I'll go for a walk, get rid of some of these cobwebs."

Nada looked around with a puzzled expression on her face. "I don't see any cobwebs."

Edgar smiled. "It's an expression, it means I'm not really fully awake, the fresh air will revive me."

"Right I will remember that. Be careful out there and don't go too far, just in case."

Startled by this Edgar nipped back upstairs and took the revolver, which Captain Leigh had said he could keep, from under his bunk.

Edgar opened the door and stepped outside. The cold, fresh air hit him immediately but he resolutely marched off, looking around at the fantastic views. Across the valley, sticking above the ridge, he could make out the tops of snow-covered mountains, the sun reflecting off the white covering. He strode briskly on, past the barn, and up the slight slope, where he could see a faint plume of smoke rising from the nearby farm.

A quarter of an hour later he stopped, panting slightly from the exercise, and took a good look at their neighbours. The building was more modern, brick built, with a steep roof, small paned windows and an electric light above the door. He turned away, ready to start back when another feature struck him. From the back of the farm a wire, on tall poles, was carried in his direction then it disappeared into the ground

Inspired, he turned and strode smartly back. At the barn he carefully walked round the building, avoiding the collection of unused farming implements that were leaning against the walls or piled in heaps on the floor, just waiting to trip the unwary.

"Well I'll go to the bottom of our stairs!" A narrow, rusty, metal pipe appeared from the ground and disappeared through the wall.

He quickly nipped round to the front and stepped inside. Sure enough, there it was, an electric cable connected to a junction box mounted on the wall.

Returning to the farmhouse he pulled out the box with spare parts for the wireless and a set of tools. Quickly he fashioned a crude current tester and ran back to the barn. With trembling fingers he connected it to the junction box, held his breath and flicked the switch. Immediately the valve lit up. They had power, there was no more need for the Partisans to steal batteries.

He disconnected his tester and sprinted back. Nada watched him run cross the yard and now had her rifle in her hands, fearing the worst, so she was very surprised when Edgar burst in, gave her a big hug and exploded into a hurried explanation of what he had found. "So all we need is a drum of cable and we will be up and running," he concluded.

Nada picked up her coat and put it on. "I know where I can get that but I need to go to the village. Will you be alright until I get back?"

Edgar took out his revolver and spun it round his finger. "Me and my trusty iron," he said in his John Wayne voice. Unfortunately the effect was ruined when the gun slipped off and clattered onto the floor.

Nada picked it up and handed it back. "A good job the safety is on."

"Wouldn't have mattered, I took all the bullets out to be on the safe side."

Chapter 49

Nada returned in the afternoon with not only a drum of cable but also an electrician, a small, wizened man who looked about a hundred years old but was loyal to the Partisans. With surprising nimbleness he scuttled round the barn, climbing over the assorted piles of rubbish with the dexterity of a mountain goat, and disappeared. When he returned a few minutes later he spoke rapidly and excitedly to Nada then dashed off again.

"He says you are right and that he will have it connected very shortly."

"He seemed to say a lot more than that."

Nada flushed slightly with embarrassment. "He also asked if you were one of the brave commandos that blew up the cavern."

Sensing there was more, "And what else?"

"He said I should not wait but marry such a brave warrior."

Now it was Edgar's turn to colour up. "Good job he wasn't talking about me then, I'm definitely not a warrior nor am I brave." He gave a quick grin and disappeared outside to see how the ancient was doing, then changed his mind, he didn't want to hear anymore in that vein, life here was complicated enough as it was. He stood by the door and lit up a cigarette, gazing across at the woods.

It was only a vague flicker but it caught his attention. Now he wished he hadn't removed the bullets from the revolver. "There's people in the trees," he shouted.

Ey Up Adolf

Rifle in her hands Nada took up position by the window while Edgar dashed upstairs to load his gun.

Tense seconds passed, then a lone figure appeared, hidden by the shadows. Cupping his hands to his mouth he called out.

Nada shouted back and instantly other figures emerged from concealment, slinging their weapons over their shoulders. A few minutes later they were all inside the house, sitting round the large table.

"What have you been up to today?" Captain Leigh asked. "Taking it easy after your excitement?"

Edgar was about to reply when the door flew open and the old electrician burst in, only to stop abruptly, staring down the barrels of two revolvers, held in rock-steady hands.

Edgar thought, if it had been him, he would probably have had a heart attack but the elderly villager merely cackled with pleasure and launched into a torrent of Croatian. When he stopped, Javor translated, saying that the old man was honoured to meet the people who had blown up the cave

Then he nodded to everyone and left.

"He has finished and you have power." Nada pointed to a bare wire that dangled through a gap near the ceiling. "All you have to do is connect that to your set and you are in business."

"Good," replied Captain Leigh. "Get a move on Edgar, we have an important message to send."

*   *

John and Ann stood side by side at the station, waiting for the train to arrive. Already it was half an hour late and he would have missed his connection at Sheffield. Ann had been given the time off by Mr Munroe when he knew that John was coming home on leave. "You look a bit peaky," he had said, "I'm certain you're starting a cold and, since I don't want everyone coughing and spluttering, I suggest you have a few days sick leave."

A cloud of smoke and the unmistakable sound of a steam train announced the arrival of John's transport. "I'll be home as soon as possible, but I don't know when that will be." He didn't need to add that it would also depend how lucky they were. Already his crew were nearing the end of their second tour of duty, something that only a few had managed, the mortality rate among bomber crews was high.

"Well write then."

"Whenever I can, but don't worry if there are any gaps, it is not always possible, security you know."

The train entered the station and ground to a halt with a billow of steam and a screech of wheels. They kissed for the last time and he climbed aboard, closed the door to the carriage and lowered the window so that he could wave to the already dwindling figure standing on the deserted platform.

The journey back to base was slow, tedious and took far longer than it should have, so it was late in the evening before he arrived. Technically John was AWOL, but he wasn't worried, as long as he did return no-one usually bothered. As he entered the gates an armed guard appeared in front of him. "Your pass expired three hours ago."

"I know but the train was delayed. I'm here now and that's what really matters. Now clear off!"

The guard stood his ground. "I'll have to report this to the CO."

After his long journey, and having to leave his new fiancée, John was not in the best of moods. "You can report it to Churchill for all I care. Let me in, unless of course you want to navigate over Germany tomorrow." He pushed past the annoyed guard and made his way to the darkened building ahead and a few hours sleep.

Ey Up Adolf

The next morning he was woken by Tom shaking his shoulder. "How did it go?" All the crew were dying for news.

"She accepted."

"Great, we'll have to celebrate the first chance we get."

"What's wrong with tonight?"

"We can't, we're posted to a new camp, leaving this afternoon." John groaned, moving was always chaotic. "Also the CO wants to see you right away."

John climbed out of his bunk, washed and dressed, wondering what the CO wanted.

He made his way across the base, reported, and was shown in.

"Morning, sergeant. I have had a serious matter reported to me by last night's guards. Apparently you were AWOL."

"I wasn't, just a little late, there were problems with the train."

"Hmph," said the CO, clearing his throat. "Still, this has been reported and I must do something about it. According to regulations I should send you to detention in Sheffield, but let me see, where do you come from?"

John began to understand where this was going. "Chapletown, Sir."

"And where is that exactly."

"Just outside Sheffield."

"Then that would not be suitable. Seven days confined to camp."

"Yes Sir."

As he turned to leave, the CO added, "When are you are transferring to your new base?"

"This afternoon."

"No way the paperwork for this can be done by then, I'll just file it."

As John closed the door he saw the CO tear up the charge report and put it in the waste-paper bin.

Chapter 50

John lay on his bunk, stared at a cobweb, and contemplated his life. He had become engaged, now all had to do was survive long enough to get married. They were scheduled for a training flight today, their plane had been repaired and needed testing before it could go back in action.

After breakfast he reported to the briefing room and was surprised to find that they were to go to RAF Errol, a base in Scotland, near Perth. Instantly he was suspicious, there was more to this than met the eye.

"Oh and by the way, while you are there could you pick up a few boxes for us?" commented the Flight Lieutenant. "Some vital parts and stuff."

"Now we are getting down to it," thought John. "I wonder exactly what is in those containers," but considering the location of the airfield, near the Spey Valley, he had a good idea.

The flight north was uneventful, the sky was clear and the plane was handling well, all the repairs seemed to be holding up. The four big engines roared on, the propellers reflecting the sunlight, driving the huge Lancaster over the uninviting water of the North Sea. The white wake of a fishing boat could be seen, a little piece of normality, but then a brace of Hurricanes flew across their path, waggling their wings in recognition. After that everyone was more vigilant, scanning the sky for movement. John hoped radar had not picked up a flight of Focke-Wulf Fw 190s, the aptly named 'bomber destroyer'.

Ey Up Adolf

A course change took them over the coastline, skirting Edinburgh and finally they arrived at Errol.

The crew disembarked and made their way across to the motley selection of Nissen huts in search of a canteen. Once they were fortified John went hunting for the boxes. He walked to the sergeants' mess and within minutes had located a small, balding scouser who was in charge of stores.

"Right, Wack, I know what you want, it's all ready for you. Six boxes, the pride of Scotland, direct from the distillery, for the officers' mess."

"I don't suppose you have any more of those for the sergeants' mess?" John inquired.

The Liverpudlian scratched the back of his head then took his pencil and altered the six to a five on the manifest. "Tell your officer there were delivery problems and I could only get five boxes, I'll credit him next time," then he lowered his voice, "if I remember."

John carefully carried his prize across to the Lancaster and secured it in his little office. "Guess who is going to be in favour tonight?" His next port of call was the weather office to check for the return journey. When he came out he had a worried frown, heavy fog was forecast for Lincolnshire, it would be touch and go if they would be able to land. He hurried off to round up the rest of the crew, the sooner they were airborne the better.

The Lancaster flew south. "Radio ahead and find out the weather conditions," asked John. The reply was not what he wanted, the mist was closing in and visibility was dropping fast.

"D-Dog requesting clearance for landing."

A brief moment of static followed then, "Sorry D-Dog, visibility poor, divert to alternative field inland."

"That's it," said the radio operator in a resigned voice. "Guess we need another heading."

They both realised the tower was still on the air and another voice could be heard in the background.

"What was that call sign?"

"D-Dog Sir, returning from a training flight to Scotland."

"D-Dog, well bloody get them down then."

"But visibility is below the safety limit."

"I don't care, as long as they can land without pranging I want them on the deck, they are carrying material vital to the war effort."

"I wonder what's in those boxes," queried the radio operator turning to John, "it must be important to fly us all the way to Scotland then be so insistent we land."

"Very," thought John. "Five cases of finest scotch whisky for the officers, plus one for us poor sergeants."

As the Lancaster sank lower the bank of fog became evident, a thick white blanket that covered the ground, hiding the houses and trees.

"Is this a good idea?" asked the co-pilot.

"The tower obviously thinks so."

As the plane descended into the murk visibility dropped, the temperature plummeted, vague shapes flashed beneath them then, abruptly the landing lights appeared dead ahead, large yellow orbs as the beams reflected off the heavy drops of water suspended in the air. With ground level defined the pilot felt far happier and seconds later the wheels touched the tarmac with only the slightest of bumps, the brakes came on and the huge plane, so graceful in the air, became a lumbering brute. Staring out of the window the pilot could hardly see the edge of the runway, the mist was thickening that fast. A few minutes more and it would have been impossible to land at all.

No sooner had the propellers stopped turning than a little Austin pickup surged from the fog and pulled up alongside, a

Ey Up Adolf

flight officer driving. He leapt from the vehicle and climbed aboard the plane, followed by a burly aircraftman.

"Well done chaps, a spectacular piece of flying that. Now, have you got the boxes?"

John poked his head out of his office and said, "Yes, but I was told to inform you there are only five, apparently there were problems and the paper work will follow."

The officer looked disgruntled but shrugged his shoulders in acceptance. "Can't be helped I suppose, the war and all that. Where are they?"

John indicated where they were stored. The burly aircraftman carried them out, then, accompanied by the officer, climbed back into the pickup and drove away.

"Well that's us finished," announced Tom as the crew started to disembark from the bomber. "Come on John, hurry up."

"I've a few things to tidy, I'll catch you later." It really wouldn't be a good idea to be seen leaving the plane with a box that was identical to ones that had just been collected, especially as the order was one short.

*　　*

"Sorry mate, bad news."

Instantly Edgar was wide awake. There was nothing like that statement to get the blood flowing. He sat up, attentive and ready for action.

"We've just heard from one of our informants. The Germans are sending in additional troops to look for the group who blew up the cave, namely us, a crack regiment, not the young lads and old men that we usually encounter. We have to get to a big Partisan camp further up the valley.

When Edgar made his way downstairs he found it a hive of activity. Everything had been hidden in a secret cache in the woods, including Edgar's wireless equipment. Even the power supply had been removed and the cable concealed under a pile of well rotted compost. Nada thrust a piece of black bread and a chunk of cheese into his hand. "We've already eaten, have those as we go." They picked up their rucksacks and weapons then left. At the edge of the trees Edgar looked back at the old farmhouse and wondered if that would be the last time he would see it. Would he be located at a new base or would he be captured and shot as a saboteur? The next few days would decide.

* *

John was leaving the sergeants' mess when he was told to report to the CO. Half an hour later he was back, cradling a cup of tea and considering the importance of the information he had received. The public were being kept in the dark about the huge losses that RAF Bomber Command was suffering. As a result the crew was being removed from active duty and could be going to Canada to train airmen. He made a decision. He was going to ask Ann to marry him straight away, by special licence, before he left. He wasn't taking any chances and leaving behind the prettiest girl he had ever met without making her his wife first.

* *

After several hours of arduous tramping up the steep paths through the forest Edgar's group came out into a clearing that contained several tents covered with netting and bracken to hide them from the air. Groups of men, and some women, sat around and stared when they arrived as news of their coming had already spread.

Off to the left a tent flap opened and a short, cocky figure in the uniform of an officer stepped out and looked at their ragged band. Edgar stared back in amazement. The last person he expected to see was Nicholas Ridiculous.

Chapter 51

The sun was creeping over the horizon when Edgar was woken by a prod in the ribs and the pungent aroma of burnt acorns. He opened one eye.

"What's this?"

"Coffee, well roasted acorns, but you get used to it," answered Nada. Edgar jumped at the sound of her voice, he had automatically assumed it was Captain Leigh bringing even more bad news. Now wide awake he sat up and took the proffered tin mug.

"Thank you." Then he noticed the faint sunlight stealing between the trees. "Why the early start?"

"You have a long journey to make. You need to be at the railway sidings by tonight then you will be taken to Murska Sobota by train."

"I hope you have the money for tickets, I'm broke."

"I'm not coming with you, I travel a different route."

Edgar took a sip of his drink, but only one. Putting the mug down he muttered, "Somehow I don't think it'll be a commercial success, the makers of Camp needn't fear."

Half an hour later he was on his way climbing higher into the rugged hills, aiming for a narrow pass that would lead them to the other side of the peaks and the railway line. Behind he could see Nada waving from the edge of the trees and he wondered if he would ever see her again. He wiped his nose on the sleeve of his jacket, swallowed, took a deep breath and trudged after the others.

*   *

Ann was sitting at the table drinking a cup of tea. Each day Mr Munroe asked her if she had any news from John, especially where he had been. Ann suspected Mr Munroe had friends in Germany, although he never said so. Well today she had some momentous news as far as she was concerned.

It had been a shock when she arrived home last night and found John sitting there, but nothing compared to the next few minutes as he first told her he might be going to Canada and then took her breath away completely by suggesting they get married straight away.

She smiled briefly at her first thought, it was not exactly romantic. "That'll set the neighbours tittle-tattling, they'll be convinced I'm pregnant and that's why the rush. Well it'll make a change from them talking about Mrs Fernleigh and her latest in a long line of lodgers. There seems to be a different pair of trousers on the line every week."

Afterwards they had gone to the Playingfields where there was a Fair, the usual site in the centre of town being considered too dangerous, and as they wandered around she noticed that one of the stalls was playing the tune, 'You'd be so nice to come home to,' and she thought, "How true."

*   *

The sun was sinking behind the horizon as Edgar and his guides approached the railway sidings. He needed to get on the train undetected so Javor had advised brazenness, just stroll across, trusting that if they seemed to belong no-one would question them. They casually sauntered forwards, stepping over the shiny rails. Fortunately they found a wheelbarrow and a couple of spades and, carrying them and chatting loudly, they were the picture of innocence, a gang of labourers finishing for the day. As they approached one of the engines the smaller guide stopped talking and started to whistle, a short meandering phrase he repeated over and over.

Within a few seconds the same tune came from the cab of the engine, then a grimy face wearing a battered cap and sprouting the obligatory bushy moustache appeared from the glassless side opening.

Edgar felt his guides relax then they shook his hand and disappeared back towards the hills, their job was done.

The engineer indicated for Edgar to climb into the cab then robustly shook his hand, uttering a babble of Croatian of which Edgar did not understand a word. He led the way over the coal tender, where Edgar carefully examined the load for dead rats, and into the box car behind. Here a second railway worker was waiting, keeping a watch for any passing Germans.

The engineer indicated to climb through an open trap door in the ceiling. Aided by the two men Edgar clambered into the cramped space, along with the emergency tools; giant spanners and wrenches, portable signs and numerous oil lamps, many of which appeared to leak judging by the layer of sooty oil that lay in puddles everywhere. He found that it was so small that no matter which way he turned it was not big enough for him to stretch out, only curl into a ball.

"Great, by the time I get out of here I'll look like the Hunchback of Notre Dame. The bells, the bells," he muttered then started to move things about to make his stay more comfortable. A few minutes later he gave up, and wondered what on earth he was doing here. Why hadn't he followed his county's motto? "See all, hear all and say nowt," especially the last part when asked to volunteer by the cruel-eyed Colonel Hudson. With this thought in mind he drifted into a fitful sleep.

The next morning he woke, with a mouth like the bottom of a parrot's cage and excruciating backache. He sat up to ease it and banged his head on the roof which brought him back to reality with a bump. As he lay there rubbing the bruise he felt the trap door tremble then drop away, leaving him precariously balanced on the edge. He opened his mouth to complain but was stopped by the sight of the engineer with his finger over his mouth in the universal sign for silence.

"Germans," he whispered, indicating all around, then he passed a metal flask and a cloth bag up to Edgar and disappeared. The trap door was closed leaving Edgar in the darkness, apart from a sliver of light that streamed through a crack in the floor.

"A private room with service what more could I ask for?" Edgar tried to stretch his legs and failed. "A bit more space would be nice." He opened the stopper on the flask and took a drink. The water tasted of metal but to a parched throat it was better than a sparkling mountain spring. When he had drunk half of the container he opened the bag and found black bread, goat's cheese and slices of cured ham. Contentedly he started to munch then he heard voices and the sound of boots on the wooden floor beneath him. He stopped chewing and very carefully turned onto his side so that he could peer through the crack. A shadow passed into view followed by a grey arm, an arm holding a submachine gun.

Edgar held his breath and waited. Through his tiny spy-hole he kept getting glimpses of soldiers as they poked around the box car, chatting to each other as they did so. He wished they would get a move on and leave. Then the smell of cigarette smoke drifted up into his small compartment. "That's not fair," he thought to himself, "I'm already suffering torture stuffed inside this box and now they're tormenting me with smokes."

As the German voices moved away he relaxed, the inspection was over. He raised the bottle to his lips then spilt some of the contents down the front of his jacket as the train gave a sudden and violent start; there were a series of clangs and squeaks and they were off.

*   *

As Ann entered her office she took in the new, utility furniture that had replaced the previous oak and mahogany ones damaged by the bomb blast but today she did not feel so saddened by it. Mr Munroe looked up and took in the self-satisfied expression. "I take it you've heard from John then."

A huge grin appeared on Ann's face. "More than that, he's home on leave. We are getting married as soon as possible as he might have to go to Canada. But don't worry, I'm staying here."

"That's great news!" he exclaimed. "I hope you didn't bring any sandwiches today, you won't need them, I'm taking you out to celebrate instead."

Chapter 52

Edgar ached in every joint in his body, stiff from being cooped up so long in the cramped, uncomfortable compartment and wished the journey would end. He took a last sip, savouring the final few drops of tepid water, carefully placed the flask down beside him, then felt the train slowly grind to a halt. Were they in a station or had the Germans stopped the train to search for Partisans, or even worse, English saboteurs?

Painfully he edged onto his side and squinted through the crack. Outside the train he could hear several voices, all speaking Croatian so he assumed they must be at a station. A few minutes later the noise receded, the train jerked forwards, moving slowly and swaying from side-to-side as it changed direction. Edgar realised they must be in sidings then with a final squeak of brakes the train halted and everything went quiet.

A shadow crossed his limited vision, there was a gentle knocking on the trap-door and the moustached face of the engineer appeared, indicating for Edgar to climb down. Feeling like a cross between an octogenarian and a snail he crawled out and dropped to the floor, held onto the side of the box-car then slowly and painfully straightened his back.

"Those mediaeval guys could take lessons from that place as a means of torture," he muttered as he regained his full height. He gazed at the grinning engineer who indicated for Edgar to follow as he jumped onto the trackside and scuttled between the wheels.

Ey Up Adolf

Slowly Edgar emerged just in time to see his guide disappear between two sheds which led to a high, wire fence with a barbed top. "Don't expect me to scale that. In my present condition I couldn't even climb a stepladder."

The engineer grasped the bottom firmly in both hands and pulled, creating a gap. Edgar immediately understood, dropped to the floor and crawled through. As he stood up the engineer pointed towards a narrow alleyway then he extended his hand through the fence. Edgar grasped it firmly while offering his thanks. Then he turned and, as quickly as his aching legs would carry him, scuttled off.

* *

John only had one more day's leave and intended to make the most of it, a meal at one of the cafes in town then the cinema. The next day he would return to base and find out what the future held, more tours over Germany or the long journey across the Atlantic to Canada.

* *

Edgar slowed at the end of the alleyway, uncertain what to do next, a figure materialised from a doorway and indicated for him to follow. With Edgar tagging along like a faithful spaniel he knocked on a plain, brown door which was immediately opened. Stepping aside, the Partisan pantomimed for Edgar to go inside then quickly retraced his steps and disappeared.

Uncertain, Edgar entered and found himself in a dark corridor with a flight of stairs in front and a wizened old man beckoning from the top. "I must be daft trusting all these strangers," he mumbled to himself, "the entire German army, complete with tanks, could be hiding in the bedroom for all I know," but realistically had no other choice so he slowly made his way up the steps.

At the top a rickety ladder led into a large, spacious attic, with an ancient armchair, half the stuffing missing, a small skylight that provided light and a large, lumpy mattress, obviously filled with hay. "I've seen one of those before," he thought, remembering happier times in his early basic training in Liverpool.

Edgar turned to thank his host but already the old man had gone, taking the ladder away with him and closing the trapdoor. Not for the first time Edgar felt very alone and isolated. There was a wooden box and set on it was a plate of cold meat and bread, a bottle of water and, miraculously, a glass containing plum brandy. Gratefully Edgar lifted the glass, toasted his comrades and took a long swallow, feeling better than he had done for some time. He slumped on the mattress, closed his eyes and wondered what Jimmy was doing at this moment, probably chatting up some pretty, young lady, unless he had been arrested for some new scam of course.

Edgar woke and opened one eye. The early morning sun was streaming through the skylight, forecasting a pleasant day and illuminating his hiding place. He turned sideways, the dry straw crunching then the trap-door opened and a pair of shining, brown eyes appeared, followed by a wide smile and he found himself gazing straight into the pretty face of Nada.

"What a lazy bones!" she exclaimed. "Missing me?"

"No, just worried about my own skin, if you were captured I'd have no-one to take me to the local."

"Local what?" she inquired.

"Local pub, inn, hostelry. Somewhere I could get a beer."

"Sorry, we have no time for that, we need to get you back on the air." She hauled herself into the attic, followed a few seconds later by Javor. Edgar sat up straight, rubbing the last

Ey Up Adolf

vestiges of sleep from his eyes. "Now are you going to get up or stay there all day?"

Edgar followed them down the swaying ladder then into the kitchen where he was greeted by a nod and a toothless smile from the elderly man who had been there the previous day. An old lady, who must have been at least a hundred and was probably the man's mother, placed a plate of cold food in front of him and indicated to eat.

"Her grandson is fighting with Tito, in fact you have probably seen him, he has a big, dark moustache," said Nada.

"As has everyone who is not female," Edgar thought to himself, "and I wouldn't be surprised if some of them didn't as well, it seems to be part of the uniform."

As he picked up a chunk of bread Edgar paused.

"It's alright, they are proud to help, they hate the Germans being in their country and are happy to assist anyone who is fighting them, especially someone as famous as you."

Edgar spluttered at that. "Me, famous, you are joking."

"Well not you personally, but the raid on the cave has entered local folklore so anyone involved is a hero."

"So what now?"

"We are moving you to a new, temporary base which is being set up as we speak, the wireless equipment is a bit more basic but it will do."

Once on the street Edgar looked anxiously around for any sign of German soldiers or suspicious looking characters but Nada laughed at him when she realised what he was doing.

"Don't worry, it's not like some other places, this is Partisan territory, you are safer on the streets than a German would be, the locals would just as soon slit their throats as look at them and any collaborators have long since gone."

Whether she meant left the district or were six feet under Edgar was not certain but he was inclined to the latter.

*   *

When John arrived back at the base he went in search of his crew. He discovered Tom sitting in a battered armchair outside the tower, reading a lurid, paperback novel. "Well, what news?" he asked, squinting as he gazed up.

John squatted down next to him. "Ann's accepted. We're getting married."

"Great! I take it we are all invited?"

"Of course. Now what's happening here?"

"Nothing official but the scuttlebutt is there are some new planes arriving so we'll be back up to operational strength."

Now they were returning to active service John wasn't certain that insisting on getting married straight away was a good idea. Perhaps he should have waited to the end of the war and made sure he survived first.

Chapter 53

Edgar was making his way through the outskirts of Murska Sobita, towards the distant hills. The sun was shining through the trees, dappling the leaf strewn floor and the occasional bird could be seen flitting from branch to branch. The entire scene reminded him of Sunday walks, then he caught a glimpse of Javor's sub-machine gun and the similarity disappeared. This was not a carefree stroll with friends but a march through enemy territory, where discovery would mean imprisonment or a bullet-ridden corpse.

After a couple of hours tramping they emerged from the trees into a small clearing in the middle of which stood an abandoned wooden lodge.

"Welcome to your new home," announced Captain Leigh, opening the door. In one corner was a wireless set and high speed sender but Edgar could not see the perforator that produced the punched strips that were necessary.

As if reading his mind Captain Leigh answered, "Sorry about that, it was lost during the drop, the parachute failed to open. They found most of the bits, about twenty of them, but they were like Humpty Dumpty, impossible to put together again. We have come up with a substitute though." He picked up two wooden handles which he handed to Edgar who examined them carefully. On the bottom were inserted two metal cutters, the exact size and shape as the ones needed. "They were salvaged from the wreckage and one of the Partisans fixed them onto the handles. I know it will be slow and laborious but it should work. Sorry to be a slave driver but could you get operational as soon as possible, we have a few important messages that need sending."

"How long are they?" inquired Edgar. "I could always transmit them by hand if necessary."

"Good idea. They are quite short and I'll see if I can condense them even further. How long will you need before you can start?"

"Five minutes for a brew."

*   *

John was reading a letter and chuckling softly as Tom approached. "From Ann?"

"No from my sister."

"So what's funny?"

"My dad. He was in the garden when this kid came running up the street, shouting and screaming. A bull had escaped and was coming their way and the lad was terrified. Anyway, my dad went to look and there was this bull, a big, black one, snorting and looking confused. Well, my dad is only quite small, about five foot three, but quite stocky so he just picks up his garden fork and marches out into the street, heading straight for the bull."

"You are joking, attacking a bull with a garden fork."

"It's true. My sister was watching from the window and she thought my dad was stark, staring mad. Anyway, there they were, like a couple of cowboys in the westerns, facing up to each other, with my dad bearing down, clutching his trusty fork. The bull's nerve must have gone, faced with this shrunken maniac 'cause it just turned round and ran all the way back to the pens where the farmers managed to get it inside again."

"I bet they were grateful to him."

Ey Up Adolf

"Probably and I'll bet he was drunk before lunch time on the strength of it." John folded up the letter and put it in his pocket.

"Oh, I forgot," said Tom, "CO says will you do canteen inspection today?"

"Do I have to, I hate that job?"

"'fraid so," then as he walked away he added, "it was either you or me and I told him you were better at it."

John looked around for something to throw, but with nothing to hand he climbed to his feet. If it had to be done, now was as good a time as any.

The room was full and he had to squeeze between the tightly packed rows of airmen who were already eating their deep-fried spam. When he reached the middle he called out, "Any complaints?" then glared around him. One or two airmen looked in his direction, noted his stripes and the glower on his face and decided that the food wasn't really that bad after all. "No, good." he turned and left the room, closing the door on the quiet, disgruntled mutterings. He hated paperwork and as there weren't any complaints he wouldn't have to fill out the forms. Perhaps that was why he seemed to get this duty more than anyone else, the CO was no lover of forms either.

*   *

Edgar settled into his new existence, it was peaceful and in the evening there was a fantastic smell of pine. One morning he had come out early and disturbed a young deer then on another occasion found a wild boar staring at him. Fortunately Nada was just behind and before the animal could move she had shot it. The roast that night was the best he had ever tasted.

Javor and Captain Leigh had left last evening with a group of Partisans to meet important visitors who were parachuting in. Edgar wondered who it could be to warrant such impressive bodyguards.

Edgar's hands were sore and he had a large blister on the side of his thumb from using the makeshift punches. He stood up, stretched and made his way to the window as a figure stepped out of the forest and waved. Edgar recognised the unmistakable shape of Captain Leigh then another man, older and wearing the uniform of a Brigadier General. Although he knew such a rank existed Edgar had never met one before but it did explain the need for the extraordinary firepower in the escort. Instinctively Edgar started to tidy his clothes but quickly realised he was wasting his time, they were so worn, bedraggled and scruffy that nothing was going to improve them, apart from throwing the lot on a bonfire. Brigadier or not, he would just have to lump it.

The door opened and Javor entered, his eyes sweeping the room, alert for anything amiss then allowed the rest to enter.

Apart from his comrades there were two others, both wearing the uniform of senior officers, but the ease with which they carried their weapons showed they were not desk soldiers.

"Hi Edgar," announced Captain Leigh "We're not stopping but we have an important message to send. London needs to know our visitors have arrived safely. Just one word and it can go in clear."

He nodded to the visitor who said in a slight Scottish accent, "Macbeth."

Edgar scuttled across to his set, glad to get away, and rapidly tapped out the single word. He wondered if Jimmy would be on the receiving end as it would pass through Section X which handled all the transmissions for clandestine organisations.

Nada ladled out helpings of the omnipresent stew, the final remnants of the wild boar. "Are you joining us?"

"No thanks, still things to do, I'll get some later."

Once they had eaten the group collected their gear and left, as quietly and mysteriously as they had arrived, leaving Edgar no wiser. Now that the table was clear he helped himself to a bowl of stew and pondered.

"Why did you lie earlier? You had finished your messages way before they arrived, I heard the tapping stop."

"Long held prejudices I guess, I'm never happy around bosses, especially big ones, they usually want to make you feel small and insignificant."

"I don't think he's like that, he's a fighter. I heard that he was in the SAS and that seemed important."

Edgar remembered hearing those letters before, referring to Colonel Hudson. If this guy was like him then someone had better watch out as trouble was on their way. "What are they doing here, any idea?"

"Going to see Tito to persuade him to meet with your leader, Winston Churchill."

"That should be interesting," Edgar commented, remembering his own very brief encounter. "Job'd be a good un."

Nada gave him a mystified look then left the table. Sometimes she wondered if Edgar spoke the same language that she studied such a long time ago.

Chapter 54

Ann and John were sitting on the train travelling to Edinburgh, watching the scenery passing outside the carriage window, occasionally obscured by clouds of steam that belched from the engine. She had to pinch herself to make sure it wasn't a dream, but a glance down at the golden ring on her finger assured her. The wedding had gone without a hitch, all John's crew were there as well as the staff of the fire station. Her mother had excelled herself with the food and they even had a bottle of sherry for the toasts, her mother had been persuaded to put aside her beliefs for this one special occasion. "Everyone will expect it," Ann had stated. "John's family are not teetotal and will think we are very stingy if we don't even have something for the toasts," so her father was sent out to queue for a bottle.

Eventually they managed to get away and now they were speeding towards Scotland. As the guard made his way down the train, announcing the next station, Ann realised that she was back in her native Geordieland, approaching Newcastle.

John must have reached the same conclusion, "Do you miss it?"

"Sometimes. It was very different, we lived in a small village right up on the edge of the moors, in fact we had a couple of goats that were tethered there. We owned two detached houses, one that was ours and one that was left to us, but during the depression we sold them both and moved to Rotherham for work. We had just enough from the two houses to buy our semi.

Ey Up Adolf

In winter, when it snowed we couldn't get out of the village. As the men came home from the pit they would dig a way through but the wind would blow and fill it in again by the next day. Everyone made wine from fruit or what grew in the hedgerows, potent stuff but not considered to be real alcohol so everyone could drink it."

They continued chatting all the way to Edinburgh, getting to know more about each other and making plans for the future, each aware that no matter what they said it might never happen unless John was very lucky. His crew was beginning a third tour of duty, something that very few managed to start, let alone complete.

*   *

Edgar was busy bashing away with his punches when Javor arrived and immediately took Captain Leigh to one side. The Captain's expression changed to one of concern.

"Better hurry up, Edgar mate, we're leaving."

"Why, what's the problem?"

"The Germans are making a big push to get rid of the Partisans and we're stuck bang in the middle. They're throwing everything at this one, top troops, tanks, air support, the lot. We're already ringed in and the noose is tightening. Heavy fighting is already going on to the south where the Partisans are attempting to break through and it won't be long before the Germans get here. A plane is coming this evening to airlift us out."

"What about Nada and Javor, are they coming with us?"

"No," replied Nada, "We will join up with one of the brigades and help fight. It is our country and we will defend it."

"So hop to it," added Captain Leigh. "Get that finished and sent."

Ten minutes later they closed the door and set off through the trees, Javor out in front as usual accompanied by Nada then Captain Leigh and Edgar.

"Well Edgar, you'll soon be back in England so then what, home to see the girlfriend?"

"No!" said Edgar firmly and trudged on in silence.

After a few minutes Captain Leigh tried again, "What happened? Do you want to talk about it?"

"No. The war happened, that's all."

They both lapsed into silence.

*   *

With John carrying the cases they made their way through the massive front door and approached the reception desk, where a dark- haired young lady with freckles looked up and smiled, instantly recognising his airforce uniform.

"Mr and Mrs Whyke," said John and together they handed over their ration books.

The girl took them and glanced at the covers then her eyes widened as did her smile. Ann wondered why, then the penny dropped, hers were still in her maiden name, it hadn't been changed since the wedding as it couldn't be done without a marriage certificate. What would the receptionist be thinking?

"It's my maiden name," Ann blurted out quickly, "we've just got married."

"I thought so. When?"

"This morning," Ann answered, blushing.

"Congratulations! I hope you enjoy your stay."

As they walked to the lifts John whispered, "Why did you tell her that?"

"Because it's better than the alterative, with us having different names on the ration books."

At first John looked perplexed then as the meaning of her words sank home he too blushed.

*   *

As the seconds ticked by Edgar became more and more concerned. A hand touching his shoulder made his heart stop until Nada whispered in his ear. "The Partisans have prepared the airstrip, move forwards ready to leave."

As he reached the edge of the trees Edgar saw a narrow road cutting through a meadow. Along the edge were oil lamps and dark figures standing patiently, moonlight reflecting off the barrels of their weapons. The slight breeze brought the scent of pine and a low drone that that was rapidly becoming louder. As he peered into the darkness a dark shape flickered against a pale patch of rock-face then the roar of engines split the night air as the Havoc dropped onto the road and rapidly taxied to a halt.

Captain Leigh materialised alongside Edgar and said jovially, "All aboard the Skylark," then he was gone, sprinting across the grass towards the aeroplane that was drawing to a halt while the Partisans gathered like ants round a sugar cube.

*   *

The next morning John and Ann entered the large dining room and were met by the head waiter who escorted them to their table. When they scrutinised the menu it was a disappointment. Both of them thought that it would be more impressive, food they could not get at home, but it was very ordinary. John decided that since they were in Scotland he should try the porridge while Ann chose scrambled egg. They chatted excitedly about what they would do with the rest of the day, a visit to the castle or a walk down the Royal Mile, until they were interrupted by the waitress arriving with their order.

John had just picked up his spoon when he was stopped by a disgusted snort from his new wife. "What's the problem?"

"These eggs, they're powdered!"

John was going to say it was wartime but one look at Ann's face cut that short. He was not the only one who noticed the angry expression, the waitress scurried across but stopped when she saw that the head waiter would get there first.

"Pardon Madam," he said in his most diffusing voice, "is there a problem?"

Ann stabbed the offending mass with her fork then replied, "Yes, this!" Again she stuck the congealed mass.

"Is it not cooked to your satisfaction?"

"It's not the cooking, it's the content," answered Ann, her anger rising because of his attitude. "You have my ration book and that includes a proper egg and that is what I want!"

Now several of the other diners were looking in their direction, their breakfast disturbed. The head waiter appeared uncomfortable, he had expected to either gloss over the problem or use his position, and the impressive surroundings, to overawe this young lady but he was wrong.

"Perhaps Madam would like to change her order?"

"No Madam would not, she would like what she ordered, scrambled egg, made with a real egg!"

Realising he was beaten the head waiter signalled for the waitress to remove the plate. "Certainly Madam, it will only take a few minutes."

John resumed eating his porridge, married life was certainly going to be interesting.

Chapter 55

Edgar entered the front door at Eaton Square as Jimmy was coming out. "Edgar, great to see you!" Then he took in the tattered clothes, unshaved chin and bags under the eyes. "What have you been up to, you look like a tramp?"

Edgar felt too exhausted to answer, especially as he couldn't tell the truth. Even though the flight back had passed uneventfully it had still been long and uncomfortable. He had parted from Captain Leigh at the RAF base then cadged a lift to London in an army truck. "I'll tell you some day, at the moment all I want to do is sleep for a week. I'll see you later."

He pushed past and glanced at the shelf where mail was placed, noticing a letter with his name on it. "Nothing important," he mumbled incoherently, "I'll read it later." After dragging his weary body up the stairs he collapsed on the bed and was dead to the world in seconds.

When Jimmy returned he found Edgar asleep, still in the threadbare jacket. As he started to close the door Edgar stirred, opened one eye and said, "Ey up, mate."

"Sorry, didn't mean to wake you."

"What's up, did you forget sommat?"

"You're joking!" exclaimed Jimmy. "I've just come back from work, you've been asleep for twelve hours."

Edgar sat up, wiping sleep from his eyes. "I thought I'd just dozed off. What's that?" he asked pointing to a parcel that Jimmy had under his arm.

"Don't know, it was waiting downstairs, it's got your name on it."

Edgar took the parcel and untied the string, allowing the brown paper to fall to the floor. Inside was his uniform, neatly pressed and folded up, but he could feel something else, something hidden in the middle, something hard and cylindrical. Carefully he unfolded the clothes until he revealed the mysterious object, a bottle of coloured liquid with a strange label.

"What's that?" asked Jimmy, taking the bottle from him and peering at the label. "Slivovitz?"

Edgar chuckled and then noticed the note tucked into one of the pockets of his tunic. 'Thanks for your help. Try to keep out of trouble.' He took the bottle and pulled the cork, instantly smelling the unmistakable aroma. "Plum brandy, a present." When it was obvious that he was not going to say any more Jimmy went off in search of glasses while Edgar changed into his uniform. As he was finishing he noticed the envelope that had arrived earlier. Inside was a single sheet, the letters written in capitals and unsigned. All it said was 'ANN MARRIED TODAY'.

Edgar crumpled it into a ball and threw it into the fireplace. "Thanks mate, whoever you are." Then he raised his voice and called, "What's taking so long, I could die of thirst up here?" He picked up the note from Captain Leigh, placed it with the letter in the grate, took a match from a box on the shelf and set fire to them both.

*   *

Edgar strolled into the communications room under the 'building site' with a smug expression on his face that was explained a few seconds later when Jimmy entered, a glazed look in his eyes. The previous night they had visited a couple of local pubs, partly to allow Edgar to sample English beer again and partly to pick up any messages for their sending service. Later they had returned to Eaton Square and sampled some more of Edgar's present which explained the searing headache that Jimmy was suffering while Edgar was clear headed, several weeks of drinking the powerful stuff had given him immunity from its after effects.

When the sergeant came across and shook his hand he was aware that the grapevine had announced something about what he had been up to, but not the whole story, of that he was certain.

As he started work he caught the blister on the side of his thumb, a reminder of his recent exploits, and thought about the old farm and almost missed being in the fresh mountain air, but only almost, there was something to be said for having several feet of reinforced concrete between you and anyone who wanted to do you harm.

*   *

Returning from his honeymoon John had to make the long journey back to his new base in Cambridgeshire. After surviving the light-hearted ribbing and occasional personal question he found out what was happening, the flight was back up to strength and was scheduled to fly that night, a combined attack with an American squadron of Flying Fortresses. They were not happy about this as the Americans flew higher and dropped a large number of smaller bombs than the Lancaster. It was quite common for them to make a mistake and drop their bombs on the planes below. Feeling disgruntled John made his way across to the briefing room, wishing all the time that he was back in the large, sumptuous accommodation in the Waverley with his new bride.

The moon was shining from a clear, starlit sky as the Lancaster thundered through the night, the crew tensing as they crossed the German border. Ahead was the industrial heart along the Rhine where the large formation of bombers was heading. Inside his office John was busy plotting not only where they were going but also the best way back. Now, more than ever, he was determined that they would return unscathed.

In the nose of the plane the bomb-aimer was poised ready, thumb on the release button, watching the dark ground beneath when suddenly bright orange fires appeared. "Markers dead ahead."

"Right on target," acknowledged John. "Drop when you are ready."

The searchlights weaved across the sky, hunting for a target but John knew they were too late, in seconds their bombs would be released, thousands of pounds of deadly explosive, then the plane would be gone, heading to the coast and safety.

As the countryside of France flashed beneath them the crew finally relaxed, in less than an hour they would be back on the ground heading to their beds. Suddenly the intercom burst into life, an American voice with a strong southern accent. "Listen up guys, does anyone have any idea where we are?"

Seconds later another voice with that unmistakable Texan drawl joined in, "Sorry partner, we were following you, we thought you knew the way."

"Haven't they an ounce of gorm between them," John muttered to himself. "If the Germans pick up all that chattering we'll have the entire Luftwaffe on our tails before long." Switching on his microphone he said, "Tom patch me in to those cowboys then, when I say, give a tiny flick of the lights." He waited a second then announced. "Relax lost sheep, the shepherd is here, just follow us. Now Tom."

The landing lights on the bomber flashed for a second then disappeared again.

"Got you, we'll fall in behind."

Ey Up Adolf

Leading a convoy of huge Flying Fortress's D-Dog ploughed on towards the English Channel. "Well with all this fire-power we should be safe from any prowling fighter," John thought, as the American planes were bristling with machine guns making them well capable of causing serious damage on any fighter unwise enough to attack.

Shortly afterwards they radioed ahead to secure an early landing slot. John made a quick call to the following Americans, "That big, water-filled V to your right is the Thames Estuary. Do you think you can find your own way from here?"

"Thanks, partner, and if you're near our home town drop in for a drink."

In the tail turret Bob watched the huge Fortresses swing away, heading for their own base, as the Lancaster began its descent back to earth, food and sleep.

Chapter 56

Occasionally, especially if he had a bad day, Edgar would wonder what had happened to Captain Leigh and his merry band but eventually the mad and dangerous times drifted into the dark areas of his memory. Even the news of the war, such as it was, was more encouraging, except the constant rumours that the enemy had developed a new weapon, a flying bomb that could deliver itself to the heart of the country. There was obviously something afoot though, the flow of messages had more than doubled generally and Section X was extremely busy.

Edgar took a second to stretch and gaze about the room, watching the bustle of activity, even Jimmy was hard at it, which was a change, usually he could be found chatting to an attractive, dark-haired young lady who worked in the far corner. The area that handled the RAF traffic seemed especially busy. "Something unusual must be brewing," he thought to himself.

* *

Ann was sitting on an ancient, wooden bench outside the small inn near Cambridge where she was staying for a couple of days to be with John. Even on duty he always managed to sneak out for a few hours, but today he had to return early. Something big was happening. The inn was close to the RAF base and all day she could hear the sound of aircraft engines being

Ey Up Adolf

tested, all the crews were back on base and lorries trundled down the narrow lane in front of her carrying heavy loads.

The staff knew that she was newly married and that her husband was stationed at the base, in Bomber Command. A teenage girl who helped out came and asked, "Would you like a cup of tea?"

"Yes please."

The girl started to leave then turned back. "He'll be alright I'm certain. You just wait and see."

Ann smiled up at her, but deep down she was not sure. Perhaps it wasn't a good idea her being here. So far he'd always come back safely, but what if she brought bad luck. As a small tear formed in the corner of her eye, she took out a handkerchief, dabbed at it then grinned as she saw the embroidered emblem in the corner, a thistle, a memento of their honeymoon in Scotland. As if this was a sign she smiled, now she was certain he would come back safe.

*   *

The sun was sinking when Edgar emerged from the bunker, the heat of the day waning and the shadows lengthening. Jimmy still had things to do but Edgar had a sneaky suspicion that the 'thing' was about five foot six, slim, pretty, with long black hair and small, white teeth. This time he felt Jimmy had met his match. Feeling hungry he decided to eat in the canteen at Scotland Yard, a few blocks down Whitehall. He sauntered along, taking his time and enjoying the sunshine after a shift underground. On days like this it was almost possible to forget that there was a war going on.

Gradually he became aware of a high pitched hum, obviously from machinery. He gazed around then realised that the noise was not coming from ground level but in the sky. He peered upwards, shading his eyes from the sun, and spotted a small dot, coming towards him and growing rapidly. Within seconds he saw it was like a long tube with a pointed front end, stubby wings and a jet of flame issuing from the back. The whining sound was getting much louder, until with a screech it passed over his head. He listened to it continue then suddenly there was silence. Before he had time to consider what this meant there was a tremendous explosion and he could see a plume of dark smoke rising into the sky.

The rumours about a secret weapon, a doodlebug, were true and he had just seen exactly what they could do. The war had just entered a new, very deadly phase because what could you do about something with no pilot to kill.

*   *

The sun had set when the first of the Lancasters left the runway and soared over the inn with a noise like thunder. Ann was sitting in the small bar nursing a glass of cider and she glanced up towards the ceiling.

"You get used to it," stated the elderly lady sitting at the next table, "happens all the time. I'll tell you what though, I'd rather be here than where they drop them bombs." Ann managed a small smile then the old woman said, with insight that comes with age, "Is your fella' on one of those planes?"

"Yes," Ann replied.

"Boyfriend?"

"Husband, just married." She held out her hand to show the narrow band of gold.

"You poor dear, you must be worried out of your mind, but don't fret he'll come back safe, I have a talent for this sort of thing, my grandma was part gypsy."

"Thank you, I'm certain you're right," then thought to herself, "not that it helps."

Ey Up Adolf

*   *

The bell had just sounded, calling time, and Edgar was waiting for Jimmy to finish his last tune when he became aware of someone standing next to him. Thinking it was a reporter he turned and was surprised when he found a well dressed man and woman.

"I understand that you are the pianist's manager," he stated in the drawl of the upper class. Edgar nodded. "We are having a little party and wondered if your friend would come and play for us. You will be invited as well of course."

"Ta, mate," replied Edgar. "How much?"

"Would ten pounds be acceptable?"

"Ten pounds! You do know who that is don't you?" When the couple looked blankly Edgar continued, "That's Jimmy Parr, from Workers' Playtime. He comes here to relax and plays as a favour to the landlord." He omitted to mention the free pints that went with it. "He doesn't perform for nowt tha' knows."

"I'm sorry," the man spluttered, "I didn't understand. Sorry to bother you," and he turned to go.

Edgar realised that perhaps he had been too strong with his indignation. "Just wait a minute, we're all in this war together and I suppose there will be some serving officers there." The woman nodded in agreement. "I'll tell you what, sithee, since it's for a good cause I'll persuade him to play for you for, let's say, twenty pounds."

"Agreed! Do you know where Eaton Square is?" Edgar nodded, hiding his smile. "Good, number 40, say in half an hour."

"Deal." Edgar refrained from spitting on his hand to seal the transaction, he thought that might be carrying the cloth cap image a bit too far then he sauntered off to inform Jimmy.

*   *

Lying in the dark, listening to the creaks and groans of the old building there was nothing to stop Ann picturing the bomber in the black sky, searchlights, detonations, fire and smoke, aircraft dropping in flames. She sat up, stared around then walked to the dresser, poured herself a glass of water and took it to the window where she stared out over the silhouettes of the trees. It was going to be a long night waiting to see if he returned safely.

*   *

Half an hour later Edgar and Jimmy made their way along Eaton Square, using the faint moonlight to read the numbers, until finally they found the right one. Climbing the steps they knocked on the door.

"Do you think the butler will answer?" Jimmy asked.

"No chance, not with a war on, it's one of the hardships the toffs have to put up with, that and a lack of caviar." Footsteps approached down the hall and the door opened a small way, allowing a shaft of light to escape and an aged retainer to peer out. Edgar heard Jimmy let out a muffled chortle.

The butler looked them up and down with disgust, taking in their worn battledress and dusty boots. Before he had time to close and bar the entry Edgar stuck out a foot, jamming an army regulation boot in the door preventing it from closing. "Hold on a minute, this is Jimmy Parr, he's the entertainment."

He expected further argument but instead the old guy's face lit up. "From Workers' Playtime?"

"The very same."

The door opened and they were ushered inside. "I'll inform the master you have arrived but not everyone is here yet, so I suggest I take you to the pantry and find you some refreshment first."

"Lead on McDuff," said Edgar then to Jimmy, "job's a good 'un."

*   *

On board D-Dog John was hunched over his maps plotting a way back home. They had already dropped their deadly load of explosives and the night sky was awash with the reflection of thousands of fires, now all they had to do was make it back in one piece. Over the radio John could hear other planes in front of them reporting heavy opposition, anti-aircraft fire and radar equipped night fighters and made a decision. "Let's take the scenic route, divert ten degrees east." As the bomber swung onto the new course he hoped he had made the correct decision. Now they were on their own, losing the safety of numbers for stealth and secrecy, if a loud and massive Lancaster bomber could ever be described as secret.

Chapter 57

Edgar and Jimmy had just finished a ham sandwich and a bottle of beer when the butler returned, "They are ready for you now." As Jimmy rose to his feet, "Before you go could I have your autograph, it'd make my wife's day." Jimmy took the proffered pencil, asked the lucky lady's name and quickly wrote on the sheet of paper.

Led by the butler they entered a large room filled with elegantly dressed people. Jimmy strode confidently to the baby grand and sat down while Edgar sneaked into a corner by the window, his army uniform, complete with sergeant's stripes, was distinctly out of place, the lowest rank he could see was a Colonel.

Quickly Jimmy was announced and he started playing. Edgar managed to snatch a glass of wine from a passing waiter and leant against the wall, listening to the music, until a voice in his ear made him choke on his drink.

"Hello Edgar, I'm surprised to see you here, I would have thought it was against your northern principles, hanging about with the gentry."

When he stopped spluttering he gaped at a face he had last seen on a cold airfield. "Captain Leigh, what are you doing here?"

"I am allowed a few days off occasionally you know, killing people is quite hard work." The words seemed even more incongruous then ever, spoken in the lush and opulent surroundings. "Besides the host is my cousin. Now, how come you are here?"

Ey Up Adolf

"I've come with my friend Jimmy Parr, he's playing the piano."

"Well make the most of it, I am coming to see you in a few days, there's a little job pending, I thought you might like to help again."

Suddenly the very expensive champagne in Edgar's glass tasted like vinegar.

*   *

D-Dog had crossed the coast and was on the last leg of its long and dangerous flight back when the wireless operator called the base for landing permission. In the middle of the transmission another aircraft cut in, its radio breaking up all the time. "F…..dy…..two engines ……fire……emergency land….."

"Sorry D-Dog take up holding pattern," then the operator continued to try and establish communications with the stricken plane.

"Sounds like they're in trouble," announced Tom.

"And I'll bet they are not the only ones," added John, glad that his gamble had worked out, giving them a clear run without any serious problems. Now all they had to do was circle round until they received instructions to land, as long as they had enough fuel he added as an afterthought.

*   *

Ann woke from a fitful sleep feeling like a wet rag when the chamber maid, a middle aged woman with a mournful expression, entered with a cup of tea. Ann sat up and glanced towards the window where a chink of light was creeping in through the blackout curtains.

The maid put down the cup and said, "The news isn't very good today."

"What isn't?"

"The government is raising the school leaving age to fifteen, that means my lad will have to stay on for another year just when I've got him a job at the local abattoir. It's not right."

Ann relaxed. "Was there anything about the war?"

"Not certain, I don't really listen, too depressing." She made to leave then paused. "There was one thing, the bombers last night had a hard time, over sixty were destroyed. I hope they weren't from up the road, it'll affect the takings something horrible."

Remembering there was a phone box across the lane Ann ignored the tea, jumped from bed and dressed.

Grasping the handle she hauled the protesting door open and entered the stuffy confines, wracking her memory for the number. The black receiver seemed to weigh a ton as she lifted it off the cradle and held it tightly to her ear. Searching in her bag she fumbled for her purse, quelling the panic that was rising. Selecting a couple of coins she pressed them in the slot, hearing the metallic clunk as they dropped.

"Stop being so silly," she said to herself sharply, "there were hundreds of planes on that raid last night and John has always come back safely so why should this be any different?" She started to replace the handset but still there was that nagging doubt.

Very slowly she turned the dial then released it, watching, mesmerised as it quickly returned. What if the news was bad, did she really want to know? For what seemed an eternity she stood there motionless, the black handset held to the side of her head and her heart pounding, then with determination she dialled the remaining numbers, she had to know one way or the other.

She heard ringing then a deep male voice.

"Can I speak to John Whyke, it's his wife?"

"Hold on, I'll inquire. John Whyke?" She heard a faint voice in the background. "I'm sorry, no-one has seen him today,"

Ey Up Adolf

Ann felt her heart stop, "but that doesn't necessarily mean anything, it was a bit hectic round here last night. What plane was he on?"

"D-Dog." She heard the call sign repeated and a muffled reply. The seconds ticked by, each lasting a hundred years, until the voice came back on the line. "My colleague has seen Jack Archer, the bomb-aimer. Would you like me to send for him?"

"No thank you, thank you very much!" she exclaimed, "that's alright." She replaced the handset and smiled. If Jack was there then they had returned safely. She opened the door and stepped out into the light, smelling the newly cut grass and fragrant flowers, hearing the songs of the early morning birds and feeling the warmth of the sun. Suddenly everything had taken on a new freshness, God was in his Heaven and all was right with the world.

She returned to her room, picked up the cup of cold tea and took a deep drink. This morning it tasted like the nectar of the gods.

*   *

Edgar was sitting in the canteen when Jimmy came in and joined him. "You know that guy you were chatting to last night, the captain, he's just walked in." Edgar peered over Jimmy's shoulder, Captain Leigh was talking to their CO. "Why do you think he's here?"

"I don't know, but I'll bet it's something that will not be good for my health. He wants to involve me in some dark and dangerous mission and for once I don't want to play." With that he stood up and, without a backwards glance, strode out of the room.

*   *

Ann had finished her breakfast when the landlord appeared, an envelope in his hand. "There's a message for you, from the base," he paused for a moment then continued, "I hope it isn't bad."

"Its fine, I already checked that John came back safely." She was rewarded with a relieved smile then slit the top with her knife, leaving a smear of jam. John would be on duty this morning but would be able to meet her in the afternoon. She saw the three crosses after his name and thought, "That won't be enough."

*   *

Edgar wasn't shocked when the CO came across, a puzzled frown on his face.

"Ah, Edgar," he said. "I had a strange visitor this morning."

"I bet you did," Edgar thought, "Now stop messing about and come to the point."

"The Captain said you had been in his unit recently and you had done a very good job."

"Ay, but I bet he didn't tell you which unit," Edgar thought.

"Anyway he has suggested that you be sent on a junior leaders' course. I can't remember hearing of that before and I don't really want to lose you, especially since you have just come back from…" he paused but Edgar made no attempt to enlighten him, "so I told him it wasn't really viable." Edgar continued looking, giving no clue to his thoughts. "So you'll be staying here."

"Want to take a bet?" thought Edgar.

He turned back to the message that had just been received but his concentration wasn't on it, he was wondering exactly what this course was and when he would be going.

*   *

John arrived at the wheel of a battered van, badly painted in the colours of the RAF with the word 'butcher' showing faintly through. "Come on, I've got a picnic in the back."

Ann stared at the decrepit vehicle, "How have you managed this?"

Ey Up Adolf

John laughed. "A liberal outlay of my private stash of chocolate. This fine piece of machinery has just been repaired and needed testing so the sergeant asked me if I minded taking it for a spin then the catering sergeant discovered he had produced one too many pies and it seemed a pity to waste it, plus a couple of sausages, some green salad and a piece of cake. It's only a small piece but I'm certain we'll manage."

As the van stuttered down the road Ann said, "I didn't know you knew how to drive a car?"

"I don't," as the gears crashed and protested loudly.

*   *

"The cheek of the man!" exclaimed the CO. "I said clearly that I couldn't spare you, especially to go traipsing off on a silly course, but he's obviously got some sort of influence. That's what you get with these desk officers, you know, not proper soldiers at all." As he paused to take a breath Edgar struggled to suppress a grin. The CO had probably never held a gun in his entire army career let alone fired one, unlike Captain Leigh who could shoot a German in the pitch dark with his eyes closed and probably had.

"Anyway you are to be sent off to Scotland in the near future. I just hope it rains the entire time." He spun on his heels and stormed back to his office.

"A bit harsh. Never mind, Scotland is the home of whisky."

"What did he want? He didn't look a happy bunny."

"I'm being sent on a course, Scotland."

"I'm surprised he agreed, we're short staffed as it is."

"I don't think he had any choice."

Chapter 58

"Are you flying tonight?"

John hesitated, "Yes but don't worry, we aren't going over Germany," then reluctantly added, "it's somewhere in France, I don't know anything more."

"Don't know or won't say," thought Ann, everyone had become accustomed to the phrase, "careless words cost lives."

*   *

"Come on Jimmy," Edgar muttered, standing on the pavement in Whitehall. He had left his friend chatting to Debs, the dark haired beauty, in the corridor, a common occurrence these days, it seemed to be developing into something serious.

"In a hurry to go somewhere?" Edgar jumped then Captain Leigh continued, "I'm surprised to still see you here, I thought you'd be off on your course by now."

"Just what am I getting involved with this time?"

The captain did not reply immediately. Instead he stared into the sky behind Edgar, his eyes narrowing as he squinted into the sunlight, concentrating on the rapidly moving flash of light that was speeding towards the earth. Suddenly he caught Edgar by the arm and dragged him into a nearby doorway.

Edgar started to complain when there was a loud explosion, the ground shook and a cloud of smoke appeared above the surrounding buildings. "Was that a doodlebug, I didn't hear anything?"

Ey Up Adolf

Shaking his head Captain Leigh replied, "No, a V2, the latest weapon. They have a longer range and can be fired from a mobile launcher, like a train or large lorry."

Edgar stepped out into the street, straightening his tunic, just as Jimmy and his new girlfriend appeared.

Captain Leigh whispered, "Must be going. I doubt if we'll bump into each other for a bit, I'm off for some decent wine and see if I can't cause a bit of bother."

*   *

With the setting of the sun fog formed over the English Channel and rolled in banks across both coastlines. For the second time that night John had checked the weather forecast and found his flight had been put back. He returned to his bunk and rested his head on the pillow, he had been told to report again in two hours, just not quite long enough for a snooze. He closed his eyes and pictured the little river with the bright, dappled sunlight reflecting off it and his new wife paddling in the shallows. The image made him even more determined to make sure that D-Dog returned safely tonight.

Two hours later the fog had lifted and the raid was on for Le Havre. He knew the only strategic target was the port, so why there and why now. There was only one logical conclusion, the long awaited invasion of Europe was about to happen.

Below the Lancaster the waves of the Channel rolled along but ahead could be seen the coastline, the moonlight reflecting off the surf as the waves broke on the golden sands. In front the searchlights were probing the night sky, the crews alerted by the monotonous drone of the heavy bombers. There was little danger from fighters, the RAF had mastery of the sky so close to England

Suddenly the air around the bomber was filled with detonations, hurtling metal and the smell of cordite from the exploding shells.

On the ground the German gunners were firing as fast as they could, then a cheer went up, one of their shells had scored a direct hit. The wing had been blown clean off and the aircraft was spiralling down to the ground in flames. Their celebrations were short lived as the next second a massive bomb landed straight on top of them, released a second before the plane was destroyed, and men and gun disappeared in a blinding flash to be replaced by a huge crater in the ground.

John picked himself off the floor of the Lancaster and straightened his flying helmet. "Sorry about that," came the pilot's voice, "is everyone alright?"

"What happened?"

"The plane next to us copped it, a direct hit."

"Anyone get out?"

The silence that followed answered the question. When D-Dog finally landed a very quiet and sombre crew climbed down and walked across the tarmac to the debriefing, no-one liked to report the loss of one of their own.

*   *

When the news of the D-day landings were announced as a success it came as a great relief to the entire nation, at last an end to the war was in sight. Edgar found himself even busier than usual with hundreds of signals a day passing through Section X. Glancing sideways he could see Jimmy toiling away just as industriously. "Good, it'll keep him out of mischief," then a slim figure with long black hair walked past and give Jimmy a gentle squeeze on the shoulder and receive a tired smile in return. "They look good together, nearly as …." He stopped himself in mid-sentence, that was a well trodden path that went nowhere.

He returned to the next signal as the sergeant strode across. "CO wants to see you and he's not happy about something, what have you been up to?"

"Honestly I haven't a clue." Then he paused, "Or perhaps I have."

A new guard had been on duty yesterday. Edgar was busy listening to Jimmy tell him about meeting Vera Lynn and hadn't noticed when he presented his soup can label instead of his pass. It had taken several minutes of abject apologies and production of numerous official papers, including the correct pass, before he was allowed to continue. This made him late for duty and officially AWOL.

Ten minutes later Edgar found out that he was correct as the CO finished with, "… so you are docked a day's pay and it will be entered on your record." A bit harsh thought Edgar for only a few minutes then he discovered the real reason for the CO's displeasure. "Also I have received orders to send you on that course, immediately, most inconsiderate since we are short staffed and very busy. I don't suppose you'd consider turning it down?" He raised his eyebrows in enquiry.

"I'd love to," Edgar thought, "but I don't think it would do any good, they'd probably just kidnap me anyway."

When Edgar didn't speak the CO handed across the papers. "I forgot to say, you have to pick up your travel documents from Goodge Street station. A bit strange that, I thought they only dealt with the underground."

"And one or two other matters," Edgar muttered. Suddenly things became crystal clear.

*   *

Goodge Street was becoming a familiar sight to Edgar so he was very surprised when he found a military guard on duty and numerous soldiers, mainly officers and many of them American, coming and going through the entrance. He presented his orders and was allowed in. "SHAEF is housed here now," the guard confided, "the place is full of brass." Edgar nodded, knowing that SHAEF stood for Supreme Headquarters Allied Expeditionary Force, the invasion army.

Making his way down to the subterranean tunnels Edgar arrived at the usual counter and handed over his orders, wondering what he would receive back, a smart suit or scruffy rags so he was surprised when it was a brown envelope and a sealed cardboard box. Once outside he opened the envelope first and found it was a travel warrant to Dover and a new set of orders, which he put to one side.

He balanced the box in his hand, feeling the weight then untied the string, broke the seal and lifted the lid. Sitting in the bottom was a revolver in a holster, the same one that he had left behind when he had to rapidly vacate the base in the mountains. Placed next to it was a short note that said, "Remember the bullets. Love, Nada."

Replacing the lid he turned to the orders and received his second shock.

Four hours later he found himself standing on the swaying deck of a sleek grey Motor Torpedo Boat watching the sailors unfastening the mooring ropes. With a gentle burble the engines moved the craft away from the dock and out towards the harbour entrance, nosing through the slight swell. "This isn't too bad," thought Edgar, who had never considered himself to be a good sailor. He gazed forwards, the waves were much larger and travelling faster. He staggered and lost his balance.

The powerful engines had been cranked up to speed and the grey, low-hulled boat leapt forwards, the front lifting from the water, skipping over the smaller waves and battering its way through the larger ones. As it crashed down into trough between waves Edgar's knees buckled and his spine felt as if it had been compressed by six inches. Ahead was over twenty miles of this and the twin torpedo tubes and mounted machine guns showed that those miles were filled with danger.

One of the sailors, dressed in a thick jacket, came and stood next to him. "Must say I expected someone more important."

"What do you mean?"

"When the orders came to transport you across the ditch, top secret mission and all that cobblers. Thought it would be general or somebody." Then glancing at the revolver strapped to Edgar's side he continued, "Taking on the whole German army on your own are you, turning the tide."

Thinking what was in his orders Edgar just nodded, "Something like that." He turned away seemingly to watch the approaching waves but in fact so that he could concentrate on keeping the contents of his stomach where they should be.

Chapter 59

For the first time in weeks D-Dog was airborne in daylight, heading towards the front line of the invasion force. As they flew over the grey water they could see the tiny shapes of boats, heavy warships, transports and occasionally the white wake of a fast moving vessel like a Motor Torpedo Boat (MTB). Ahead the golden sand of the French beaches shone in the afternoon sun.

"If there were any landing strips we could pop in for a paddle," announced Jack from his forward perch.

"A bit too polluted for my liking," John replied. "All those mines floating about, jellyfish are bad enough but those things can do some real damage."

The plane thundered onwards, flying low so they could see the burnt out tanks and other vehicles lining the sides of the roads, showing the price that had been paid by both sides. Somewhere ahead the Germans were dug in, defending heavily fortified positions.

"An excellent tactic if you are being attacked by soldiers with rifles and bayonets but not so good when a Lancaster is overhead with a full payload," thought John. By now the troops would be able to hear the deep drone of the engines and would know exactly what was in store for them.

Ey Up Adolf

*   *

The MTB throttled back, sneaking alongside the temporary landing, and Edgar was helped ashore, glad to be back on dry land instead of this bucking, jarring monster. With a cheery wave the captain reversed engines and they sped off looking for the reported enemy destroyer out in the Channel.

"What is it about this war that turns perfectly normal people into mad hatters. That thing is like a toy compared to a destroyer but there he goes, like David and Goliath, happily trying to get killed," murmured Edgar.

He walked up the beach, the sand clinging to his boots and the wet ends of his trousers, in search of transport for the rest of his journey, with part of him hoping that none would be available. He had been in some manic and dangerous situations so far this war but this could easily turn out to be the worst yet, with the might of the German army poised only a few scant miles away. He just hoped that, for once, he was on the correct side of the lines, surrounded by his own people rather than the enemy.

*   *

The Lancaster roared onwards, the patchwork of fields hurtling past beneath them. At this height every little detail was visible, cows in back gardens, tiles missing from roofs and the occasional French peasant waving at them. Ahead puffs of smoke from exploding ordinance were drifting into the air marking their destination. The Lancaster swung into a wide loop that would run them down the length of the German fortifications, a series of pill-boxes interlinked with trenches full of infantry. The phrase 'shooting fish in a barrel' popped into John's brain.

Neil Whyke

In his forward position Jack could see the trenches clearly and the white blobs which were the upturned faces of the German troops, cringing as deep in the trench as possible, each one fully aware of the sheer hell that was going to erupt around them in the next few seconds and there was absolutely nothing they could do to alter that or escape from the terrible destructive force that was going to happen.

A click of the button in his hand and the stick of bombs dropped from the bay and hurtled downwards. Seconds later bright blossoms of light spread across the ground followed by mighty detonations that sent clouds of smoke, debris and human parts hurtling into air, almost as high as the speeding bomber, then they were gone, leaving the scene of carnage behind. Even though the view had disappeared Jack knew that the image of those condemned men would stay with him forever.

*   *

The camouflaged lorry ground to a halt depositing Edgar in front of a motley collection of tents. Thanking the driver he approached the largest and entered. Inside was the usual commotion that went with a hastily constructed base, numerous people trying to make sense from chaos, and all totally ignoring the intruder. They had enough problems of their own without taking on someone else's. Edgar looked round for somebody of a lesser rank than himself. This would be one of the few occasions when the chain of command would be useful. Spying a mere corporal he stepped up to the unfortunate and attracted his attention. The man turned irately then noticed the sergeant's stripes. "Can I help you Sarg?"

"Who do I report to?"

"The General's at the front at the moment but the Captain's over there?"

"He'll do."

Edgar strode across the muddy floor of the tent, stood to attention and saluted. "I've been told to report here, Sir."

The officer looked at him with a weary expression then took the proffered papers. After a quick glance he said, "Out of the tent and turn left. Three tents down is where your lot are based."

As Edgar left he was still wondering who 'your lot' were exactly. He trudged through the mud, cursing the typically wet weather, it was summer after all.

He found the correct tent and entered. Inside was a standard communications set-up, a small table and a rather scruffy looking individual smoking a foul smelling cigarette.

Removing it from his lips the man looked him up and down then mumbled, "Bonjour."

"Ey up, mate," replied Edgar, a feeling of satisfaction at the man's look of blankness. "Two can play that game," he thought, "your French or my Yorkshire, both equally incomprehensible." Then he continued, "I'm the wireless operator."

At this the stranger's expression brightened and he continued in thickly accented English, "Glad you've arrived. I'm Pierre, Free French, a sergeant like yourself." he fished in a pocket and produced a battered packet of Gauloise.

"No thanks, I don't like smoking old slippers soaked in garlic." He received a Gallic shrug of the shoulders. Turning to the set, "I'll get organised then start transmitting. Are the messages ready?"

"Not yet."

Edgar was taken aback, he thought, having been hurried across on the MTB, this was an urgent, rush-job. "What's the problem?"

The Frenchman waved a nonchalant hand in the general direction of the distant gunfire from heavy artillery. "That is, my agents can't get through at the moment."

"My departure was a bit hasty, what exactly am I doing here?"

Pierre squinted as the upwards curling smoke drifted into his eyes then replied, "Saving lots of lives. The Germans have mounted their V2s on large trailers that they can move about quickly. My men are locating the rockets and bringing me the co-ordinates then you send them to England. Once you know their position they make easy targets for your bombers."

"Why not just transmit directly?"

"We tried but took too many losses, the transmissions were slow and easy to locate. It is better for us this way."

Edgar stared open-mouthed at this revelation. He was risking his neck just to make life easier for these garlic-eating Frenchmen.

A couple of hours later Edgar was disturbed by a commotion outside his tent including several loud voices speaking French. His companion listened for a few seconds then rushed outside, closely followed by Edgar. A bedraggled and disreputable group were gathered in the centre of the cluster of tents and Pierre was going round shaking each of them by the hand then crushing them in an embrace. Off to one side was a smaller group of three, one standing, one squatting and one sitting on the ground, hugging a blood soaked arm.

Captain Leigh looked up from where he had been examining the wound. "Hi Edgar." He peered intently round the tents. "Which one is yours?" When a dumbfounded Edgar indicated he marched off.

Chapter 60

The next few weeks settled into rhythm, every few days the camp would be dismantled, they all climbed into trucks and moved a few miles deeper into France.

Abruptly it all came to an end, the Allies had finally broken through and the Germans were in retreat. Edgar received a message saying his work was done and to hitch a lift back to the coast where he would disembark on a Corvette that was arriving in two days. Shortly afterwards he was back in England.

"Where have you been this time?" demanded Jimmy when Edgar wearily entered the billet at Eaton Square.

In reply Edgar delved into his pack and produced a long garlic sausage, a baguette and a bottle of brandy. "Nuff said?" he inquired and received a nod in return.

"So you'll be ready for a proper pint then."

"Lead on Macduff."

Sitting round a small table in the nearest pub Jimmy brought Edgar up to date, the CO had started ranting about Edgar's continuing absence, phoning the regimental headquarters until one day a very hard looking colonel had arrived and taken him to one side. Edgar nodded, acknowledging he knew who they were talking about. "Anyway," continued Jimmy, "after that he didn't say another word."

"I'm not surprised," replied Edgar, "he's not someone to argue with. What else, how are you making out with Debs?"

Jimmy paused, "Fine, we get along well." Edgar realised there was more to this than his friend was letting on and gave him a hard stare. "It's a bit complicated, she's related to all sorts of theatrical people, top people, but she has seen too many relationships fall apart so she doesn't like me performing. It's alright for a hobby but not as a career. It's difficult."

"Not really mate, to me it seems a simple decision, a gorgeous lady or a dodgy job, never knowing where the next money is coming from. Stick with the day job, the war will be over soon and you can go back to the GPO. You can still play for fun and beer if you want to, I don't suppose she'll object to that, but you'll both be happy and have a future together."

"Thanks, I knew you'd put me straight."

"Too true, mate, too true."

Work in the communications room continued at a hectic pace as the allies advanced until one day a huge volume of very short messages shot around.

"Something's up," stated Edgar when he met Jimmy for a short break. "I wouldn't be surprised if the war is over."

Sure enough a few days later the official announcement was made that Germany had surrendered and the war in Europe was at an end. That night saw the largest party in history, every single inhabitant of London appeared to be out on the streets celebrating. The next morning Edgar and Jimmy carefully made their way down the steps, both nursing sore heads.

"Well, soon we'll both be on our way back home, civilians again," stated Jimmy. "Mind in some ways I'll miss it, especially the opportunities to make spare cash. Will you go back to Rotherham?"

Edgar considered this question, what was there for him now? He could return to his job at the GPO but after his adventures would it seem too tame and also what about Ann? Rotherham was a small place, he was guaranteed to bump into her at some point, then what? "Not certain, mate, perhaps I'll stay on for a bit."

Ey Up Adolf

"What, in the army?"

Edgar had meant in London, the idea of remaining in the army had not occurred to him. "Maybe."

Section X had slowed dramatically since the announcement of cessation of hostilities. Edgar wondered if the people he had met had survived, Captain Leigh, Nada, Javor, Nicholas Ridiculous and more recently Pierre. He certainly hoped so.

"Sergeant Stanton," came the CO's voice.

"Now what," mumbled Edgar. "It could be we were a few minutes late for duty this morning but then so was the entire population of the country. Mind it would be typical, officious twit right until the end."

"I have received a message from Corps headquarters, we are sending a unit to the Far East, India, to set up an additional base to handle communications out there. The war here is finished but there is still the matter of the Japanese. It has been suggested you might like to go." Edgar's first thought was who had recommended him and what murky business would he be involved in, but if the CO knew about it then it must be kosher. "You would be promoted to sergeant major and extra pay of course," the CO continued.

"Well it will put off making any decision about what to do," Edgar thought. "Yes Sir, I'll go."

"Good, you embark from Portsmouth on the 15th July."

*   *

John sat in the sunshine looking out at the line of Lancasters. He had been asked to stay on in the RAF, take a commission, become an officer then train the next generation of navigators. He had thought about it for all of two seconds. Ann would never go for the idea, leaving her family in Rotherham and living on a succession of bases all over the world. Politely he had refused, he would return to the hard, manual work in the

Neil Whyke

iron foundry, putting up with the steam, the dust and the danger to be with his new bride.

*   *

His shift having ended Edgar wandered down Whitehall, lost in his own thoughts. Had he made the correct decision, what would be waiting for him in India? Jimmy had obviously not taken up the offer and was planning to settle down with Debs and now Edgar was having second thoughts, would it be the same without his best friend?

*   *

The troop ship was steaming through the azure sea, the sun beating down on the soldiers sitting about on deck playing cards, reading or merely dozing when the tannoy suddenly burst into life. "This is the Captain. We have just received some momentous news. The American airforce dropped an atomic bomb on two Japanese cities, totally destroying them."

As he took a breath the man next to Edgar muttered, "I'm surprised they managed to hit the right country, knowing the Yanks."

The tannoy continued, "As a result the Japanese government has surrendered. The war is finally over."

The last few words were almost drowned out by the tumultuous barrage of cheers that rang round the boat. Everywhere soldiers were on their feet, slapping each other on the back, shaking hands and jumping up and down. One short, plump squaddie took off his helmet, looked at it then threw it high in the air, watching it arc over the rail and plop down in the ocean where it bobbed up and down like a small dinghy. A second and third followed then suddenly the air was filled with a storm of helmets like a swarm of bees. As the ship

Ey Up Adolf

sailed on it left behind a veritable armada of floating metal that slowly dispersed in the wake, until finally the last one disappeared from sight to the strains of Rule Britannia and Roll Out The Barrel from the massed choir of servicemen on deck.

Edgar stood by the rail and watched. "So now what?" he wondered.

Lightning Source UK Ltd.
Milton Keynes UK
177328UK00001B/1/P

LIVING & WORKING

in San Francisco

FRANCES GENDLIN

·K·U·P·E·R·A·R·D·

In the same series

Argentina	Egypt	Korea	Spain
Australia	Finland	Laos	Sri Lanka
Austria	France	Malaysia	Sweden
Bolivia	Germany	Mauritius	Switzerland
Borneo	Greece	Mexico	Syria
Britain	Hong Kong	Morocco	Taiwan
Burma	Hungary	Myanmar	Thailand
California	India	Nepal	Turkey
Canada	Indonesia	Netherlands	UAE
Chile	Iran	Norway	Ukraine
China	Ireland	Pakistan	USA
Cuba	Israel	Philippines	USA—The South
Czech Republic	Italy	Singapore	Venezuela
Denmark	Japan	South Africa	Vietnam

A Student's Guide
A Traveller's Medical Guide
Living & Working in Barcelona
Living & Working in Chicago
Living & Working in Havana
Living & Working in Jakarta
Living & Working in Kuala Lumpur, Malaysia
Living & Working in London
Living & Working in New York
Living & Working in Paris
Living & Working in Rome
Living & Working in San Francisco

Living and Working Abroad—
  A Practical Guide
Living and Working Abroad—
  A Parent's Guide
Living and Working Abroad—
  A Wife's Guide

Living & Working in San Francisco
First published in Great Britain 2001 by
Kuperard
311 Ballards Lane, Finchley, London N12 8LY
Tel: 020 8446 2440 Fax: 020 8446 2441
Email: kuperard@bravo.clara.net

Kuperard is an imprint of Bravo Ltd.
All rights reserved. No part of this publication may
be reproduced, stored in a retrieval system, or
transmitted, in any form or by any means, electronic,
mechanical, photocopying, recording or otherwise,
without the prior permission of the copyright owner.

© 2001 Frances Gendlin

Illustrations by TRIGG

Printed in Singapore

ISBN 1-85733-243-1

CONTENTS

Acknowledgments and Notes 6

Introduction 8
The city 8; Getting settled 11; A closer look 12; Poking fun 14; Gays in the city 15; Familiar problems 16

1 **The City by the Bay** 19
Then 19; And now 21; Climate 22; Earthquakes 23; Cable car 24; Thinking about place 25; North of Market 27; Two hills and a valley 35; West of Van Ness 38; Moving south 40; South of Market 42; The Castro and Noe Valley 47; The mountainous center 50; The Haight and 9th Avenue 52; The avenues 53; The southwest 55; The southeast 56

2 **Around the Bay** 59
Suburban living 59; East Bay 61; North Bay 63; South Bay 65; The peninsula 66

3 **Housing: Problems and Solutions** 68
Situation 68; Rent control 70; Thinking about rent 71; Search 72; Apartment 74; Short-term rentals 75; Apartment complexes 77; Purchasing a home 79; Starting the search 80; Thinking about price 83; Student housing 84; Roommates 84; Retirement living 85

4 **Logistics of Settling In** 86
General information 86; Electricity hookup 86; Telephone service 87; Telephone books 88; Television and radio reception 88; Accessing the Internet 89; Mail delivery 89; Trash collection 90; Earthquake insurance 90; Opening a bank account 90; Finding a laundry 91; Getting your hair cut 92; Reading a newspaper 93; Foreign publications 94; Finding your spiritual home 95; Gay and lesbian worship 97; Registering to vote 97; Storage lockers 97

5 **Formalities for Foreigners** 99
Immigration 99; Visas 101; Employment-based visas 101; NAFTA 103; Student visas and permits 103; Diversity Immigrant Program 105; Petition by a relative 107; Citizenship 107; INS in San Francisco 108; Foreign consulates 108; Bringing belongings, appliances, car, pets, money, medications 109

6 **Bringing the Children** *113*
Great for the kids 113; Thinking about schools 114; Public schools 117; For non-native English speakers 119; Charter schools 119; The Open Enrollment Request 121; Public school registration requirements 121; Preschools 122; Private schools 124; Regulation/Accreditation 125; Types of private schools 125; Admissions process 127; After-school programs 127; Child care 128; Educational entertainment 129; Recreation and Parks Department 130

7 **Options for Study** *132*
Opportunities galore 132; English language schools 133; State-wide education systems 134; University of California 134; California State University 135; City College 135; Private universities 135; Specialized and technical schools 136; Extended education 137; Courses for seniors 138; Libraries 138

8 **Staying Healthy** *140*
Medical care in SF 140; Health insurance 140; Emergency services 142; Pharmacies 143; Women's health 144; Alternative medicine 145; Free clinics 146; Dentists 147; HIV/AIDS 148

9 **Work and Business on the Pacific Rim** *149*
Job search 151; Career help 152; Employment agencies 153; Starting a business 154; Business setup advice 155; Networking 156; Office space 158; Temporary/shared office space 159

10 **Up and Down the Hills** *161*
Understanding the city 161; Thinking about transport 162; Walking 163; Bicycling 164; MUNI 164; Cable cars 165; BART 166; Commuter transit 168; Taxis 169; Driving in the city 170; Parking problem 172; Driver's licenses 174; DUI 175; Registering your car 175; Automobile insurance 175; Purchasing a car 176; Handicapped access 177; Call of nature 177

11 **Gastronomic Delights** *178*
San Francisco—the best? 178; Attitude of San Franciscans 179; Resources 181; Reserving a table 183; Opening times 185; Menu 185; What will it cost? 186; Paying the bill 187; Smoking 187; San Francisco's own 188; California Cuisine 189; The old 190; The new 191; The basic 192; Fish 193; Vegetarian and kosher 194; Latin American 196; Italian 197; Pizza 198, Grabbing a bite 199; Weekend breakfast 201; Coffeehouses 202; Ice cream 204

12 **Eating Out in Asia** *205*
    An Asian town 205; First, the Chinese 206; Differing cuisines 207; Dim sum 211; Japanese cuisine 212; Southeast Asian cuisines 213; Pan-Asian 215

13 **Exploring the Markets** *216*
    Outdoor markets 216; Supermarkets 218; Health food supermarkets 219; Discount supermarkets 219; Shopping from home 220; Shopping in Asia 220; Small ethnic groceries 223; Bakeries 224; Cheese 226; Fish 226; Meats and poultry 228; Kosher meat 229; Coffee beans 229; Eating out at home 230

14 **Watering Holes** *232*
    Fruit of the vine 232; Exploring wine country 233; Trying wines 235; Purchasing wine 236; The wine label 237; Brew pubs 238; The bar 239; Drinking age 242

15 **The Sporting Life** *243*
    All year 'round 243; Resources 244; Spectator sports 244; Baseball 244; Football 245; Soccer 245; Basketball 245; Horse racing 245; Walking 246; Running 246; Enjoying nature 247; Farther afield 249; Bicycling 250; Inline skating 251; Multi-sport fitness clubs 252; Gyms 253; Tennis 254; Swimming 254; Other water sports 256; Golf 258; Skiing 259; Other sports 260; Spas 262; Dogs 263

16 **Shopping At Your Door** *264*
    All day, every day 264; Where to shop 265; Prices and paying 267; Shopping centers 268; Clothing 270; Beyond the city 272; Children's clothing and equipment 273; Toys 274; Sports clothing and gear 275; Setting up house 276; Furniture 278; Furniture rental 279; House plants 280; Filling your bookcase 280; Foreign language bookstores 282; Computers 283

17 **The Entertainment Scene** *284*
    The city that knows how 284; Infinite resources 285; Getting tickets 287; Museums 288; Theater 289; Classical music 290; Dinner with music 293; Rock concerts 294; Blues 295; Jazz 295; Dance 296; Films 297; Interesting and unusual 297; Foreign films 298; Prices and bargains 298; Film festivals 299; Comedy clubs 300; Gay and lesbian resources 300; For men 301; For women 302; Calendar of national holidays and local events 302

The Author *308*

Index *309*

ACKNOWLEDGMENTS AND NOTES

San Franciscans, as you will come to understand, are an opinionated lot. My friends and colleagues, many of whom have lived in the city as long as I have, gave me helpful suggestions for material to be included in this book, and they will no doubt either be gratified or disappointed upon reading it. Nonetheless, I thank them all, for I truly did appreciate their comments, their willingness to try new restaurants with me, to drive around neighborhoods in the far reaches of the city, to participate with me in my musings about what makes San Francisco tick, and to read early versions of chapters that I hoped would interest them. In these regards, thanks especially to Fred Allardyce, Eleanor Burke, Helen Cohn, Jean Coyner, Robert Domush, Connie Easterly, Jaem Heath-O'Ryan, Allan Jacobs, Edith Jenkins, Faye Jones, James Keough, Sarah Keough, Andy Leakakos, Peter Linenthal, Ann Magennis, Ronda Nasuti, Les Plack, Candida Quinn, Ken Rosselot, Newby Schweitzer, Linda Sparrowe, Patricia Unterman, Al Williams, and John Zaugg.

Regardless of all our efforts, there may be a mistake here and there concerning a business that might no longer exist, or perhaps a neighborhood that has changed almost overnight. If there are any such errors, they are, of course, mine alone. Some things are sure, however. There is an old joke among chauvinistic San Franciscans, that "one of these days there will be a big earthquake here, and the rest of the country will fall into the sea." But as of the book's publication, at least, the city was intact: the "big one" had not hit and San Francisco and the rest of the continent were still firmly attached. In addition, all the establishments mentioned in the book were going concerns as of this writing, but since San Francisco thrives on change, don't be surprised when looking for a particular address if something newer, more trendy, more crowded, and even more expensive has replaced what once was.

In terms of format, note that important places, organizations, and other entities are shown in **bold face** where they are first described. The few foreign words are in *italics*, but not those that have entered the standard American vocabulary—sushi, for instance. Readers may be surprised to find some spelling inconsistencies and should understand that this has more to do with the current American psyche than a malfunction of the word processor. Although our American ancestors rebelled against the British and forged their own language and spelling of certain words—theater and center, for example—some current Americans seem to find British spelling more elegant. Thus there will appear here a shopping *centre* or two and a *theatre* or two amid the centers and theaters, but no matter how spelled, they are American in every important regard. The same holds true for the word cafe, which is American, but which may variously be spelled *caffè* or *café*, depending on the nationality or whim of the owner of the establishment.

Note that where services or shops will be sought out owing to their location (*e.g.* bakeries), they are listed by the neighborhood closest to them; where the services might be needed no matter where they happen to be (*e.g.* churches), they are listed alphabetically or by category. Also, Internet addresses have been included for information that readers might reasonably want to access online—such as housing options, visa formalities, business advice—but not for every Internet address in this totally cyber-friendly city.

Last, the area code for all telephone numbers in this book is 415 unless indicated otherwise.

INTRODUCTION

I have always been rather better treated in San Francisco than I actually deserved.
— Mark Twain

THE CITY

Welcome to San Francisco, certainly the most open city in the United States, and probably the most tolerant. Here is a city where you can not only openly *be* who you are, you can also try out whatever it is you *want* to be. Just about anything goes, whether you've come to make a fortune or to squander one, whether you've decided to join the established culture or any one of the myriad counter-cultures that call San Francisco home. Some nicknames this freewheeling city has acquired over its two-century history can begin to provide some clues: "The Barbary Coast" during the 1850s, when the rowdy behavior of gold miners recalled the old-time Barbary pirates, to the current, exotic "Baghdad by the Bay." Yet the city for its residents is much more than these appellations would indicate, and other nicknames demonstrate their pride: "The City That Knows How," "The City by the Bay," or as some residents sometimes call it, just "The City," as though it were the only one—as for many residents it is. One nickname it does not ever have—at least for locals—is Frisco. Don't call the city Frisco.

About 16 million visitors a year come to "everyone's favorite city." You might think the reasons obvious: San Francisco is the most beautiful—ravishing—cosmopolitan city in the United States, with clean air, sparkling water on three sides, steep hills rising in the middle of the city, and breathtaking views. Quaint cable cars clang up and down the hills, and exotic aromas waft through the streets. People are outgoing and friendly. And when the sun shines and the sky is bright blue, it feels as though there is no other city in the world where you would want to be. But although beauty and charm stretch far, they do not tell the entire story. The deeper story unfolds as you come to understand the city and its residents, as time goes on.

Some of San Francisco's substance, of course, is in plain view. Perched on the Pacific Rim, the city is home to some of the most important banks and trade institutions in the country. It is the northern focus of Silicon Valley—an area that may not appear on any map, but which nonetheless commands most of the world's high technology development and trade. It is a major port for passenger cruises. It has an outstanding opera company, symphony orchestra, and ballet, plus impressive art museums and galleries. It has excellent universities, hospitals, and research institutions. It has a glorious climate and beautiful parks and promenades from which to enjoy it. And it has some of the best restaurants in the country.

Introduction

The Golden Gate, discovered in 1769 by Spanish soldiers, now spanned by the famous Golden Gate Bridge.

You will find all this in a tourist guide book, and you should keep one handy at first. Such guides describe the city and its unique attractions in detail, review restaurants, and suggest hotels of all categories. Each tries to present the material in an eye-catching manner, and each has its own approach to capturing the spirit of this enchanting city by the sea. All, however, have one thing in common: they are designed for people visiting for a short while — those visitors who think that what they see in a week is what the city is all about.

The truth is that you need to dig a little deeper to see what makes this city hum and to understand why *Money* magazine in 1999 rated San Francisco as the best city in the country to live in. Certainly, many of the things you've heard about Baghdad by the Bay do ring somewhat true. Definitely it is charming at its core, and it is also always vibrant, ever pushing toward the future. And its beauty goes far. That Tony Bennett has sung to the world "I left my heart in San Francisco" is no mistake. But it is also odd, offbeat, perhaps even outrageous in some ways, and its outright iconoclasm contributes a great deal to its delicious mystique. When you begin to understand the city's acceptance of the unusual and its constant search for any next frontier, you'll realize that it wholeheartedly embraces the new, which should be important to you as you settle in.

GETTING SETTLED

First, you need to get to know your new home. This book, thus, starts where tourism ends and is designed to offer advice and assistance in understanding daily life in San Francisco. Whether your stay is for a month or two or a year or two, the type of information you need for a successful stay is different—deeper and more detailed than that found in tourist guides. How to choose a neighborhood that suits you, how to cope with the difficulties of finding affordable housing or the right school for your children, how best to get up and down the hills or commute in from other towns, how to find out what's going on, and where to find the most interesting markets and shops are just a few examples of basic information that should help you move comfortably onto the San Francisco scene.

With the basics out of the way, you can then meet your neighbors, not as a tourist but as someone who has settled in. Tourists compare San Francisco with their own city and others they have seen, saying, "San Francisco is so European," or "so Asian," or "it's not like home at all." All those things are partly true, yet it *is* like home, because it *is* home to 750,000 San Franciscans—of all ethnic backgrounds, religions, political persuasions, and sexual preferences—who have created a city in their image. San Franciscans, whoever they have decided to be, are in love with their city, adore its views (visual, political, and social), appreciate its eclectic population, and in general are convinced they live in the best, most exotic city in the United States, if not the world. And, sometimes tediously, they never stop telling everybody so.

A CLOSER LOOK

One way to look at San Francisco is to understand that it is a city of minorities, for no ethnic, religious, or societal group represents more than 50% of the population. Of the 750,000 people who live in the city, there are some 185,000 Asians, 60,000 Latinos, sizeable populations of Russians, Italians, and African Americans, and throughout all these ethnic groups, some 175,000 gays and lesbians. This leads tourist guides to devote separate sections to Chinatown, Japantown, the Mission, or the Castro, describing them to people passing through. But in a guide designed for people moving to San Francisco, no such delineation would help you understand how the city works, for these areas and their peoples are each just a part of the overall scene. Part of what makes San Francisco so interesting is that each separate community is open enough that anyone can feel welcome, but closed enough not to lose its sense of place.

San Francisco, with all its idiosyncrasies, remains a town to take seriously, and people coming for the lifestyle soon find out that "everyday life" rules: if San Franciscans are known for playing hard, they work hard, too. In the soaring office buildings of the Financial District and in the funky warehouses of Multimedia Gulch, workers earn salaries that, on average, are among the highest in the country; more than half of the city's residents hold college or professional degrees. Locals spend their dollars in almost 13,000 retail businesses and eat out in more than 3,500 restaurants, all of which must appeal to a population that demands creativity and excellence—and something ever new to tickle its changing fancy. Even the municipality itself has done its best to make its urban life attractive and rewarding. Where other cities have seen their downtowns collapse as people fled to the suburbs, San Francisco has conscientiously upgraded its own with the Moscone Convention Center, Yerba Buena Gardens, Museum of Modern Art, the light rail system, the refurbished waterfront, and the downtown baseball park.

Businesses that manage to capture the changing, eclectic tastes of San Franciscans tend to succeed. Yet those that do not often see failure as an opportunity to start again, to reinvent themselves with a different—even more novel—approach. The city has always been known for its creative energy, and, since Gold Rush times, for risk taking. If San Francisco is on the cutting edge of technology and finance now, think back to 1853 when Levi Strauss came to San Francisco to work with his brother-in-law. By 1871, they had received a patent for securing the seams of their duck twill work pants with copper saddlebag rivets. Now the headquarters of the multi-million dollar Levi Strauss & Company sits in its own lovely green park along the Embarcadero, and the company provides some 2,000 people with work.

On the other hand, there is a lot not to take seriously in The City by the Bay: the attitude that makes living here downright fun. This book also describes the area's myriad sporting opportunities, the varying Chinese cuisines, and some cultural—and decidedly non-cultural—events. What it cannot impart in detail—but you'll soon find out for yourself—is how the lighthearted and mischievous nature of the city's population contributes to the whole. If Americans have found that it's easier to get along together by avoiding talk of politics, sex, and religion—San Francisco doesn't agree.

Where else would you find the citizens of a city irreverently twitting their rather imperial mayor Willie Brown by referring to him as "His Williness?" Where else would you find a group of gay men forming an "order" of nuns, "The Sisters of Perpetual Indulgence," with one of those men — Sister Boom Boom — running for the Board of Supervisors, as "nun of the above?" (Some 23,000 voted for him, but not enough for him to win.) And where else would the electorate, countermanding the police department's prohibition, vote to allow a friendly policeman to carry a ventriloquist's dummy wearing a little police uniform on his beat? Stories like these abound and quickly go into the city's legends and lore.

POKING FUN

If some of the humor is not to your taste, just roll your eyes and shake your head, for San Francisco's enjoyment of the outrageous goes far back and it has encompassed all strata of the city's society. Take the case of one Joshua Abraham Norton. Having left San Francisco in the mid-1850s a financial failure, he returned just a few months later styling himself as "Emperor of the United States and Protector of Mexico." His proclamations were published in the newspapers, and he became the "darling of everybody in town." For twenty years Emperor Norton sported regal finery, was fed for free at various establishments around the city, and pontificated at corporation board meetings, and when he died in 1880, he was given a fittingly royal funeral, to which ten thousand of his "subjects" came.

More recently, when Tom Ammiano, a gay politician, was sworn in as President of the Board of Supervisors in 1999, his predecessor gave him a tiara and feathered scepter she had received at the beginning of her term, and declared him "queen of the realm." Acknowledging the change in the city's leadership and in societal tolerance, Ammiano responded by quoting from *The Wizard of Oz*, a movie favorite, "We're not in Kansas anymore."

GAYS IN THE CITY

In fact, San Francisco from its beginnings was a town of men: the priests and soldiers who adventured north to Alta California to settle the area two centuries ago, the Chinese fleeing famine who sailed the Pacific, and the adventurers who flocked to the California frontier in 1849 seeking gold. That the miners also sought booze and bawdy women convinced some moralists that the city should be punished, and after the 1906 earthquake they thought it had been. But a port city it was and it remained, welcoming more sailors after the opening of the Panama Canal in 1914 and ship workers through World War II. During the war, San Francisco was a military port of embarkation, where eagle-eyed officers mustered out men who were homosexual, many of whom then decided to stay. By the 1960s, when it was said that the 70,000 gays who lived here frequented "decadent" gay bars, national newspapers stereotyped the city as a haven for sexual deviates. Far from having the desired effect, the news spread throughout the country that this was a place for gays and other iconoclasts to feel at home.

Unfortunately, there's still occasional "gay bashing," despite the city's official stance on affording equal rights to domestic partners of any persuasion. Although other "hate crimes" occur from time to time, they are rare, for San Franciscans tend to get along together. That you can find a beautifully dressed society matron at the opera sitting just one row away from a Rastafarian sporting dreadlocks and wearing blue jeans isn't a paradox. That you can find a middle-aged straight couple eating dinner at Asia SF, a transvestite "gender illusion" bar, isn't unusual. That you can find the best martini in town at a bar in the seedy Inner Mission doesn't keep anyone away. And that a distinguished looking gentleman driving a Mercedes can order take-out ribs from a shack called Brother-in-Law's #2, in the problematical Western Addition, means only that he has good taste. (And no one cares that there is no Brother-in-Law's #1.) Since its beginnings, San Francisco has carried the country's vision of the "melting pot" where differing societal cultures and attitudes enrich the whole. What is different about San Francisco is that each mini-society in its own way embraces this vision and is—at least for the most part and on most days—proud of it.

FAMILIAR PROBLEMS

San Francisco, of course, has its problems. Although the city is often rated near the top of "quality of life" surveys, and its workers earn above the national average, the cost of living in the Bay Area also ranks among the highest in the country and is the highest in the state. This is owing to a lack of affordable housing, brought about by a shortage of housing in general and the willingness of newly wealthy cyberspace professionals to pay high rents and purchase prices. Housing in the Bay Area costs three to four times more than in most areas of the country, and rents run about double the national average. If this trend continues, some people are concerned that San Francisco may in the future become a city dominated by the interests of the rich.

Other top problems are a public transport system that too often does not transport very well and, as in other major urban areas, too many homeless people on the streets. A succession of mayoral candidates has used homelessness as a campaign issue, and those elected come into office with big plans, only to find that, without being able to address the causes of homelessness, few "Band-Aid" solutions work. Mayors also set out to address the problems of transportation and parking, housing, and more serious crime, and occasionally it seems—at least temporarily—that some progress is being made.

San Francisco also has its true undesirable elements, its occasional robberies and muggings. Yet women need take only the usual precautions of staying on well-traveled streets and jogging in the parks with friends on designated paths and in daylight hours. And there should be no reason at all for anyone to enter the Tenderloin alone at night—that area between Union Square and the Civic Center that might in other cities be termed "skid row"— or Hunters Point to the south. Some other neighborhoods that are trendy in some spots—the Mission, Western Addition, Lower Haight—also have their pockets of disagreeable streets and attitudes.

Unlike some other cities, however, San Francisco copes— even triumphs—in its own unique way. The intensity San Franciscans bring to their lives translates into a civic activism that cuts through all levels of society. As Mayor Brown has said, "Here in San Francisco, you have 750,000 people, and each and every one of them is informed, interested, and has an opinion on everything." It is true. Residents volunteer at food banks that feed the homeless, at non-profit cultural institutions, for environmental and political causes, and at organizations for needy kids. They form groups to protest injustice and to call for reform. They insist volubly on better transport, more parking, and more affordable housing. They vote in higher percentages than in most other major cities, and if it appears that San Francisco is to the far side of "liberal," look at the issues and see that residents vote for the very things that make their city work: good social programs, preservation of cultural institutions, improvement of the downtown areas, and equality and tolerance for all.

Where else would all levels of society flock to an elegant restaurant on the Embarcadero (Delancey Street) that is staffed entirely by former drug addicts and felons who now are on their way back up? And where else would a Methodist church in the gritty Tenderloin (Glide Memorial) that feeds hundreds each day at its soup kitchen, also draw San Franciscans of all strata and religious beliefs on Sunday mornings to its rafter-raising, rocking, gospel message? This is San Francisco at its best.

Introduction

All in all, as you will shortly discover, San Francisco is—and isn't—just like any other city. This book should help you find that out as you begin to settle in. Scout out the neighborhoods it describes, stroll the outdoor markets, experiment with unfamiliar dishes in offbeat Asian eateries. Get to know your neighbors and your colleagues at work, for San Franciscans are welcoming folk. Volunteer in your community. Spend Sundays in one of the city's beautiful parks, go whale watching not far offshore, and find the view that best makes your own heart soar. San Francisco's Convention & Visitors Bureau says that the three commandments when visiting San Francisco are to "explore, experience, and enjoy." When you join long-time San Franciscans in following these "commandments," soon you too will understand what led the city's beloved writer Alice Adams to term San Francisco "the last lovely city." Welcome home.

— CHAPTER ONE —

THE CITY BY THE BAY

THEN ...

When the founding fathers of the United States were signing the Declaration of Independence in 1776, what is now San Francisco had only recently been discovered and was still wild lands and sand dunes as far as the eye could see. That people date this "discovery" to 1769 by Spanish soldiers looking for Monterey Bay of course doesn't take into account the thousand years the area had already been inhabited by the Miwok, Ohlones, and Wintuns, hunters and gatherers who were quickly subjugated by the intruders and then overcome by their diseases. The soldiers and missionaries coming to control and convert these native peoples very shortly did them in.

One wonders whether those Spanish soldiers were as awed by the beauty of their find as we are today. The sandy shoreline they took over was backed by soaring cliffs. Rocky hills were covered with live oaks and sweet-smelling grasses, and the ever-shifting sand dunes reached toward little inland marshes and streams, borne by the constant ocean breeze. But, as with the native peoples, even the bay we currently see, spectacular as it is, is not as the Spaniards found it, for some 40 percent has been filled in. Bay waters originally came as far as what is now Montgomery Street, lapping at Kearny Street, and the Marina was dredged only for the 1915 Panama-Pacific Exposition. By Francisco and Taylor Streets there once was a protected sandy cove called North Beach, but now all that remains is the name.

The Spanish named the area Yerba Buena, after those herbal grasses on the hills. By 1776, Juan Bautista de Anza and his contingent of 200 Spanish soldiers had established the Presidio, a military fort that commanded a strategic overlook of both ocean and bay, and it remained a base until just the last decade. By 1776, too, the priest Junipero Serra had founded the sixth of the Franciscan missions that stretched up the 600-mile Alta California coast, several years later dedicating what is now known as Mission Dolores, an adobe building which still stands.

Although the areas that are now the Mission District and the Presidio were the first to be settled, the original village of Yerba Buena was founded along the city's easternmost waterfront. Yerba Buena Plaza, now Portsmouth Square in Chinatown, was the heart of the village, which was first Spanish, then Mexican, and finally, in 1846, American. The town also rolled down the hill to the waterfront and today the old brick buildings on streets with names such as Balance Street and Gold Street still attest to their role during the Gold Rush, a century and a half ago.

It may be that only a few buildings remain, but the spirit of a city determined by the 1849 discovery of gold persists today. While thousands of adventurers seeking quick fortunes came to the Sierra foothills, clever merchants of all sorts readied their wares to take some of that fortune for themselves. Restaurants, bordellos, hotels and rooming houses, groceries, baths, and laundries almost exploded overnight around the Barbary Coast. Banks and financial services set themselves up toward Montgomery Street. Levi Strauss started producing his trousers. And a sleepy town that a short while before had counted only 500 residents, one newspaper, and one school became a city of 35,000 on the country's western edge. By the end of the century the city held ten times that number, and today, with the population having doubled once again, the frontier spirit holds—in the soaring steel and glass downtown office buildings, with this century's financial adventurers looking out, this time over the Pacific Rim.

San Francisco's colorful history may not be long—just over 200 years—and earthquakes and fires have taken their toll. But the city's background is still visible in some of its streets, and it is also evident in its residents' continuingly iconoclastic attitudes towards life, focusing on opportunities seen and grasped. Learn how these diverse factors have shaped, and continue to influence, the development of the city: for an excellent history of San Francisco, neighborhood by neighborhood and street by street, look for *San Francisco: The Ultimate Guide* by Randolph Delahanty, and for a detailed overall tourist guide, *Time Out: San Francisco*.

And Now ...

Today, the City of San Francisco makes up the entire San Francisco County, the most important of the nine counties comprising the Bay Area (see Chapter Two). Yet it is the smallest of the nine, and almost half of it is water, most of it San Francisco Bay. In fact, it is the smallest county in the state. Situated on about the same latitude as Tokyo and Washington D.C., the beautiful, hilly, wind-swept city sits at the top of a peninsula, and it encompasses 46.6 square miles, just seven miles across. Only since 1937 has the city been connected to the north and east by its two famous bridges, and ferries that have long brought people to the city still traverse the sparkling bay. The city itself swells like the ocean tides: each day it accommodates 200,000 workers who commute in from around the Bay, plus, over the course of a year, 16 million visitors—tourists and conventioneers—who filter through.

CLIMATE

Climate may be a general factor when choosing a place to live, but in San Francisco, and indeed in the extended Bay Area, there are so many microclimates that if weather is important to you you'll find what you want somewhere in the area, from warm and sunny to cool, windy, fog. As to San Francisco itself, surrounded on three sides by cold water and buffeted by strong ocean winds, its bracing, changeable climate makes some people joke that the city does have four seasons—they just take place in a single day.

To be simple about what is truly complex, the city's climate is determined by the ocean, by the 40 or so hills that break or conduct the ever-present wind, and by the long Central Valley that cuts down the middle of the state. When the Central Valley swelters in the summer and the hills are golden and dry, the hot air rises, as it must. This forces cold ocean air to whip through the natural opening of the Golden Gate and across the bay to cool the valley, but bringing to the city foggy days and brisk winds that move bitingly through the streets. Sometimes the fog burns off by late morning and early afternoons can be clear and warm. Other times, however, the fog hovers and doesn't move for days, leaving visitors surprised that they need a jacket in mid-summer and residents amused by the tourists in their shorts and tee shirts, hunched against the wind. Conversely, when the Central Valley cools off in September and October, San Francisco can have its sunniest summer days, perhaps even reaching about 90°F for a day or two. This is when diehard San Franciscans complain the most, bemoaning the absence of their beloved fog.

Winter itself is cool and damp, but not really cold. Although climate is changeable in San Francisco, as it seems to be everywhere, there has traditionally been a winter "rainy season" and a summer "dry season," but there is never a season of snow. Rains can be gentle or hard, but there are rarely thunderstorms, and usually part of each day is clear. With the city rarely seeing temperatures below freezing, flowers bloom outdoors in the winter, athletes play tennis in shorts and sweatshirts, office workers eat their sandwiches at outdoor tables, and people walk to work wearing light wool jackets—perhaps carrying an umbrella, just in case. On those rare occasions when a flake or two of snow does appear, so do the amazed telephone calls: "Did you see the snow?" People love snow, though, as long as it is in the Sierra, so they can head past the vivid green hills, up to the mountains to ski.

Within the city are about a half-dozen separate microclimates, depending on which side of which hill or valley you are looking at and the patterns of the winds. No matter where, however, the climate is bracing and the average annual temperature is about 55°F. Generally, the areas near the ocean are the foggiest and cool, as are the summits of the highest hills. Areas away from the ocean and on the lee sides of hills—the Mission, Noe Valley, and the Castro, for instance—are often sunny when other parts of the city are socked in, and in fact, these are the warmest parts of town, occasionally called "the banana belt." But if having four distinct seasons is important to you, or if you hate wind and fog—or earthquakes—perhaps one of the other counties around the Bay would be your best bet.

EARTHQUAKES

It's a fact one has to admit: San Francisco sits directly above the intersection of several of the earth's tectonic plates. Earthquakes regularly assault the entire Bay Area, owing to adjustments in the rifts of those tectonic plates: the famous San Andreas and Hayward faults, as well as the San Gregorio, Greenville, and Calaveras faults.

Two major tremblers, two "big ones," are still remembered with awe: the 1906 quake, registering 8.2 on the Richter scale, whose aftermath all but destroyed the city, and the lesser one in 1989, registering 6.9, which caused great damage and a restructuring of the downtown waterfront.

No matter how long people have lived here, everyone talks about the minor occasional quakes, and few people get used to the even rarer large seismic jolts. Despite nervous jokes about "waiting for the big one," the dangers earthquakes present do not seem to drive people away. All recently constructed apartment and office buildings in the city must be "earthquake-proof," which means they should sway during a quake, but not collapse. Nonetheless, earthquakes remain dangerous, and if they worry you, you might consider living away from the faults in one of the other counties of the Bay Area where the risk is perhaps somewhat less. Scientists are now saying there is a 70 percent chance of a major quake within the next 30 years, and although no one knows exactly when the next "big one" will come, everyone knows that it will.

But earthquakes, for better or worse, bring new beginnings. After the 1906 "big one" destroyed some 25,000 buildings in the eastern part of the city, a modern, well-planned city rose from the ashes, today's downtown districts. And after the 1989 Loma Prieta quake damaged the freeway that hid the city's waterfront, San Franciscans—who had always grumbled about tearing the eyesore down—voted to demolish it and to refurbish the five-mile strip, reclaiming it beautifully for their own. Now the Ferry Building and clock tower that withstood both "big ones" are visible at the foot of Market Street and can once again be a symbol of city pride.

THE CABLE CAR

Although an omnibus system of horse-drawn carriages was in operation in the city by 1851, the heavily laden horses could not climb the steep hills, whose summits remained out of reach as residences. Thus, the availability of efficient, mechanized public transportation—especially the cable car that tourists find so charming today—affected the development of the modern city as much as its climate and geology. In their heyday at the end of the 19th century, some 600 cable cars traversed more than 100 miles of tracks, bringing what had been distant or inaccessible areas of the city into easy commuting distance, transforming those daunting rocky summits—Nob Hill, Russian Hill—into areas of prime real estate. Although the poor had long trudged partway up those and other hills to their small cottages (enjoying the best views in town), the advent of the cable cars opened up the city in a way that nothing else had. The Castro, Diamond Heights, the Mission—all seen as distant from the city's commerce—were suddenly vital neighborhoods of their own. If these working class neighborhoods were not as fashionable as Nob Hill, Pacific Heights, or the then aristocratic residential Van Ness Boulevard, one hundred years later that is certainly no longer the case.

THINKING ABOUT PLACE

San Francisco is, by and large, a residential city. Its major businesses and largest banks cluster in the eastern portion that became the city's financial hub during the Gold Rush, and the rest—extremely diverse residential areas—maintain the local services and shops that residents of each area would expect. The city calls its widespread areas *districts*, and their names often reflect their history, such as the Mission or Cow Hollow. Yet the hills and their microclimates, and the lifestyle each area has molded, have created myriad little neighborhoods with names of their own, and it shouldn't be surprising that in such an individualistic city each area has its own character, often fiercely defended. Some of these neighborhoods may take more understanding than others, and some may display distinctly different characteristics even just from block to block, such as in the Mission or Western Addition. Many are charming and welcoming. Some are warm, sunny, and relaxed, some foggy, wind-swept, and brisk. Some are known for their social activism, some clearly defined by their ethnicity. Some are slightly more reasonably priced than others, but in any neighborhood worth considering, this will not last. And a very few are not worth considering at all.

Some San Franciscans regard the eastern part of the city as urbanized and progressive and the western parts as more suburban and conservative. It is true that although neighborhoods overlap and populations change as prices rise and older districts become gentrified, people still tend to be characterized by the districts they call home. This, however, is beginning to change. In fact, the ethnic and social population is diffuse, and the city's balanced cultural diversity constitutes a great part of its cosmopolitan charm. While Pacific Heights is known to be predominately wealthy Caucasian, the Castro gay, Chinatown Chinese, the Mission Latino, and the Western Addition African-American, in general there is a pleasing—and sometimes surprising—ethnic distribution throughout the city. Asians are now predominant in the area around Clement Street, and a diverse mix of San Franciscans is moving into the Mission, Bernal Heights, Potrero Hill, and the Haight—all areas where people have been taking advantage of the remaining reasonably priced housing—of course then driving prices up. In fact, young professionals with an abundance of discretionary dollars to spend on housing are moving into all the different neighborhoods, bringing life and color to those areas that were once uninspired, or, conversely, that were once considered only private enclaves of the rich.

As in any city, some districts are more open, beautiful, or well-kept than others. No matter where you live, however, you will have access to open space, whether it is the sandy strips that form the miles of ocean beaches or the beautiful concrete promenade that runs alongside the bay. If the eastern half of the city, destroyed in the 1906 earthquake, does not see as many leafy streets as its western counterpart, green squares and large landscaped plazas nonetheless pleasantly dot the area, allowing spectacular views of the nearby mountains and the often bright blue, almost iridescent, sky. Away from downtown, large parks, both sculpted and wild—Buena Vista, Glen Canyon, McClaren, and Harding—offer as many attractions, in their own ways, as the city's most famous, the Presidio and Golden Gate.

Each district, naturally, abuts at least one other. Sometimes there is a dividing boulevard or street or a hill, but sometimes just a subtle sense of change. In some areas, just one small street will mean the difference between an area you might consider for housing and one you would not. Although all the districts are given a broad look here, some mini-neighborhoods may not be mentioned, only partly for lack of space. Some are too small to describe and, given the overwhelming need for housing, some are in the process of change or rebirth; these may lose their longtime flavor to gentrification, or they may not, if residents of those areas have their way. In any case, change is what San Francisco is all about.

THE DISTRICTS

North of Market

Named after the pro-Union rallies held here during the Civil War, **Union Square** is San Francisco's downtown shopping and theater district. Although there are some pleasant rental apartments north of Geary and on the southern foothill of Nob Hill as it heads toward Polk, others may be shabby, and some may be too close to the seedy Tenderloin, which stretches out toward Polk Street. Nonetheless, reasonable rents are drawing a younger, student population that finds access to public transportation convenient.

A century ago this area that nestles around the 2.8 acre park was wealthy residential, but when the cable car made the steep hills more accessible, the wealthy moved up or out toward the new elegant residential district along Van Ness. Yet the high-quality shops and artisans that had served the residents stayed on when the neighborhood changed, and after the 1906 fire,

THE CITY BY THE BAY

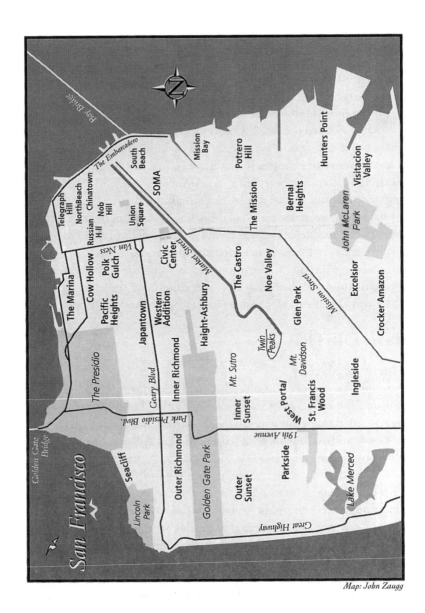

Map: John Zaugg

commerce moved back as soon as it could.

Today the pleasantly landscaped green square is ringed by luxury hotels and modern department stores; although most of the original shops are long gone, a few—such as Shreve's Jewelers—still exist. Hotels and theaters cluster near Geary, and chic restaurants that cater to both tourists and locals nestle in the side streets, along with small, interesting boutiques.

Until recently this vibrant downtown district stopped abruptly on the south at Market Street, but now it heads well across to what is known as SOMA (South of Market Area), embracing the Museum of Modern Art, the spectacular Yerba Buena Gardens entertainment complex, and the Moscone Convention Center. Restaurants and hotels are opening up, and this area is becoming more exciting day by day. To the west, however, Union Square is bordered by the Tenderloin, a seedy area of low rents and transient residents. New Asian immigrants, especially the Vietnamese, are bringing businesses and ethnic restaurants to this grubby area that stretches out toward the **Civic Center,** but improvement is slow.

Straddling Van Ness Boulevard, the Civic Center, with its beautiful Beaux Arts buildings, is the city's center for government and culture. It is interesting that almost a century after the 1906 fire destroyed it, the Van Ness corridor is once again becoming an upscale residential area, with its new condominiums, supermarket, multi-screen theater, and chic restaurants in all directions.

Stretching east to the Bay from Union Square is the **Financial District**, the "Wall Street of the West." As people hurry down the windy corridors of Montgomery and Sansome Streets, they probably don't think about the early days of San Francisco, when everything east of Kearny was mud flats, and the waters of the bay came up to what is now Montgomery Street. Having solidified its hold on the city's commerce during the Gold Rush, the Financial District (along with Los Angeles) is now the Western capital of the Pacific Rim, and some 300,000 people work here in about 50 million square feet of office space. The Financial District—with just a few steel-shell buildings remaining from before the 1906 earthquake—is home to almost all of the city's modern high-rise office buildings.

Here, however, the wind can whip through the concrete canyons, and here quite often is a "neighborhood" deserted when the corporate types go home after work. Some restaurants thrive on lunchtime customers and close early in the evenings (except in upbeat Belden Street), and a few close on weekends. But because so many people work in this area, it is filled with little treasures of restaurants and shops; the closer to Union Square, the more expensive they become. There are one or two mixed-use high-rise buildings—offices below, apartments above—but true residential districts are within easy walking distance in any direction except east.

To the west, **Nob Hill** is closest. Perhaps the best known of the city's hills, Nob Hill still houses some of San Francisco's wealth, but not in any of the palaces ostentatiously constructed at the end of the last century by San Francisco's "Mother Lode" and railroad tycoons. The opulent lifestyle that allowed for 50-room homes came to an end in 1906, and today only one old mansion remains, a private club whose facade allows us a glimpse at what once was.

Today, residents at the summit live in elegant apartment buildings, sharing the impressive views with Grace Cathedral and upmarket hotels. The little park in the middle holds a playground for the area's children, but except for this slight nod to residents of this expensive aerie, conveniences for daily living are found down the hill.

Until the end of the 19th century, Nob Hill was too steep for horse-drawn carriages, and it was workers who built little cottages along the lower slopes. But although cable cars allowed the tycoons to claim the summit, after the 1906 earthquake most rebuilt on safer terrain. Small frame apartment buildings began to appear, and these buildings—refurbished and modernized—remain

The summit of Nob Hill.

convenient today for people working in the Financial District or Chinatown. High-rises appeared at the summit in the fifties, but here, as in other areas, height limits were instituted, limiting the amount of skyline that could be blocked. Now there is a six-story limit on new construction, but that doesn't affect those fortunate few who are already there, enjoying the view.

The 1-California bus has made this steep hill convenient for Asians, as Chinatown expands up Clay and Sacramento from the east. On the west, low-rise apartment buildings line the narrow streets heading down to the Polk Gulch corridor. You probably won't find housing on the top of Nob Hill itself, although on its slopes apartments do come available.

Down Nob Hill to the north is **Chinatown**. You may not want to live here, but no discussion of San Francisco would be complete without a bow to this colorful, iconoclastic area that — the Mission and military Presidio aside — formed the original

The Chinatown Gate.

settlement of Yerba Buena and that in its own way dominates much of the spirit of the modern city.

Chinatown, until recently contained from Bush to Broadway, and from Kearny to Powell, now crosses over Broadway into North Beach and up Russian and Nob hills. The Chinese community has also expanded out to Clement Street and into the Sunset, but Chinatown remains home base, and no matter where people live, many come back on a Sunday for shopping and a family lunch. Although residents complain that their traditional area is becoming too homogeneous in its commercial effort to lure tourists, Chinatown is still a crowded warren of streets and alleys, of small Chinese-speaking shops and apartments above them, perhaps with an open window and laundry waving in the breeze. In fact, behind some of the shabby, unmarked doors in the little alleyways is where the most interesting—and quietly private—business of this sometimes secretive community takes place. The tantalizing aromas from the restaurants and the inexpensive markets crowded with elderly women carrying their grandchildren on their backs in cloth sacks also conspire to give Chinatown an air of other-worldliness.

Although only about half of the city's 150,000-strong Chinese population lives here, this 24-block area is one of the city's most densely populated districts. Its constant bustle is perhaps at least slightly reminiscent of the original Chinese quarter founded in the 1850s, when Cantonese immigrants flocked to these shores. During the Gold Rush they were cooks, launderers, and shopkeepers, even brothel keepers, and then workers on the railroad. By 1881, some 25,000 Chinese were resident in the city, and so many were coming to the United States that the Chinese Exclusion Act of 1882 was passed to stop the influx, meaning that until its repeal in 1943 the Chinese population became older—and poorer. Only in the post-World War II period did immigration begin once again and did the Chinese come again to Chinatown.

The main local shopping streets are to the north, on Stockton and Powell, which leaves Grant to the tourists looking for gifts. But the spiritual heart of the community is Portsmouth Square, which as Yerba Buena Plaza was originally only one street away from the shoreline. Until commerce moved south to Montgomery Street, this was the center of town, and it was at Yerba Buena Plaza that the discovery of gold was announced.

Rents in Chinatown are reasonable, but conditions may not be particularly agreeable. This is not the cleanest part of the city by any means, nor is there anything leafy green. Many of the area's renters are poor and elderly, speaking no English, and they often live in substandard housing without knowing the recourse to city agencies that could help them, exploited by landlords who have little incentive to make improvements to their holdings. Yet this is certainly the most exotic part of the city, and although you might easily enjoy living nearby—along the Embarcadero, up Russian Hill, or in North Beach—think carefully if Chinatown appeals. Chinatown is another planet, deep in the heart of San Francisco.

Down along the bay, as the working piers along the eastern edge of the city head north toward Pier 39 and Fisherman's Wharf, which draw 10 million tourists each year, the refurbished **North Embarcadero** becomes more pleasantly residential on its inland side. Long in decline, the area took on a new life in the 1960s, when an old produce market was demolished and warehouses were spruced up to hold offices, television studios, and art galleries. At Jackson Street, the Golden Gateway Center added more than one thousand apartments and townhouses, creating an instant neighborhood. Expensive though it is, the Golden Gateway is convenient to the massive four-building office, shopping, and restaurant complex of the Embarcadero Center—an extension of the nearby Financial District—which is almost a city in itself.

This flat land-filled area was once the Barbary Coast, its dance halls, boarding houses, and bawdy night life catering to the boisterous goldminers down from the hills. Now the surviving red brick buildings dating from the 1860s have been turned into antique shops and art galleries in an area called the Jackson Square Historic District, and with restaurants, cinemas, and theaters open late, the area is once again offering somewhat more sedate succor to those looking for fun.

There are several open plazas in this sunny area, in addition to the splendid promenade that runs along the bay. Sidney Walton Park, with its sculptures and fountain, brings office workers to its grassy knolls at lunchtime. Overlooking the park are the Golden Gateway Commons, spacious red brick condominiums built around private landscaped walkways. These town homes are sometimes rented out by their owners; when they come up for sale, the prices are extremely high.

Farther along, nestled below the eastern granite outcropping of Telegraph Hill, several condominium complexes bring quiet residentiality to an area that was enhanced by the construction of Levi Strauss Plaza, with its fountains, streams, and grassy lawns. Some of these condominiums along Lombard or Montgomery are rented out by owners and some come up for sale, and the prices are what one would expect. Unfortunately, as yet, there are few commercial services, and residents must head over to Bay Street or back toward Jackson for supermarkets and pharmacies. Up Telegraph Hill — on the sheer eastern side that no car can traverse — are the Filbert Street Steps, a landscaped walkway with charming clapboard cottages along lanes and terraces that might seem precarious, but that (at least so far) have survived earthquakes, rains, and whatever else the San Francisco climate (or politicians) might inflict.

Two Hills and a Valley

Over the top of the hill is **North Beach**, a sunny valley nestled between the western slope of **Telegraph Hill** and the eastern edges of **Russian Hill**. One hundred and fifty years ago there were a few docks and a little beach along the northern waterfront. Fishermen lived close by, some Basque and Portuguese, but primarily it was the Italians in what came to be called Little Italy who gave the area its flavor, one that still remains. Italian restaurants, coffee houses, bakeries, and delis draw the crowds, and old Italian-American gentlemen sit in the sun at Washington Square, the heart of the community, watching the passers-by. That this working class area of cheap rents was also home to the "beat" poets in the fifties brought a rather bohemian feel to the area, but prices today are no longer cheap. And the atmosphere has also changed: Chinese restaurants and groceries have crossed their erstwhile boundary at Broadway, and now along Stockton they compete noisily for attention, while in the early morning Washington Square is filled with Chinese practicing tai chi. The result is an agreeable mix, one that tourists and San Franciscans appreciate to their full. North Beach is one of the most treasured areas of the city.

As a residence, North Beach is popular with people who work in the Financial District, as it is only a 15-minute walk away. Reasonably priced low-rise apartments hover above interesting shops and restaurants. On the east, the quiet residential neighborhood of Telegraph Hill rises slowly, and as it does, many of the three- and four-story apartment buildings command excellent views. Long-term residents live in cottages or in old buildings that new arrivals would love to get their hands on to refurbish. Some do become available from time to time, and the prices vary, according to the view and the work needed. Not all of these buildings have garages, and finding parking on North Beach streets is always a challenge.

Heading up the winding road to Coit Tower, private homes of all sizes and apartment buildings command prices that are as steep as the hill; the hill is on bedrock and its buildings less liable to damage during earthquakes, and the views can be grand. The old beach itself may be gone, but beach town it remains: keep your windows open at night and you'll hear the sea lions barking at Pier 39 and the foghorn piercing through.

This holds true, too, for parts of steep Russian Hill, which climbs up from North Beach to the west. Its location couldn't be better. With trendy Polk Street on the west, North Beach to the east, Cow Hollow down past the western slope, and Chinatown to the south, Russian Hill is ringed by every convenience one could want. If the area took its name from the Russian seal hunters who 150 years ago were said to have buried their dead up here, the area is now very much alive.

People don't talk much about Russian Hill, and few tour buses labor up the hill—which suits the residents very well. The businesses here cater to locals, and in general this is a rather peaceful district with many enchanting pockets of almost-hidden charm. On Russian Hill, with its varied residential opportunities, you can probably find something you want. What everybody finds is a well-kept residential community with an active community

THE CITY BY THE BAY

The eastern side of Telegraph Hill is too steep for roads and cars.

association to keep it so. People may live in small apartments above neighborhood shops, in large buildings that push up against the fog, in luxurious condominiums on little landscaped lanes, or even in single-family homes—small, large, or enormous—that persist despite the desire of development to encroach. Some streets have Mediterranean villas or simple redwood homes, and some cul de sacs even have houses with gardens in front. Russian Hill seems to have it all.

West of Van Ness

Past North Beach and the commercial **Fisherman's Wharf** area, the exquisite, residential **Marina** sits on marshland dredged for the 1915 Panama Pacific Exposition celebrating the opening of the Panama Canal. If the Exposition was designed to show the world that the city was once again on its feet after the 1906 earthquake, the quake of 1989 that damaged so much of this landfill district showed how fragile that footing actually was. Nonetheless, defying nature's whims, most Marina residents decided to stay, rebuilt their homes and are today enjoying spectacular views of the Bay, the Golden Gate Bridge, and the distant hills—at least until the next "big one" hits.

Looking majestically out over the broad, grassy strip of Marina Green, a line of elegant Mediterranean-style private homes stands as entry to the peaceful, often fog-shrouded neighborhood within. Grand stucco houses, smaller homes, and gracious Art Deco apartment buildings that impose on broad, winding, windy streets are home to a smart set of young professionals—many singles but also some families—who enjoy the proximity to the Marina Green, the eucalyptus-fragrant Presidio, and also to Chestnut Street, the Marina's vibrant commercial and nightlife scene. The area here may be flat, but the rents are quite steep.

Across Chestnut and the broad, commercial Lombard Street, **Cow Hollow** bridges the Marina below to aristocratic Pacific Heights above. An area of tranquil dairy farms 150 years ago, the restaurants and nightspots of Union Street—from Franklin to Divisadero—are today a playground for the upscale singles crowd. Interesting apartments and homes line just about every street, and climbing the steep hill up to Pacific Heights, the houses along Green and Vallejo are generally Victorian. On Union Street itself, the old Victorians have been converted into offices and trendy shops.

Combined, the Marina and Cow Hollow are great areas for living and hanging out. It's hard to park in these areas, so if you're interested in living here, make sure of a garage for your car. Yet services, supermarkets, and shops are all within walking distance, and public transportation to the Financial District is so convenient that you may not need a car.

Just up the hill, **Pacific Heights** is the most expensive residential district in the city. In Pacific Heights, luxurious apartment buildings near Broadway and Fillmore quickly give way to beautiful single-family homes, and even these give way—as the broad streets head west toward Divisadero and Presidio—to the exquisite mansions of the truly rich. The tranquil, empty streets climb hills and dip into valleys, making the outer part of Pacific Heights a rather removed enclave, with little to disturb its serenity. Once seen as almost a suburb of San Francisco, in places the area does feel remote. Properties occasionally come on the market here, and the prices soar above the unbelievable.

Yet streets to the sides of Fillmore, although still decidedly Pacific Heights in character, see rental apartments nestled among large private homes. This area is less removed, more in touch, as residents are seen with their children at Alta Plaza or Lafayette Park, or walking dogs. Upper Fillmore Street itself, from Washington to Pine, is becoming trendier by the day, with restaurants, chic boutiques, an international cinema, a high-quality supermarket, and crowds of people strolling and browsing the shops.

An extension to the west, **Presidio Heights**, is perhaps slightly less aristocratic in demeanor than Pacific Heights, but the grand, well-landscaped houses lining Clay, Washington, and Jackson nonetheless offer extremely gracious living in the heart of the city, with tree-lined streets, few passers-by, and the security that a rather suburban lifestyle might provide. Proximity to shopping in Laurel Village and to the Sacramento/Presidio intersection make the area feel connected to city life, while the leafy Presidio and its edge of Mountain Lake Park make it feel less so. Apartment buildings ring the edges, but vacancies are rare and prices are high. The beautiful houses do come up for sale from time to time; they sell quickly and well.

Out beyond Arguello (technically the dividing line into the Inner Richmond) the atmosphere of wealthy tranquility continues on the avenues east of Lake, with large single-family homes, some of which are divided into flats. Certainly **Presidio Terrace** is one of the most exclusive and beautiful enclaves in the city.

Starting at California and reaching to Geary are the almost hidden, overlapping communities of **Laurel Heights** and **Jordan Park**, whose broad, clean streets are often swept by fog and wind. Quiet neighborhoods of apartments and private homes, they are rather underrated, except by those fortunate enough to live there.

Moving South

The **Western Addition** is one of the districts you should know well before you consider making it home. Although parts of it — near the Panhandle (a green belt leading to Golden Gate Park) or upcoming Hayes Valley, Alamo Square, or the Lower Haight — may offer pleasant homes and welcoming communities, the entire area is in transition and has always been so, in one way or another. Its image and population makeup change, but the area starting south of Geary, extending to the Panhandle, and centering between Fillmore and Divisadero has long been controversial, riddled by problems and perhaps only now on the way to some solution.

Originally **Japantown** (to the east of that great concrete swath called Geary Boulevard) was considered a part of this district, but now it has a character of its own. By the end of the 19th century, while the Chinese population was diminishing, the Japanese population increased. Many Japanese immigrants lived south of Market, but others moved out to the Western Addition, buying small houses and settling in the area they called *Nihonjimachi*, or "Japanese people's town." After the Chinese Exclusion Act, the Japanese bore the brunt of racism, setting the atmosphere for Order 9066, during that infamous period of World War II, when Japanese Americans were sent to "relocation centers," forcing them to abandon their homes.

By 1942, ship workers—many African Americans—found empty buildings and low rents. Ultimately the Western Addition became known as a "black neighborhood," and when the Japanese came back, most settled in the Richmond and the Sunset. Only a small percentage of the city's 12,000 Japanese lives in Japantown now, separated from the rest of the Western Addition by Geary's concrete. But the area is once again the central focus of the community: the 5-acre Japan Center shopping, cinema, and restaurant complex at Post and Fillmore draws people from all over, but *Nihonjimachi* remains firmly and locally Japanese.

Across Geary, the Western Addition was an area that had long been poised to go downhill. Fillmore Street near McAllister, the commercial center of town after the 1906 devastation, was more or less abandoned by 1912, when commerce moved back downtown. The lovely 1890s Victorians on Alamo Square—and just about all the others—went to seed. Eventually the area became known only for its shabby housing projects, dilapidated homes that lined the once-tranquil streets, and for crime and drugs, which it still has in some small pockets.

Finally, urban renewal stepped in, as did people looking for affordable homes. The Victorians on the once again chic (but not always tranquil) Alamo Square have been restored to their brightly colored glory. The development of a shopping center and several large modern apartment complexes just south of Geary are bringing more stability to the area, and people throughout are sprucing up apartments and single-family homes. Restaurants of all levels are becoming popular, and more services are moving in.

Some streets remain rough, but others are cleaning themselves up. On the eastern edge of the district, **Hayes Valley,** which was formerly known for crime-ridden housing projects and drugs, is a neighborhood that blossomed almost overnight after the demolition of the freeway that loomed over it. Now, stretching out to Octavia Street, it is home to little restaurants, boutiques, art galleries, and apartments that are being refurbished, and it is becoming both an extension of the Civic Center and a lively neighborhood in itself.

South of Market

South Beach, as the eastern edge South of Market is coming to be known, is an important area to watch. After the "big one" of 1906 destroyed what had been a wealthy residential district, South of Market was left to wither, becoming a seedy area of industry, shipyards, and cheap rooming houses; this atmosphere only increased during World War II with the influx of men who came to work in the yards. Now, however, modern entrepreneurs have found this frontier—starting at Mission Street and moving south past the old dockyard areas of Mission Rock and China Basin—and San Franciscans are once again moving back into the sun. The demolition of the freeway that obscured the view of the waterfront allowed the development of a spectacular promenade along the Bay, and this plus a new light-rail transportation network has made apartment living in this area both convenient and fun, a chic neighborhood that will soon take on a new life of its own.

Old warehouses are being converted into residential lofts or artisans' studios, and scruffy empty lots are being developed. Rental and condominium complexes now line the waterfront, with more to come. Prices vary wildly. The Rincon Center, once the main post office, has long been a moderately priced rental residential and commercial complex, but just a few streets away, the expensive condominium in the old Hills Brothers coffee factory sets a different tone, and new residential complexes—both rental and condominium—are not cheap. Although the new baseball stadium has brought trendy businesses in, currently there are few services for a residential population—no supermarket-pharmacy complex, for example—and some areas remain deserted at night. There is no doubt that this will change, as people increasingly flock to South Beach. Fueled by the influx of a new set of professionals to the area, those who have caused the area just a few streets inland around **South Park** to be referred to as Multimedia Gulch, this entire area is on the way up.

More is yet to come at **Mission Bay**, past China Basin and Pacific Bell Park, at a new development that is already beginning to retake a wasted industrial area between Potrero Hill and the bay. This sunny area that was long ago the hunting grounds for the native peoples will eventually hold some 6,000 homes, schools, parks, and stores, all anchored by a 43-acre campus of the University of California, San Francisco. It encompasses an area called **Central Waterfront** and is just beyond the Mission Creek community of houseboats, whose residents are fiercely protective of their neighborhood and have successfully sought legal protection so that they may stay.

Between Third and Fifth streets, in a reclaimed area now called **SOMA**, the huge Moscone Convention Center, the beautiful Yerba Buena Gardens, the Sony Metreon entertainment complex, and the Museum of Modern Art have become a southern extension of Union Square. Although these streets are always full of people, Fifth Street is currently a kind of boundary, as trendy South of Market disappears, and streets moving west toward South Van Ness are solidly commercial. Repair shops, wholesalers, light industry, and automobile garages line the uninspired streets, still solidly entrenched despite the steady encroachment of modern life. Factory outlet stores come and go, and several enormous discount chains — Costco, Office Max, Bed Bath and Beyond — have established their large centers here. Although there are popular nightspots here, some of the streets are unwelcoming after dark.

This holds true of the neighboring **Mission District**, where in several sections crime rates are high. This is one of the sections of town that you should understand well before choosing: some pockets of the Mission are charming and some will be charming soon, but others are not charming at all.

Yet this is where it all started, and where, after more than 200 years, it seems to be starting once again. Since the Spanish priests established their mission here in 1769 the area has maintained a Latin tone, and despite waves of other nationalities that have left their mark on the Mission, Latino it remains. Some 60,000 people currently live in the Mission, in a melting pot of races and nationalities, yet it is the 60 percent Latino population that gives the area its colorful, uninhibited flavor.

Mission Street, which centuries ago linked Mission Dolores to the port at Yerba Buena, is the city's longest; as it cuts to the southwest, it takes on the character of each surrounding neighborhood. Here it is a Latino main street, with businesses displaying their wares on the sidewalk, *taquerias* offering inexpensive meals, and neighborhood folk volubly carrying on an outdoor life. The 24th Street intersection is the heart of the *barrio*. Many of the side streets are uninspired, with three-story, bay-windowed flats and other low-rise apartments perched over the neighborhood stores. Although now in the process of a great change, this has long been — and still is — a poor, working class area. Some streets are noisier and dirtier than others, and occasionally there are turf battles between gangs of differing nationalities.

This wasn't always a poor neighborhood: toward the end of the 19th century, it was solidly middle class. Yet this was one area that did not benefit from the advent of the cable car, for when the hills became accessible, many people moved up. As industry developed near the waterfront, Irish, German, and Italian workers flocked to this sunny area from which they could walk to work. Although the area had been international for decades, what solidified it as Latino was the establishment of international fruit and coffee companies that dealt with Latin America. Many people think of the district as solely Mexican, yet from the early 20th century it has had a mix of Latin cultures. Unfortunately, despite the bilingual ballots and campaign materials, this neighborhood has traditionally voted less than many others, and its political clout has been low.

Now, however, the Mission has been rediscovered by San Franciscans, especially by cyberspace entrepreneurs, who see an area ripe for investment and for refurbishment of old, decaying houses. The Mission is a booming town.

Drive around the district and you will be convinced. Hundreds of restored large Victorians and small bungalows line side streets between Valencia and Guerrero. See well-maintained grassy Dolores with its Canary Palms, Fair Oaks with its Chinese elms, and streets such as Capp Street or Hill Street with Italianate Victorians on one side and Stick Victorians on the other. Here a few are already brightly restored, others no doubt soon will be. Chula Lane to Abbey Street is a cul-de-sac of Victorians as well. Crossing over Cesar Chavez, the Precita Park area that backs up on Bernal Heights Park is a community of small homes on short streets that is suburban in feel. These are all areas new home buyers are finding, and when you look around you'll see beautifully restored homes perching majestically over some that look as though they would fall over in the next breeze, and new apartment complexes rising in any inch of space.

Rents and purchase prices in the Mission may still be low in comparison to other parts of town, but they are quickly climbing. Chic non-Latin restaurants, hip bars, galleries, and charming boutiques are following the money, raising prices even more, especially around Inner Valencia, which in its current trendiness is now sometimes called Valencia Gulch. Some traditional businesses are being forced out by the rise in rents. In addition, the rent for a two-bedroom apartment may now approach $1,800, and this may ultimately mean a displacement of low-income families. But not yet, and the Mission remains a mixture of cultures like nothing else in the city, for better and for worse. Again, if this area appeals to you, make sure you understand it well.

East of the Mission, sunny **Potrero Hill** has traditionally been a working class district, removed from San Francisco's downtown more in spirit than in distance. Few early tourists braved the hill and the wind, and in fact, there was little to explore in what was a rather sedate, residential quarter settled by Scottish and Irish shipbuilders. Yet a few decades ago, as prices around the city escalated, this area became ripe for gentrification. Now artists and professionals, straight and gay couples, and young families are mixing pleasantly with old-timers in a neighborhood that is viewed as an easy commute to the Financial District and Multimedia Gulch. Houses here are in demand, especially those "fixer-uppers" that then increase in value, although people who come to live on Potrero Hill tend to stay. A rather iconoclastic ambience persists, but for how long?

Although industrial sites, furniture shops, and offbeat businesses dominate the northern flats, local commerce is clustered up and down the 18th Street hill. Residential areas that follow the hill's contours seem quiet, and lining the leafy streets are small clapboard houses, large spaces converted into lofts, multi-story Victorians, attached single-family homes, and apartment buildings—a pleasant mix that looks sunnily out over other parts of the city that may already be enveloped in fog. Potrero Hill is bordered on the east by several public housing projects, and their proximity to the hill has contributed over the years to robberies and auto break-ins. Yet, a new condominium complex is transforming the southern section near 24th and Wisconsin, and ongoing building and restorations are making this area increasingly attractive. Potrero Hill is the kind of neighborhood for which its residents swear they would never live anywhere else.

There are no supermarkets or banks on the hill, but the Potrero Center down on the flat at Potrero Boulevard is becoming a neighborhood hangout. Multimedia Gulch is quickly expanding out here, and its proximity to the Mission makes some people call it Baja Mission; but except for the hilly Utah Street with its little houses, this area is not residential—yet. What much of it is, at least today, is a superficially arid stretch of warehouses and old buildings—that inside house some of the city's newest restaurants and breweries, avant-garde theaters, and multimedia businesses. It will be interesting over the years to see which of the districts claims it as its own.

The Castro and Noe Valley

Certainly no discussion of San Francisco would be complete without some understanding of the **Castro.** In San Francisco geography it is actually Eureka Valley, although no one calls it that any more. Originally part of a large ranch owned by José de Jesùs Noe, whose name remains on the next valley over, this colorful district that begins around Market and 16th Street, and climbs up the steep hill to its south, is known simply as the Castro, although little of the Castro is simple at all.

Until the end of the 19th century, this was one of those hilly areas that was seen as remote by San Francisco's elite, and so it remained rural and agricultural longer than its neighbors closer in. But when the cable car made the hill with its 18.4 percent grade habitable, real estate speculators laid out a grid of streets, built Victorian houses and peak-roofed cottages and sold them to the working class Irish, Scandinavians, and Germans, who created a traditional Catholic neighborhood—or so they thought.

Look at the Castro today. To outsiders it may look like the city's "gay ghetto," but to most San Franciscans it is much more than that. It truly is a small town with its own set of urban pleasures and problems, its local services and shops, its particular sense of what a community should be. Look at the bright, rainbow-colored flags waving from windows, and you will understand this community's pride. Both light-hearted and serious, this is a community that will no longer be anything but bold.

Some of the Irish population still lives in the warm, sunny Castro, but most moved away as the neighborhood changed, leaving the then-shabby Victorians their families had inhabited for almost a century. And the white-collar workers and professionals stepped in, refurbishing the houses, setting up shops. This is what gregarious Harvey Milk did in the seventies, and his subsequent rise in city politics and tragic assassination drew together what had been a rather disparate community, one that has stood its ground ever since. Do not underestimate its political clout; politicians now understand that, like everyone else, gays need public transportation, affordable housing, and reasonable zoning laws. Unlike everyone else, however, they often get out to vote as a bloc. Now, although gays—like all San Franciscans—live anywhere they can afford, the Castro is the community's spiritual and political home. Castro Street is bustling with men doing their daily shopping and errands, cruising, frequenting the late-night clubs, or going to the Castro Theater, along with other San Franciscans who come for the film festivals and for the trendy restaurants nearby.

As a residential area, the center of the Castro is a sunny valley. Steep hills shelter the small houses, and flowers bloom in backyard gardens or in pots on the sunny decks. As the streets rise steeply toward Twin Peaks, the homes become larger—Victorians and Queen Anne cottages—and these, when they come up for sale, are snapped up in the blink of an eye, no matter the cost. Rentals are also climbing; one-bedroom apartments in the center may rent for as much as $1,200, a two-bedroom for $2,500.

Across Market, up toward Corona Heights and Buena Vista Parks, the Castro's suburbs have large, well-landscaped homes on winding, hilly streets. This is a more traditional, less noticeable area, agreeable and calm, and prices are rising considerably here. And farther in is the Duboce Triangle, less wealthy but always in demand.

Just to the south, **Noe Valley** takes and gives to both the Castro and the Mission, but is in fact a village unto itself. Some old German and Irish still live here, as they do in the Castro, but it is now one of the most sought-after areas of town by young couples, by lesbians and gays spilling over from the Castro, and by artists and others with a bohemian outlook. Protected from the fog by three steep hills, this sunny valley is one of the city's most popular areas for young families; mothers pushing their children in strollers do their shopping on 24th Street or sit with their friends at outdoor tables in front of any of the area's charming little cafes. Twenty-fourth and Church is the main shopping intersection, but the shopping district really stretches from Diamond to Dolores. Since the J-Church streetcar line comes here, it is as convenient to downtown as any other district.

The entire area is relaxed in feel, less frenetic than the Castro, more solidly comfortable. Streets are fairly wide, and the small houses that line them are painted in light colors. The streets leading up to Diamond Heights are steep and the large Victorians have exceptional views, although the higher the climb, of course, the denser the fog. The residents of Noe Valley value their village and are trying to keep out the big businesses and chains, successfully so far.

Just a few years ago you wouldn't have paid much attention to Noe Valley's eastern neighbor, a rather placid, uninspired—sometimes rundown—area of small private homes nestled on low-rising hills. Now, however, sunny **Bernal Heights** is on the way up. The area's excellent location—with borders also on Diamond Heights and the Mission—meant that it was a logical expansion for those neighborhoods, as well as for men and women who might also have thought of the lively Castro or Inner Mission as their home. Pleasantly winding streets heading up low-rising hills, several welcoming green parks, gentle breezes, and lovely views from Bernal Hill drew a new generation of San Franciscans, ready to spruce up the Victorian bungalows and Queen Anne cottages, many of which were suffering from neglect. Bernal Heights is now an area with its own cachet.

Fortunately, the area has not lost its traditional multiracial, multi-ethnic character, but it took the work of community activists opposed to excessive gentrification to bring about a moratorium on "certain types of development." It is true that new businesses and restaurants are moving in, but so far the neighborhood ambience persists, even on Cortland Avenue, the district's main commercial street, which offers to residents all the conveniences and services that a small town would want.

Bernal Heights thus remains a mixed area, one of agreeable proportions. Old-timers still inhabit their homes, young professionals and artists are fixing up cottages throughout, and Latino families are finding their way out from the crowded Mission to homes that are still within financial reach, both for rental and purchase. But the good prices here will not last long. Home prices increased nearly 18 percent in just one recent year, to the point that now the median price for a two-bedroom, one-bath house has reached $320,000. Rent control means that a long-term renter might be paying $650 per month, but a young professional who is just moving in might pay $1,800. Clearly, this is a neighborhood still in transition, and fortunate is the person who can seize an opportunity here.

The Mountainous Center

To the south and west of Noe Valley the highest hills in the city impose themselves over a dozen interesting communities. Windswept and foggy for the most part, Twin Peaks, Mount Davidson, and Mount Sutro command the city's geographical center; many of their neighborhoods are blessed with exquisite views and park-like settings, some a bit sheltered from the cold ocean wind. Despite the winding and dead-end streets, each area is convenient to—or overlaps—another of interest, and all are in proximity to the city's major universities, making them attractive to faculty and students. There are pockets of mansions and grand private homes, small cottages, and well-maintained apartments, but what you'll find depends on where you look, for each area has its own character.

Diamond Heights, which is the major district on the eastern slopes of Twin Peaks, was developed in the 1960s, and its modernity shows in its large apartment complexes and well-designed, single-family homes. Its proximity to its eastern neighbors makes it ever more desirable, as prices in Noe Valley and the Castro soar. Being "discovered" also is the attractive hilly **Glen Park** district to the southeast, with its many rental apartments, Victorians, and almost reasonably priced homes, although it had long been a sedate, well-kept neighborhood. And the Glen Park BART Station makes the Financial District even more quickly accessible than some areas closer in. Nearby, the steep Glen Canyon Park offers a wilderness park, although playgrounds, tennis courts, and a baseball field have tamed it somewhat.

Mount Davidson's summit is foggy and wild, but on its western downslopes some incredibly beautiful neighborhoods are almost a surprise in this outer part of the city. That they are near the universities and Stonestown makes them very much in demand. Drive around **Sherwood Forest** and **St. Francis Wood**, for example, to see the lovely homes on impeccably landscaped grounds. Houses occasionally come up for sale here, but as in Pacific Heights, the prices are astronomical. The pleasant homes of **West Portal** bridge toward the more ordinary **Miraloma Park**, **Westwood Highlands**, and **Westwood Park**, where some areas and streets are more appealing than others.

Just above the UC Medical Center, Mount Sutro and its fragrant eucalyptus forest may be the city's best-kept secret. On the hill's eastern edge, within walking distance of the hospital, the charming enclave of **Sutro Heights** backs on the forest, and here are several of the most beautiful and flowery streets in the city, especially Edgewood Avenue, which is paved in red brick. Circling the hill, wild, foggy Sutro Forest sees private homes and apartments in addition to institutional housing for medical students. And around the hill to the west is **Forest Knolls,** a grouping of more than one hundred small, uniform homes on winding streets, each facing the forest itself.

The Haight and 9th Avenue

Just to the east is the **Haight**, which for some is still identified by its most famous moment—the flower children's 1967 "Summer of Love." Yet time has moved on, and funky shops and eateries are coexisting with the upmarket boutiques and restaurants that are gentrifying an area that had become extremely seedy. Haight Street itself doesn't seem to have changed, a colorful street with cluttered storefronts and this generation's anti-establishment youth lounging the sidewalks. These street people mix with—or more likely ignore—the new home owners who are refurbishing the Victorians that line the side streets and the Panhandle.

In fact, the district has a rather surprising appeal. The neighborhoods that abut—**Upper Haight, Cole Valley, Parnassus Heights, Buena Vista**—offer an extremely appealing mix of large and small private homes on tree-lined, sometimes winding, streets. These are still inhabited by long-term residents, by young couples who value the backyards for their children, and by faculty and researchers at the UC Medical Center, for whom this area is prime. Rentals are available throughout the district. In terms of purchase, although this is not one of the city's most expensive areas, the homes are often large and thus prices can be steep. Nonetheless, some houses that need refurbishment do come available and sell very quickly. This is also true for **Lower Haight**, east of Masonic, which is just beginning to come up.

The Haight's attraction for the flower children is not hard to understand. This area along the Panhandle was once quite fashionable, as the Victorians attest. But during the economic depression of the 1930s, it was hard to maintain the large homes, and during the war, some were split into apartments with cheap rents. When North Beach became too popular and expensive, many Beat Generation poets and "beatniks" moved here, and by 1962, the entire area was rather bohemian. By 1967, very hippie. But years of decline took their toll. Finally the City stepped in to subsidize the refurbishing of buildings and to limit the building of new units, which encouraged people sensing bargains to buy and restore the lovely old homes.

All these areas—and indeed some of those in the previous section—are near Golden Gate Park and the hilly Buena Vista Park, with its cypress, pines, and redwoods. They are also near commercial but charming Cole Street, and residents also head down the hill to the west, toward 9th Avenue and Irving.

Years ago, the sleepy intersection at 9th and Irving (which is actually in the **Inner Sunset**) held a few shops, restaurants, and local services, but not much else. Now, despite the fog that whips in early, it is one of the city's liveliest scenes. As with many other areas that have been discovered, however, small businesses are being forced out as rents are raised, allowing chain eateries and cafes to move in. Yet residents of this area—students, faculty, artists, and young Asian families who live in low-rise apartments or two-story stucco homes—are fighting back, trying to force businesses to keep the scale and size of stores appropriate to their sites. Several large chains were rejected, and at present the area is invitingly trendy, but with its community ambience intact.

The Avenues

To the west of Arguello are "the avenues," grid-like streets that start at 2nd Avenue and go west until they can go no more. They stretch on both sides of Golden Gate Park, and it is the park that divides its two adjacent districts, the **Richmond** and the **Sunset**, which have much in common, although slightly less as time goes on. In terms of climate, these are the foggiest districts in the city, and on some days when downtown areas are still basking in the sun, the Outer Richmond and the Outer Sunset are shrouded in mist, buffeted by wind. Both these large residential areas were developed only in the 1920s and 1930s; pleasantly culturally diverse, they are solidly middle class, known for their two-story, stucco, pastel-colored homes, sitting side by side, street after street. In each district, however, there are pockets of luxury, of magnificent views, of exquisite homes—to be had at a price. These roomy communities—safe, comfortable, and well-kept—are seen by some as far from the city life, and some residents rarely feel the need to go downtown.

As mentioned, Richmond's eastern edges remind one of Pacific Heights, from Arguello all the way out to Seacliff, with its mansions standing stately in the fog. Just across California Street, however, the Richmond is increasingly Asian: some 35 percent of the Chinese community has settled here, making Clement Street the focus of a "new Chinatown." Geary, its neighbor to the south and one of the city's longest commercial thoroughfares, has long been the stronghold of the Russian community, marked by the impressive gold-domed Cathedral of the Holy Virgin; all along Geary there are Russian delicatessens, bakeries, and stores, firmly ensconced in the increasingly Asian strip.

South of Geary begin the alphabetically consecutive streets, starting at Anza. Residentially, there are low-rise homes and apartments on wide, straight, rather bland streets. As the area heads out toward the ocean, however, it begins to feel like the wild beach town it is. At the very edge of the continent, past the tourist attractions at Cliff House, the condominiums of **Ocean Beach** sit along the Great Highway, behind the sandy dunes.

South of Golden Gate Park, in the Sunset, the alphabetical streets start again at Lincoln and end far to the south at Wawona.

The trendy area around 9th and Irving begins to fade, and the straight wide streets carry on as far as they can to the west and into the chilling fog. Despite seemingly endless rows of small, undistinguished single-family bungalows and semidetached homes, the Outer Sunset has some attractions, including Asian commercial districts on Irving and Noriega, especially around 19th Avenue. With access to beaches and several large parks, and close to the major Stonestown Galleria and San Francisco State, the residents seem content. All along the westernmost stretches, past 19th Avenue and surrounding the long Sunset Avenue greensward, a few of the discreet, pleasantly residential communities — **Parkside, Pine Lake Park** — seem part of a more tranquil world. Prices here are reasonable in relation to the rest of the city.

The Southwest

Just south of the "avenues" and still in proximity to the university and Stonestown sits the **Oceanview Merced Ingleside (OMI)** set of communities. These green, fragrant areas are often totally socked in by fog, but their residents enjoy the coastal winds and the smell of the sea. Revolving around Ocean Avenue and 19th Avenue, these are three middle class neighborhoods trying to form a cohesive whole. In general, they are known for pleasant, single-family homes with neatly kept yards. Some apartment areas exist around Stonestown, inhabited by both long-term local residents and students who come and go. Park Merced, adjacent to the university, is an extensive apartment and townhouse complex.

To the west, near the university in its wooded and garden-like setting, near large Harding Park, near Lake Merced, and close to the ocean with its crashing waves, the area begins to take on the aspect of the coastal town it is. Lining the western side of the lake, along John Muir Drive, a large complex of rental units can be seen in a community known as **Lakeshore.**

Ocean Avenue, the northern border of the district, is gently residential to the west of 19th Avenue, but commercial to the east.

This is one of the commercial areas that service Ingleside Terrace, known for the looping residential Urbano Drive that follows the course of the long-gone Ingleside Race Track. The comfortable, well-kept houses here give off the atmosphere of suburban living, and, fortunately, one may occasionally come up for rent.

Yet Ingleside and Oceanview themselves are in transition, and in fact have long been so. Fifty years ago, when the decaying Fillmore districts were being redeveloped, African American families were evicted with a promise they could return to new housing. Instead, many families migrated outward to the OMI and affordable homes, as the traditional White communities bought automobiles and moved to suburban living. Decades later, centralized shopping centers and large cinema complexes forced small local businesses to close, and the area declined. Recently, however, although some parts still remain rough, an active citizens' effort is striving to bring the area back to its residents, with rebuilt and expanded public facilities and an overall sense of renewal.

The Southeast

Also at the south, but on the city's eastern edge, are several districts that seem not to fit into the vibrant San Francisco mold. Separated from Bernal Heights by Interstate 280, **Portola** is a generally lower-middle class melting pot. Originally an Italian neighborhood, then Jewish, it is now truly multicultural, as evidenced along San Bruno Avenue, with its Latin American establishments, Italian butchers, and Asian restaurants of all kinds. People buying their first homes often settled here, but now prices are rising as everywhere else, and especially in this area so near Bernal Heights.

Surrounding the large John McLaren Park are several neighborhoods—**Excelsior, Visitacion Valley,** and **Crocker Amazon**—that are generally characterized by middle-income and working class families living in bland single-family homes. Originally Italian, these areas now see more Latinos and Asians. The foggy, rather uninspired streets with their rows of little houses are convenient to Daly City, to San Francisco State, and to the city by BART. In this area there are also some apartments, flats, and duplexes, many needing refurbishment, and these present opportunities for neighborhoods to come back, which they will eventually do. Crocker Amazon has some slightly newer homes on more interesting streets such as Chicago Way.

But just across the Highway 101 corridor are **Hunters Point,** an area of city-wide concern, and **Bayview**, which seems now to be on the upturn. During World War II military shipyards here bustled with some 35,000 workers. Now, however, with much of the city's public housing—some of it still in use since the war— these are the areas most beset by poverty and crime. Yet, a few artists have their studios at the old naval base, and the city is perhaps beginning to address the problems.

This broad look at the city should help you get a feel for it as you explore it on your own. As you do, you will discover that it still has its little mysteries which no doubt will eventually be resolved. Will the charming enclave of private homes around the University of San Francisco continue to be considered part of the nearby Western Addition, which currently has so little charm? Will the industrial South of Market become gentrified to match its eastern edge at the upcoming South Beach? Will the enormous mixed-use development planned for China Bay succeed? Is Corona Heights a suburb of the Castro? And will the formerly commercial Van Ness corridor, now sparkling with new condominiums, supermarkets, and theaters, coin a name for itself? The answers to these puzzles will certainly unfold. In any case, the architect Frank Lloyd Wright summed up his own understanding: "What I like best about San Francisco is ... San Francisco," he said. For overall, as San Franciscans believe, the city is unique.

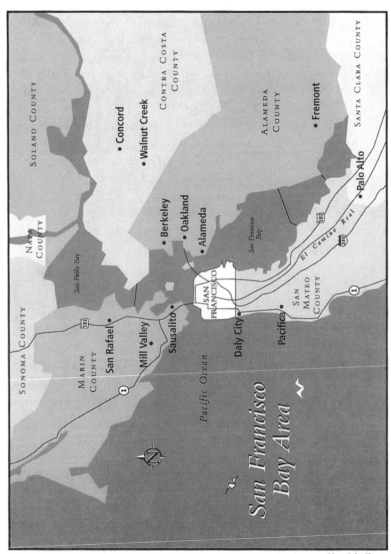

Map: John Zaugg

— Chapter Two —

AROUND THE BAY

SUBURBAN LIVING

The eight outlying counties of the Bay Area stretch about fifty miles south toward the major metroplis of San Jose, east past the industrial port of Oakland, and north to Sonoma, up toward what is known as the Delta. Bay Area counties are generally referred to by their position in relation to the Bay: the North Bay (Marin, Sonoma, Napa, and Solano counties), the South Bay whose farther reaches are called the Peninsula (San Mateo and Santa Clara counties), and the East Bay (Alameda and Contra Costa counties). Thousands of people commute to the city from the nearer portions of these counties, and now even some of the farther reaches are beginning to be seen as within commuting distance. People choose to live in the greater Bay Area rather than in San Francisco for a variety of reasons: a tranquil suburban or even rural lifestyle, lower housing costs (in some places), good public and private schools, low crime rates, fewer earthquakes, or perhaps even a more "normal" climate. Although the details of the towns and villages of the Bay Area are beyond the province of this book, they are well worth considering in terms of residence.

Unlike San Francisco, the rest of the Bay Area sees four distinct seasons. While San Francisco is enjoying its natural summer air conditioning, it is warmest inland, away from the bay. Temperatures in the rest of the Bay Area can soar in the summer, but even in these areas, winter climes are mild, with perhaps a touch of snow in Sonoma, on the peaks of Mount Diablo, or on Mount Tamalpais.

All these counties are dotted with delicious little towns, gentle and leafy green, linked by country roads and, for the most part, touched by major highways. Living here, thus, requires keeping a car, perhaps more if two people in a household are working, or if a child needs to be taken to school. If living outside the city appeals to you, think about living along the BART line, which goes from San Francisco under the bay to the east, and somewhat toward the south (see Chapter Ten). Commuting by car during rush hours is slow and tedious, but BART is reliable and fast. From the North Bay, commuting is most often by car, crowding the lanes of the Golden Gate Bridge; there too, however, the public commuter buses and even ferries are reliable and practical. And from the south also come the buses and BART (from Colma), and, unfortunately, long lines of cars.

Rents and purchase prices vary from the merely expensive to the outrageous, depending on the home's size and its views of the Bay, and the town's amenities. Some of the communities have new subdivisions with planned developments of single-family and multi-family homes, some clustered around golf courses. Whereas the towns close to San Francisco were considered an easy commute to the City, now communities as far north as Petaluma or Novato, or as far east as Concord are being developed and considered within commuting distance. Whatever the price range, the beauty and lifestyles of these more relaxed areas are considered by many — especially young families — to be essential for a well-balanced life. Towns around the Bay Area are never called suburbs, but the life is truly suburban.

EAST BAY

Across the $8^1/2$-mile Bay Bridge is the East Bay, known for its warm climate and beautiful grassy, rolling hills rising toward Mount Diablo, the highest peak in the region. It is home to **Oakland**, the Bay Area's major shipping port, and its contiguous neighbor, **Berkeley**, with its prestigious University of California campus. Both are in **Alameda County**, which has the highest population of the Bay Area. Yet there are many almost rural towns to consider, both in Alameda County and, farther east, in **Contra Costa County**. Formerly seen as less desirable than the upscale counties to the north or south of San Francisco, the East Bay — although recently "discovered" by young, upcoming professionals — is still characterized by lower rents, and a more traditional lifestyle. This won't last long. Providing its own cultural attractions, modern shopping and extensive services, good schools, and lovely parks and outdoor recreation areas, the East Bay is even known for its efficient public transit, including access to BART, and the Oakland International Airport, increasingly used by travelers trying to avoid SFO.

In the mid-1960s, Oakland, which had refitted its waterfront to handle the new container ships, became the the area's major international shipping port, when San Francisco decided to spend its public funds to draw tourists instead. Unfortunately, Oakland's new industries did little to make the sprawling city into a desired residential locale, and it became known for drugs, crime, and poverty, a situation that is finally being addressed. Currently, the city is in the process of an exciting renewal. New construction is changing the skyline, neighborhoods are being spruced up, businesses are moving in, and Oakland is striving to show itself as on the move.

The new spirit of Oakland—and its still reasonable rents and purchase prices—is drawing people from across the Bay and from Silicon Valley. Prices are beginning to climb, and as in San Francisco, long-term residents are concerned about the gentrification of the city and about being forced out as prices increase. The market is definitely heating up. Yet construction of rental units is part of the overall renewal plan, and you can look for graceful apartments near trendy, waterfront Jack London Square and around the large Lake Merritt, a man-made, saltwater, tidal lake which serves as a recreational haven for the area's residents.

Towns close by which heretofore appealed to those looking for lower rents—**Alameda** and **San Leandro**, for example, and down to **Fremont**—are also experiencing a surge in housing costs, but none of these as yet approach the prices in San Francisco. Some areas have always been expensive and will remain so: in **Piedmont**, an exclusive enclave of large homes and an understated yet elegant atmosphere, there is little to rent, and purchase prices are high. This is also true of the Oakland hills, a prestigious, wealthy aerie between Oakland and Berkeley that was all but destroyed by a massive fire a decade ago, but which was quickly and splendidly rebuilt.

Berkeley, Oakland's neighbor to the north, may no longer be called "berserkeley" for its once-strident mixture of radical politics and New Age sensibilities, but this is still a city on the cutting edge of the nation's intellectual and political life. You can find whatever you want in Berkeley, whether it is a beautiful home in the secluded hills or a moderately priced room near the university and the student life along Telegraph Avenue. Whether student or faculty, or neither, the residents are activists in all senses, and this is a lively, well-kept community that never hesitates to make its opinions known. There is a lot to be said for Berkeley: a generally sunny climate, the university atmosphere, the beautiful Tilden Park, excellent theater and concerts, some of the best restaurants in the Bay Area, and good schools.

Inland and through the Caldecott Tunnel are the small communities of **Contra Costa County: Orinda** and **Lafayette**, and the charming, comfortable city of **Walnut Creek**. Continuing along the line are **Pleasant Hill** and then **Concord**. Some 880,000 people live in these "bedroom" communities of Contra Costa County, but nestled among the green rolling hills or under Mount Diablo, some of it feels almost bucolic. Check out towns such as **Martinez, Antioch, El Cerrito**, or **Clayton**, which are still affordable and which have good access to public transportation and BART for commutes into the City or Oakland.

NORTH BAY

Like San Francisco, **Marin County** is fairly surrounded by water. More than 100 miles of its borders are ocean, lagoons, or bays. Marin is two counties in one. East of the coastal mountains are trendy towns with lovely homes and elegant, peaceful living. To the west is the rugged coastline with its cliffs and surf. The weather to the east is sheltered, warm, and sunny, and the towns and their services and conveniences easily available to all. On the coast, however, are foggy, tiny villages that draw hearty lovers of wild beauty. One winding, narrow road links them. A quarter million people live in Marin, from corporation executives who commute to San Francisco from their $4 million homes, to solitary artists and writers who leave their cottages to brave the winds and stroll the beaches, but who rarely want to come out "over the hill."

Just over the Golden Gate Bridge, picturesque **Sausalito** was once a sleepy fishing village. Now, however, tourists dominate the spectacular waterfront with its restaurants and boutiques. But the dramatic hills, steep and green, with their winding narrow lanes, are held by residents, many of whom commute into the city, escaping San Francisco in evening traffic back to their beautifully landscaped homes with striking views of the city they just left. Sausalito's quaint Mediterranean atmosphere is drawing young professionals who are bidding against each other for the few available properties and who are driving prices up from the merely expensive to the outrageous.

Farther out along Highway 101 are the charming towns of **Mill Valley**, **Larkspur**, **San Rafael**, **Corte Madera**, and **San Anselmo**. In these family towns, the pace is slower, the tourists at a distance. There is a mixed blue- and white-collar population that mingles easily with the corporate or artsy set. Small homes may approach the affordable, but hillside houses appeal to those who want the lifestyle no matter the cost, a situation that is increasing throughout the North Bay. Charming San Rafael, one of the oldest cities in California yet one of the most well-maintained in terms of schools, services, and atmosphere, is convenient either to a commute to the East Bay over the Richmond Bridge, or to the city by ferry, bus, or car.

San Rafael is the area's largest town, but it is Mill Valley, stretching from the flat up to the tip of Mount Tamalpais, that provides in gentle microcosm much of what Berkeley is known for: artists, writers, an annual film festival, lovely little galleries and boutiques. All these towns are accessible to San Francisco by commuter bus, but the ferries at Sausalito, **Larkspur**, and **Tiburon** make commuting even somewhat pleasant.

Tiburon and **Belvedere**, at the end of a causeway heading east from Highway 101 toward the bay, are almost hidden communities of astronomically expensive, lovely houses. Close to the natural harbor and to the local commerce are modern upscale condominium apartments, which sometimes come up for sale. Quiet, remote Belvedere is home to the truly rich.

Yet Marin has its pockets of affordable rental housing, in any of the towns mentioned above. Where you live here will depend also on whether you will commute daily into the city. The western and northern portions of Marin, heretofore seen as too remote, are currently enjoying an upswing for people who telecommute, for those who work in the North Bay, and for those who will put up with the commute for the lifestyle—and almost reasonable housing costs—these towns allow. Look at towns such as **Fairfax,** or **San Geronimo** and **Nicasio**, where new housing developments are under way.

SOUTH BAY

Mirroring Marin, **San Mateo County**, which stretches from **Daly City** to **Menlo Park**, has two distinct climates and lifestyles, and as would be expected, the stretch that is oceanside of the coastal mountains is often socked in by fog. Unlike Marin, however, the beach town of **Pacifica** is close to Interstate 280, making a commute into the city feasible for those who want to live in the fresh ocean air. This is less true of **Half Moon Bay**, about 20 minutes farther south, for winter mud slides sometimes make the commute difficult. Yet these charming coastal fishing communities are populated by families and singles who live in small, comfortable houses or in affordable apartments, often with a view of the waves.

Inland, past the southern edge of the city but still well within its fog belt, are the working class Daly City and **South San Francisco**. Here people commute into the city on BART, but they also work in the industries that line the Highway 101 corridor, at the airport, at the huge shopping complexes in **Serramonte** or **Colma**, or at San Francisco State. Colma is the southern terminus for BART, making for an easy commute into the city. These are areas of small, square, stucco homes, apartments, duplexes, townhouses, and condominiums. This part of the South Bay may not be the most exciting place to live in, but its price and convenience may be appealing to some.

But this is not all there is. Just beyond the fog belt, **San Mateo**, **Belmont**, and **Burlingame** offer pleasant ranch houses on wide, tree-lined streets. Here the residential areas are varied and prices may be quite reasonable. Yet here, too, they are rising, for at the end of the century, the median price of a single-family detached home in San Mateo County was $461,000; **East Palo Alto** had the most affordably priced homes, and in general condominiums are reasonably priced. Along the long north-south artery of El Camino Real, an Asian business community makes itself known, and to the east of "the Camino" interesting, well-priced homes become available from time to time. At about 15 minutes south of the airport, **Foster City,** between 101 and the bay, is a lovely, sprawling town of upscale rental and condominium apartments, plus well-landscaped streets of private homes. Sheltered by the hills from the fog and wind, its climate is moderate, its parks pleasant, and its proximity to the highway makes it convenient both to San Francisco in the north and Silicon Valley in the south. If you look for housing close to the airport, inquire about flight patterns and noise.

THE PENINSULA

Santa Clara County accounts for more than one million of the six million people living in the Bay Area. The geography of the area is beautifully varied: flat areas along the 101 corridor, green rolling hills, wooded retreats, agricultural lands, horse farms farther east toward Highway 280, and charming towns. The county starts around **Menlo Park** on the north, encompasses the major highways of Route 101 and Interstate 280, flanks El Camino Real, and heads south to the edge of **San Jose,** a bustling, forward-looking city with a population larger than its more celebrated neighbor to the north.

Santa Clara County is now famous as "Silicon Valley," headquarters for most of the country's high-tech industries that have brought some 800,000 well-paid jobs to the area and a younger set of entrepreneurs looking for housing they can easily afford. What is sometimes called "dot.com" money has caused a doubling of housing prices in just the past few years, in an area that was already quite dear. That housing prices range from the merely upscale to the astronomical shouldn't be surprising in an area in which the median family income is currently $82,000, the highest in the United States. Yet condominiums do come available, temporary rentals come up from time to time in the homes of faculty members at Stanford University who are off on sabbaticals, and in some flat pockets near commercial areas, almost affordable homes can still be found.

The leafy campus of Stanford is nestled in the charming town of **Palo Alto**, which is known for its Craftsman-style bungalows, although in recent years houses have become larger and prices have climbed considerably. Palo Alto is home to the Stanford Shopping Center, an extensive and popular mall that serves this part of the Peninsula.

Nearby, the exquisite towns of **Hillsborough** and **Atherton**, with median home prices hovering in the $2 million range, are becoming home to those who commute into San Francisco, work in Silicon Valley, or head down to San Jose. These and the elegant **Los Altos** and **Los Altos Hills** are gentle towns with high-quality services and impressive homes hidden on large, well-landscaped grounds. Farther into the rolling hills to the west, the horse farms and estates of **Woodside** off Interstate 280 are remote and rarefied in atmosphere—and price.

Yet, the sections of any of the towns that are on the flats closer to the industrial 101 corridor than to the less developed Interstate 280 are for the most part pleasant, middle class "bedroom communities." Here, rents for the smaller houses and apartments—as well as more affordable purchase prices—give access to worlds in all directions. Check them out.

— CHAPTER THREE —

HOUSING: PROBLEMS & SOLUTIONS

THE SITUATION

As small and compact as it is, San Francisco offers a wide range of housing, from elegant mansions and single-family homes with gardens to semidetached row houses, from high-rise complexes to low-rise apartments over neighborhood stores, to flats in two-story homes. Thousands of charming Victorian houses and small homes coexist peaceably with the few tall modern structures, and each of the almost thirty distinct neighborhoods has its own eclectic blend. In general, San Franciscans are apartment dwellers. Of the more than 330,000 residences in the city, some 229,000 are multi-units, and only about 105,000 are single or semidetached one-family homes.

Fortunately, San Francisco is a city of renters. Some two-thirds of the population rent their homes, while only slightly more than one-third own theirs. Unfortunately, San Francisco is a city whose boundaries are fixed by water, and its expanding commercial areas have reduced residential possibilities just as an influx of affluent newcomers is demanding more space. This has pushed prices up to the point where the city is rated as one of the least affordable housing markets in the United States. That the city has decided to keep its residential ambience and put height restrictions on new building construction has also created a low inventory of available apartments, and increasing demand has fueled a difficult price situation. This holds true for both purchase and rental units.

In fact, San Franciscans themselves consistently rate the lack of affordable housing and the city's high rents as the city's most pressing problems. Rental vacancies hover around 1 percent, and apartments listed for sale may well be snapped up after a bidding war with the winner paying hundreds of thousands of dollars *above* the asking price. In the last four years of the 20th century, the number of transactions doubled, but price per sale also doubled.

The problem began with the construction boom after World War II. Just about all the high-rent commercial skyscrapers in the city were built during what critics called the "Manhattanization of San Francisco," which stopped only because there was no more space downtown. Small businesses were driven to the outer reaches, some lower-end apartments were demolished to build hotels or upscale apartments, and some former rental units themselves converted to expensive condominiums.

Yet, the most important part of why housing costs are so high is that the economic boom of the nineties brought new high-tech and multimedia entrepreneurs into the city, people who were willing to pay even more than the asking price for a place they liked. Despite a commute to Silicon Valley, many of the "dot.com" entrepreneurs prefer to live in San Francisco; sometimes San

Francisco itself seems a bedroom community as cars create a new, southbound morning rush hour. These people work hard, have little time for private life, and they want to be where the surroundings are vibrant. Thus, they are willing to pay whatever it takes for the finest location and most spectacular view, ignoring traditional purchase procedures, forcing the market to become even more competitive.

It is beginning to hold true, as some people say, that in San Francisco nothing worth living in is inexpensive. Don't be shocked, don't be upset, it's just the way it is. Finding the right home at the right price is not an easy matter, but eventually you will, especially if you understand that you will have to compromise. But do not expect to arrive in San Francisco and stay in a hotel for two or three days before moving into the "just right" inexpensive apartment with a spectacular view. San Francisco doesn't work that way. Expect instead to find a short-term apartment or residence hotel (see below), and to spend several months in search of a home.

Yet the news is not all bad. Although the cost of living in San Francisco is higher than the United States average, income levels in the Bay Area are generally commensurate. Costs other than housing are not particularly high: the mild climate allows customers to spend less on household utilities than in some other cities, for instance, and San Franciscans are always happy to say how little they paid for something, whether clothing bought at a discount or a delicious meal in an Asian restaurant.

RENT CONTROL

Another plus is that renters do have some protection under San Francisco law. Apartments in San Francisco have been rent controlled since 1979, meaning that rents for tenants with leases may only be raised a certain percentage each year, determined by a formula tied to the Cost of Living Index. Currently, the rate of increase is $2^1/_2$ percent. Rents may be raised to "market levels," however, when a tenant leaves and before a new tenant moves in;

this sometimes encourages landlords to force tenants out under one pretext or another, or to insist on month-to-month contracts, rather than leases.

In some apartment complexes, tenants who have held leases for twenty years are paying only a fraction of what a new tenant pays. This may seem unfair, but without some regulation to protect tenants, rents in San Francisco would be even higher than they are. Although some people claim that rent control is forcing the higher rents and that a free market would bring rents down, the unregulated commercial market has not shown this to be true.

Some landlords are taking advantage of a law that allows them to evict tenants if they themselves, or their families, are planning to move in. Such evictions rose some 200 percent in the last years of the nineties, and not all landlords actually moved in; new tenants did, paying higher rents. In addition, the controversial Ellis Act allows landlords to take their properties off the market, evicting existing tenants. In just six months in 1998, some seventy buildings were taken off the market—sometimes just temporarily. These are issues that the Board of Supervisors are constantly struggling with, to be fair both to the renters and landlords in the city.

THINKING ABOUT RENT

Rental units are strewn throughout the city; the areas to the north and east have more apartments, and to the west and south, more private homes. Their price, of course, depends on the neighborhood and the view; the more central or trendy the neighborhood, the higher the price. Even areas that were once seen as lower-priced are no longer so, and this at least benefits the long-term tenants who are protected under rent control. It is said that less than one-third of the people who moved to an apartment in the Mission a decade ago could afford to move in today; even in this formerly low-rent area, the current median rent for a two-bedroom apartment is approaching $1,600. In terms of luxury housing, the

1,000 apartments of the Golden Gateway Center that were offered as moderate-income housing in the sixties are now charging up to $2,950 per month for a studio and up to $3,995 for a two-bedroom apartment. In fact, the median price for an available apartment in the city is now $1,500, having risen from $860 just six years ago. Nonetheless, you should be able to find housing in your price range, but it might take some time and compromise.

It is hard to predict the type of rentals in any given area. Older apartments may be found in newly trendy areas, and some recent construction may be found in areas thought of as traditional. And some reasonably priced rentals may be just on the edge of higher-priced districts, in areas called the Outer Mission, Lower Haight, or Upper Market. Except for a few areas near the Tenderloin and down by Hunters Point, there are practically no areas of the city that are not appropriate for the apartment search, although some — the Mission and the Western Addition — require some caution.

STARTING THE SEARCH

You can begin to understand the San Francisco rental market in advance of arrival by looking online. Some listing services charge a small access fee, usually good for three months; these services, however, allow search by location or by housing requirements (number of rooms, elevator, etc), and they often offer advice on moving and landlord requirements. See also Roommates below.

- San Francisco daily newspapers: classified ads (www.sfgate.com) provide links to Spring Street, Metro Rent and Rent Tech, listed below
- *Renter's Digest*: advertisements for large complexes that have a fair amount of tenant turnover, as well as some short-term options (www.aptguides.com)
- *Bay Area Rental Guide*: Advertisements for housing in the Bay Area (www.rentalguide.com)

- **Spring Street**: $75 for rental listings; $65 for roommate listings. Nationwide service; one of the most extensive (www.springstreet.com).
- **e-Housing**: Covers East Bay. $60 for rental listings; $25 for roommate listings (www.e-housing.com).
- **Metro Rent**: Rental and roommate listings from San Francisco to San Jose; $85–95 for two months of access; $65 for 90 days for roommate listings (www.metrorent.com)
- **Rent Tech**: San Francisco and East Bay rental listings; $85 for access to rentals; prices vary for roommate services (www.renttech.com)

Once in San Francisco, you can read the local publications and walk around the neighborhoods you are interested in to spot the "for rent" signs in apartment windows, which give a telephone number to call. Some people also rent bicycles for leisurely explorations of neighborhoods that interest them (see Chapter Fifteen). If you can afford it, however, work with a real estate agent, who knows what is available in the various neighborhoods. You will have to pay a commission, but it may be worth it to streamline the search. Although most real estate agents and roommate services handle rentals (see below), **Hill & Co**, at 2107 Union, is especially known for its rental properties (rental tel: 921-3040).

Daily newspapers are excellent sources for rentals, but if you see something you like, act immediately. Fast-spreading news of the availability of a good apartment may mean that by the time an ad appears in the paper, the apartment might well have been taken. Nonetheless, both the *San Francisco Chronicle* and *The San Francisco Examiner* are important resources. The *San Francisco Weekly* has apartments at the lower end of the scale, and shares (www.sfweekly.com). For apartments and shares throughout the Bay Area, try the *Bay Guardian* (www.sfbg.com); in the East Bay, look for the *Oakland Tribune* and *The Express*, but for housing farther out—in Walnut Creek and Concord—try the *Contra Costa County*

Times. The best resources in the South Bay are the *San Mateo Times* and, farther south, the *San Jose Mercury News*. In the North Bay, look for the *Marin Independent*.

THE APARTMENT

San Francisco real estate makes a distinction between an apartment and a flat. A flat is an entire floor of a small apartment building or two-story house, and it has its own entrance. Thus, you might walk up an outdoor flight of stairs to your door, and inside, the entire floor is your own. An apartment, however, is one of several — or many — on a floor. Foreigners should understand that, in the United States, the first floor is the ground floor, and the second floor is the next floor up.

If you are bringing a car, pay attention to the parking situation. Although new buildings must include off-street parking, older dwellings may have no garages, and parking in San Francisco is a problem in all but the western neighborhoods. Some areas have public garages that rent spaces by the month; in addition to price, which varies from district to district, inquire about hours of access. If you intend to park your car on the street, you may need a city-issued parking permit (see Chapter Ten).

On the other hand, you should also determine the closest access to public transportation. Even people with cars often take public transport or walk to work, to avoid congested traffic and expensive parking.

Landlords generally ask for an application fee, which covers the cost of a credit check, plus the first and last months' rent, and/or a security deposit when the application is approved. Be prepared to provide a credit reference and the names of your past and current employers and landlords. Identification might include your driver's license, bank account numbers, and Social Security number. Many places don't allow pets, but it is illegal for a landlord to prohibit children.

A lease must specify a beginning date and termination date (not when you are required to move out, but when the lease must be renewed). If there is no termination date, the contract is not a "lease," but an "agreement," which will run month to month indefinitely, may be terminated by either party at any time, and, of course, is beneficial to the landlord. It's not wise to accept an oral agreement, which has no legal validity.

Before signing, ask your landlord for procedures for breaking a lease, should you decide to move. In general, you should give as much notice as possible, in writing, and expect to pay the entire remainder of the lease should a new tenant not be found.

Security deposits are used to cover damage to the apartment (deducted upon your departure). Thus, when you are returning the signed lease, make sure you have checked for any irregularities in the apartment, and specify them in writing—every crack in the walls or chip on an appliance—so that upon leaving you will not be charged for damage. No laws apply as to what constitutes a furnished apartment, so you should inquire about some of the items you require, such as a desk, a microwave, or a toaster. Ask the landlord for a detailed inventory of what is in the apartment and make sure it matches what is actually there.

Short-term Rentals

If you cannot come to the city and spend time looking for an apartment before your actual move, consider either a short-term, furnished, fully equipped apartment or a residence hotel. Short-term, furnished apartments are less expensive than hotels, and with housing so tight, you might as well be comfortable during your search.

- **American Marketing Systems**, at 2800 Van Ness, is an agency that handles short-term (monthly) furnished and unfurnished apartments throughout the city (tels: 447-2000, 800/747-7784; fax: 440-1008; www.we-rent-sanfran.com).

- **Executive Suites**: (tel: 800/258-1973; fax 776-5155; www.rent.net/ads/executivesuites). Short-term furnished luxury studios, one- and two-bedroom apartments in San Francisco, the East Bay, and Sausalito.
- *Civic Center*—**Ashlee Suites**: 1029 Geary, at Van Ness (tel: 771-7396; fax: 771-7455). Studios to two-bedroom fully equipped apartments.
- *Downtown*—**The Steinhart**: 952 Sutter Street (tel: 928-3855). An older, restored, landmark building. Studios to two-bedroom furnished apartments, maid service.
- *Embarcadero*—**Golden Gateway Apartments**: 460 Davis Court, at Jackson (tel: 434-2000; fax: 989-5034). Stays of three months or more in an elegant complex. Health facilities and pool. Parking available.
- *Nob Hill*—**Nob Hill Place**: 1155 Jones Street, at Sacramento (tel: 928-2051). Quiet residence offers studios to two-bedroom apartments at prices fitting the area. Parking garages in the neighborhood.
- *Nob Hill*—**Pierre Suites/Nob Hill**: 835 Pine, near Powell (tels: 800/570-0252; 544-0252). Fine apartments of various sizes by week or month.
- *Nob Hill*—**Grosvenor Suites**: 899 Pine, at Mason (tel: 421-1899; fax: 982-1946). Studio to two-bedroom fully equipped suites, some with exquisite views of the city. Parking available.
- *Nob Hill*—**Nob Hill Chateau**: 795 Pine Street (tel: 986-5145; fax: 392-8161). Fully equipped studio and one-bedroom furnished apartments for rent by the week or month. Computer and fax lines, answering machines.
- *Wharf*—**Northpoint Executive Suites**: 2211 Stockton at Bay (tel: 989-6563). Fully furnished apartments of various sizes and amenities. Parking available. Swimming pool and health club.

Another option, although not particularly suitable for families, is the residential hotel, which offers one room and meals in a common dining room.

- *Downtown* — **Ansonia**: 711 Post Street (tel: 673-2670). Inexpensive hotel; breakfast and dinner served daily; no Sunday dinner.
- *Downtown* — **Cornell Hotel**: 715 Bush Street (tel: 421-3154; fax: 399-1442). Charming French-style hotel offering rooms and excellent meals, except Sunday.
- *Van Ness Corridor* — **The Kenmore**: 1570 Sutter Street, near Gough (tel: 776-5815; fax: 776-9659). Residence club in a quiet area, yet close to public transportation, supermarket, restaurants. Most meals included.

Apartment Complexes

For permanent housing, some large apartment complexes handle their own rentals. These generally have a management office on the premises, which — at least theoretically — should make it efficient for repairs and service. In addition to considering these for long-term leases (if there are any available) you might also consider one of these complexes for the short term, so you can have some place to live and keep your furniture while looking for permanent housing. Some offer six-month leases or month-to-month contracts; in fact, six months is not unreasonable in thinking about finding satisfactory permanent housing.

- *Civic Center* — **Trinity Plaza**: 1169 Market Street, at 8th Street (tel: 861-3333). Studios and one-bedroom apartments, heated swimming pool. Moderate prices.
- *Embarcadero/Mission Street* — **Rincon Towers Apartments**: 88 Howard Street (tel: 777-4100). Two-tower set of apartments, from studios to two bedrooms. Short-term rentals available.
- *Embarcadero* — **Golden Gateway Center**: 460 Davis Court, at Jackson (tel: 434-2000; fax: 989-5034). Luxury apartments

and townhouses. Fitness center, tennis courts, swimming pool. Parking additional.
- *Embarcadero*—**Bayside Village**: The Embarcadero at Brannan (tel: 777-4850; fax: 777-2410). Studio to two-bedroom units, parking. Free shuttle bus to Financial District. Swimming pools, fitness center.
- *Lake Merced/San Francisco State*—**Parkmerced**: 3711 19th Avenue (tels: 888/218-0373; 587-6322). Moderately priced single-family townhouses and apartments in a large development near San Francisco State.
- *South of Market/Multimedia Gulch*—**City Lofts**: 175 Bluxome Street (tel: 495-8885). One- and two-bedroom live/work lofts, with a business center, a fitness room, and parking.
- *South of Market*—**St. Francis Place Apartments**: One St. Francis Place, 3rd Street at Folsom (tel: 888/704-8844; fax: 777-3972). Long- and short-term rentals of furnished one- and two-bedroom apartments.
- *Sunset*—**Sunset Towers**: 8 Locksley Avenue, at Kirkham (tel: 681-6800; fax: 681-1501). Near University of California Medical Center and Golden Gate Park. Studios to two-bedroom apartments. Parking, laundry, all conveniences.
- *Union Square*—**Trinity Towers**: 888 O'Farrell Street, near Polk (tel: 885-3333; fax: 885-3294). Loft apartments, townhouses, fitness center and swimming pool, underground parking, 24-hour doorman.
- *Van Ness*—**Fox Plaza**: 1390 Market Street (tel: 626-6900; fax: 863-3190; ARW Hospitality rental tel: 565-0625; fax: 554-0573). Rents and furnishes short-term and long-term apartments in this complex of studios to two bedroom apartments. Cats allowed, but no dogs.
- *Western Addition*—**Webster Tower and Terrace**: 1489 Webster Street, at Geary (tel: 931-6300). Modern studios, one- and two-bedroom apartments, and penthouses. Parking, rooftop terraces, shopping convenience.

- *Western Addition* — **The Fillmore Center**: 1475 Fillmore Street (tel: 921-1969; fax: 563-2019). Studios to three-bedroom apartments, penthouse, townhouse. Health club on premises. Shopping convenience.

PURCHASING A HOME

Since most homes for sale are listed in the centralized database of the San Francisco Board of Realtors' Multiple Listing Service, real estate agents have access to the broadest range of available housing. Only about 10 percent of homes do not come to the open market; instead the owner of a top-end residence might ask a particular realtor to find a buyer privately. In San Francisco's tight market, where there are fewer homes for sale than buyers, this works well for realtors, but it also affects their commissions. Generally, realtors hope for a 6 percent commission (paid by the seller), but in a competitive market where homes turn over quickly, agents have become flexible and sometimes accept 5 percent.

The "fair market value" of a home is what a buyer will pay and a seller will accept. As mentioned, the lack of available properties and an influx of suddenly rich Internet entrepreneurs has created a "seller's market" in which buyers are very often forced to offer several hundred thousand dollars *over* the asking price to be the successful bidder, whether for a house or apartment. Generally, a home does sell at a price within the price range of similar homes on the market in its area, and your real estate agent should be able to give you an estimate of what each neighborhood's homes are going for.

Price ranges do fluctuate over time. When the stock market is rising (and the dot.coms are doing well), a seller may receive multiple offers, and when the stock market "corrects," these bidding wars may slow. Given this new type of buyer in the city, most attractive homes will receive multiple offers, so you will need to make a competitive bid immediately and be prepared to raise your offer quickly. In addition, because properties move so quickly, you will need to have a mortgage up to a certain amount and the schedule of inspections and appraisals all pre-approved.

Work, if possible, with an agent with experience in the San Francisco market and with solid references; recommendations from friends and colleagues should help. Unfortunately, the best agents may be overbooked and may not have as much time as one who is fairly recent in the field. Nonetheless, in all cases be specific with your agent about your price limits and your needs; also indicate where you might be willing to compromise. Ask also about their relocation services. Below are three of the most well-respected throughout the city. All have several branches.

- **Tri-Coldwell Banker**: 1699 Van Ness (tel: 474-1750; fax: 771-1264; www. coldwellbanker.com)
- **McGuire**: 2001 Lombard (tel: 929-1500); 560 Davis (tel: 296-1000; www. mcguire.com)
- **Pacific Union:** 601 Van Ness (tel: 474-6600; www.pacunion.com)

Your agent should inform you of the weekend "open houses" in the neighborhoods you are considering. By looking at what is available in different areas and price ranges, you should quickly begin to understand values and how you may need to modify your own positions.

Starting the Search

Most apartments for sale are condominiums in which each unit is privately owned along with a percentage of the common space. The few "community apartments" are what other cities call co-operative apartments, where residents share in the corporation that owns the building. These apartments are generally in buildings constructed in the 1920s, and as that was a time when real estate was inexpensive, these co-ops had large, open floor plans. Today, however, only a few of the biggest condominiums may have 2,500 square feet, and in general a new one-bedroom apartment averages

900 square feet and a two-bedroom about 1,200–1,300 square feet.

Small, stucco single-family bungalows line the streets in the western sections of the city, and large, well-designed homes are more frequent in the northern districts of Pacific Heights and the Marina, farther west at Seacliff, and in enclaves such as Cole Valley, Diamond Heights, and Sherwood Forest. All areas have low-rise apartment buildings, some have high-rise apartment complexes, and just about all have some semidetached row houses.

Victorian houses are San Francisco's pride. Although thousands disappeared in 1906, some 14,000 survived the fire and have been preserved, primarily throughout the Mission, Cow Hollow, Pacific Heights, and Alamo Square districts. Victorians may be garish or gracious, they may appear in a number of styles such as Queen Anne, Italianate, or Stick, they may be single-family homes or two-flats, or—as along Union Street—they may have been converted into stores and offices. No matter what their state, Victorians are always sought after and do not come cheap; a few still needing restoration are left, but for the most part they have already been refurbished and decorated in the glorious colors that have earned them the name of "San Francisco's painted ladies."

But Victorians, famous and expensive as they may be, are not all the city offers. If you are interested in historic houses, look also for the Brown Shingles popular in the 1890s, single-family homes built in reaction to the ornate Victorian. Made of natural materials, used simply and frankly, with cedar shingles and window trims of plain broad planks, they were still fairly Victorian in attitude. It wasn't until the early part of the next century that the one-story Craftsman Bungalow led the city away from its previous era. By the twenties, the compact California Bungalow, with its front porch and stucco walls, had become predominant in the then-developing western portions of the city. All these interesting styles still exist in the city and occasionally come up for sale.

HOUSING: PROBLEMS AND SOLUTIONS

The right side of this Victorian was built in 1876 in the Italianate style, and the addition built in 1895, in the Queen Anne style.

Thinking About Price

First you should remember that San Francisco rates among the ten most expensive housing markets in the world and is the most expensive in the country. That said, you should next figure out which are the best resale locations in the city, such as in good school districts, in sunny areas, or in upcoming parts of the city, although these of course are the most expensive. Some districts — the Marina, Pacific Heights, Noe Valley, the Castro — are always in strong demand. Others are in upward transition, both in atmosphere and price — Hayes Valley, SOMA, Potrero Hill, Bernal Heights. Note that most neighborhoods have their own improvement associations, local residents who are vigilant about keeping the character of the area intact, which will, of course, maintain the value of real estate as well as that area's lifestyle. A general rule is "the better the view, the higher the price; the farther out into the fog, the lower the price."

Neighborhoods that are "coming up" are doing so quickly: a house that cost $180,000 in Bernal Heights just five years ago, for instance, may cost $350,000 today. The California Association of Realtors has said that "only 20 percent of households would be able to buy the city's median-priced home at $331,100." But "median" prices include the 10 percent that sell for above $1 million, as well as the 90 percent that may sell for $280,000, so affordable apartments and houses do exist. Yet the high end of the market is expanding and going higher: in 1998, some 11 homes in the city were sold for $5 million or more, and one outstanding two-bedroom 5,000 square foot apartment on Russian Hill sold for $15 million. Although these are exceptions, it is true that some 75 percent of the best properties receive multiple offers; in 1998–99, the winner bid at least 5–10 percent over the asking price.

If a job is bringing you to the area, inquire of the Human Resources department (during your compensation negotiation) as to whether the company offers housing incentives or a relocation package. Some do.

STUDENT HOUSING

Fortunately, universities have housing offices to help find students appropriate housing; some have on-campus housing. For temporary and inexpensive accommodations, San Francisco has several youth hostels that offer basic domitory-style rooms for basic prices. Currently, the price per night runs to about $15, and there is a two-week maximum stay. If you are bringing valuables such as computers or printers, inquire as to their safekeeping; some have provision for safe storage, others do not. The two below are members of Hostelling International (www.hiayh.org), but there are others; see the Yellow Pages under Hostels. For the HI hostels, membership in Hostelling International is required: membership may be purchased on-site.

- **HI Fisherman's Wharf**: Fort Mason, Building 240 (tel: 771-7277; fax: 771-1468; www.norcalhostels.org). One hundred and fifty beds in an urban park on the Bay, formerly a military base. Credit cards accepted; reservations advisable. At the Marina and close to Fisherman's Wharf.
- **HI Union Square**: 312 Mason Street (tel: 788-5604; fax: 788-3023; www.norcalhostels.org). Two hundred and twenty beds in the heart of the downtown area; reservations required.

Roommates

Sharing apartments is common, and roommate services offer referral services. In addition to the agencies below—most of which also handle regular rentals—look on bulletin boards at universities or at the Rainbow Grocery (see Chapter Thirteen).

- **Original San Francisco Roommate Referral Service**: 610-A Cole Street (tel: 558-9191; 800/446-2887; www.roommatelink.com)
- **Spring Street**: 3129 Fillmore Street (tel: 441-2309; www.springstreet.com)

- **Rent Tech**: 4054 18th Street, in the Castro (tel: 863-7368; fax: 552-8447; www.renttech.com); also at 1212A Union Street

RETIREMENT LIVING

If you are planning to retire to San Francisco, as many people do, you might consider one of the attractive urban complexes that offer independent-living apartments plus assisted living and medical care programs. These complexes are convenient with respect to cultural events, the city's restaurants, and downtown shopping. Others dot the Bay Area, up into the Sonoma and Napa Valleys. *San Francisco* magazine frequently runs an advertising section on retirement living.

- **San Francisco Towers**: 1661 Pine Street (tel: 776-0500)
- **The Sequoias**: 1400 Geary Boulevard, near Gough (tel: 922-9700)
- **Coventry Park**: 1550 Sutter Street (tels: 921-1552, 800/722-1414)
- **The Carlisle**: 1450 Post Street (tel: 929-0200)

— CHAPTER FOUR —
LOGISTICS OF SETTLING IN

GENERAL INFORMATION
For general information on living in San Francisco, dial **Local Source**, an automated 24-hour service that covers a variety of helpful subjects (tel: 808-5000; www.localsource.net/sanfrancisco). A listing of the four-digit subject codes can be found at the beginning of the Yellow Pages.

ELECTRICITY HOOKUP
In most rental homes you will be expected to pay for your use of electricity and gas, but in some they are included in the rent. The electric utility industry in California has been deregulated, meaning that home owners may choose their own electricity provider. **PG&E (Pacific Gas and Electric)**, formerly the public monopoly

in the state, continues to maintain the poles and lines for all electric service in California, and it is still the major provider of residential electricity and gas. PG&E's offices are open 8:30 am–5:30 pm weekdays (tel: 800/743-5000). New customers may be asked to pay a deposit, which will be applied (with interest accrued) to the monthly bill after one year if all bills have been paid on time.

For information on other registered electric service providers that meet the State's financial, technical and operational requirements, call **Electric Education Call Center** (tel: 800/789-0550). When considering a provider, consider the initiation and sign-up fees, length of contract, and how the electricity is generated.

Note that in the United States electricity is 110 volts, 60 hertz, and appliances brought from abroad that run on 220 volts will not run as they should. Fortunately, all housing comes with major appliances such as refrigerators and stoves, and sometimes with clothes washers and dryers. Otherwise, appliances in the United States are not particularly expensive, so it would be most efficient just to plan on purchasing what you need here. See Chapter Sixteen for appliance shops.

TELEPHONE SERVICE

Local telephone service is provided by **Pacific Bell (Pac Bell)**. Long distance service may be handled by any one of a number of providers. Rates and services among carriers vary widely, so shop around; advertisements appear regularly in the media. Owing to inexpensive options and the advent of the Internet, rates are dropping rapidly. At this writing, plans costing 7¢ per minute nationwide at any time of day are being offered by **AT&T**, **MCI**, and others; some offer free or discounted service on low-use days. People who make international calls regularly should inquire about international telephone rates, which are also dropping quickly.

To connect your residential telephone, consult the White Pages, which details the rates, hookup and repair procedures, and all options such as call-waiting and voice mail; then call Pac

Bell (tel: 800/310-2355). Customer service responds in English, Cantonese and Mandarin, Spanish, Korean, Vietnamese, Filipino, and Japanese; see the telephone book under Pacific Bell for their specific telephone numbers.

Telephone Books
Pac Bell delivers current telephone books when your new service is hooked up. New telephone books are issued annually in September. They are generally left in the lobby of apartment buildings or delivered to the door of private residences. Informational pages at the beginning of each book are multilingual, in English, Chinese, and Spanish.

The San Francisco **White Pages** are in one volume and include Brisbane, Colma, and Daly City; city, county and federal government listings are first, located by a blue edge to their pages. Business listings are edged in pink. The remainder, on plain paper, are residential listings. The **Yellow Pages**, also in one volume, are arranged alphabetically by category; a center insert also lists services with Internet addresses by category.

TELEVISION AND RADIO RECEPTION

Basic television channels—the three national networks and some local stations—are free, but reception may not be good, depending on the area. Most people subscribe to cable television, which offers good reception on all channels and the option to subscribe at an extra charge to various movie channels. Call **AT&T Cable Services** (tel: 877/824-2288). The daily newspapers detail each evening's television programs, and the Sunday papers publish a weekly schedule.

With some 80 radio stations in the Bay Area, you can probably find just what you're looking for, in whatever language. FM reception may depend on what side of a hill you're living on, and you may need an outside antenna. AM reception is generally clear. The newspapers list the radio stations.

ACCESSING THE INTERNET

All of the nationwide Internet providers have local access numbers in San Francisco and the Bay Area. If you have to find a new provider, you might ask your colleagues for their recommendations or take a look at the Internet magazines. If you need to check your e-mail before you are set up, try one of the Internet access points listed below, which should also have information about Internet providers. The **San Francisco Main Library** in the Civic Center provides Internet access, as do the Sony and Microsoft shops at **Metreon** in Yerba Buena, but they are usually crowded and suggest a time limit for access. **Kinko's** copy shops have Internet access and most are open 24 hours. Try also these cybercafes:

- **Club-I Internet Cafe**: 850 Folsom Street (tel: 777-2582)
- **Circadia Coffee House**: 2727 Mariposa Street (tel: 552-2649)

MAIL DELIVERY

The Post Office delivers mail addressed to you at your new address without official notification, although you will have no doubt submitted a Change of Address card to your previous post office. There is one mail delivery per day, Sundays and holidays excepted. Until you have a permanent mailing address you may have mail sent to your name at General Delivery, San Francisco CA 94142. Pick it up at the Civic Center Station, 101 Hyde Street, at Golden Gate Avenue; hours Monday–Saturday, 10:00 am–2:00 pm. Bring identification.

Each postal "zip code" has a post office. All are open weekdays from 8:30/9:00 am to 5:00 pm; most, but not all, are open Saturdays for some portion of the day. For the post office nearest you and its hours of operation, see the informational section in the Yellow Pages; calling a central number also connects you to any post office (info tel: 800/275-8777).

TRASH COLLECTION

Almost all new apartments and houses have in-sink garbage disposals to handle most food waste. For the rest, in large buildings, both trash collection and recycling of paper, glass, and metal are taken care of by the management. In small buildings, tenants themselves may have to place the blue recycling boxes by the curb on the days specified for that neighborhood. If you live in a house, you will have to arrange for garbage collection. Ask your neighbors or the previous owner of your home which scavenger company is used in your area. Bills are generally sent quarterly, and costs average about $12 per month.

EARTHQUAKE INSURANCE

Homeowners may want to take out earthquake insurance, as part of the homeowners' insurance policy; inquire of your insurance agent. The **CEA**'s **(California Earthquake Authority)** "mini-policy" is available through many insurance agencies (CEA tel: 916/492-4300); other companies offer policies that are not part of the CEA system.

On a practical note, no matter where you are in the Bay Area, you should have a working flashlight in your home and perhaps some candles, a portable radio, a standard, non-electric telephone, and a few gallons of water—just in case. Always keep enough medication to tide you over and a small reserve of cash. Many stores in the Bay Area sell earthquake kits.

OPENING A BANK ACCOUNT

Opening a bank account is easier than in some other countries. You will only need to provide a picture identification, an address, and enough money to make your initial deposit. When choosing a bank or a savings or loan association, make sure it is part of the federal insurance systems FDIC or FSLIC, to ensure that your funds will not be at risk. Consider a credit union, for they often offer good terms, both on accounts and fees, and on interest paid on time deposits and savings accounts.

Inquire as to all options open to you, especially their charges; with a sizeable deposit you may avoid the various user and monthly fees, and some offer no-fee checking. Ask if you may bank by Internet. Banks are affiliated with major networks such as CIRRUS or PLUS, which allows withdrawal of cash from automatic teller machines (ATMs); when choosing a bank, inquire whether it charges for using other banks' ATMs. Many shops and groceries accept bank cards, which, unlike charge cards, debit your account immediately.

You may be asked whether you wish to apply for a Visa/Master Card. Inquire as to the rates of interest charged, for rates vary and low-interest cards are available. Note that it is illegal in California for merchants to use your credit card as identification; they may not write its number down on your check. Don't let this happen.

The two largest banks in California are Wells Fargo and Bank of America (BofA), and both have branches throughout the city. In any case, your bank should be convenient to your home or workplace. Banks are open weekdays only and are also closed on holidays.

FINDING A LAUNDRY

You can find self-service laundromats in every neighborhood. Machines generally accept quarters only. Although many sell soap powders, it's better to bring your own; it's cheaper, and you can choose the kind you like. If you would like to be entertained while doing your laundry, try **Brain/Wash** at 1122 Folsom, between 7th and 8th Street (tel: 861-3663); wash your clothes, eat a meal and drink some wine, and listen to music or comedy.

Ask your neighbors for recommendations for dry cleaners, for there are many. Cleaning of standard items generally takes about three days, but most cleaners have "early bird specials:"

clothes that are brought in before a certain time (8:30 am or 9:00 am) may be picked up the same day after 5:00 pm; of course, many have home pickup and delivery. Hard-to-clean items take longer, as do items that require repair. **Meaders**, established in 1912, has four locations. Cleaners that advertise "hand finishing" or "French cleaning" do well with more delicate items; **Locust** at 3585 Sacramento Street (tel: 346-9271) and the nearby **Peninou French Laundry and Cleaners**, established in 1903, at 3707 Sacramento (tel: 751-9200) are two high quality cleaners. Cleaners do laundry as well as dry cleaning. See *Cleaners* in the Yellow Pages.

GETTING YOUR HAIR CUT

Many of the city's hair salons are unisex. Prices vary widely, depending primarily on location. Salons near Union Square charge more than a local hairdresser in one of the outer districts. Tips are not included in the price, and every person—shampoo person, hair stylist, coat check—gets a tip based on level of service. A few chains—**Supercuts, The Beauty Store**—offer good prices and standard services. Of course the quality varies with the particular hairdresser at any salon, so you just have to experiment until you find someone you like. Salons may offer more services than you are used to: massage, music, art exhibits, etc; see also Chapter Fifteen under Spas for **Elizabeth Arden** and **77 Maiden Lane**, two elegant multi-service salons. Almost all shops are closed on Sunday and many on Monday. See *Beauty Salons* in the Yellow Pages.

- **Architects and Heroes**: 2239 Fillmore, near Sacramento (tel: 921-8383). Consistently voted one of the best hairdressers in the city. Open Sunday. Also at 580 Bush Street (tel: 391-8833).
- **Cowboys & Angels**: 207 Powell Street, Suite 400 (tel: 362-8516). Trendy, fun salon for young people who want to look wild and for corporate types who don't.
- **Mister Lee Beauty, Hair & Health Spa**: 834 Jones (tel: 474-

6002). Rated among the best in the city.
- **Snippity Crickets**: 3562 Sacramento (tel: 441-9363). Welcoming atmosphere for children's haircuts. Also in Berkeley. Open Sunday.
- **Vidal Sassoon**: 359 Sutter (tel: 397-5105). Popular salon, part of a nationwide chain.
- **Yosh for Hair**: 173 Maiden Lane (tel: 989-7704). Among the top hair styling salons in the city.

READING A NEWSPAPER

As of this writing, San Francisco has two daily newspapers, the *San Francisco Chronicle* and the *San Francisco Examiner*. Both papers have recently been sold, however, and their future directions remain uncertain. Currently, on Sunday the two papers put out one combined issue. The *Oakland Tribune* and the *Berkeley Barb* serve the East Bay, as does the *Contra Costa Times*. In the South Bay, the *San Mateo County Times* and the *San Jose Mercury News* are the standards, and in the North Bay, the *Marin Independent*. All are available for subscription to be delivered to your door before dawn, as are such national newspapers as the *New York Times* and the *Wall Street Journal*.

Some of the most interesting and popular local newspapers, however, are free. *The Bay Guardian* is a liberal weekly that covers issues of interest throughout the Bay Area and reviews events and cultural activities. The *San Francisco Weekly* basically covers the same for the city. Both are issued on Wednesday and can be found in news boxes on street corners.

Most city districts have their own newspapers, with articles of local interest and ads for neighborhood services. *San Francisco Downtown*, for instance, covers the Financial, Retail and South or Market areas, *The Nob Hill Gazette* covers Nob Hill, and, obviously, *North Beach Now* covers North Beach, plus a section on South Beach. The *San Francisco Observer*, which serves "the heart of San Francisco," covers neighborhoods around the Haight, Hayes

Valley, Fillmore, and Duboce Triangle. Look for the tabloid for your community; many are delivered each month.

Various ethnic communities have their own newspapers. The *Tenderloin Times*, for example, is published in English, Chinese, Cambodian, and Vietnamese. Look for *Asian Week* at news boxes on city streets and in Japantown for *Nichi Bei Times*, a Japanese-English daily. The national *Sing Tao Daily* has an extensive section on California and is read by 100,000 Asians. *El Mensajero* is the bilingual weekly for the Latino Community, and *El Latino* is only in Spanish. *San Francisco Bay View* is a free weekly newspaper for the African-American community. There are others.

Leading the long list of gay publications are the bi-weekly *Bay Area Reporter* (Bar) and the *San Francisco Bay Times*. *Icon* is a lesbian newspaper, published monthly.

Foreign Publications

European and Asian publications and some American hometown newspapers are found in a few shops around the city, and **Borders** on Union Square has a good selection. Chinatown's newsstands sell a good selection of Chinese papers, and you may find the free *Chinese TV Guide* tabloid in some restaurants and Chinese shops. **Kinokuniya Bookstore** in the Japan Center has an outstanding selection of Japanese publications. One news kiosk, on Sansome between Bush and Sutter, has a good selection of foreign and hometown newspapers, as do some newsstands such as **Eastern News**. See also Chapter Sixteen, under Foreign Bookstores.

- *Union Square* — **Harold's International News**: 524 Geary (tel: 441-2665)
- *North Beach* — **Cavalli Italian Bookstore**: 1441 Stockton (tel: 421-4219)
- *Chinatown Gate* — **Café de la Presse**: 352 Grant (tel: 398-2680)
- *Pacific Heights* — **Juicy News**: 2453 Fillmore Street (tel: 441-3051)

FINDING YOUR SPIRITUAL HOME

Finding the right place of worship shouldn't be difficult. Generally the city's churches and synagogues are welcoming of anybody who wants to worship, whether affiliated with that religion or not. San Franciscans practice their religion in the way they do everything else—according to their own reasons and tastes—and it is said that only some 35 percent of the population is identified with a major religious denomination. Nonetheless there are multilingual options for daily or weekly worship for just about any faith. Most churches and synagogues sponsor educational and social programs for their congregants.

There are so many faiths—traditional denominations, evangelical, messianic, and those that worship in their own ways, such as the **Church of Saint John Coltrane,** an African Orthodox church that uses the music of the great jazz saxophonist in its liturgy—that they would be impossible to list here. And there are so many worship sites that they, too, would be impossible to mention. Instead, this small sampling should serve to show the diversity of opportunities in San Francisco. See the Yellow Pages under *Churches* or *Synagogues*. Some print their worship schedules.

- *Baptist*—**19th Avenue Baptist Church**: 1370 19th Avenue, at Irving (tel: 564-7721). The most active of the Baptist congregations. Services in English, Cantonese, Vietnamese and Arabic. Bible study in all languages.
- *Buddhist*—**Zen Center**: 300 Page Street (tel: 863-3136). Buddhist temple and information point for Buddhism in the Bay Area.
- *Catholic*—The major Catholic cathedral is **The Cathedral of St. Mary**, at 111 Gough Street, at Geary (tel: 567-2020). Masses in English and Spanish. For information on the Catholic community, schools, and churches, contact the Archdiocese office at 445 Church Street (tel: 565-3600).
- *Christian Science*—**First Church of Christ, Scientist**: 1700

Franklin Street (tel: 673-3544). Call for other places of worship and reading rooms.

- *Church of Christ* — **Civic Center Church of Christ**: 250 Van Ness Avenue, at Grove (tel: 861-5292). An international and multi-ethnic congregation of Caucasians, African Americans, and Asians.
- *Episcopal* — **Grace Cathedral**: 1051 Taylor Street, at California (info tel: 749-6310). This "modern Gothic" cathedral is the seat of the Episcopal Church in San Francisco, and hosts lectures, concerts, etc. Evening prayer, Evensong on Thursdays, carillon recitals and concerts, in addition to regular scheduled worship.
- *Islam* — For information on worship, call the **Islamic Center of San Francisco** (tel: 552-8831) or the **Islamic Bookstore and Islamic Society**: 20 Jones Street (tel: 863-8005).
- *Jewish* — **Congregation Emanu-El**: 2 Lake Street (tel: 751-2535). Reform temple. For information on any aspect of Judaism in San Francisco, call the **Jewish Community Information & Referral Service** at 121 Steuart Street (tel: 777-4545). Inquire about the annually issued *Resource*, an extensive guide to Jewish life in the Bay Area.
- *Methodist* — **Glide Memorial United Methodist Church**: 330 Ellis Street, at Taylor (tel: 771-6300). In the heart of the Tenderloin, Glide is the city's most celebrated religious gathering place. Sunday services are always crowded. This is the church most known in the city for social activism, feeding and providing job training for the poor and homeless.
- *Methodist* — **Park Presidio United Methodist Church**: 4301 Geary Boulevard (tel: 751-4438). Services in English, Chinese and Korean. Congregation involved in community projects.
- *Presbyterian* — **Noe Valley Ministry**: 1021 Sanchez, at 23rd Street (tel: 282-2317). The *de facto* community center for Noe Valley, this church is an interfaith gathering point, providing social events, meetings and concerts.

- *Quaker*—**Friends Quaker Meeting**: 65 9th Street (tel: 431-7440) Unprogrammed meeting. Socially active.
- *Unitarian*—**First Unitarian Universalist Church**: 1187 Franklin Street (tel: 776-4580). Congregation has worshiped here since 1888.

Gay and Lesbian Worship

San Francisco's churches and synagogues are openly welcoming of gay and lesbians, singles or couples. Although active and integrated into the city's spiritual life, gays and lesbians are also forming supportive spiritual groups and worship sites of their own. Progressive in outlook, these communities are usually open to people of all sexual identities.

- *Catholic*—**Dignity San Francisco**: 1329 7th Avenue (tel: 681-2491)
- *Interfaith Christian*—**Metropolitan Community Church**: 150 Eureka at 18th St (tel: 863-4434)
- *Jewish*—**Congregation Sha'ar Zahav**: 290 Dolores Street (tel: 861-6932)

REGISTERING TO VOTE

There are no time-linked residency requirements for voter registration; all citizens over the age of 18 with proof of a permanent address may vote. Call the **Department of Elections** at 633 Folsom Street, Room 109, for a registration form up to one month before an election (tel: 554-4375). Otherwise, before each election or primary there are usually people outside supermarkets registering voters.

STORAGE LOCKERS

Last, if your new home is smaller than you had imagined and you need to store some belongings, consider a self-storage locker. Sizes range from those that would hold a few items to those in which you might store all your furniture while looking for housing. In these dry, well-maintained warehouses, there is 24-hour security; you retain the key to your own locker and have daily access. Sometimes there are waiting lists, but lockers do come available, and new warehouses are opening up. There are others outside the central districts, in the East Bay, and in Marin. See the Yellow Pages under *Storage—Self Service*.

- **Attic Self Storage**: 2440 16th Street (tel: 626-0800)
- **American Storage Unlimited**: 600 Amador Street (tel: 800/863-5820)
- **City Storage Loc-N-Stor**: 144 Townsend Street (tel: 495-2300); 500 Indiana Street (tel: 436-9900)
- **Crocker's Lockers**: 1400 Folsom Street (tel: 626-6665)

— Chapter Five —

FORMALITIES FOR FOREIGNERS

IMMIGRATION

Perhaps the streets of the United States were not paved with gold as so many immigrants imagined when they came to these shores, but America has nonetheless been, since its earliest days, a land of opportunity. Whether people came to escape poverty or politics, America has always seemed to be — and often has been — the world's most beneficial haven. America has, in fact, gained its strength by being a "melting pot" of cultures, and it is immigration and assimilation that have created the world's most successful multi-ethnic nation. Immigration has waxed and waned over the centuries, owing to external factors such as wars or internal factors such as changes in societal attitudes. During the 1990s, the population of the United States grew by only 8 percent, but the percentage of foreign-born residents grew by some 30 percent. In 1996, some 900,000 immigrants came to the United States from 206 nations; Mexico and then the Philippines are the largest sending countries. One-third of all immigrants come to California, and about one-quarter of California residents are not native-born.

Although both the citizens and the government of the United States understand and believe that diversity enriches society, the country has always had mixed feelings about immigration: the subject of limiting immigration always comes up during economic downturns, for it is widely held that immigrants take jobs away from low-skilled American citizens.

The problem is compounded by the number of illegal immigrants who cross untended borders. For instance, since 1990, one million Mexicans have immigrated into the United States, some 80 percent of them illegally. Efforts to strengthen the borders have had some effect, but it is difficult to police the long border between the United States and Mexico. Thus, although some 170,000 illegal immigrants were deported in 1998, official efforts to limit immigration also tend to focus on legal immigration. A 1997 report to the United States Congress by the Commission on Immigration Reform recommended some immigration reform, but at this writing it is not yet clear which recommendations will be implemented.

Nonetheless, immigration laws are currently—and will no doubt remain—very complex, and it is important to consult the American Embassy in your country (or the consulate nearest you) long in advance of your desired emigration and to receive the most current information. Have ready as much documentation as possible concerning your personal history, health, qualifications, financial condition, and plans for your stay in the United States. You can receive detailed information on eligibility and requirements for immigrant visas on the Internet, from the websites of the State Department (www.state.gov; www.travel.state.gov) or the **Immigration and Naturalization Service (INS)**, an agency of the Department of Justice (www.ins.usdoj.gov). In the United States, you may also call the INS Forms Request Line (tel: 800/870-3676).

Visas
All people entering the United States must have a valid passport, although in most cases Canadians may provide only legal proof of residency. Citizens of most western European countries, the United Kingdom, Argentina, Australia, New Zealand, Singapore, and Japan do not need visas for stays of under 90 days, but must complete the I-94 Nonimmigrant Visa Waiver upon arrival; almost everyone else must have a visa, obtained before departure from the American Embassy in your country or the nearest consulate; you will also need to complete the I-94 Form and keep it with you during your stay. Leave enough time to apply for and receive the visa; lines at visa offices can be long and employees harried. Depending on your country and situation, you can sometimes apply for the visa at your travel agent, while booking your flight.

Upon arrival at a port of entry, be prepared to wait in line at the immigration booth, to show your passport, visa, and return ticket (if appropriate), and to explain the reason for your visit. If you need help, immigration officers at the airport have information. In dire situations, you may wish to call your country's embassy in Washington, D.C. or its consulate in San Francisco (see below).

Employment-based Visas
Do not expect to enter the United States and then to look for and find a permanent, legal job. There are, however, a variety of options for coming to the United States to work, depending on your skills, abilities, and experience in your field. It also often depends on how much an employer needs your unique services. The INS issues a booklet *Instructions for Completing Petition for a Nonimmigrant Worker, Form I-129*, which spells out in considerable detail all the categories of people eligible to work in the United States, the

circumstances of the employment, and how to apply. For immigrant worker visas, it is the would-be employer who makes the application for the I-140, which allows certain workers to apply for one of the E1-4 visas; these forms are not available outside the United States. Often, particular educational levels must have been reached, professional-certification requirements must have been met, or the applicant's experience so unique that the employer can show that no American citizens are qualified to fill the particular position. People with other specialty occupations such as licensed nurses are likely to receive permission to enter without much difficulty. Artists and entertainers must have demonstrated recognized achievements in their field, or national or international acclaim. The H1B visa is for high-tech workers; as of this writing, the annual allocation is 115,000 visas, and the cap is generally reached early in the fiscal year.

The publication mentioned above also spells out the requirements for those who may come to work permanently and those who may come to work temporarily. An example of a temporary position might be an internationally renowned professor who comes to a university to teach, or an acclaimed artist or entertainer who is coming to perform on tour. In California, applications may be had from the **Employment Development Office** in Sacramento (tel: 916/464-3400).

There are many categories for eligibility, including those for religious workers and those for entrepreneurs who are investing at least $1 million in an enterprise that creates a minimum of 10 new jobs in the United States. It is extremely helpful to check the State Department website.

Finally, do not expect to come and find illegal work, despite tales from your friends of how easy it is to find work in a restaurant or bar. Employers face stiff fines if caught employing non-documented foreigners, so this kind of job market is drying up.

North American Free Treaty Agreement

To enter the United States under the North American Free Trade Agreement (NAFTA), Canadians and Mexicans should understand the conditions that apply to entry for business or work purposes. These are set forth in Justice Department Form M-316, *The North American Free Trade Agreement (NAFTA) between the United States, Canada and Mexico*, available at immigration offices, at United States consulates, and from Free Trade Specialists at most of the ports of entry between the United States and Canada/Mexico.

- *Canada* — **United States Embassy**: 100 Wellington Street, Ottawa, ON K1P 5T1 (tel: 613/238-4470)
- *Mexico* — **United States Embassy**: Paseo de la Reforma 305, Cuauhtémoc 06500, near the Monumento a la Independencia (tel: 01/5209-9100); consulates in Cuidad Juarez, Hermonsillo, Guadalajara

Student Visas and Permits

Some 480,000 foreigners are studying in the United States, the majority in California. The highest percentage are Asians from Japan, China, and Korea. Universities welcome foreign students, providing their credentials meet the institutions' standards and all immigration criteria are met.

In most countries the **United States Information Agency (USIA/USIS)** maintains an Educational Advising Center. Centers can be found at U.S. embassies, Fulbright Commissions, non-profit organizations with overseas operations, and at local universities. These centers provide general information about the system of education and the admissions process in the United States, and they also offer individual advising (sometimes for a fee). Inquire of the American Embassy in your country. You can also get information from the State Department's website: click on "The Department," then on the region and country you are coming from; highlight the option "education" or "study."

To receive the visa that will allow you to enter the United States to study, you must already have been accepted at an accredited institution. Upon acceptance, you will receive from the Admissions Office the I-20 Certificate of Eligibility, which allows you to enter the school on a particular date. Take the I-20 to the American Embassy or your nearby consulate to apply for the appropriate visa: F1, J1, or M1. In addition to your passport and the I-20, you will need to show that your finances (or the finances of your sponsor) allow you to study without relying on income from working, although some work is permitted. Visas are generally valid during the duration of study. If you decide to postpone the entry date for any reason, you will have to start the process again and get a revised I-20 from the institution.

Although most universities have health clinics on their campuses, they all require foreign students to have health insurance, and most sell insurance plans that meet at least the minimum levels of the National Association for Foreign Student Affairs (NAFSA); if you have insurance, it must meet NAFSA's minimum criteria. Insurance requirements appear on the institution's application forms.

Part-time work on campus may exist at some universities, especially for graduate students who may be offered teaching/research assistantships. Although almost all foreign students must have taken the TOEFL test for admission to an American institution, the TSE (Test of Spoken English) may also be required for those interested in teaching assistantships. Spouses who enter the country with an F2 visa (dependent of an F-1 holder) may not work but may study full- or part-time as long as they are living with the holder of the F1.

For work and study programs, internships and seasonal work, contact the **Council on International Educational Exchange (CIEE)** or access their website for extensive information (www.ciee.org):

- *Australia*: University Center, Level 8, 210 Clarence Street (tel: 07/3849-8463; fax: 07/3849-8556)
- *France*: Centre Odéon Franco-Américain: 1, place de l'Odeon, Paris 75006 (tel: 01.44.41.74.74; fax: 01.43.26.97.45)
- *Japan*: Cosmos Aoyama Gallery Floor, 5-5367 Jingumae Shibuya-Ku (tel: 03/5467-5502; fax: 03/5467-7031)
- *United Kingdom:* 52 Poland Street, London W1V 4JQ (info tel: 171/478-2000; fax: 171/734-7322)
- *United States*: 205 East 42nd Street, New York, NY 10017 (tel: 212/822-2600; fax: 212/822-2699)

While in the United States, carry your student identification card with you. Also get the **International Student Identity Card (ISIC)**, an internationally recognized document which shows your student status and offers discounts on a variety of services and travel; you will need to bring proof of your registration as a student. Cards cost about $20, and travel agents often carry them, as does **Council Travel**, which is part of CIEE; for their offices worldwide, see their website above. In San Francisco offices are at 530 Bush Street (tel: 421-3473) and at 225 West Portal Avenue (tel: 566-6222). In Berkeley, Council Travel is at 2846 Channing Way (tel: 510/848-8604).

Diversity Immigrant Program

The Diversity Immigrant Program is a lottery that offers 50,000 permanent residence visas each year. The program is divided into six regions: Asia; South America, Central America, and the Caribbean; Europe; Africa; Oceania; and North America (the Bahamas). No one country receives more than 3,500 diversity visas in any year. Applications for a visa date of two years in the future are generally due toward the end of October. Applications that arrive after the deadline are not considered. Check for current deadlines.

Certain countries within broad categories above are not entitled to apply, owing to the large number of applicants from those countries under other immigration programs. This includes Canada and Mexico, which have special programs under the North American Free Trade Agreement. At this writing, other countries excluded are China and Taiwan, Colombia, Dominican Republic, El Salvador, Haiti, India, Jamaica, Mexico, Philippines, Poland, South Korea, United Kingdom (except Northern Ireland), and Vietnam.

In general, an applicant must have been born in an eligible country and have either a high school education or its equivalent, or have two years of work experience in a job that requires at least two years of training to perform.

Inquire at the consulate nearest you for current information or search the INS website (www.ins.usdoj.gov). Basically, there are no entry forms: on a plain sheet of paper, type or print (in the English alphabet) your full name (surname first, and underlined), date and place of birth (and the same information for your dependents), plus your full mailing address. Attach with tape one recent photograph of 1.5 inches (37 mm). Sign the entry form; an original signature is required.

Put the entry form into a business-size envelope and as the return address put your full mailing address and place of birth. Mail it (regular mail only) to the address below. Note that the address for each of the six areas is the same, but that the zip code is different. If the application is sent to the wrong zip code, it will be disqualified. The address is: DV Program (add year of application, such as "DV01" for 2001) National Visa Center, Portsmouth NH USA. The zip code for each area of origin is:

- Asia: 00210
- South America, Central America, Caribbean: 00211
- Europe: 00212
- Africa: 00213
- Oceania: 00214
- North American: 00215

Petition by a Relative

A U.S. citizen may petition to have a family member come to the United States. "Family members" include a spouse, parents, children, or siblings. First, the INS must approve an immigrant petition (INS Form I-130) filed by the relative in the United States. Upon approval, the State Department allocates an immigrant visa number to the overseas relative. With this, the overseas relative applies for the immigrant visa at the U.S. Consulate. This, unfortunately, is not a particularly efficient method of immigrating into this country, nor is it the most sure, for the number of immigrant visa numbers are limited and there is a preference system. First come spouses, parents and unmarried children under the age of 21; next come all the rest. Thus, even after the forms have been filled out, the $110 fee paid, and the appointment made for the interview, it may take many years for the application to take effect. Nonetheless, if you wish to follow this path to immigration, ask your relative in the United States to request the Department of Justice Form I-130, the *Petition for Alien Relative*. If you want to estimate the time it will take to receive the immigrant visa number, you can access the State Department's Visa Bulletin (http://travel.state.gov/visa_bulletin.html). Compare your number with the number the Department is then working on.

CITIZENSHIP

After you have received your "green card" that allows you to stay and work in the United States, start thinking about citizenship. With certain exceptions, citizenship may be applied for after holding the "green card" for at least five years. Apply three months before the residency requirement is fulfilled.

An applicant for citizenship must be able to speak, read and write English (again, with certain exceptions, such as being over 55 years of age and having lived in the United States for 15 years), know the fundamentals of United States government and American history, and be of "good moral character."

INS IN SAN FRANCISCO

The San Francisco District Office of the INS is at 444 Washington Street, near Sansome (tel: 705-4411). It is open from 6:45 am to 3:00 pm weekdays except Wednesday, when it closes at 2:45 pm. Waits can be extremely long. The office has forms and information; you may also order forms by telephone, if you know the number or name of the form you need (tel: 800/870-3676), or order them by fax: 844-5270, 855-9950).

If you need passport or immigration photographs or fingerprint documentation, try the two shops below, across from the INS building. Both are open weekdays only.

- **Leetone Photo Center**: 615 Sansome Street (tel: 391-9890)
- **Corning Gold Photography**: 501 Washington Street (tel: 392-2223)

FOREIGN CONSULATES

In the United States, embassies are in Washington, D.C., but countries with many residents or visitors in San Francisco maintain consulates here as well. Consulates are most helpful to their country's citizens during times of crisis: they replace lost passports and help in medical or legal emergencies by making referrals to appropriate doctors, dentists, or lawyers. They do not, however, help people get out of jail. Yet in all emergencies, they act as liaison between the family abroad and the person in the United States. It is a good idea to carry the telephone number of the consulate in your wallet; should trouble befall, it can be easily contacted.

For non-emergencies, embassies and consulates renew passports, record births, marriages and deaths, notarize documents, and provide advice on matters pertaining to citizenship in their country, such as filing taxes. Sometimes they offer information on local services, including lists of doctors and attorneys who speak your language, and translators.

Most consulates are open for consular affairs weekdays in the mornings only. Some have afternoon telephone hours. Find out when your consulate is open before going. On the national holidays of the United States and of your own country, the consulate will no doubt be closed. For a complete list, see the Yellow Pages under *Consulates & Other Foreign Government Representatives*.

- **Australia**: 1 Bush Street (tel: 362-6160)
- **Brazil**: 300 Montgomery Street (tel: 981-8170)
- **Britain:** 1 Sansome Street (tel: 981-3030)
- **Canada**: (visas and passports tel: 213/356-2700)
- **El Salvador**: 870 Market Street (tel: 781-7924)
- **France**: 540 Bush Street (tel: 397-4330)
- **Germany**: 1960 Jackson Street (tel: 775-1061)
- **Ireland**: 44 Montgomery Street (tel: 391-4214)
- **Israel**: 456 Montgomery Street (tel: 844-7500)
- **Italy**: 2590 Webster Street (tel: 931-4924)
- **Japan**: 50 Fremont Street, 23rd Floor (tel: 777-3533)
- **Malaysia**: 2 Embarcadero Center (tel: 421-6570)
- **Mexico**: 870 Market Street (tel: 392-5554)
- **New Zealand**: One Maritime Plaza (tel: 399-1255)
- **Philippines**: 447 Sutter Street (tel: 433-6666)
- **Russian Federation**: 2790 Green Street (tel: 202-9800)

BRINGING

…Your Belongings

If your appropriate visa for residency is in order, there are no particular formalities for bringing your personal effects into the United States for your own use. If you have owned them for more than one year, there is no duty on import; antiques are also free of duty if they are more than 100 years old. It is, however, helpful to have an inventory and valuation of the belongings. For information, call the **United States Customs Service** (tel: 782-9210;

www.customs.ustreas.gov). Most international shippers are familiar with the paperwork and bureaucratic requirements for international shipment, and they are affiliated with moving companies in the United States.

...Your Appliances
As mentioned earlier, the United States uses 110-120 volt, 60 hertz electricity. Importing European appliances may be more trouble than it is worth, for appliances—large and small—are fairly inexpensive in America, and discount shops are found in every city. Most apartments and houses are equipped with stoves and refrigerators, and some with clothes washers and dryers.

...Your Car
All cars and vehicles coming into the country must conform with U.S. safety, bumper, and emission standards; the vehicle must have written certification that it meets emission requirements before it may be brought into the country. This may either be in the form of a statement from the Environmental Protection Agency (EPA), or a manufacturer's label in English that is affixed to the car. Unless the car was manufactured in the United States and exported, it is not likely that it will meet all standards. For information, write or telephone the EPA Programs and Compliance Division/Imports (6405-J), at 401 M. Street, S.W., Washington D.C. 20460 and ask for the *Automotive Imports Facts Manual* (tel: 202/564-9660; fax: 202/564-9596).

To bring a car into the country, you will need the shipper's original bill of lading, the bill of sale, foreign registration, and any other documents that cover the vehicle. The undercarriage of the car must be free of foreign soil, which can be accomplished by having the car steam-cleaned before shipment. Make sure you know in advance from your shipper the date the car will arrive, so that Customs can clear it. Imported cars (except some from Canada) should also have the International Registration Marker.

Except for the vehicles of returning U.S. government employees (including the military) and some citizens returning from employment abroad, foreign-made vehicles are generally dutiable at about 2.5 percent based on price paid. Contact the U.S. Customs Service at the Department of the Treasury, Washington D.C. 20229 (or any Customs office) for the brochure *Importing or Exporting a Car*.

...Your Pets
All dogs and cats being brought into the country must be examined at the port of entry before being allowed into the United States. (This also applies to pets that were taken out of the country and are being brought back in.) Dogs must be accompanied by a health certificate stating that they are free of diseases communicable to human beings. Both dogs and cats must be vaccinated against rabies at least 30 days before entry into the United States (except for animals under three months old). If the dog has been living in an area free of rabies, no rabies certificate is required; otherwise the dog should have a valid rabies vaccination certificate. For more details—and for details about other animals and birds—request the brochure *Pets, Wildlife: U.S. Customs* from The U.S. Customs Service, Department of the Treasury, Washington D.C. 20229 (or any Customs office).

...Your Money
There is no limit to the total amount of monetary instruments—cash, traveler's checks, negotiable securities—that may be brought into the United States, but if you bring in more than $10,000 (or if you receive that amount), you must file Form 4790 with the Customs Service.

...Your Medications
To bring medicines containing habit-forming drugs or narcotics (prescription-strength cough medicine, diuretics, heart drugs,

tranquilizers, etc) into the country, make sure all are properly identified and that you have a physician's prescription (or written statement that the medicine is used under a doctor's direction). Bring an amount that will tide you over until you can get a new prescription in the United States.

— Chapter Six —

BRINGING THE CHILDREN

GREAT FOR THE KIDS

San Francisco is a wonderful place to raise children. The area's moderate climate means that outdoor play is available just about any day of the year: parks and playgrounds dot the landscape, wide beaches offer endless play in the sand, and schools offer extensive extracurricular sports programs. The ethnic diversity of the city means that children will have a culturally stimulating environment in which to grow and learn. And the open friendliness of the city means a generally nurturing environment to those who avail themselves of opportunities presented. Well-behaved children are welcome in most restaurants, and even the most elegant restaurants have booster seats. Theaters, museums, private organizations,

Children at play in a neighborhood park.

the parks and other city agencies all have enriching programs for children. And the options for schooling, although seemingly complex and perhaps slightly discouraging at the outset, can offer a well-rounded education. Whatever you want for your child, you will no doubt find it in San Francisco.

THINKING ABOUT SCHOOLS

First, think about schools. Choosing a school in San Francisco, whether elementary, middle, or high school, is not as simple as showing up on the first day of school in your neighborhood and expecting your child to receive a good education. In fact, it is wise to think about schooling well before you decide on the neighborhood where you might want to live, for the suburbs are an extremely attractive option in terms of schooling. With research and care, you should be able to find a good public school for your child, or you may choose one of the excellent private schools, if tuition fees that may run as high as $15,000 per student are within your budget. If you can make a trip to San Francisco before your actual move, investigating schools should be among your priorities. Get advice from the Human Resources Department of your company, visit the San Francisco Unified School District headquarters, tour the schools you are considering, and talk to parents of children in those schools. Then, when you have found the right schools, follow carefully every procedure for application, for the most popular schools have the most applicants, and acceptance is not always assured.

There is no easy solution to schooling in the city of San Francisco. Public schools tend to be overcrowded and in the upper grades the large class size is not conducive to individual attention. Not all schools are equal in their facilities, programs, educational approach, or results, and budget cutbacks have forced major reductions in staff and in enrichment programs in areas such as art and music. Unfortunately, state and federal funding of schools is often inadequate; Gray Davis, the governor elected in 1998, has made raising the standard of education in California one of his highest priorities, but the enormous task will be difficult at best. Owing to the sheer number of children in public schools — some 5.6 million — California spends less per pupil than the national average and in 1997-98 ranked a low 46th in the country for *per capita* expenditures on education.

The above notwithstanding, the San Francisco school system educates the city's children. Public school students consistently rank above the national average in reading and math on the CTBS (Comprehensive Test of Basic Skills), a test that is given to every student to measure progress in those areas; another system-wide test, the Stanford 9 Test, compares ranks within the state and throughout the nation. But parents should remember that it also takes active parental participation to educate children in any city. Join parents' groups to understand the strengths and weaknesses of your school. If arts or music programs in your child's school have been cut back, for example, make sure your child attends outside enrichment programs, either in structured public programs or through private lessons. Everything is available in San Francisco to supplement basic public school education; it just takes determination on the part of the parent to find it.

Other options exist. If you have several children to educate, you might want to consider a public elementary school and then perhaps a private high school. Legislation has recently lowered the number of students permitted in each public elementary school class, but public high school classes tend to be overcrowded, sometimes with upwards of 40 students in a class. Private high schools generally take a fair number of students from public schools, especially those who have tested well or who were in GATE programs (see below).

Private schools have distinct advantages. Although each has its own character, basically they all have smaller class size with a better teacher/student ratio, and they can give more individual attention to each child. Private schools (see below), of course, are expensive, but some do offer scholarships or other financial aid. And, although they are usually filled to capacity and the application process is stringent, there are many different types to choose from.

Try to start your research before arriving in San Francisco. Check the **San Francisco Unified School District (SFUSD)** website (www.sfusd.k12.ca.us). You might also contact **School Match, Public Priority System**, which has detailed statistics on public and private schools across the country (tel: 614/890-1573; www.schoolmatch.com). School Match can do a full search for the right school for your child. After you fill out a questionnaire detailing all your priorities, School Match will suggest schools in the area that match your preferences. The full search costs $97.50; individual reports and "snapshots" cost less.

The Public Schools

In San Francisco, some 65,000 children attend the 77 public elementary schools (kindergarten through grade 5), 17 middle schools (grades 6–8), and 21 high schools (grades 9–12). Although a few schools offer grades K–8, most children attend a middle school. Not all schools are the same. Schools at all levels offer differing educational themes and teaching approaches; some offer academic programs while others stress technology, two are year-round, a few have language immersion programs (the language depending on the district), and some have better educational track records than others.

It is interesting to note that the highest percentage of the city's students are Chinese (27.4 percent), followed by Latino children (21.5 percent), and that Caucasians account for about 13 percent of the schooling population. Thus, no ethnic or cultural background dominates. Until 1999 the city officially maintained an ethnic and racial balance in the schools, but this was successfully challenged by the Chinese community on the grounds of discrimination. The SFUSD thus has been changing its procedures for application; it may no longer use ethnicity as a primary consideration in enrollment decisions, but may factor it in with location and economic need. One effect of the decision was the loss of almost $40 million in state funds for equalizing academic opportunities for African Americans and Latinos.

Every school offers a required core curriculum, and in addition to the themes mentioned above, some stress Bilingual Education, English-as-a-Second Language (ESL), Special Education, or the Gifted and Talented Education program (GATE); almost 15 percent of the city's students are enrolled in GATE programs. A wealth of information on public schools is available at SFUSD. SFUSD provides descriptions of each school's programs and their current "accountability report card." Much of this is also available on SFUSD's website, so if you have access to the Internet, you can obtain the information before you have to

The Marina Middle School.

make your decisions. SFUSD, at 135 Van Ness Avenue (tel: 241-6000), also has information about the **OER (Open Enrollment Request)** application process (see below). In addition, information can be had from the **Parent Information Center** of the **Educational Placement Center**, within SFUSD (tel: 241-6085).

Every block and every street of the city is assigned to a public school "attendance zone." The sizes of these zones vary according to the number of school-age children living in them. The zones include all children, even those going to private schools. It would be ideal if popular schools were in each neighborhood and if each neighborhood had schools to accommodate all the area's kids, but this isn't the case. Thus, parents must apply for the public schools they believe would be best for their children. There is no guarantee, however, that they will be accepted. Yet, the application process is crucial to your child's education in this city.

A *regular* school is one in which children are assigned based on where they live. Most of the city's children go to schools in their attendance zone. Some of these schools can't accommodate all the children in their zone, so even if you are planning to send your child to the neighborhood school, you should apply for a place in that school during the OER process.

An *alternative* school may offer special curriculum programs or have higher standards for academic programs than a regular school. It may also have a higher degree of parent involvement. Sometimes students from particular zip codes which have had lower average performance results may be given higher priority for acceptance into an alternative school. Otherwise, acceptance is by lottery and based on the OER application.

Because they are so in demand, a few of the top high schools, the *application* schools, require a special application in addition to (or instead of) the OER. These include **Lowell, School of the Arts (SOTA), Galileo,** and **Balboa.**

For Non-native English Speakers

Several elementary schools within the school district (as well as preschools mentioned below) offer language immersion programs for children whose native language is other than English, and whose ability in English would not yet allow them to integrate fully into a regular English-language school. Languages include Japanese, Spanish, Chinese, and Korean. Inquire at SFUSD. In addition, **Newcomer High School** at 2340 Jackson Street offers a transitional program for newly arrived high school age students who lack adequate English language proficiency (tel: 241-6584). Students study at Newcomer High approximately one year before transferring to other high schools.

Charter Schools

An increasingly recognized but somewhat controversial development is the use of public school funds to contract out the management of schools to private concerns. The almost 1500 "charter schools" nationwide have greater flexibility than municipality-run schools in that they have autonomy in management of the schools, in hiring of teachers, and in the development of curricula and enrichment programs. Charter schools must, however, adhere to public school norms. In California, for example, they must keep track of the number of minutes of instruction for each age level, keep attendance records, and administer the annual achievement test. But standards are high: class size is usually reasonable and students receive more individual attention than in many public schools. Students often study longer hours each day and may have a somewhat longer term than a regular public school schedule. Included in the curriculum are enriched art, music and language programs which, unfortunately, have been reduced at the city's cash-strapped public schools. Teachers, who must hold teaching certificates, are also paid somewhat higher salaries. In San Francisco, the charter schools are the once-ailing Thomas Edison Elementary in Noe Valley, the Creative Arts Charter School, the Life Learning Academy, the downtown Leadership High, and Gateway High, for students with learning difficulties.

Charter schools are gaining popularity nationwide, and in 1999 President Clinton proposed spending $95 million in the following three years to bring the number of charter schools to 3,000. Yet the schools remain controversial: some educators believe that the schools are not accountable enough for their educational results across a broad spectrum of students. As in private schools, however, if the results are not forthcoming, parents will no longer support the schools. Ongoing parent involvement is fairly high, and standardized testing gives an indication of a child's progress. Nonetheless, allocating public funds to private concerns (rather than the community's voting for funds to improve the quality of municipality-run education) will remain controversial until the results are in. For information on charter schools, you can access the website of the **California Department of Education** (www.cde.ca.gov/charter).

The OER

Selecting a child's school, of course, will be based on many factors other than just a school's location or reputation: the age, character, and language ability of the child should be considered, as well as the expected length of stay in San Francisco, whether permanent or temporary. The best way to determine which school is right for your child is to do your research: get the descriptions of schools and their "accountability report cards," visit schools if you can, and talk to parents of children in those schools. Then, begin the application process; the most popular schools have the highest number of applicants and the fewest openings.

The key to acceptance in the school you want for your child is the **OER (Open Enrollment Request)**. Each autumn the OER forms become available at schools or at SFUSD's Education Placement Center. The deadline for application is in January and it is strictly enforced; each year the date is slightly different, so make sure you are apprised of the date. Rank the schools you are applying for in order of preference. You are allowed to ask for four schools; one of them should be the regular school in your attendance zone if that is an option for you. SFUSD then compiles all the requests and matches them with the number of slots available in each school.

By March, the first round of acceptances are announced and the appeals process begins. In April, appeals are reviewed and the waiting lists are determined. In June, students who have not been placed are assigned to a school. Occasionally, vacancies occur at the last minute for students on waiting lists, but they should not be counted on, unless the school is in the "regular attendance district" of the child, meaning the neighborhood lived in.

Public School Registration Requirements

A child must have turned five years old before December 2 to enter kindergarten during that year. Proof of birth date is required for entrance into a public school; this might be a birth certificate or passport, for instance. As students must be legal residents of San Francisco, a proof of current address might include a recent utility bill in the name of the parent/guardian, a valid California driver's license, or a dated lease or property tax statement. Records from other schools attended should also be brought.

Kindergartners and first graders must have a complete physical examination before entering a public school. You will need to produce the child's immunization record. (Records from a foreign country must be reviewed by a local health facility.) DTP (Diphtheria, Tetanus, Pertussis), MMR (measles, mumps, rubella), Hib (Haemophilus influenza type B), and polio vaccination records will be reviewed. All children entering school are required to have a Tuberculin Skin Test, and if positive, will then need a chest x-ray. Immunization against Hepatitis B is required for incoming kindergartners.

Preschools

Preschools are for children aged two to five. Preschooling has long been important in San Francisco, a city in which both parents are likely to work outside the home, and to which people migrate without having other family in the area to help take care of the kids. But preschool is important on other grounds: it is widely held that children who have been "socialized" by attending preschools perform better in their early school years than children who have not.

When investigating preschools, consider only those facilities that have been licensed by the State Department of Social Services. Licensing means that the facility has met the state's criteria concerning the physical plant (amount of fenced playground areas, number of toilets per child, safe food preparation area, etc) and that the staff has met stringent educational and experiential qualifications. But these are minimum criteria: when you visit a school, inquire about its staff-child ratio, its activities and play materials, its teaching approach (the ratio of teacher-provided structure to child-directed play), and its general philosophy for young children. Ask also about parent involvement and the process of feedback and evaluations concerning a child's progress.

Each school is different. No matter how positive a recommendation you receive from someone you know, you should visit the schools you are considering and determine for yourself whether the facility, the teaching methods, and overall environment are suitable for your child. First, you should decide which kind of preschool fits the personality of your child and your budget (and see if those have places available). There are independent, private preschools, those sponsored by religious agencies, and public preschools sponsored by the San Francisco Unified School District (SFUSD). See *Schools: Academic-Preschool & Kindergarten* in the Yellow Pages: in addition to alphabetical listings, many private preschools advertise their qualifications and special features on these pages.

The SFUSD's **Child Development Program** operates 43 Children's Centers that provide "supervision and instruction" for children from the age of two, provided they are toilet trained. Parents must be San Francisco residents. Eligibility is determined by income of families, and lowest income families are considered first; parents who can afford at least a portion of the tuition pay on a sliding scale. Some of the most popular centers have waiting lists. Call the Child Development Program for information (tel: 750-8500). Information can be had in English, Chinese, and Spanish.

You may be surprised by how costly the private preschools may be, despite some being incorporated as non-profit: fees may reach $500 per month, but some may offer financial aid, depending on need. *Cooperative* schools, in which the parents are expected to participate regularly, cost less, but you should be prepared to make a commitment to a particular time and activity at your child's school.

- *Independent* preschools are not affiliated with public or religious agencies. Many are neighborhood schools, serving the ethnic mix of that area. Some have bilingual programs, also depending on the neighborhood. There are dozens of these private, independent schools, so shop around. In addition to the Yellow Pages, if you are interested in a particular bilingual program, ask for information at the elementary school in the area you are considering, or of people who share your native language.
- *Agency-affiliated* preschools are sponsored by an organization such as the Jewish Community Center (JCC) or the Young Men's Christian Association (YMCA). Both have schools throughout the city. Each school sets its own approach; some have a religious component to the program, but others do not. *Religious* preschools are sponsored by a particular church or synagogue, not the agencies above. If you are interested in a religious component to your child's schooling, ask your church or synagogue for recommendations.
- *College and university* preschools are sponsored by the city's institutions of higher learning, servicing their faculty and students. Inquire of the university.
- *Montessori* schools are similar worldwide. They follow the teachings of Dr. Maria Montessori, who advocated stimulating, non-competitive activities in a structured atmosphere while providing creative freedom.

PRIVATE SCHOOLS

Some 23,600 students attend the city's 36 private schools, and others commute to private schools in nearby towns. Private schools generally provide a high standard of education, small classes with a low student/teacher ratio, individual attention for children, and enriching extracurricular activities, all in a safe, nurturing, and stimulating environment. But this comes with a price tag. Tuition and other fees at private schools in the Bay Area are high, but they are generally in line with other private schools around the country. Some schools have financial aid programs and some offer reduced tuition if there are siblings in the school—it's worth checking them out. All in all, if you can afford it, you should at least check out private schooling during your investigation of schools. Some of the schools outside the city (especially in Marin) are extremely popular.

Regulation/Accreditation

Private schools are not regulated by the California Department of Education, except that the physical plants of the schools themselves must meet the state's standards for any public business or building, relating to earthquake or fire. Thus, they may not conform directly to the same minimums for days or hours of school attendance, nor are their teachers asked by the state to meet particular experiential or educational requirements. This does not in any way mean that the schools do not meet—or even exceed—the minimum standards of the state. It only means they are not governed by state regulations. In general, parents send their children to private schools to exceed the minimum standards set by the state.

Elementary and high schools are generally *accredited* by one of a number of governing bodies, such as the Accrediting Commission for Schools or the Western Association of Secondary Schools. Religious schools may also (or instead) be accredited by their own religious accrediting body, such as the Western Catholic Education Association or the National Association of Episcopal Schools. Accreditation is a lengthy process during which the school must meet the requirements of the accrediting body, including standards for curriculum, teaching philosophy, etc.

Types of Private Schools

There are several types of private schools and within them, their philosophies, goals, teaching approaches and curricula may differ widely. Some are traditional, others may be innovative in approach.

There are boys' schools and girls' schools, but most are co-educational. All should be able to provide detailed information during the application process. Some schools advertise their programs and philosophical approach in the Yellow Pages: see *Schools-Academic-Secondary & Elementary*. For a directory of California private schools ($17.50, plus tax and shipping), contact the California Department of Education: P.O. Box 271, Sacramento CA 95812 (tel: 800/995-4099). Unfortunately, the directory contains no evaluative statistics on the schools, but these can no doubt be had by writing to the schools directly. School Match, mentioned above, may have information as well. The schools themselves should be able to provide the parents of potential students with all the information necessary to make an informed decision.

Non-profit (or *independent*) schools are just that, and they are overseen by a Board of Trustees, often with parents on the Board or on committees that advise the Board. Many independent schools are eligible for outside funding and grants, and in order to receive them must meet the requirements of the funding agencies.

Proprietary schools may be a corporation or partnership, incorporated to make a profit, and although they are not necessarily governed by a board, they often have parents' committees that advise the administration, and being entirely dependent on tuition, are responsive to parents' concerns.

Most of the *parochial* (religious-based) schools in San Francisco are Catholic, although there are Jewish, Episcopal, and Baptist schools as well; inquire of your church or synagogue. Of the Catholic schools some are attached to parishes, some are independent and incorporated not-for-profit, and some — those affiliated with churches that were closed for budget-cutting — are now administered by the Archdiocese itself. Most have parent-teacher committees and some have advisory boards. For information, contact the **Archdiocese of San Francisco, Office of Catholic Schools**: 443 Church Street 94114 (tel: 565-3660).

The request must be in writing, and in addition to providing your name and address, you must indicate why you are requesting the information.

The Admissions Process

Private schools are usually filled to capacity. Thus, any new slots are filled according to a priority system: first to be considered are children who have other siblings in the school, children who have attended that school's pre-school, or children of the school's alumni or teaching staff. Only after these children have been considered are outside applications taken.

In fact, the application/admission process is quite stringent and is lengthier and more detailed than application into a public school. The process starts earlier, and each school may have a slightly different schedule. Schools generally require an interview with both parents, and a "play" period with the child to evaluate readiness for the program. References from previous schools attended may be required. Most schools charge an application fee.

Have all your questions ready. Inquire about teaching philosophy, curriculum, amount of homework, ethnic diversity, after-school programs, expectations for parent participation, and information about all costs, not just tuition. For example, there are often extra costs for after-school "extended care," or for uniforms, if the school requires them.

AFTER-SCHOOL PROGRAMS

As in any major city, children need to be supervised by an adult in their after-school hours, whether by a parent or in a structured program. Working parents should inquire about after-school "extended care" on the school premises, and whether there are places available and at what cost. The Child Development Program mentioned above offers after-school programs; call for information (in English, Chinese, or Spanish).

The **Recreation and Parks Department** sponsors a year-round after-school **Latchkey Program** for children 6–12 years of age. Programs are held in more than 30 of the Department's recreation centers around the city. During the school year, the hours are weekdays 2:00–6:00 pm, and during the summer 9:00 am–6:00 pm. These are structured programs: during the school year leisure and craft activities are encouraged (according to the specialty of the staff at a particular center), homework is supervised and a snack is provided. Summer programs feature arts and crafts, athletics, and field trips. These programs use a priority registration system, and there is a waiting list, especially for the most popular sites. Children in the Latchkey Program sign in upon arrival, sign out upon departure, and are expected to stay on site. Other "drop in" programs at Department centers are less structured and not as strictly monitored. Call for a brochure (tel: 337-4712).

Private schools also offer after-school programs for their students, invariably at extra cost. Each school's program is different, so if this is important to you, inquire during the application process.

CHILD CARE

If you need child care, consider the non-profit **Marin Day Schools**, based at 100 Shoreline Highway, Mill Valley (tel: 331-7766; fax: 331-7066). It has 14 campuses around the Bay Area, including San Francisco, and has since 1981 provided child care and a developmental curriculum for children 6 weeks to 10 years old.

You might also contact the **Children's Counsel of San Francisco**, which has offices downtown, in the Mission, and at Bayview-Hunter's Point (downtown tel: 243-0700; www.childrenscouncil.org). Among its services, the Council provides workshops and counseling for parents needing child care, and referrals to licensed child-care providers in San Francisco; it does no screening of individual providers, so all interviews and reference gathering are up to the parent. Some subsidy funds are available for needy parents. **Wu Yee Children's Services** at 831 Broadway provides much the same services, with bilingual (Chinese) resources (tel: 391-4721).

Providers should be licensed by the Community Care Licensing Agency, and they are checked annually by the agency. Arrangements for child-care providers vary: some come to the parents' house and others take children into their own homes. Because some providers follow their own children's schedules, they maintain flexible hours, so inquire in advance about days when they might not be available and about vacations.

EDUCATIONAL ENTERTAINMENT

Below is a small but representative sample of the range of opportunities for enriching entertainment in the area. Check occasionally with the San Francisco Visitors Center on Powell Street, for it has brochures on ongoing commercial activities and events that young children enjoy, including a list of city playgrounds. One commercial attraction is the **Basic Brown Bear Factory and Store** at 444 De Haro Street at Mariposa, a factory offering tours during which kids can see stuffed animals being made and stuff their own bears (tel: 626-0781); also at the Cannery (tel: 931-6670). For outdoor activities, make sure to bring a jacket for your child.

- **Rooftop at Yerba Buena Gardens**: A city block devoted to kids of all ages. Ice skating and bowling complex (tel: 777-3727), carousel, child-care center, and landscaped gardens. **Zeum** is an art and technology center for hands-on experience in exploring the high-tech and performing arts (tel: 777-2800).
- **Exploratorium**: 3601 Lyon Street, at the Palace of Fine Arts (tel: 561-0360). Hands-on science museum for kids of all ages (adults like it, too). Closed Monday.
- **Bay Area Discovery Museum**: 557 McReynolds Road, East Fort Baker, in Sausalito, just over the Golden Gate Bridge (tel: 487-4398). Hands-on multi-building museum for the entire family, focusing on natural sciences, art and multimedia. Hours change according to the season.

- **California Academy of Sciences** in Golden Gate Park (info tel: 750-7145). This complex includes an aquarium, planetarium, and natural history museum. Across the way is the **Japanese Tea Garden**, a pavilion with traditionally dressed waitresses serving tea. Also nearby is the 55 acre **Strybing Arboretum**, with its 7,000 plant and tree species, ponds, aquatic birds, etc.
- **M.H. De Young Memorial Museum**: Tea Garden Drive, Golden Gate Park (tel: 850-3658). Children's creative workshops, tours, and an "education room" with computer stations, reading areas, and art-appreciation activities.
- **Randall Museum**: 199 Museum Way, at Roosevelt (tel: 554-9600). Hands-on nature and history museum, with a petting zoo, woodworking shop, environmental learning garden. Summer classes. Closed Sunday and Monday.
- **Alcatraz Island**: Until 1963 a maximum security prison, now it is a tourist attraction, showing the daily lives of prisoners and guards. Check ferry schedules.
- **San Francisco Zoo**: Sloat Boulevard at 45th Avenue (tel: 753-7080). Extensive zoo with many attractions, including a children's zoo, a lion house, primate center, playground.
- **Underwater World**: Pier 39 (tel: 623-5300). Visitors progress on a moving walkway through this wraparound aquarium to see marine life of the Pacific Ocean.
- **San Francisco Maritime National Historical Park: Hyde Street Pier**: Foot of Hyde Street, near Fisherman's Wharf (tel: 556-3002). Explore 19th century sailing ships, a side-wheel ferry, schooners, and, incongruously, a World War II submarine. Operated by the National Park Service.

RECREATION AND PARKS DEPARTMENT

Get to know the offerings of "Park and Rec," located in Golden Gate Park at McLaren Lodge, 501 Stanyan Street. Latchkey is only one of many programs for children; others include sports lessons, programs, and events. One of the most popular is the affordable **Camp Mather**, a rustic summer camp in the Stanislaus National Forest that allows families to spend a week together swimming and playing sports, participating in camp-like activities. Applications are taken in April and are selected by lottery; San Francisco residents are given priority.

— CHAPTER SEVEN —

OPTIONS FOR STUDY

OPPORTUNITIES GALORE

The Bay Area has 35 degree-granting universities, colleges, and specialized technical schools, some the finest of their class in the country. Non-degree courses are also available in a surprising number of fields, traditional or New Age, and can further your life—or your lifestyle. Some representative samples of schools are listed below; their names should give an idea of what they are about, their websites should allow you access to their substantive information, and their addresses should allow you to contact them. The major universities are extremely competitive for admission. Even small technical schools require application in advance, and you may be asked to provide academic transcripts, references, proof of financial independence, and health insurance.

Foreigners wishing to study in the United States should follow the procedures detailed in Chapter Five. Be prepared to take the Test of English as a Foreign Language (TOEFL) as part of the application procedure. If you want to study in the United States, learn English first.

ENGLISH LANGUAGE SCHOOLS

San Francisco is actually a multilingual city. Corporations that trade around the Pacific Rim are used to doing business in several Asian languages, staff in tourist shops can sell to just about any of their international clients, and the city-wide ethnic groceries and restaurants speak the languages of their clienteles. You'll hear more Chinese than English in Chinatown and along Clement, and more Spanish than English in the Mission—all with regional differences or dialects. But there are also communities of Russians and Koreans out along Geary, Vietnamese in the outer Tenderloin, and Japanese both around the Japan Center and in the Sunset. Pockets of other ethnic communities are multilingual as well.

Nonetheless, foreigners should make every effort to learn English as quickly as possible. If you do not speak English well, you will certainly be at a disadvantage with your competitors in business or your fellow students in school. Despite the plethora of multilingual publications, if you don't read English well you will not know as much as your neighbors as to what is happening in the city at any given time or even what opportunities are available. There are many registered English language schools in the Bay Area; choose one that suits your schedule and purse. For people who wish to apply for further study in the United States, the schools all offer TOEFL preparation. See also *Language Schools* in the Yellow Pages.

- **St. Giles Language Teaching Center**: One Hallidie Plaza (tel: 788-3552; fax: 788-1923; www.stgiles-usa.com). Morning or full-day programs, preparation for TOEFL and Cambridge exams, social occasions, and the I-20 for a student visa.

- **Brandon College**: 830 Market Street (tel: 391-5711; fax: 391-3918; www.brandoncollege.com). English as a Second Language, preparation for TOEFL and OTEIC, plus Business English. Housing assistance and social programs. I-20 for student visa.

STATE-WIDE EDUCATION SYSTEMS

Four higher education systems are funded by the State of California. The most prestigious and stringent belong to the University of California system: in the Bay Area its major campus is in Berkeley, and its medical and other health-profession schools are in San Francisco, as is one of its law schools. Next come the enormous California State Universities, which in the Bay Area are San Francisco State, Sonoma State, San Jose State, and Cal State Hayward. Last come the city and community colleges: in San Francisco, San Francisco City College.

UNIVERSITY OF CALIFORNIA

The University of California system offers some of the best education in the country, whether in its undergraduate colleges, graduate programs, or professional schools. The University of California, Berkeley, is one of the country's finest teaching and research universities, as is the Medical Center in San Francisco. Admissions are extremely competitive, and priority is given to California residents. Of some 30,000 applicants, only about 8,000 are accepted. No one ethnic or racial group constitutes a majority, which makes for an eclectic and diverse population.

- **University of California, Berkeley**: 110 Sproul Hall, Berkeley 94720 (tel: 510/642-6000; www.berkeley.edu)
- **UCSF Graduate Medical School:** 500 Parnassus (tel: 476-4044); also pharmacy (tel: 476-2372), nursing (tel: 476-1435), and dentistry (tel: 476-2737)
- **University of California Hastings College of the Law**: 200 McAllister Street (tel: 565-4600; www.uchastings.edu)

CALIFORNIA STATE UNIVERSITY

The widespread California State University system is known for educating the bulk of California high school graduates. Although the number and type of high school courses required for admission are almost identical to that of the University of California system, the admissions process is less competitive. In San Francisco, **San Francisco State University** is at 1600 Holloway Avenue (tel: 338-1111; www.sfsu.edu). This 25,000 student "commuter" university offers undergraduate and graduate degrees, a law school, and several certificate and credential programs.

- **San Jose State**: One Washington Square, San Jose (408/924-1000)
- **Sonoma State**: 1801 East Cotati Avenue, Rohnert Park (tel: 707/664-2880)
- **California State University Hayward**: 25800 Carlos Bee Boulevard, Hayward (tel: 510/885-3000)

CITY COLLEGE

City College of San Francisco, at 50 Phelan Avenue, is a community college that offers associate degrees and certificates, international trade programs, and a small-business institute (tel: 239-3000; www.hills.ccsf.cc.ca.us). It has ten campuses and more "instructional sites" in the city.

PRIVATE UNIVERSITIES

In a class by itself among private universities, the beautiful campus of **Stanford** is nestled in the hills on the Peninsula, at Palo Alto. Its address is Stanford University, Stanford CA 94305 (tel: 723-2300; www.stanford.edu). Its undergraduate application process is extremely competitive: only around 13 percent of applicants are accepted; among those, 99 percent maintained a 3.0+ grade average in high school, and 86 percent were in the top 10 percent of their class. In the city are:

- **University of San Francisco**: Parker and Fulton Streets (tel: 422-6563; www.usfca.edu). Jesuit university founded 150 years ago. Undergraduate and graduate degrees in business, education, law, and many other fields.
- **Golden Gate University**: 536 Mission Street (tel: 442-7000; www.ggu.edu). Undergraduate and graduate degree programs at a university in the heart of downtown. Law school.
- **Academy of Art College**: 79 New Montgomery Street (tel: 274-2222; www.academyart.edu). A leading arts and design educator. Courses and degree programs in 10 visual arts majors, including film, computer art, video, graphic design, photography, advertising and industrial design. Bachelor of Fine Art and Master of Fine Art degrees.
- **New College of California**: 777 Valencia Street (tel: 888/437-3460; fax: 626-5171; www.newcollege.edu). Since 1971, this small college fosters "inquiry and critical thinking, and the integration of education with social action." Accredited by the Western Association of Schools and Colleges, NCOC offers BA degrees, weekend BA programs, a teacher credential program, a public interest law school, MFA and MA degrees.

Specialized and Technical Schools

Specialized schools may offer full degrees or professional certificates and other credentials in particular fields. This representative sample should give you an idea of the range of education offered.

- **Heald Business Colleges**: 350 Mission Street (tel: 808-3000; www.heald.edu)
- **The San Francisco Law School**: 20 Haight Street (tel: 626-5550; www.sfls.edu). Long-established evening law school.
- **California College of Podiatric Medicine (Pacific Coast Hospital)**: 1200 Scott Street (tel: 563-8070; www.ccpm.edu)
- **American College of Traditional Chinese Medicine**: 455 Arkansas Street (tel: 282-7600; fax: 282-0856; www.actcm.org)

- **San Francisco Conservatory of Music**: 1201 Ortega Street (tel: 564-8086; www.sfcm.edu)
- **California Culinary Academy**: 625 Polk Street (tel: 800/229-2433, 771-3500; www.baychef.com)
- **University of the Pacific School of Dentistry**: 2155 Webster Street (tel: 929-6400; www.dental.uop.edu)
- **American Schools of Professional Psychology**: 999 Canal Boulevard, Point Richmond (tel: 510/215-0277; fax: 510/215-0299; www.aspp.edu). Graduate programs in clinical psychology.
- **San Francisco Art Institute, Extension Division**: 800 Chestnut Street (info tel: 771-7020; admissions tel: 749-4554; www.sfai.edu). Ten-week classes in painting, photography, filmmaking, figure drawing.

EXTENDED EDUCATION

Extended education courses and workshops may be short in duration but may offer certificates in some professional or technical fields. Others offer lifestyle courses such as "Wine Appreciation," or "Learning the Internet."

- **San Francisco State University, College of Extended Learning**: 425 Market Street (tel: 405-7700; www.cel.sfsu.edu). Continuing education opportunities, with classes held evenings and weekends.
- **University of California Berkeley Extension**: 55 Laguna Street (tel: 510/642-4111; www.berkeley.edu/unex). San Francisco campus for continuing education. A wide variety of courses and certificate programs, from "art to business and education to engineering." Call for catalogue.
- **The Learning Annex**: 291 Geary Street (info tel: 788-5500; www.learningannex.com). Non-credit courses on a variety of subjects, including computers and the Internet, health and healing, personal development, business and careers, and

finance and investing. Locations vary. Look for free catalogues in news boxes.

COURSES FOR SENIORS

The universities and colleges all have programs that allow older adults to audit courses or, with some qualifications, to enroll as a student. The extension divisions welcome older students, and there are some opportunities specifically tailored toward seniors.

In Berkeley, look for **Alternative Lifelong Learning**, a member-run senior education program held at the North Berkeley Senior Center. Six-week courses, guest speakers, field trips. Note that as this is staffed entirely by volunteers, contact numbers may change (current tel: 510/530-3609).

- **Center for Learning in Retirement**: 55 Laguna Street (tel: 863-4518). UC's Extension Center offers workshops and study groups in a wealth of disciplines. Also offered are monthly walks and tours.
- **City College Older Adult Department**: 106 Bartlet Street (tel: 550-4415). Several campuses offer classes to people over 55. Call for a catalogue.
- **San Francisco State University, Urban Elders Program**: 22 Tapia Drive (tel: 338-2127). SFSU's "60 Plus" program offers either credit or audit classes. Call for a brochure.
- **Fromm Institute for Lifelong Learning (USF)**: 2130 Fulton Street (tel: 422-6805). "Retired" professors offer classes to people over fifty.

LIBRARIES

To obtain a library card that allows book borrowing from any of the city's neighborhood public libraries, bring your driver's license or other picture identification, plus a document that shows your current address. There are libraries in many neighborhoods; some, in multilingual districts, offer books and periodicals in the languages primarily spoken in that area.

- **San Francisco Main Library**: 100 Larkin Street, in the Civic Center (tel: 557-4400). Extensive collections, a local history wing, work stations for connection to the Internet, and special-interest sections on history, gay and lesbian studies, art and music.
- **Mechanics' Institute Library and Chess Room**: 57 Post Street (tel: 421-1768). Long-established private reference and lending library. Periodicals, video and audio cassettes. Author readings and events. Chess Club is open to all members at any skill level. Classes and tournaments.

— Chapter Eight —
STAYING HEALTHY

MEDICAL CARE IN SF
The quality of medical care in San Francisco is excellent. Practicing physicians who are also researchers at the area's major medical research centers and hospitals bring cutting-edge knowledge and techniques to their patients, assuring the best of care. There is no question of availability of excellent health care. There is a question, however, as to accessibility—how much access any individual has to the best care—and this concerns finances and health insurance.

HEALTH INSURANCE
The United States has no national health insurance plan, but there are many options for obtaining insurance, provided you can pay for it. Workers may be covered through their employer's health

plan, and some employers offer several to choose among. While discussing health benefits with your future employer, ask what the company's plan covers; many people don't know which health conditions or treatment procedures are covered until they are unexpectedly denied payment for some treatment. Not all companies offer health insurance to their employees; small businesses often do not, and employees thus must find coverage elsewhere, through their spouse or domestic partner, through associations or unions, or through an individual plan, which is more costly.

Even among individual plans there are several types. Some allow the holder to see any doctor at any time, others specify physicians belonging to their plans. Most usually have an initial amount that the patient must pay before the insurance begins to reimburse at the percentage allowed, and these "deductibles" vary. And not all insurance plans have the exact same coverage, not even within the same company. It's best to shop around, but not to take too long, for people without insurance are at great financial and health risk. See the Yellow Pages under *Health Plans*.

When choosing your physicians, inquire as to the insurance plans they accept. A few specialists—including some dentists—prefer not to allow insurance companies to dictate how they practice their profession and do not participate in insurance plans. Instead they require payment to be made at the time of treatment and, furnishing the appropriate diagnosis and treatment statements, ask patients to submit the insurance claims themselves. Invariably, the patient using non-participating doctors receives a lower percentage of reimbursement.

Kaiser Permanente is a major membership Health Maintenance Organization throughout the state of California and in other western states. With its own hospitals and physicians, its Personal Advantage membership offers comprehensive health care on all levels (tel: 800/464-4000). A Senior Advantage Program is also available for Medicare recipients and disabled persons (tel: 800/777-1238). Inquire about the Delta Care dental program.

Veterans of any branch of the United States military are entitled to use the services of the Veterans' Administration: contact the **San Francisco Veterans' Affairs Medical Center**, at 4150 Clement Street (tel: 221-4810).

Emergency Services

In a dire emergency, dial **911** for police or ambulance response; for poison assistance also call the 24-hour poison control service: (tel: 800/876-4766). Response to a 911 health emergency call will be by a Fire Department ambulance. Paramedics will stabilize the patient, if necessary, and then transport to a hospital. In the case of accident or sudden trauma, the hospital will probably be San Francisco General, known for its trauma services, or for burns, St. Francis Memorial. In other cases, the ambulance will probably be directed to the nearest hospital, unless that hospital's Intensive Care Unit (ICU) has no beds available, and the ambulance is diverted to another emergency center.

All public hospitals have 24-hour emergency rooms, and many of them provide bilingual staff (Spanish, Russian, Chinese). All emergencies are treated, regardless of a person's ability to pay; once in stable condition, however, the patient may be transferred to a different facility. Each hospital has its own procedures for payment or insurance reimbursement. If you are covered by insurance in the United States, you should have no trouble sending the itemized bill to your carrier; most hospitals will do that for you. If you are covered in another country, you may be required to pay in advance and submit the itemized bill to your own carrier. The hospitals below with 24-hour emergency room telephone numbers are known for excellent care; those with specialties are also noted.

- *Castro/Hayes Valley* — **California Pacific Medical Center/ Davies Campus**: Castro and Duboce (emergency tel: 600-5555; tel: 600-6000)
- *Haight* — **St. Mary's Medical Center**: 450 Stanyan Street (emergency tel: 750-5700; tel: 668-1000)

- *Mission* — **San Francisco General Hospital**: 1001 Potrero Avenue (tel: 206-8000). The city's public hospital. Especially known for its trauma center.
- *Pacific Heights* — **California Pacific Medical Center/Pacific Campus**: 2333 Buchanan (emergency tel: 600-3333 tel: 600-6000)
- *Polk Gulch* — **St. Francis Memorial Hospital**: 900 Hyde Street (emergency tel: 353-6300; tel: 353-6000). Known for treatment of burns and spinal injuries.
- *Presidio Heights/Inner Richmond* — **California Pacific Medical Center/California Campus**: 3700 California Street (emergency room tel: 600-3333; tel: 600-6000)
- *Sunset* — **University of California, San Francisco**: 505 Parnassus Avenue (emergency tel: 353-1037; tel: 476-1000). Excellent hospital, attached to medical school.
- *Western Addition* — **Kaiser Permanente Medical Center/Geary Campus**: 2425 Geary Boulevard (tel: 202-2000). Care for members of Kaiser Permanente insurance plan.

Pharmacies

When you first arrive in San Francisco, have with you enough medications to tide you over until you have found a doctor and pharmacy of your own. Foreigners should understand that many medications that are "over-the-counter" in other countries may require a doctor's prescription here. Ask your physician to write new prescriptions using both the trade and generic name of the medication. Bring a copy of your eyeglass prescription and an extra pair of glasses.

In addition to prescription medications, drug stores carry over-the-counter medications, vitamins, and a wide variety of familiar brands of health- and beauty-related items, plus foods, cold drinks, magazines and stationery, candies, and more. Cosmetic brands are generally well-known, and are less expensive than those found in the department stores. Neighborhood drug stores stay open late, depending on the traffic in their area, sometimes until 8:00 pm or 10:00 pm. Most are open on Sunday.

If you have a health-related emergency and go to a hospital's emergency room, you will receive the appropriate prescription to treat your condition and enough medication to last until pharmacies open the next morning. The pharmacies below have 24-hour prescription departments. For over-the-counter remedies such as cough medicine or aspirin, you can also try 24-hour supermarkets.

- *Castro/Noe Valley*—**Walgreens**: 498 Castro Street (tel: 861-3136)
- *Outer Richmond*—**Walgreens**: 25 Point Lobos, at 42nd Avenue, near Geary (tel: 386-0736)
- *Pacific Heights/Marina*—**Walgreens**: 3201 Divisadero Street, near Lombard (tel: 931-6417)
- *Richmond*—**Rite Aid**: 5280 Geary Boulevard (tel: 668-2041)
- *Daly City*—**Walgreens**: 395 South Mayfair Avenue (tel: 650/756-4535)
- *South San Francisco*—**Walgreens**: 2238 Westborough Boulevard (tel: 650/873-0551)
- *South San Francisco*—**Walgreens**: 399 El Camino Real (tel: 583-8685)

WOMEN'S HEALTH

The **University of California at San Francisco (UCSF)** has two centers in the Bay Area devoted to women's health care (at the Parnassus campus mentioned above and at UCSF Mount Zion on Divisadero Boulevard, at Post). Care includes cardiology and gynecology services, obstetrics, and breast cancer screening and treatment. The Great Expectations Women's Health Library and Resource Center offers resource materials and classes on women's health, including a Healthy Baby Program (tel: 476-6667).

The **Women's Program** of California Pacific Medical Center at 3698 California Street also consults on and treats all aspects of women's health (tel: 750-6500). Its comprehensive Planetree Library is at 2040 Webster Street (tel: 923-3681).

Natural Resources, at 1307 Castro, is a pregnancy, childbirth and parenting center, providing many excellent resources (tel: 550-2611). It offers classes and support groups during pregnancy and for new parents, has referrals listings for birth and child professionals, has a reference library, sells supplies and clothing at good prices, plus health-care products for mother and baby.

ALTERNATIVE MEDICINE

San Francisco is one of the foremost cities in the United States for alternative medicine, including Eastern techniques and homeopathic healing. Traditional Western physicians in San Francisco are open-minded, probably to a greater degree than those in other American cities; for the most part they are willing to discuss non-traditional techniques and remedies with their patients, as well as to consider alternative options their patients present to them. Some of the hospitals also have Eastern-oriented medical clinics, and the major insurance companies now accept claims for acupuncture. Licensed acupuncturists work on their own or in conjunction with Western colleagues, and herbalists and homeopaths prescribe natural remedies. Therapeutic massage of varying internationally recognized techniques is available, as are classes for yoga and other relaxation methods. Massage is sometimes covered under health plans if prescribed by a physician or chiropractor.

Chiropractic, considered an alternative medicine in some countries, is considered mainstream in the United States, and chiropractic treatments for muscular and skeletal difficulties are generally covered by health insurance carriers, depending on the condition. There are many licensed Doctors of Chiropractic in the city; it's best to ask among your friends and colleagues for a recommendation.

For an excellent guide to services for natural living, look for the free semiannual publication *Bay Area Naturally* in natural food shops and outlets. It includes descriptions and advertisements for holistic health professionals, "green" products and services, natural food restaurants, and natural food markets. *Common Ground*, another free tabloid, offers "resources for body, mind, and spirit." *Open Exchange*, which advertises courses and seminars in healthy living and healing, can be found in news boxes around the city.

- **American College of Traditional Chinese Medicine**: 450 Connecticut Street (tel: 282-9603). The clinic of this accredited school offers acupuncture and Chinese herb treatments for a variety of difficulties: upper-respiratory, gastrointestinal and cardiovascular problems, and more.

Free Clinics

The **Community Health Network of San Francisco** provides low-cost health care to residents (tel: 206-4785). Funded by the city, clinics provide both primary and specialized care for people who have no health insurance and cannot afford access to traditional health care providers. In most, patients pay on a sliding scale geared to their ability to pay. Many of the clinics are staffed by professional volunteers—physicians, nurses, residents, interns—who donate their expertise to people who could not otherwise afford health care. Look in the City Government section of the White Pages under the *Health Department* and the subhead of *Health Centers*, and for emergency treatment, see above. The clinics listed below are well known:

- *Haight-Ashbury* — **Haight Ashbury Free Clinic**: 558 Clayton Street, at Haight (tel: 487-5632). Long-established clinic offering low-cost basic health services, HIV treatment, drug and alcohol detox, etc.
- *Hayes Valley* — **Lyon-Martin Women's Health Services**: 1748 Market Street, #201 (tel: 565-7667): Primary care clinic for women, providing treatment for acute and chronic conditions, physical examinations, gynecology, internal medicine, family

planning, and preventive health care. Special focus for lesbian and HIV-positive women. Sliding scale for fee payment.

- *Mission* — **Castro-Mission Health Center**: 3850 17th Street, at Noe (tel: 487-7500)

DENTISTS

Although the quality of dental care in San Francisco is extremely high, finding the right dentist might take some time, depending on your needs and preferences. Thus, before moving, have any remaining dental work done, and bring with you current x-rays and copies of your dental records to give to your new dentist.

Your friends, neighbors, and colleagues may recommend dentists, but as with choosing any professional relationship, you will have to determine whether that person is right for you. This may depend not only on your physical needs, but whether you have dental insurance and whether the dentist you choose accepts it. For a recommendation, you might also call the **San Francisco Dental Society Referral Service** (tel: 421-1435). Be specific as to the type of dentist you are seeking, the type of work you need done, and any financial concerns.

Until you have found a dentist of your own, you might try the clinics of the dental schools in San Francisco. Both schools listed below offer inexpensive dental care by dental students under the supervision of faculty members who have first made the initial evaluation of condition and treatment. In addition to their regular clinics, both have weekday emergency services seeing patients on a first-come first-served basis, and after-hours emergency assistance. For 24-hour dental emergencies, you might also try San Francisco General Hospital, listed above.

- **University of California School of Dentistry**: 707 Parnassus Street (tel: 476-1891; after-hours emergency tel: 551-9036)
- **University of the Pacific School of Dentistry**: 2155 Webster Street (tel: 929-6400; info tel: 929-6501)

HIV/AIDS

As San Francisco has been hit particularly hard by the HIV/AIDS epidemic, the city has extensive public resources for testing and care. Both San Francisco General and the Davies Campus of California Pacific Medical Center have well-known AIDS clinics (see addresses above). The **City Clinic** at 356 7th Street tests and treats sexually transmitted diseases at low cost or for free (tel: 487-5500); hours are Monday and Wednesday 8:00 am–4:00 pm, Tuesday 1:00–6:00 pm, and Thursday 1:00–4:00 pm. For an extensive list of helpful resources, see the Yellow Pages under *AIDS, HIV Education, Referral & Support Services*.

- The **Gay and Lesbian Medical Association** offers referrals to physicians and other medical services in the Bay Area, publishes helpful guides, and offers forums and seminars; it takes phone calls weekdays 9:30 am–5:30 pm (tel: 255-4547).
- **San Francisco Department of Public Health**: AIDS Health Project (tel: 502-8378). Free anonymous and confidential HIV testing.
- **California HIV/AIDS Hot-line**: (tel: 863-2437). Information on HIV/AIDS, safe sex, and a database of HIV-related services. In English, Spanish, Filipino.
- **A New Leaf**: 1853 Market (tel: 626-7000). Mental health and substance abuse programs for gays, lesbians, and bisexuals. Open weekdays, 9:00 am-5:00 pm.
- **AIDS/HIV Nightline**: Emotional support hot-line, open 5:00 pm–5:00 am every night (tel: 434-2437).
- **Stadtlanders Pharmacy**: 445 Castro Street, is the San Francisco branch of the nationwide pharmacy specializing in HIV/AIDS care (tel: 434-8600; www.stadtlander.com). Hours: 8:00 am–9:00 pm weekdays, 10:00 am–6:00 pm Saturday, noon–5:00 pm Sunday; 24-hour pharmacist available, and mail order is available on the Internet.

— CHAPTER NINE —
WORK AND BUSINESS ON THE PACIFIC RIM

From its earliest days, San Francisco has been a city of opportunities seen and grasped. Even today, whether you are coming to find a job or to start your own business, you will find that San Francisco opens its doors to those who are qualified—and who understand how the city works. Extensive informational resources are widely available and should be helpful for those who are determined to succeed.

If the Bay Area were an independent country, it would rank among the top 25 economies in the world. San Francisco plays a crucial part in the economy and trade of the vast Pacific Rim, and with some 30 of the world's largest banking institutions and offices here, it is sometimes called the "Wall Street of the West." Here are the headquarters for Bank of America and Wells Fargo, the Pacific Stock Exchange, and the Federal Reserve Bank of San Francisco. With the city's long-standing ties to Asia, finance and commerce along the Rim are increasingly becoming the most important part of the economy of the city and the region. Bay Area exports have grown more than 50 percent over just the last five years, while its overall economy grew by 9.2 percent.

You should think of the entire Bay Area as your resource, especially that geographically intangible—yet very real—concept called Silicon Valley, which stretches from San Francisco down to San Jose. Companies throughout the Bay Area are world leaders in high-tech innovation, manufacturing, and trade. This includes computers and software, telecommunications, semiconductors, other electronics, and robotics. High-tech industries in the area attract almost 40 percent of the venture capital in the country, and knowledge-based industries account for just under 20 percent of the region's exports.

The largest corporations with headquarters in San Francisco are Bechtel and Levi Strauss, both American-owned. But foreign-owned companies also maintain a major presence in the area: Fireman's Fund Insurance, for example, with headquarters in San Francisco, is German-owned; Bank of the West is French-owned; and Shaklee is a Japanese company, to name just a few. It should be said, though, that as the Bay Area relies heavily on business with Asia and Latin America—two areas that were hit hard economically toward the end of the last decade—some major corporations regrouped for a time, bringing about job layoffs and a slowing of job growth.

Yet at the end of the last decade, San Francisco was ranked second only to Dallas as the most productive city in America. Its *per capita* average income of $35,000, however, was ranked as the highest. Part of this is owing to the professional caliber of workers and the fact that San Francisco is close to some of the most prestigious universities in the country—University of California and Stanford—which means that research plays a major role in the atmosphere of the entire region. In fact, more than half of those who work in the city have college or advanced degrees.

THE JOB SEARCH

San Francisco has long been home to plentiful jobs in international trade and especially in tourism, where turnover is high. Recently, however, service-related businesses have been growing, while the economy of the region has been shifting to one based on knowledge. This means that people with all sorts of good computer skills —computer programming, telecommunications, data processing— and those who have education in the life sciences—biotechnology and scientific research—will be in increasing demand. The multimedia industry is one of the region's fastest growing, and both new jobs and new types of jobs are being created.

The above notwithstanding, unemployment in San Francisco hovers just under 3 percent. Thus, you should ensure that your résumé is attractively prepared and organized. If you have several distinct skills, for example, prepare different résumés with different emphases, depending on the job you are applying for. Be prepared also to network with any professional contact you may have and to make "cold calls" to the Human Resources departments of companies, rather than relying solely on your résumé and cover letter. Competition is fierce, and you must use every channel at your disposal. Think carefully about salary and your lifestyle, for the Bay Area has the highest cost of living in the state.

In order to apply for a job, you must prove that you are legally permitted to work in the United States; foreigners may be asked to take an English-language test. In addition, some companies will test you on the skills you claim to have and may ask for work samples and references.

If you are coming to the city without a job, start your search before arrival by looking at the website of the local newspapers to see what is available (e.g. www.sfgate.com). Once in the city, buy the combined Sunday issue of the *San Francisco Examiner/San Francisco Chronicle* which has an extensive career section containing articles, advertisements for career development, and a major section of classified ads for job openings. Some free tabloid magazines can be found at news boxes on street corners.

- *Open Exchange Magazine:* a bimonthly publication sponsored by the Community Resource Institute, which develops learning technologies for personal growth and social change. Advertisements for seminars and courses, and by professionals offering help in a variety of fields from accounting and taxes to yoga and meditation.
- *Jobs and Careers:* lists hundreds of positions open (info tel: 800/49career; http://jobscareers.com)
- *High Technology Careers*: a tabloid focusing on high-tech jobs (www.hightechcareers.com)
- *Bay Area Business Woman*, a monthly newspaper with advertisements and articles of interest to professional women, plus a calendar of events (tel: 510/654-7557)

Career Help

In addition to listing yourself with the employment agencies, try to take advantage of the organizations that help people to develop their capabilities, to present themselves well, and to understand the San Francisco job market: The **San Francisco Chamber of Commerce** (see below) sells an *Employment Guide*, listing agencies and services for job seekers.

- **Life Print** (formerly **Alumnae Resources**): 120 Montgomery Street, Suite 600 (tel: 274-4700; fax: 274-4744; www.ar.org). Career development organization offering assistance to anyone beginning, advancing, or changing a career. Resource center, career advisor network, job listings, Internet access, seminars. Membership fee allows access to career counseling, workshops, career planning, and a quarterly newsletter, calendar, and access to their job list.

- **Experience Unlimited**: 3120 Mission Street (tel: 771-1776). Free service of the State Employment Development Department. Career Counseling, résumé assistance, etc.
- **Jewish Vocational Service and Career Counseling**: 77 Geary Street, Suite 401 (tel: 391-3600; www.jvs.org). Long established non-sectarian job counseling and employment agency. Workshops, networking, English instruction. Also at 4600 El Camino Real, Suite 207, Los Altos (tel: 650/941-7922).
- **Media Alliance**: 814 Mission Street, Suite 205 (tel: 546-6334; www.media-alliance.org). Non-profit association for communications and general media professionals. $45 fee plus $20 for access to job file.
- **San Francisco Chamber of Commerce**: 465 California Street (tel: 392-4520; www.sfchamber.com). Wednesday evening Job Forum, offered as a free community service. A rotating panel of experts from business, government and academia address a variety of job-finding problems. Not an employment agency, the Job Forum offers brainstorming and problem-solving to job seekers.

Employment Agencies

The hundreds of employment agencies in the city offer temporary and permanent jobs. If you are willing to work outside San Francisco, inquire whether the agencies service the entire Bay Area. See Employment Agencies in the Yellow Pages, which has extensive advertisements, including agencies that specialize in fields such as the dental, insurance, or legal professions. The nationwide firm **Manpower** is in cities around the Bay Area (San Francisco tel: 781-7171; www.manpower.com).

- **Alpha Four**: 447 Battery Street, Suite 240 (tel: 995-9080; fax: 956-7161; www.alphafour.citysearch.com). Full-time and temporary placement for administrative, clerical, sales, finance, and graphic design positions.

- **ABAR Staffing Service**: 142 Sansome Street (tel: 773-2227; fax: 263-3690; www.abarstaffing.com). Full-time positions in finance, accounting, sales and marketing, management, and administration. Also in the East Bay.
- **Bach Personnel**: 2358 Market Street (tel: 626-4663; fax: 626-6159; www.bachpersonnel.com). "The Premier Gay/Lesbian Placement Agency," specializing in full-time, contract, and temporary positions.
- **Apple One**: 44 Montgomery Street (tels: 800/564-5644; 397-3201; www.appleone.com). Full-time positions around Bay Area. Also in Oakland (tel: 510/835-0217) and San Mateo (tel: 650/574-8252).

STARTING A BUSINESS

Many people come to San Francisco hoping to open their own small retail business. In fact, despite the invasion of nationwide chain stores and franchises, locally owned businesses continue to characterize San Francisco, from tourist-oriented kiosks and locally owned upscale restaurants of all quality and prices to the most elegant fashion boutiques and furniture showrooms. Some businesses are successful, yet many fail, often owing to an incomplete understanding of how the city works. Much will depend on the amount of knowledge you have at the outset—including that all-important aspect of location—and how organized you are in your approach.

Businesses that depend on tourism are always a draw. Tourism is big business in San Francisco, its largest industry, sustaining more than 60,000 of the city's jobs. With 30,000 hotel rooms, hotel taxes alone account for $110 million that is added to the city's coffers. San Francisco International Airport filters 38 million passengers through its corridors every year.

Some 16 million visitors spend more than $5 billion in the city each year, a city that is often rated by travel magazines as the nation's most popular vacation spot. Other than vacationers, the

200 trade shows, conventions, and business meetings draw some 1.5 million. International visitors account for just under half of all hotel guests. Tourists and business visitors explore the city every day of the year, spending their money at tourist attractions, in the downtown and outer shopping districts, and especially at the city's restaurants.

BUSINESS SETUP ADVICE

Before you do anything else, make sure you understand the legal and financial implications of opening a business and the risks involved. Start with the **U.S. Small Business Administration (SBA)**, at 455 Market Street, 6th floor, an agency of the federal government that helps people who want to open a small business (tel: 744-6820; www.sba.gov). Its Business Information Center offers informational workshops and seminars, counseling, computer access, and a resource library with information on business plans and starting a business (tels: 744-4244, 744-4242).

The SBA is also the largest source of long-term small business financing in the nation. Loans are made to qualified applicants by private lending institutions that participate in the SBA program, and a percentage of the loan (up to $750,000) is guaranteed by the SBA. Inquire of your banker or at the SBA for its booklet *Small Business Start-up Information*.

Women own some 27,000 businesses in San Francisco, and other minorities own some 15,000 businesses in the city. Women should inquire at the SBA about the Women's Pre-Qualification Loan Program, in which loan requests may be reviewed and approved by the SBA before application to the lending institution (SBA Women's info tel: 744-8491). The **Women's Initiative for Self Employment (WISE)**, a pilot program of the SBA, at 450 Mission Street, offers training in business assessment, marketing, finances and sales and counseling (tel: 247-9473). Fees are on a sliding scale.

Learn about the **Mission Economic Development Association (MEDA)** at 2601 Mission Street, 9th floor (tel: 282-3334; fax: 282-3320). This bilingual (Spanish and English) association in the heart of the Mission provides counseling, technical assistance, and loan packaging services (through the SBA and small lenders) to people wishing to set up a new business or improve an existing business.

The **Renaissance Entrepreneurship Center**, at 275 Fifth Street (tel: 541-8580; www.rencenter.org), is a non-profit entrepreneurial training organization supported by the San Francisco Community Development Fund and some private businesses. It offers classes in Introduction to Business, Business Planning, and Growing Your Business, plus courses in writing business plans and pricing products. Classes last 8 to 14 weeks.

The Business Reference Section of the San Francisco Main Library allows any card holder access to its services and database (tel: 557-4488). An excellent ongoing resource for current business information and annually issued business-related reports is the *San Francisco Business Times*, at 275 Battery Street, #940 (tel: 989-2522). Subscriptions are $70 per year.

For assistance with business plans and tax incentives, contact the **California Trade and Commerce Agency**, 801 K Street, Suite 1700, Sacramento 95814 (tel: 916/327-0079; www.commerce.ca.gov).

NETWORKING

San Franciscans are friendly and open, both socially and professionally, so you should have little trouble meeting people and becoming an active member of the business community. Consider joining the groups below for business networking. If you are interested in volunteering at any of the dozens of worthwhile non-profit organizations in the city—another way to meet interesting people—contact the **San Francisco Volunteer Center**, at 425 Jackson Street, which coordinates volunteer opportunities in many community projects (tel: 982-8999; www.vcsf.org). Or contact the **Volunteer Centers of the Bay Area** (tel: 800/227-3123; www.volunteerbayarea.org).

The **San Francisco Chamber of Commerce**, at 465 California Street, is a non-profit membership association of almost 2,000 local businesses (tel: 392-4520). Working to attract businesses to the Bay Area, the Chamber sponsors luncheons, networking socials, and committee meetings, and organizes special events for members and non-members, plus the important Job Forum mentioned above. The Women in Business Roundtable is a bimonthly breakfast meeting with interesting speakers. Consider also some of the professional networking possibilities below.

- **Asian Business League of San Francisco**: 233 Sansome Street, Suite 575 (tel: 788-4664). Membership organization for Asians in business, providing seminars, workshops, networking events.
- **Bay Area Career Women**: 55 New Montgomery Street (tel: 495-5393; www.bacw.org). World's largest lesbian volunteer organization formed to eliminate discrimination. Business networking opportunities, social events, etc. Other chapters in the area.
- **City Club of San Francisco**: 155 Sansome Street, 10th Floor (tel: 362-2480). Multi-purpose professional and social club. Breakfast speakers, networking forums, special events.
- **Commonwealth Club of California**: 595 Market Street (tel: 597-6700). Prestigious public affairs group invites well-known and interesting people to speak at meal-centered meetings (breakfast, lunch, dinner, receptions). Special and social events geared to current issues; outings to cultural and sports events.
- **Golden Gate Business Association**: 2107 Van Ness Avenue (tel: 441-3651). Nation's oldest gay and lesbian business organization. Professionals, business owners, and artists belong to this group that offers networking events and a variety of business-related programs.

- **National Association of Women Business Owners—SF** (tel: 333-2130; www.nawbo-sf.org). Monthly dinner meetings, networking, business and social contacts.
- **Rotary Club of San Francisco** (tel: 923-0399). Call for meeting and luncheon sites.
- **World Affairs Council**: 312 Sutter Street, Suite 500 (tel: 982-2541). Programs on important foreign policy issues. Dinners with special, international guests, lectures from government officials, forums on current issues, special and social events.

OFFICE SPACE

Office space in the city hovers at about a 6 percent vacancy rate. Corporate downsizing over the past few years and more stringent funding criteria have decreased the amount of new business construction in the city, which had once suffered from overbuilding and high vacancy rates. In addition, retention programs to keep business in San Francisco are fairly successful, and tenants are staying in their long-term office space. As less space is on the market, rents climb, and to compound the situation, commercial space is not rent-controlled. San Franciscans are concerned that steeply rising rents will be affordable only to national chains, and that small "mom-and-pop" businesses will be forced out. Some efforts by resident groups have been successful in keeping large chains out of their neighborhoods, but if prices continue to rise, they may not continue to be successful.

Thus, companies are beginning to colonize the heretofore industrial South of Market area, enlivened by the Moscone Convention Center, Yerba Buena Gardens (including Metreon), and the Museum of Modern Art. Multimedia companies have also established themselves in this area, which from South Park reaching out toward the Mission is now nicknamed "Multimedia Gulch." The new Pacific Bell baseball stadium is also increasing the attractiveness of the area for businesses of all sizes and levels.

Last, new development at Mission Bay is under way, and upon completion will bring more than a million square feet of university facilities, plus a varied residential and retail community.

Temporary/Shared Office Space

Shared offices provide full services without a long-term financial commitment. You may rent a conference room for a meeting, or rent offices by the day, week, or month. See *Office and Desk Space Rental Service* in the Yellow Pages.

- **HQ Global Workplaces**: 44 Montgomery Street (tel: 781-5000); 2 Embarcadero Center (tel: 835-1300). Full conference, office, electronic, and secretarial services (www.hqnet.com). Other locations in Bay Area.
- **Office General Executive Business Centers**: 580 California Street (tels: 283-3200; 800/960-1818; www.officegeneral.com). Other locations in Bay Area.

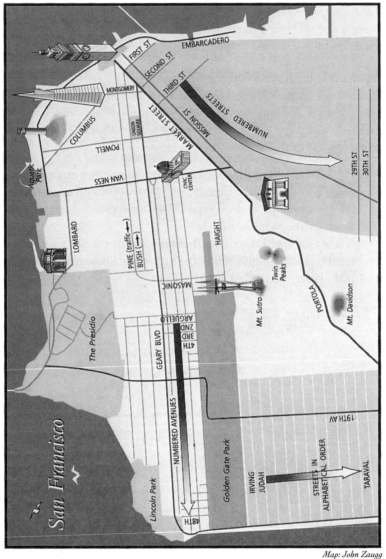

Map: John Zaugg

— Chapter Ten —

UP AND DOWN THE HILLS

UNDERSTANDING THE CITY

The city plan of San Francisco should not be difficult to understand. Streets are laid out on more or less a grid, except where one of the city's 42 hills intrudes; on either side of a hill the name of a continuing street is most likely different. To understand the city, first take into consideration the role of the diagonal Market Street, which starts at the Bay and cuts southwest through much of the city. North of Market, the streets are named; south of Market, the streets are numbered. People often refer to these areas as "north of Market" or "south of Market."

North of Market, the street names have no particular order to them; you just have to learn them. South of Market, the north/

south streets are numbered, starting with First Street and continuing regularly to 30th Street, where Twin Peaks and then Mount Davidson loom above. At Twin Peaks, Market Street changes its name to Portola, and as it winds toward Ocean Avenue, the names and contours of streets follow no plan.

The numbered streets south of Market should not be confused with what everyone calls "the avenues." These begin at Arguello, which runs from the Golden Gate Park panhandle to the Presidio. These straight streets run north/south from Second Avenue (there is no First Avenue) to Forty-Eighth Avenue, at the edge of the sea. Making orientation even easier in this area, south of Geary Boulevard begin the alphabetically consecutive streets (running east/west), starting with Anza and Balboa, and—after jumping Golden Gate Park—continuing to Wawona, just north of Sloat.

If none of this makes sense at first, take heart: most intersections throughout the city have large green signs above them, indicating the cross street, which is helpful when driving, for street signs may occasionally be missing or hidden by foliage.

Small city maps, found at bookshops, can be carried in a briefcase or purse, but there are no pocket-sized street atlases for San Francisco. Some maps—mostly of the downtown and tourist areas—may be had at the San Francisco Visitors Center. More detailed, indexed maps can be purchased at some gasoline stations, and members of the **California State Automobile Association (AAA or "Triple A")** may obtain free maps at 150 Van Ness Avenue (tel: 565-2012). A detailed street atlas to keep in your car may be bought at bookstores. The Yellow Pages have a few helpful maps of neighborhoods, downtown streets, public transportation routes, and city zip codes.

THINKING ABOUT TRANSPORT

Transportation is an important issue in San Francisco. The population of this small city almost doubles each workday, when more than 200,000 commuters file into the city—in vehicles, on ferries, on trains. Rush hours may be among the busiest in the country, as vehicle access into the city is limited to two bridges and two major highways coming up from the Peninsula. Traffic problems are compounded by the millions of tourists who come to the Bay Area every year, many of whom either drive their own cars or rent one to go out into the countryside. Traffic is also a problem on weekends, as residents themselves head to the country and suburbanites come into the city. Thus, if you decide to live in a suburb and work in the city, you will have to think carefully about commuting strategies. In the city itself, driving and parking in the city center can often be difficult, depending on time of day and the number of delivery trucks double parked.

Compounding the problem, the city's municipal transit system has been beset by problems. Mayoral candidates promise during campaigns to fix them, then once elected state that problems are being addressed. Nonetheless, San Franciscans consistently rate public transit—along with unaffordable housing—as the city's worst problems; people who use the system, however, do manage to get to work on time, and the system is more or less reliable. Many people walk to work, some use bicycles, and several banks of parking meters downtown are designated for motorcycles.

Walking

San Francisco, despite its hills, is a walking city, and people walk whenever and wherever they can. According to California law, all vehicles must stop for a pedestrian in a crosswalk (except at extremely busy intersections). Surprisingly, for the most part, they actually do. Occasionally an impatient driver will pretend not to see the person crossing, or a tourist in a rented car might not know the law, so it is still important to pay attention to traffic and cross when safe. Obey the traffic signals and the "Walk" or "Don't Walk" signs. And note that jaywalkers who cross outside the designated crosswalks do not have the right of way.

When crossing the street, watch for cars that are turning right on a red light. Also, watch out for cars that dash through the intersection *after* the light has turned red. This is a major problem in San Francisco, one the police has yet to solve. Do not assume that the instant the light has turned green in your direction, it is safe to cross.

Bicycling

San Francisco rates among the top ten urban centers in the country for bicycling. The city encourages bicycling for daily transportation, and commuting by bicycle is popular. There are a few bicycle lanes on city streets, including a major lane in both directions on Valencia Street. Color-coded signs on bike routes indicate the direction (primary crosstown routes in full color or neighborhood routes in green and white), and odd numbers indicate north-south routes while even numbers are for east-west routes. The routes try to avoid the hills. To aid commuters, bicycle lockers have been installed at several public garages, and some Muni routes are experimenting with bike racks. Always lock your bike to an anchored, solid object with a U-lock. For information on the Bicycle Program, call the Commuter Hotline (tel: 585-2453). Bicyclists are expected to obey all the laws pertaining to motorists, not that many do. For bicycling as a sport, see Chapter Fifteen.

MUNI

The **Muni (Municipal Railway)**, San Francisco's public transportation system, accommodates more than a half million passenger rides each day (info tel: 673-6864; recorded timetables: 923-6336). Muni's 81 routes are covered by diesel and electric buses, cable cars, and the city's light rail streetcars known as Muni Metro. Of the 81 lines, 16 are express buses, making limited stops along their routes. All types begin operation at about 5:00 am and run until about 1:00 am; in the early morning the city is serviced by nine Owl lines.

The front of each vehicle displays the route number/letter and name, destination, and type of service: black/white lettering indicates local buses with many stops, green/white lettering indicates limited stops, and red/white lettering means express service. Buses are numbered (e.g. 38-Geary), and streetcars are lettered (e.g. J-Church). The bus stops themselves indicate which buses/streetcars stop there and their schedule. Buses stop only at designated bus stops, and not even in the pouring rain is the driver likely to open the door for you one inch away from the bus stop.

For a single trip, exact fare is required: adults currently pay $1; children over 4, seniors over 65, and students and disabled people with a discount card pay 35 cents. If you plan another trip within a few hours, ask for a "transfer" while paying your fare. Transfers, which are free, allow two additional trips within the time limit displayed on them, usually about 1½–2 hours, although some drivers are more liberal in where they mark the expiration.

For regular use of Muni, it's best to buy a **Fast Pass**, the weekly or monthly pass that allows unlimited access to any Muni vehicle, including cable cars (and to BART and Caltrain within San Francisco). There's no need for transfers, no need to search for dollar bills or change. Fast Passes are widely available, and prices vary according to category: see the Muni Timetables booklet that is sometimes in a rack at the front of the bus. Disabled persons should get the Regional Transit Connection Discount Card (tel: 923-6070). All streetcar stations are wheelchair accessible; call for further information (tel: 923-6142).

Cable Cars

Cable cars—since 1873 the city's most famous form of transportation—are certainly the most thrilling way to see San Francisco, as they clang charmingly up and down the hills on their underground cables at just under 10 miles per hour. But for occasional use they are expensive: currently they cost $2 per ride, unless you have a Fast Pass. And during the height of the tourist season it's hard to find a seat inside. Generally it's the tourists who like to sit on the outside in the fog and the wind, while the locals head into the inside seats.

The cable cars run on three lines—the Powell/Mason and Powell/Hyde lines, which begin at Powell and Market and head toward Fisherman's Wharf, and the California Street line, which begins at Market and California and terminates at Van Ness. Stops are every few blocks and are either marked with a maroon and white sign on the curb, or by a yellow line between the rails. Wait on the sidewalk, signal the gripman to stop, and board only when the car is fully stopped. Theoretically, automobiles are supposed to stop to allow people to cross to the cable car, but they don't always, so watch carefully when stepping off the sidewalk when the cable car is approaching.

BART

BART (Bay Area Rapid Transit) is a 5-line, 72-mile commuter railway that stops at some 39 stations on its route between the East Bay and Colma/Daly City (info tel: 650/992-2278; www.bart.org); it is wheelchair accessible. Efficiently run, BART accommodates more than 250,000 passenger rides each day. Bus lines are set up throughout the Bay Area to take people directly to BART. The service starts around 4:00 am (later on weekends) and shuts down around midnight. Trains run approximately every fifteen minutes, more often during rush hours. Check the schedules, for on weekends the trains run every 20 minutes and on Sundays the service is further reduced. Several informational brochures are available at BART stations.

To determine the fare to your destination, check the information charts which are displayed in each station. For regular commuting, buy a multi-trip ticket, which saves time and money The magnetic ticket is read by the computerized turnstiles at the entrances and exits. If you buy a one-trip ticket, save it in order to exit the station at your destination.

UP AND DOWN THE HILLS

One of San Francisco's beloved cable cars.

Taking BART makes commuting into the city easy.

Commuter Transit

Regularly scheduled buses and ferries bring commuters into the Financial District each day from around the Bay Area. Most ferries have differing weekday and weekend schedules, and some also have service to tourist attractions or to sports events. For recorded information on public transport and driving in the Bay Area, call **TravInfo** (tel: 817-1717).

- *East Bay* — **AC Transit** (Alameda-Contra Costa Transit) offers bus service to San Francisco and connects to BART stations in the East Bay (call TravInfo).
- *Marin/Sonoma* — **Golden Gate Transit** (GGT) offers fixed-route bus service from Marin to downtown San Francisco, and ferry service to the Ferry Building from Larkspur and Sausalito (tel: 923-2000; Marin tel: 455-2000); modified service on weekends. Bus service to and from Marin county locations, or leave your car at the "Park & Ride" parking lots. Call for the *Bus & Ferry System Map*, which details all the services and locations. All ferries are wheelchair accessible, and **Whistlestop Wheels** is GGT's intercounty paratransit service for disabled passengers who are enrolled (tel: 454-0964).
- *Marin* — **Blue & Gold Fleet**: Commuter ferries from Tiburon to Ferry Building, all-day ferry between Pier 41, Sausalito, and Tiburon (tel: 773-1188), and service to Alcatraz and Angel Island.
- *East Bay* — **Harbor Bay Maritime Ferry** (tel: 510/769-5500). Weekday commuter ferry between Harbor Bay Isle and the San Francisco Ferry Building.
- *East Bay* — **Alameda Oakland Ferry** (tel: 510/522-3300). Commuter service between Alameda, Oakland, and San Francisco.
- *Peninsula* — **Caltrain**: Daily train service between San Francisco and San Jose, stopping at stations in the South Bay and Peninsula (tel: 800/660-4287). The terminus is San Francisco's

Fourth Street Station, at Fourth and Townsend. The new extension of Muni has made access to the Financial District easier, but to Market Street it's only about a 10-minute walk. Fares are based on distance; buy tickets at the Caltrain stations.
- *Richmond* — **Red & White Fleet**: Weekday rush hour commuter service, with two trips in each direction on weekdays between the Ferry Terminal and Harbour Way (tel: 673-2900).
- *San Mateo* — **SamTrans** (San Mateo County Transit District): Bus service within San Mateo County and commuter service to San Francisco Financial District. Also services San Francisco International Airport and the Colma BART station (tel: 800/660-4287).

Taxis

Taxis in San Francisco do not cruise the streets regularly as they do in many other major cities. There are taxi stands at the major hotels downtown, but at rush hours, on rainy days, or when there is a major convention in town, there may be no taxis to be had, even at the stands. Trying to call one on the telephone can be frustrating at any hour, but if you're out of the direct city center, it's still best to call a cab well in advance of the time you'll need it, and then confirm just before its expected arrival that it is, indeed, on the way. Some hospitals, hotels, and apartment complexes have direct lines to the taxi companies, and any restaurant will call a taxi for you when you are ready to leave.

Taxis may be yellow, blue, or red and green, but all have the name of the cab company and the number of the cab in prominent letters on the sides. The top light of the taxi is illuminated when it is vacant. If an empty cab passes you by even though you are flagging it down, it has probably been called on the radio to go to a particular address. In San Francisco, the meter does not start running until you have entered the cab. Tip about 20 percent.

You can either give the taxi driver the exact street address where you're going, or you can indicate the two cross streets, such as "the corner of Washington and Battery." If you think you know the best route to get there, tell the driver on which streets you want to go. Generally, however, the driver is aware of the traffic conditions at that time and will take you the shortest and quickest way possible.

- Citywide Cab (tel: 920-0700)
- DeSoto Cab (tel: 970-1300)
- Luxor Cab (tel: 282-4141)
- Veteran's Cab (tel: 552-1300)
- Yellow Cab (tel: 626-2345)

DRIVING IN THE CITY

The most important thing about driving in San Francisco is to drive defensively. The congested downtown streets, the few major arteries, and the hills and the sun in drivers' eyes all contribute to the highest rate of traffic accidents in the state (although not involving pedestrians). Do not let the hills intimidate you. People drive up and down the hills every day, and some major routes go over the steepest of hills. When stopping at a traffic light while driving up a hill, leave at least ten feet between you and the car ahead, in case that car rolls back a little when starting up again. On some steep hills, you may have to downshift to maintain the car's power level, and some streets are marked with the percentage of grade and warnings to trucks not to attempt them. Make sure you have a pair of sunglasses in your car when you drive. If you drive toward the East in the morning or toward the West in the afternoons—especially when maneuvering the hills—the sun can be blinding.

When parking on a hill, "curb your wheels." This means if your car is heading down a hill, turn the front wheels toward the curb, to keep it from rolling. If your car is heading up a hill, turn the back part of the front wheels toward the curb to keep it from rolling back down. If you do not, your car will be ticketed.

Streets are narrowest in the downtown area, and it is on these streets, of course, that delivery trucks routinely double park, forcing cars to merge and causing traffic jams. Try to glance two to three blocks ahead while you are driving, to determine whether your lane is clear. Drivers in San Francisco are not particularly generous in allowing cars to cut into their lanes, so it's best to leave yourself as much time as possible to change lanes.

Many of the streets east of Van Ness are one-way; past Arguello, however, most streets—except for a few major arteries—are two-way. Two important one-way streets are Bush, which heads east ("Bush to the Bay"), and Pine, which heads west ("Pine to the Pacific"), for their lights are "timed," meaning that if you maintain a certain speed (and if there are no obstacles), you should not meet any red lights once you are in the traffic flow.

Some downtown streets have "diamond lanes," reserved for buses and for cars turning right at the next corner. Cars may turn right on a red light, after having come to a complete stop and allowed all pedestrians in the crosswalk to cross; some busy intersections, however, have signs saying "No turn on red." Left turn on red from a one-way street and into another is permitted under the same conditions.

Rush hours are generally 7:00–9:30 am and 4:00–7:00 pm. Streets leading to the bridges or freeways begin to be crowded by 3:30 in the afternoon, and traffic is slow until early evening. Local radio and television stations report traffic conditions every few minutes during rush hours and regularly throughout the day. You can also call TravInfo.

Do not be shocked at the price of gasoline; Northern California motorists pay the highest prices in the country. Some San Franciscans rely on public transportation, but despite the various expenses a car entails, most people find one necessary.

Last, all car passengers must wear seat belts, and occasionally a ticket will be given for failure to do so. Children under four years of age and under 40 pounds must wear a child restraint.

The California State Automobile Association is the best source of information for cars, driving, routes and maps, licenses, and insurance and permits. It also provides its members with excellent emergency road services. Offices are open 8:30 am–5:00 pm weekdays.

THE PARKING PROBLEM

About 800,000 cars circulate each day in this city of only 750,000 people. There are not enough parking spaces, so parking is a major complaint among residents. The closer to the bay, the harder it is to find a parking space. Downtown, parking meter spaces are generally reserved until 6:00 pm for commercially licensed vehicles to load and unload merchandise. Other meters may run on a half-hour basis. People who do find a parking space tend to stay there and return periodically to "feed" the meter, which is supposedly illegal; sometimes "meter maids" (parking police) mark the tires of cars with chalk to indicate the time they passed by; if the car is still there the next time the meter maid passes, it will be ticketed.

Parking garages and outdoor lots help with the problem, but they are crowded and prices vary: it depends on their location, whether they are city-owned or private, whether you are a short- or long-term parker and what time of day you park; early morning entry may allow a flat day rate, and evening parking also may incur a flat fee, paid in advance. In the popular areas around North Beach, Chinatown and Fisherman's Wharf, a $2.00 charge for 20 minutes is common, pretty expensive if you're planning a leisurely evening out. But if you're staying only 20 minutes, it might be worth it. The garages mentioned here are reasonable in price; there are others around the city, and fortunately supermarkets and most shopping centers have their own free parking lots.

- *Union Square*: Sutter/Stockton Garage
- *Union Square*: Under Union Square, enter on Geary
- *Yerba Buena*: Fifth and Mission Garage

- *Japantown*: Entrances on Post and Geary, off Webster
- *Chinatown*: Portsmouth Square Garage, enter on Kearny, just past Clay
- *Financial District:* St Mary's Square Garage, enter from Kearny, north of Pine
- *North Beach*: Vallejo/Stockton Garage, enter from Vallejo
- *Richmond*: Geary and 16th Avenue, on second floor, above shops.

When you make a reservation at a restaurant, ask about parking; valet parking is often available, but can be expensive, for the price displayed does not include the expected tip to the parker. Some restaurants and cinemas offer validated parking in nearby parking garages; your parking ticket stamped by the restaurant or theater entitles you to a discount on the charge.

In high-traffic districts, residents may park indefinitely on non-metered streets with a permit issued by the **Department of Parking**, at 370 Grove Street (info tel: 554-5000); you must have proof that the car is registered in California and that you live where you say you do. Street signs indicate the permit needed for that area, and they also specify how long non-permit cars may park during certain hours. Signs also indicate which day of the week and time the street is to be cleaned; if your car is parked there during those hours, permit or not, it will be ticketed and towed. Unfortunately, street cleaning days decrease even further the number of available parking spaces. (If you see a street on which no one is parked, don't thank your lucky stars that you found a parking space: look to see if this is street cleaning day.)

None of this makes it easier to find a space on Chestnut Street if you want to go to a film on a Saturday afternoon or to Ninth Avenue for dinner. Nonetheless, avoid parking illegally, for anything other than an overtime meter incurs a high fine. Look on the parking meter itself to determine its hours and days of operation; don't assume that parking is free on holidays, especially in tourist areas. Fines are extremely steep for parking where the curb is painted red (prohibited) or blue (handicapped parking), in a crosswalk, or where the curb has been cut out for wheelchair access. And do not even think about parking in a bus zone. A white curb is for passenger pickup and drop-off, and a green curb is for 10 minute parking. Yellow is for commercial vehicles, and the hours and days of parking limitations should be painted on the curb. A green, yellow and black zone is for taxi cabs. As mentioned above, some downtown streets prohibit parking during morning or evening rush hours; for infractions, your car will most likely be towed. These streets are usually marked "tow-away zone."

Driver's Licenses

All applicants for a California driver's license must submit proof of legal presence in the United States. (This might include—among other documents—a birth certificate, U.S. passport, Certificate of Naturalization, Canadian Passport, or Mexican Border Crossing Card with a valid I-94.)

Residents of San Francisco—defined as people who are making their home here or who have taken a job here—must apply for a California driver's license within 10 days to the **DMV (California Department of Motor Vehicles)**, at 1377 Fell Street (tel: 557-1179; www.dmv.ca.gov). If you have a valid license from another state, you may not be required to take the driving test; all applicants, however, must take the written "rules of the road" test and a vision test. All applicants must give a thumbprint and have a picture taken. DMV offices are located in towns throughout the Bay Area. A driver's license is generally valid for four or five years, and expires on your birthday of that year.

If you are here only on a temporary basis, however, you may drive for one year with a valid license from your home state. This applies also to citizens of Western nations; others must possess a current International Driving License. If you do not drive but would like an official identification card, bring identification, Social Security number, and proof of address to the DMV.

DUI

Do not drink alcohol and drive. It is dangerous, and the police crack down on drivers who have been drinking (even if the driver doesn't appear to be "drunk"). If you intend to drink, designate a non-drinking driver for that evening. Fines for DUI ("driving under the influence") are steep, and if there is a serious accident, may even involve a term in prison. The DWI ("driving while intoxicated") is not generally used in California, for prosecutors do not need to prove that a driver is intoxicated to take the driver to court. In California it is illegal to drive with a blood alcohol level of 0.08 or more; the fact that a driver doesn't know the blood alcohol level is not an excuse under the law.

Registering Your Car

Within 20 days of establishing residency in California, you must register your out-of-state car. (Residency means paying resident-based tuition at a school, having a job, filing for home owner's tax exemptions, obtaining any kind of lease or contract, or any other benefit that non-residents do not obtain.) In order to register the vehicle with the DMV, you will need to fill out the application, pay the current fee, and produce the title to the car and a "smog certificate" (available at many full-service gasoline stations). The car must be inspected by the DMV.

If you are coming to California for only a few months, you need not register your car, and may drive with your own state's license plates. This may pose a problem if you rent an apartment in a neighborhood which requires parking permits to park on the street; you can't get a permit for a car not registered in California. In this case, it's best to rent a space in a garage nearby, or make sure in advance that your apartment has a garage space.

Automobile Insurance

California state law requires that all drivers be financially responsible for their actions while driving and for the vehicles they own;

if you have an accident not covered by your insurance, your driver's license will be suspended. In fact, car dealers do not permit you to take possession of a new car without proof of insurance; make sure to arrange for it in advance. The minimum amount your insurance must cover per accident is $15,000 for a single death or injury, $30,000 for death or injury to more than one person, and $5,000 for property damage; given the litigious nature of American society, however, these minimums may not protect you well enough, depending on your financial circumstances. If you are bringing a car with you, you may be able to transfer your insurance if the company does business in California; check in advance with your carrier. Otherwise, some major insurance companies that service California are **Allstate**, California State Automobile Association (AAA), **Farmers**, **Mercury**, **State Farm**, and **20th Century**. Rates vary considerably. Many companies have discounted rates for drivers with proven safety records, some give discounts for cars with alarm systems, some have discounts for professionals, and some offer towing services.

PURCHASING A CAR

Advertising supplements for new cars appear in each Friday's daily newspapers. Used cars are advertised in the classified ad sections, especially on Sundays. When purchasing a car, it is best to determine the dealer's factory invoice price on the car (not the "sticker price" which is affixed to the window). Several services help buyers get the best deal possible.

Members of the Cal State Auto may use its Vehicle Pricing Service to receive suggested retail prices on new and used vehicles, and to buy a new car at a fair price, without haggling (vehicle pricing tel: 800/272-2877; vehicle purchasing service tel: 800/477-1222; www.csaa.com/carbuying). When you indicate the make, model and options of the car you want, "Triple A" will tell you which dealers in the area have agreed to sell at the pre-arranged price.

HANDICAPPED ACCESS

San Francisco is wheelchair friendly. Buses have operator-assisted ramps for wheelchairs, all BART stations are wheelchair accessible, and curbs throughout the city are cut to a slope for easy access to sidewalks and crosswalks. Hotels and restaurants are wheelchair accessible, and most public rest rooms have wide stalls that will accommodate wheelchairs.

Drivers with handicaps may apply to the DMV for a permit to park in any of the blue-marked parking spaces reserved for handicapped drivers. Your doctor should have a form that entitles you to such application. As mentioned above, people with physical disabilities are entitled to a public transportation discount card.

The Department of Tourism issues *California Travel Planning Guide*, which is available at the Visitor Center in Halliday Plaza. If you have a problem, contact the 24-hour Crisis Line for the handicapped (tel: 800/426-4263).

The **San Francisco Paratransit Broker** arranges reasonably priced taxi transportation for people with physical disabilities who are enrolled in their program (tel: 543-9650).

THE CALL OF NATURE

It shouldn't be hard to find a clean public bathroom in San Francisco. Downtown, in addition to rest rooms in the large hotels and department stores, there are a few French-style coin-operated *sanisettes*, standing lavatories with toilet and sink; when you are finished, open the door to exit, and as it closes behind you, the toilet flushes and the entire facility is sterilized. Supermarkets generally have rest rooms for customer use, as do shopping centers. Fast-food restaurants, bars, and coffee shops may expect you to purchase at least a cup of coffee to use their rest room, and some small restaurants on the tourist path have clear signs indicating that rest rooms are for customers only. Rest rooms at service stations may require that you ask the attendant for a key. In most places, if you ask to use a rest room, you will not be refused.

— Chapter Eleven —
GASTRONOMIC DELIGHTS

SAN FRANCISCO—THE BEST?

San Franciscans believe their city to be the gastronomic capital of America. Residents of a few other American cities may dispute this claim, but the seemingly endless numbers of tourists who patiently await their tables at the city's crowded restaurants tend to confirm that San Francisco's offerings rise to the top. But how has this come to pass? The answer is itself a stew, combining the city's particular geography, climate, history—and attitude.

Begin with the ingredients: the area's moderate climate and the city's proximity to rich, fertile, agricultural lands, to the Pacific Ocean, and to the country's top wine-producing region. See the fishing boats coming in early each morning to the piers off

Jefferson Street, and you will never doubt that the fish is fresh, year-round. Drive south or east, passing the rich vegetable fields and flourishing orchards that supply the city's restaurants directly, and you can tell what is in season and what will be on the menu at that time. Or pass the miles of grape-laden vines as you head up to warm, sunny Napa or Sonoma—just an hour north of the city— and then don't be surprised to find outstanding wines made at those vineyards in restaurants all over town.

Now stir in a bit of history. The city's unusual approach to food combinations has grown from its own cultural diversity. From its earliest days, San Francisco was a town where people ate out. It started with the Gold Rush, when thousands of miners with money—or gold nuggets—in their pockets, came down from the hills for a taste of "civilization." Restaurants of all types flourished. Even at that time, the cooks were immigrants—Italians, Hungarians, French, and Chinese—melding their own cooking traditions with the ingredients on hand. After the flurry of the Gold Rush and the Silver Rush died down, eating establishments remained.

Since then, each wave of immigrants has taken and given to the tastes and aromas of the city: Italian food with Oriental overtones, Vietnamese food presented in the style of the French, and pan-Asian or pan-Latin cuisines. Although you might hear such appellations as *eclectic* or *international,* the more common culinary term for this bringing together of traditions and tastes is *fusion*, describing an approach in which each flavor contributes to the overall dish but is identifiable in itself. But fusion is not new in San Francisco, and in fact, fusion of cultures, cuisines, and traditions—with each contributing but still identifiable in itself—is what has always defined the city itself.

Attitude of San Franciscans

Adding spice to the answer of why San Francisco's restaurants are so exceptional, is that San Franciscans demand they be so. San Franciscans also love to eat out—at restaurants of all levels—

and with a mean household income of about $60,000, residents spend about $2,500 per household per year eating out. Thus, no one needs to settle for just a "good dinner." Although it is not true that San Francisco has more restaurants than people, with some 3,500 eating and drinking establishments, it may well have more restaurants *per capita* than other cities. Thus, diners get a wide choice, and they set the tone. In fact, the city works on the premise that the entire experience of eating should be fun. San Franciscans consider eating out to be one of their major cultural—albeit playful—experiences, and they demand, and get, the best.

"The best" does not necessarily mean the most expensive restaurant or those that are lavishly reviewed. An innovative Thai restaurant might be the best in its class, and an otherwise undistinguished Italian restaurant might well have the best calamari— to some diners' tastes. Other restaurants may tickle diners' fancy with their decor, and some now are offering entertainment— foreign movies or live music—along with the dining experience.

Also, particularity rules. Gone are the days when Italian food meant spaghetti with tomato sauce; now San Franciscans may select among their favorite Ligurian- or Roman-style restaurants, even choosing a place for one particular dish. (This holds true for fish restaurants as well, where people may throng to a particular restaurant for its way of cooking one type of fish.) And gone also are the days when Chinese food meant Chicken Fried Rice; now San Franciscans pick carefully among Hunan, Chiu Chow, or Cantonese cuisines, and they know which restaurants serve the best *dim sum*. The best San Franciscan restaurants demonstrate a strong sense of place.

But even the cuisines do not tell the entire story. San Franciscans also demand that restaurants, no matter the style of cuisine, mirror their lifestyles. The restaurants themselves should be attractive. The food they eat should be healthy and look good, whether it is a luxurious dinner in an elegant restaurant or a hearty meal in a neighborhood pub. Food in San Francisco can also be high art. What is known as California Cuisine—which originated at Berkeley's **Chez Panisse** and which has now been adopted around the globe—epitomizes this trend. Emphasizing regional, in-season ingredients, California Cuisine presents a beautiful yet simple-seeming and healthy effect (sometimes with a touch of humor) although the exotic combinations of ingredients and presentation may not be simple at all.

Yet even with California Cuisine, distinctions blur. Some restaurants known for California Cuisine also use Asian flavors and presentations, others might borrow from the Italian, some might just call themselves Modern American, or even that generic term of *fusion*. What San Franciscans want, in short, is everything all at once: excellent and healthful food imaginatively prepared, a great view, an attractive space, and friendly service. Some of the city's most inventive chefs—at luxury restaurants such as **Aqua, Fleur de Lys, La Folie, Campton Place** and **Jardeniere**—offer a "tasting menu" that allows diners to sample several of the evening's dishes, including starters, entrees, and desserts. If San Franciscans, as some people claim, "want eveything now," at least in terms of dining out, they seem to be able to get it.

Resources

It is a passion of San Franciscans to seek the best restaurant for every meal. Weekends find people out early eating hearty breakfasts or, later, a delicately prepared brunch. Weekday lunchtime sees crowds in most of the downtown business-style restaurants, people looking not just to eat but for a culinary experience. (It is wise to reserve for lunch, just as much as for dinner.) And dinner is a constant process of happy exploration in any neighborhood, sometimes the more offbeat, the better. Currently, expanding out of the tried and true districts, San Franciscans are seeking out the restaurants and bars in what is sometimes called Baja Mission (on the edge of Potrero Hill), the Inner Sunset nexus around 9th Avenue, and the new offerings near the baseball park.

It would be impossible to describe all the city's excellent restaurants here. There are so many international cuisines and traditions that these chapters can give only representative samples of the diverse culinary experiences the city offers. To aid in your pleasant search, buy one of the guides dedicated entirely to eating out in the Bay Area. The best, which covers both restaurants and food markets, is *A Food Lover's Guide to San Francisco*, by Patricia Unterman, a local food writer who knows San Francisco's restaurants better than anyone else. Loosely arranged by district and within district by category, her book makes it easy to find anything you want to know about food in the area. *Access San Francisco: Restaurants* presents a comprehensive selection, also arranged by neighborhood. The famous *Zagat's* rates restaurants according to diners' choices; in recent years, **Boulevard** has been rated the city's most popular restaurant, with Aqua the runner-up.

Although this book emphasizes establishments patronized by locals, do not overlook those in the tourist guides, for the elegant places that the hordes of tourists are clamoring to try—**Fifth Floor**, Fleur de Lys, **Farallon**, Jardiniere, **Stars**—are truly exceptional. In addition, these guides—such as the always-interesting *Time Out San Francisco*—usually describe some out-of-the-way places of all cuisines and price ranges that they believe capture the spirit of San Francisco.

Look also at the daily newspapers and weekly tabloids, which review and rate restaurants and often conduct readers' polls, which accounts for the myriad restaurants that boast that their specialty (sushi, hamburger, pizza, barbeque, salsa, etc) has been judged the best in the city. They probably all have, by one judge or another. *The Bay Guardian* and *San Francisco Chronicle* also regularly publish surveys of the "best" in dozens of categories, always interesting, always with a surprise. Beauty of the establishment is often rated, and some—such as Farallon and Jardiniere—are imaginative in their decor. If noise bothers you, pay attention to the decibel ratings in restaurant reviews, as the current trend for a lively atmosphere has resulted in large open spaces with high ceilings, which greatly increases the noise.

Reserving a Table

Most but not all restaurants take reservations. The currently fashionable restaurants require reservations to be made one month in advance, and if you do not call exactly when specified, you might not get a table; sometimes, however, tables are available at off-hours, such as 5:45 pm or 10:00 pm. As a general rule, the better the restaurant, the longer in advance you should book. This also holds true for the restaurants that play live music, or those with a view—**The Waterfront** and **Greens** at water level, or the **Carnelian Room** soaring 52 floors above. To find out about table availability and making a reservation on the Internet, you might try **Open Table** (www.OpenTable.com).

On the other hand, there's no harm in calling to see whether there has been a cancellation. Ask whether the restaurant serves dinner at the bar to walk-in customers, for bar food is of the same quality as in the rest of the restaurant. (Some restaurants have open kitchens, and sitting at the counter/bar allows you to watch the chefs perform their magic.) Sitting at the bar is an attractive option for solo diners, although San Franciscan restaurants are welcoming to people dining alone.

Most restaurants can accommodate you if you make a reservation the day before or even on the morning of the day you intend to dine, and in some, if you don't reserve in advance, you can wait for a table to be vacated. Restaurants generally figure 90 minutes for a couple to remain at a table and two hours for a party of four. The maître d'hôtel will be as honest as possible—given the unpredictable time a party may linger—in assessing the waiting time, or indeed, if there is a chance to get a table. If you have to wait, the maître d' will almost always offer a seat at the bar.

Not all restaurants take reservations. Some of the fish restaurants do not, or will take reservations only for parties of more than six people; this also holds true for the Asian establishments and many small, neighborhood restaurants. In popular places where there is a line, there will usually be a waiting list; seating is first come first served, according to the tables available and the number of people in the party.

Do not forget that tourists love San Francisco restaurants. When a large convention is in town, it can be impossible to get a table at a restaurant that might have been reviewed in a guidebook or that was recommended by the convention planners. Make your reservation as far in advance as you can and call if you must cancel; don't just not show up. No one minds if you cancel; they're glad you have called. Some restaurants require confirmation of the reservation the day before, and a few ask for your credit card number, explaining that you will be charged a fee if you do not show up.

Despite the foggy, cool evenings, San Franciscans love to eat outside; some restaurants have patios sheltered from the wind by glass screens with gas heaters under an overhanging roof. These popular establishments are likely to be crowded on warm spring or autumn nights (and always for brunch on weekends), so make sure you reserve in advance, and mention that you'd like a table on the patio or one with a view. The reservations taker usually says, "we'll see what we can do," meaning that you will probably get a table you want, given the traffic flow at the time.

Dress is generally casual, and it is rare to find a man wearing a suit, except for holidays or special occasions. In the most fashionable restaurants, a man might wear a sports jacket, without a tie, and women slacks, sweaters, and a blazer. However, it's always good to dress appropriately to the establishment and the occasion. In most neighborhood restaurants and smaller cafes, casual dress is the rule; even blue jeans and sneakers are acceptable. One casual Berkeley establishment humorously advertises "food so good, you might want to wear your nice jeans."

Opening Times

San Francisco is an "early town." Because the Pacific Time Zone is three hours behind New York's financial markets, financial workers start working before dawn and eat lunch and dinner early. Because they most often eat before performances, not after, do not expect to get into popular restaurants around Union Square or at the Civic Center in the early evening (or on days when there are matinees) unless you reserve well in advance. On the other hand, you can generally get a table if you are willing to eat a little later, after a performance has started.

Restaurants start to serve breakfast around 6:30 am, begin lunch at 11:30 am, and those that don't stay open all day may start dinner service at 5:30 pm, taking their last orders around 10:00 pm. Some restaurants in the Financial District close by 9:00 pm, and a few are open weekdays only.

A few restaurants—**Black Cat**, **The Globe**, **Chow**, **Brazenhead**, and **Absinthe**—fill the void in late-night dining, while **Lisa's on Folsom**, and **Yuet Lee** and a few others in Chinatown satisfy the need for a late-night Chinese food fix. **Sparky's**, **The Grubstake**, and **Mel's** offer burgers into the wee hours. The hours of neighborhood restaurants generally reflect the habits of the locals. Asian restaurants usually serve all day, as do the coffeehouses. Fashionable restaurants may take their last orders around 10:30, but neighborhood eateries are generally closed by then.

Most of the large restaurants serve dinner every day, but serve lunch only on weekdays. Most of the Asian restaurants are open daily as well, although any small family-run establishment may close one day a week. Days of closure vary, but generally it is either Sunday or Monday.

The Menu

The menu depends on the season. Some restaurants print their menus daily, and in others servers recite the list of that day's special dishes. These invariably reflect the fishermen's catch and the produce that is then most plentiful in the markets. Pay attention to the specials, for they generally offer the best value for the money. Do not hesitate to ask how a dish is prepared, and in the case of an oral recitation of the specials, to ask the price, if the server omits it.

If you have dietary restrictions, specify your needs to the server in advance, so that you can be assured of ordering a meal that you can eat. The server will ask the chef what is in the dish you are considering, and then you can decide. In general, you send back a meal only if it isn't cooked properly or if it is different from what is described on the menu.

Order only as much as you want. Restaurants are used to people ordering two appetizers, to splitting appetizers and main courses between two diners, or serving just an appetizer and a dessert. And every establishment, from the grungiest dive to the most fashionable temple of gastronomy, will cheerfully wrap your unfinished meal to take home.

Coffee may be served at any time during the meal and generally with the dessert, not after; all restaurants offer decaffeinated coffee and many offer espresso and cappuccino. Tea drinking is becoming trendy, and most restaurants now offer a selection of teas, including decaffeinated versions and herbal infusions.

What Will It Cost?

An excellent dinner in a neighborhood Asian or Latino restauraunt may cost as little as $10, including a beer or soda, and an excellent meal in one of the city's top restaurants may cost as much as $100 per person, with several glasses of wine. The average per-person dinner tab is currently $35, on a par with New York. Yet what matters to San Francisco diners is value for the money, and in general, eating out in San Francisco is an affordable pastime.

Chinese and other Asian restaurants may offer a lunchtime special of soup, a hearty main course with plenty of rice, plus tea for about $5.00. Dinner specials may be slightly, but not much, higher in price. In fact, because the best restaurants are crowded year-round, and the inexpensive restaurants are affordable at any time, few have "early bird specials," for people arriving (and leaving) before normal dining hours. Occasionally restaurants offer specials with a coupon from the newspapers.

Paying the Bill
All the major restaurants accept credit cards. In the United States the tip (gratuity) is generally not included in the bill, although some restaurants will add 15 percent for a party of at least six people. The standard tip is 15–20 percent, depending on level of service; 20 percent is becoming more common for good service. In San Francisco, the sales tax is 8.5 percent, and when figuring the tip, many people just double the tax that appears on the bill. This assumes the service was good; if not, point it out to the manager or tip accordingly.

It is best not to assume that the small Asian eateries accept credit cards, although many do. Even some of the popular neighborhood restaurants don't, so if this is of concern, call ahead or carry enough cash. A few will accept a local check, so long as you provide a picture identification. In some Asian establishments you may not understand the bill because it is written in Chinese on a small piece of paper only somewhat resembling a bill. On the other hand, the amount may be so cheap—under $20 for two people—that a rarely made mistake of a few cents doesn't matter much.

SMOKING
Smoking is not allowed in any public place in San Francisco, not in any public building, restaurant, theater, sports arena, nor on public transportation. A recent law passed to prohibit smoking in bars raised a loud protest, but even before the law was enacted, San Franciscans were capable of shooting dirty looks and saying something pointed to anyone they thought was smoking too close to their "smoke-free zone."

SAN FRANCISCO'S OWN

It is true that San Francisco's cuisine blends international flavors, but the city boasts its own local favorites, worth seeking out. The season (November–May) for the sweet, meaty **Dungeness crab** is eagerly awaited, and people keep track of the weather, for stormy weather makes for a bad catch. Cracked crab, served cold with a cocktail or butter sauce, or Crab Louie, a crab salad with a Thousand Island type dressing, are served in most fish restaurants during crab season. Outside crab season, the crab is likely to have been frozen or imported. Asian restaurants serve well-sauced crab dishes, and many people think the upscale Vietnamese restaurant **Thanh Long** at 4101 Judah Street in the Outer Richmond serves the best in the city; dinners only, closed Monday (tel: 665-1146).

Filet of sole is on the menu worldwide, but the local varieties—**petrale**, **rex**, or the delicate **sand dabs**—are particular to this area. Two of the oldest fish houses in the city are known for their excellent preparations:

- **Sam's Grill**: 374 Bush Street, near Kearny (tel: 421-0594). For almost 150 years, Sam's has served excellent fish. Try the sand dabs and rex sole. Closed weekends.
- **Tadich**: 240 California Street (tel: 391-1849). Perennially popular, Tadich's has been serving seafood in San Francisco since 1849, making it the oldest in the city.

If every fishing port has its favorite seafood dishes, San Francisco's is **cioppino**, a fish stew based loosely on the Ligurian *ciuppin*. It also resembles the French *bouillabaisse* and the Spanish *zarzuela*. Basically, cioppino features locally caught crab in season, other fresh shellfish and fish (especially the local rockfish, like cod), all stewed in a spicy tomato broth. Note that squid, a favorite seafood in San Francisco, is called by its Italian name *calamari*, even in some Asian restaurants. Eat the stew with San Francisco's **sourdough bread** (see Bakeries, in Chapter Thirteen).

Eating lunch by a fountain in the sun.

- **Alioto's**: 8 Fisherman's Wharf, at Taylor (tel: 673-0183). Despite the tourist atmosphere, this is one of the best cioppinos in the city.
- **Rose Pistola**: 532 Columbus Avenue (tel: 399-0499). Excellent cioppino and other Ligurian dishes. Live jazz.

CALIFORNIA CUISINE

As mentioned above, California Cuisine is a modern American style of cooking that emphasizes fresh, regional ingredients in creative combinations and presentations. **Chez Panisse** at 1517 Shattuck Avenue, Berkeley, is still the high temple of California Cuisine (tel: 510/548-5525; cafe tel: 510/548-5049). Delicious and beautiful ingredients in magically pure combinations look deceptively simple on the plate yet are addictive to the palate. Make reservations for the restaurant (downstairs) at least a month in advance and expect an outstanding culinary experience during an expensive price-fixed meal, with one entree selection per evening. In the cafe (upstairs) reserve the same day and expect a delicious, imaginative selection at more moderate prices.

- *Downtown* — **Postrio**: 545 Post Street (tel: 776-7825). A temple to California Cuisine. Outstanding dishes, creatively prepared.
- *Mission/Potrero* — **Gordon's House of Fine Eats**: 500 Florida Street (tel: 861-8900). Billing itself as "modern American," Asian overtones can be found amid the blend of American traditions.
- *Mission* — **Luna Park**: 694 Valencia, at 18th Street (tel: 553-8584). Chic yet funky atmosphere, good California cuisine, and a bar that serves up great margaritas and other trendy drinks.
- *North Beach* — **Moose's**: 1652 Stockton Street (tel: 989-7800). Eclectic menu, great bar, famous for the Mooseburger.
- *South Waterfront* — **Delancey Street Restaurant**: Embarcadero at Brannan (tel: 512-5179). Upscale "ethnic American bistro" staffed by people who have "hit bottom" and are now being rehabilitated. Closed Monday.
- *Sunset/NorthBeach* — **The House**: 1269 9th Ave (tel: 682-3898); 1230 Grant Ave (tel: 986-8612). Asian/Mediterranean/California Cuisine in a spare setting.

The Old ...

As mentioned, San Francisco became an eating-out town during the Gold Rush, when miners came down from the hills for a good time. Tadich's (see above) is the oldest restaurant in the city, and others, some dating from the 1860s, also pride themselves on maintaining traditions of "old San Francisco."

- **Fior d'Italia**: 601 Union Street, at Stockton (tel: 986-1886). Claiming to be the oldest Italian restaurant in the country, this standard, fairly expensive Italian restaurant has been in this location since 1886.
- **Fly Trap**: 606 Folsom (tel: 243-0580). Only a few streets away from its 1898 location, this rather hidden restaurant still serves grilled food in an old-time setting. Closed Sunday.
- **Jack's**: 615 Sacramento Street (tel: 421-7355). In the same

location for more than 135 years, Jack's has recently been restored, with period furnishings. Fresh and hearty food, traditional favorites, plus "California" dishes.
- **John's Grill**: 63 Ellis Street, at Powell (tel: 986-0069). Since 1908, John's has served hearty food. Live jazz.
- **Maye's Oyster House**: 1233 Polk, between Bush and Sutter (tel: 474-7674). Serving Italian food and seafood since 1867, Maye's has an old-time feel, despite its modern piano bar.
- **Schroeder's**: 240 Front Street, near Sacramento (tel: 421-4778). Solid German food such as sauerbraten and sausages, served here for more than one hundred years. Open weekdays.
- **The Old Clam House**: 299 Bayshore Boulevard (tel: 826-4880). Since 1861, this fish house has been offering fresh seafood in an old-time setting. Open daily.

... The New

Although many restaurants borrow liberally from world regions, San Franciscan restaurants excel in presenting a meld of flavors and traditions that reflect the city's own cultural diversity. Fusion cuisine may blend several culinary traditions, at least one of them Asian, and often the exotic result seems more than the combination of the parts.

- *Cole Valley* — **EOS**: 901 Cole Street (tel: 566-3063). Popular for East/West cuisine, and its excellent wine list and wine bar. Less noisy upstairs. Dinner daily.
- *Downtown* — **Oritalia**: 586 Bush Street (tel: 782-8122). Mediterranean and Eastern blends, such as a Chinese cioppino. Dinner only.
- *Marina* — **The Blue Monkey**: 2414 Lombard Street, at Scott (tel: 776-8298). Excellent Thai fusion cuisine.
- *Mission* — **The Rooster**: 1101 Valencia, at 22nd Street (tel: 824-1222). Country cooking with European, Asian, and Latin flavors, in a rustic setting.

- *Noe Valley* — **Firefly**: 4288 24th Street (tel: 821-7652). Popular neighborhood eatery preparing "American food with no ethnic boundaries." Wonderful desserts. Dinner only.
- *Polk/California* — **Crustacean**: 1475 Polk Street (tel: 776-2722). Like its sister restaurant Thanh Long: Euro/Asian menu featuring Dungeness crab, garlic noodles, and other interesting dishes.
- *Polk/Broadway* — **Yabbies Coastal Kitchen**: 2237 Polk Street (tel: 474-4088). Excellent establishment specializing in fish dishes with Asian-Mediterranean overtones.
- *SOMA* — **XYZ**: 181 3rd Street at Howard (tel: 817-7836). Popular restaurant next to W Hotel, serving seafood with Japanese overtones, and other fusion-style dishes.

... and the Basic

To the rest of the world American food means steaks, roast beef, barbeque, fried chicken, burgers and fries, and San Francisco does not disappoint. But here — although you can find **McDonalds** and other international burger chains — even the purveyors of down-home ribs and burgers do so with their own San Francisco twist:

- **Max's Diner**: 311 3rd Street (tel: 546-6297). Huge sandwiches, burgers, and desserts, plus a sports bar.
- **Big Nate's Barbecue**: 1665 Folsom, near 12th Street (tel: 861-4242). Ribs, chicken and sausage links in this takeout storefront owned by Nate Thurmond, the famous basketball player. A few tables for eat-in.
- **Bill's Place**: 2315 Clement Street (tel: 221-5262). For more than 25 years, consistently rated among the best for burgers and crispy fries.
- **Brother-in-law's Barbeque #2**: 705 Divisadero Street (tel: 931-7427). Delicious brisket and "short-end ribs," plus greens, beans, spaghetti, and corn bread. Take out, for there are only two small tables in front for eating-in.

- **Cliff's Bar-B-Q & Seafood**: 2177 Bayshore Boulevard (tel: 330-0736). Ribs of all sorts, spicy or not, excellent brisket, fish and turkey burgers. A few tables.
- **Hamburger Mary's**: 1582 Folsom at 12th Street (tel: 626-5767). A city tradition, advertising "Great food, Fun Bar, Crazy Staff." Excellent meals served to a rather interesting clientele.
- **Memphis Minnie's Bar-B-Que Joint**: 576 Haight Street (tel: 864-8461). Great smokehouse ribs, brisket, Andouille sausage, and a good selection of sides. Closed Monday.
- **Mo's Place**: 1322 Grant Avenue (tel: 788-3779). Among the best burgers in town. Also at Yerba Buena Gardens on the second level of the bowling alley-ice skating rink.
- **Powell's Place**: 511 Hayes Street (tel: 863-1404). Delicious fried chicken, yams, and greens. Pork chops, beans and rice, and other soul food. Daily specials.
- **Harris' Restaurant**: 2100 Van Ness Avenue (tel: 673-1888). Excellent steaks, good decor, from a famous California cattle rancher.
- **House of Prime Rib**: 1906 Van Ness Avenue (tel: 885-4605). Succulent prime rib, carved at your table.

FISH

Expect all restaurants to serve fish, and for it to be fresh. As the menu depends on the day's catch, the entire city pays close attention to the weather and fishing conditions. It is a disappointment when the Dungeness crab catch is low, or when storms prevent the taking of sand dabs and rex sole. Restaurants that don't print their menus every day generally announce fish dishes as specials of the day. Often they will give the origin of the fish. If they don't, you can ask where the fish was caught.

In a restaurant, a serving of fish is generally about $5^1/_2$ or 6 ounces. Don't neglect the fish dishes in Asian restaurants: although the portion of fish may be smaller, the flavors meld together with the vegetables and sauces of each region's culinary traditions.

The elegant, trendy Aqua and Farallon specialize in fish, and **Scott's** in the Embarcadero Center is always reliable. Sam's and Tadich's (see above) remain favorites, and if their ambience is staid, the quality of the food is not. There will no doubt be a good fish restaurant in your own neighborhood. Try also these below, and see the following chapter for Asian restaurants.

- *Castro* — **Anchor Oyster Bar**: 579 Castro Street (tel: 431-3990). Small restaurant serving delicious pastas, seafood, and clam chowder, with a delightful aroma of garlic throughout.
- *Civic Center* — **Hayes Street Grill**: 320 Hayes Street (tel: 863-5545). Great fish on a menu that changes daily. Tell the staff if you have a performance to make in the Civic Center, and service will be speedy.
- *Inner Sunset* — **PJ's Oyster Bed**: 737 Irving Street (tel: 556-7775). Long before 9th Avenue became chic, PJ's was serving fresh oysters, chowder, and other excellent Southern dishes to neighborhood locals, and it still does.
- *Polk Corridor* — **Swan's Oyster Depot**: 1517 Polk Street (tel: 673-1101). Lunch only at the counter of this excellent almost century-old fish market. Outstanding chowder, oysters, seafood salads.
- *Western Addition* — **Alamo Square, a Seafood Grill**: 803 Fillmore Street, at Fulton (tel: 440-2828). Fish any way you like it. Dinners daily; Sunday brunch.

VEGETARIAN AND KOSHER

Catering to a healthy, fitness-oriented crowd, even the best "carnivore" restaurants offer well-presented vegetarian selections. Italian restaurants offer meatless pasta dishes and the ubiquitous Asian restaurants have vegetarian dishes. The city's totally vegetarian restaurants offer the same high-quality food as the others.

You will not find many kosher restaurants under rabbinic supervision in San Francisco. The preponderance of vegetarian restaurants, however, should allow people who keep kosher to enjoy the cuisines of San Francisco with few problems.

- *Chinatown* — **Lotus Garden**: 532 Grant Avenue, in Chinatown (tel: 397-0707). Chinese vegetarian restaurant. Closed Monday.
- *Chinatown* — **Lucky Creation**: 854 Washington Street, near Stockton (tel: 989-0818). Very popular local vegetarian eatery in the heart of Chinatown. Try the tofu roll with mushrooms. Closed Wednesday.
- *Civic Center* — **Ananda Fuara**: 1298 Market, at 9th Street (tel: 621-1994). Hearty breakfasts, curries, pizza, salads, and sandwiches, vegetarian and vegan. Open until 8:00 pm Mon–Sat; closed 3:00 pm Wed.
- *Civic Center* — **Millennium**: 246 McAllister, near Hyde (tel: 487-9800). This "optimal health cuisine restaurant" serves elegant and imaginative combinations of vegan, organic, low-fat foods … and luscious desserts.
- *Downtown* — **Sabra Grill**: 419 Grant Avenue (tel: 982-3656). Glatt kosher Middle Eastern restaurant.
- *Haight* — **Ganges Vegetarian Restaurant**: 775 Frederick Street (tel: 661-7290). Curries and regional Indian dishes in a pleasant setting across from Kezar Stadium.
- *Marina* — **Greens**: Building A, Fort Mason, next to the Marina Green (tel: 771-6222). Always crowded, this upscale restaurant with its big windows sits almost in the bay. The delicate vegetarian creations all have a "Zen" flavor. Closed Monday, open Sunday for brunch. Reservations a must.
- *Outer Sunset* — **Shangri-La Vegetarian Restaurant**: 2026 Irving Street (tel: 731-2548). Good neighborhood restaurant, with an extensive menu and low prices. Vegetarian but not vegan.
- *Outer Sunset* — **Joubert's Restaurant**: 4115 Judah, at 46th Avenue (tel: 753-5448). Vegetarian and vegan cuisine from South Africa. Dinners Wed–Sun.
- *Union Square* — **This is It Grill**: 430 Geary Street (tel: 749-0201). Glatt kosher Middle Eastern restaurant.

FOREIGN CUISINES

Because Asian restaurants are found on just about every commercial street, the next chapter is devoted solely to "Eating Out in Asia." Yet so many other foreign cuisines are represented in the city that it would be difficult to mention only a few of the French, German, Spanish, or Moroccan. Quite naturally, given the history of the city, other prominent cuisines are the Latin American and Italian, and those described below are merely a few suggestions of the diversity San Francisco offers.

Latin American

As with most ethnic cuisines, Latin American cooking in San Francisco is not just "Mexican food." It is true that *taquerias* abound, but in San Francisco the ingredients are regionally based, using good-quality meats and fish, relying on fresh vegetables and fruit, and with rice and beans as tasty side dishes. Some places advertise, for the healthy set, that they use no lard. Spicy *salsas* are often competitively rated, and some restaurants will boast that they were judged to have the "best salsa in S.F." by some panel at some time. What this means is that the tomato salsa is made with fresh ingredients, but the degree of chunkiness and fire varies from place to place. The Mission, as one would expect, is home to the most authentic Mexican establishments, plus Peruvian, Salvadoran and Nicaraguan restaurants, which have slightly different flavors and traditions. Combinations of cuisines are coming to be known as *nuevo latino*. Note that the **Taqueria Can-Cun**, often rated as the best Mexican restaurant in the city, has several locations in the Mission.

- *Cuban/Puerto Rican* — **El Nuevo Frutilandia**: 3077 24th Street (tel: 648-2958). Only 10 tables in this eatery that serves authentic Caribbean cuisine: Cuban pork sandwiches, plantains, and delicious fresh-fruit smoothies. Closed Monday.
- *Mexican* — **Los Jarritos**: 901 South Van Ness Avenue (tel: 648-

8383). Small family restaurant offering excellent Mexican dishes at low prices. Wonderful menudo.
- *Mexican* — **Mom Is Cooking**: 1166 Geneva Avenue (tel: 586-7000). Excellent, inexpensive outpost in the Excelsior District.
- *Mexican* — **Cafe Marimba**: 2317 Chestnut Street, at Scott (tel: 776-1506). Upscale, interesting combinations, good margaritas, in a lively Marina atmosphere. Closed Monday.
- *Mexican* — **Maya**: 303 2nd Street (tel: 543-6709). Elegant Mexican seafood dishes, beautifully prepared.
- *Nicaraguan* — **Nicaragua Restaurant**: 3015 Mission Street, near Cezar Chavez (tel: 826-3672). Locals have been coming here for more than 20 years for the delicious Central American regional dishes.
- *Peruvian* — **Fina Estampa**: 2374 Mission, near 20th Street (tel: 824-4437). Peruvian specialties such as fish soups, ceviche, marinated beef dishes. Spanish-style *tapas*. Closed Monday.
- *Salvadoran* — **El Zócalo**: 3230 Mission, near 29th Street (tel: 282-2572). *Pupusas* (like a filled tortilla). Fish soup and other excellent fish and shrimp dishes, fried plantains, etc.
- *Salvadoran* — **De Rosario**: 1796 San Jose Avenue (tel: 334-1863). Comfortable Mission restaurant serving pupusas, *platanos*, and other Salvadoran basics.

Italian

Although traditional southern Italian cuisine — pasta, tomato sauce, and garlic — can still be found in just about any Italian restaurant, even this basic combination is becoming increasingly refined and imaginative. Some restaurants now feature the buttery, rich cuisine from the north, fish dishes from the coasts, the simple yet flavorful dishes of Rome, or even the specialized hearty cuisine of a small area past Trieste that is now part of Yugoslavia. And, of course, each restaurant features its region's wines. (For pizza, see below.)

In the old days, Italian workers coming back to North Beach could eat a full meal for fifty cents. Wine — especially during

Prohibition—was made in the basement and served in coffee cups. Now, this area is still the focus for Italian restaurants—although prices are slightly higher. Yet there are dozens of interesting Italian restaurants in all corners of the city; here are just a few favorites.

- *Embarcadero*—**Il Fornaio**: 1265 Battery Street, at Levi's Plaza (tel: 986-0100). Monthly specials feature the differing regions of Italy; the standard menu always authentic. Outdoor dining.
- *Fillmore*—**Laghi**: 2101 Sutter (tel: 931-3774). Excellent pastas, main courses, breads, and an interesting wine list from the Emilia-Romagna region.
- *Hunter's Point*—**Dago Mary's**: East on Evans, off 3rd Street, just past the entry gate at the Hunter's Point Shipyard (tel: 822-2633). Since 1931, this old-world, basic Italian and fish restaurant has thrived in an unlikely location. Weekday lunch only, 11:00 am–3:00 pm.
- *Mission*—**Delfina**: 3621 18th Street (tel: 442-4055). Small, reasonably priced, and friendly restaurant serving simple yet elegant and imaginative combinations.
- *North Beach*—**Albona**: 545 Francisco Street, in North Beach (tel: 441-1040). Unusual spices from the Istrian region on the Adriatic make the Yugoslavian/Italian combinations interesting. Closed Sunday and Monday.
- *North Beach*—**Ideale**: 1315 Grant Avenue, in North Beach (tel: 391-4129). Roman specialties, lightly sauced fresh pasta dishes and roast meats.
- *Polk/Van Ness*—**Acquerello**: 1722 Sacramento Street, off Polk (tel: 567-5432). Luxurious restaurant, with north Italian specialties, homemade pastas, wonderful antipasti.

Pizza

Although a few restaurants serve the individual Italian-style, thin-crust pizza cooked in a wood-fired oven (**Il Fornaio** and **Pazzia** come to mind), most pizzas are American, in that they come in a number of sizes suitable for sharing, and the toppings are more dense. Most of these noted neighborhood favorites also serve pasta and other Italian dishes. Most chains offer home delivery.

- *Broadway* — **Tommaso's**: 1042 Kearny Street (tel: 398-9696). The city's oldest pizzeria, and some say still the best. Dinner only; closed Monday. Parking is difficult.
- *Downtown* — **Blondie's Pizza**, at 63 Powell, at Market (tel: 982-6168). Dead center in the tourist area, this is nonetheless a popular pizzeria for locals who are downtown.
- *Fillmore/Cow Hollow* — **Extreme Pizza**: 1730 Fillmore Street (tel: 929-9900) and 1980 Union Street (tel: 929- 8234). Some of the city's best pizza. Create pizza the way you want, and take it home to bake.
- *Mission* — **Pauline's**: 260 Valencia St, near 14th (tel: 552-2050). Try the pesto pizza. Dinner only; closed Monday.
- *North Beach, etc.* — **North Beach Pizza**: 1499 Grant Avenue at Union (433-2444). Popular pizzeria, serving a wide variety of pizza toppings, plus Italian entrees. Several other locations.
- *Potrero Hill* — **Goat Hill Pizza**: 300 Connecticut, at 18th Street (tel: 641-1440). Sourdough crust, excellent pizzas, live music on weekends. Monday night, all you can eat.
- *Union Street* — **Amici's East Coast Pizzeria**: 2033 Union Street (tel: 885-4500). Also in North and South Bay.

GRABBING A BITE

Eating fast in San Francisco does not necessarily mean "fast food." Storefront sandwich shops and cafes provide sandwiches, salads, and hot dishes with an international flavor for eating in or taking out. San Franciscans love to eat lunch out of doors. Eating *al fresco* is not always easy, for the wind is often fierce, and frankly, the air can be cold. This does not deter San Franciscans, who pour out of offices, off construction jobs, or out of delivery trucks, to eat outside under any feeble ray of sun.

Chinese restaurants generally serve their eat-in clientele quickly, and these eateries are jammed at lunchtime; almost all have takeout menus. Some office, shopping, and entertainment complexes (**Rincon Annex**, **Metreon**, and **Crocker Galleria**, for example), have food courts, with stalls lining a central set of tables for fast eating, and the four-building **Embarcadero Center** abounds with quick-eating solutions. Small chains such as **Briazz** sell sandwiches to go, and even their ready-made items cater to the tastes of San Franciscans, with many vegetarian and low-fat offerings. The latest trend is the wrap—interesting combinations of foods wrapped in a tortilla—and **World Wrapps** and others offer inexpensive, interesting lunches. But hearty lunches such as burritos or chili can be had to take out from small storefronts around the city, or slices of pizza at any of the dozens of pizza storefronts. Juice bars such as **Jamba Juice** offer smoothies and protein drinks for those who really have no time.

- **Peasant Pies**: Two locations (Noe Valley and Sunset districts). Individual filled savory and sweet pies to take out. Some stuffed with seafood or poultry, others vegan; the dessert pies are all vegan. Addresses: 4108 24th Street, at Castro (tel: 642-1316); 1039 Irving, at 11th Street (731-1978). Pies also available at some supermarkets.
- **Pasta Pomodoro**: Nine restaurants offering inexpensive Italian food to eat in or take out.
- **Fuzio Universal Pasta**: Chain of inexpensive pasta restaurants with dishes to eat in or take out.
- **Noah's Bagels**: City-wide chain. Bagel sandwiches featuring smoked salmon and cheese spreads make for an inexpensive and hearty lunch. Hot bagels to take out.
- *Civic Center*—**Saigon Sandwiches**: 560 Larkin Street, at Eddy (tel: 474-5698). Vietnamese sandwiches of meatballs, roast chicken, or pork, plus vegetables, spices, and a delicious sauce.
- *Embarcadero*—**Yank Sing**: 427 Battery Street (tel: 781-1111).

San Franciscans dining al fresco.

Takeout department adjacent to the ever-crowded *dim sum* house. Also at 49 Stevenson Street (tel: 541-4949) and (weekdays only) Rincon Center (tel: 957-9300).
- *Haight*—**Two Jack's Seafood**: 401 Haight Street (tel: 431-6290). Excellent takeout fried fish dinners, in a funky Haight atmosphere.
- *Tenderloin*—**Ba Le**: 511 Jones, near Geary (tel: 474-7270). Vietnamese grocery with prepared food ready to take home. Spring rolls, sausages, rice noodles, meat on skewers, and everything for a delicious Vietnamese meal. Table service.

WEEKEND BREAKFAST

Sunday brunch can be found on the menu of numerous restaurants and hotels, but eating a hearty Sunday breakfast—pancakes, red flannel hash, French toast and omelettes—is also a distinct social occasion, at places like **Mel's Diner** or **Max's Diner**, or at a number of rather sparsely decorated neighborhood cafes. These are wildly popular, so be prepared to add your name to the list and to wait.

Some of the cafes open only for breakfast and lunch, and many are closed Monday, after the Sunday crush. A few take cash only.

- *Cow Hollow* — **Doidge's**: 2217 Union, near Fillmore (tel: 921-2149)
- *Downtown* — **Dottie's True Blue Cafe**: 522 Jones Street (tel: 885-2767). Closed Tuesday.
- *Glen Park* — **Tyger's Coffee Shop**: 2798 Diamond (tel: 239-4060)
- *Haight* — **Pork Store Cafe**: 1451 Haight Street, near Ashbury (tel: 864-6981)
- *Hayes Valley/Castro* — **It's Tops**: 1801 Market Street (tel: 431-6395)
- *Lower Haight* — **Kate's Kitchen**: 471 Haight Street, near Fillmore (tel: 626-3984)
- *Mission* — **Boogaloos**: 3296 22nd Street, at Valencia (tel: 824-3211)
- *Pacific Heights* — **Ella's**: 500 Presidio (tel: 441-5669)
- *Potrero Hill* — **Just For You Cafe**: 1453 18th Street (tel: 647-3033)

COFFEEHOUSES

Cafes in each neighborhood reflect the character of their clientele, but North Beach seems driven by the mystique of coffee. Once, North Beach's coffeehouses welcomed Italian workers coming back from the docks, and now they comfort anyone who wants to sit for a while and relax. Many of the most famous of the North Beach coffeehouses — **Caffè Puccini**, **Steps of Rome**, **Caffè Greco**, **Caffè Roma** — line a few short blocks of Columbus, between Broadway and Union. Others, such as **Caffè Malvina** and the famous **Cafe Trieste**, are nearby.

Of the 100 coffeehouses in the city, most offer some kind of pastry selection to go with the coffees, teas, or Italian sodas, and some also serve light meals and salads. What is important is that in any coffeehouse, you may order something refreshing and then sit for as long as you like. Even in the most undistinguished-looking establishment, the quality of the coffee (and selection of aromatic teas) may be very good. As with everything else, San Franciscans are espresso snobs, knowing just which cafe serves the type of coffee they like (often it's **Illy**). Some people rail at the ubiquitous **Starbucks** intruding into neighborhood businesses; others like the chain's coffee and reliable atmosphere. For Irish coffee, try the ever-popular **Buena Vista Cafe**, at 2765 Hyde, near Ghirardelli Square (tel: 474-5044). (See Chapter Thirteen for coffee roasters.)

- *Financial District* — **Torrefazione Italia**: 295 California (tel: 274-1634). Deep leather couches and a friendly atmosphere in which to enjoy the good Italian coffees.
- *Lower Haight* — **Bean There**: 201 Steiner (tel: 255-8855). Modern, airy coffeehouse, with pleasant decor and welcoming ambience.
- *Noe Valley* — **Lovejoy's**: 1351 Church Street (tel: 648-5895). Probably the most charming tea room in the city, with antiques and a cosy English atmosphere.
- *North Beach/Chinatown* — **Imperial Tea Court**: 1411 Powell Street, at Broadway (tel: 788-6080). Unusual Chinese teas to purchase in bulk or to enjoy on the premises, each one brewed to bring out its unique flavor.
- *Outer Sunset* — **Java Beach Cafe**: 1396 La Playa Boulevard, at Judah (tel: 665-5282). A beach atmosphere, good coffee, and a relaxed atmosphere.
- *Pacific Heights* — **Tea & Company, World Tea House**: 2207 Fillmore Street, at Sacramento (tel: 929-8327). Nice place to relax with a cup of tea or coffee and a fresh pastry.
- *Potrero Hill* — **Farley's**: 1315 18th Street (tel: 648-1545). Funky and popular neighborhood coffeehouse.
- *Richmond* — **Caffe Dante**: 3101 Geary (tel: 386-2057). Friendly Italian coffeehouse with excellent coffee, pastries, and sandwiches.

GASTRONOMIC DELIGHTS

ICE CREAM

All national brands of ice cream, frozen yogurt, and sherbet are available in supermarkets, and **Ben & Jerry's**, **Häagen-Dazs**, and **Baskin-Robbins** have outlets in the city. Better, however, are the neighborhood ice cream parlors, some of which are listed below, and most of which create their own offbeat, exotic flavor combinations. **Double Rainbow, Ghirardelli Chocolate Shop and Soda Fountain**, and **Swensen's** are famous San Francisco institutions, and the **Gelato Classico** shops offer Italian-style preparations.

- *Castro/Pacific Heights* — **Rory's Twisted Scoop**: 1300 Castro Street (tel: 648-2837); 2015 Fillmore Street (tel: 346-3692). Homemade ice cream. Tables outside at Fillmore Street.
- *Inner Richmond* — **Toy Boat Dessert Cafe**: Clement at 5th Avenue (tel: 751-7505). Welcoming, traditional ice-cream parlor on inner Clement.
- *Mission* — **Mitchell's Ice Cream**: 688 San Jose, near 29th Street and Guerrero (tel: 648-2300). Extremely rich (16 percent butterfat) concoctions, often rated the best in the city.
- *Mission* — **Bombay Ice Creamery**: 552 Valencia Street (tel: 431-1103). Flavored with Indian herbs and spices. Closed Monday.
- *Outer Sunset* — **Marco Polo Italian Ice Cream**: 1447 Taraval Street (tel: 731-2833). Exotic Asian flavors, plus delicious traditional combinations.
- *Potrero Hill* — **Daily Scoop**: 1401 18th Street (tel: 824-3975). Friendly, neighborhood ice cream parlor.
- *Richmond* — **Joe's Ice Cream**: 5351 Geary, near 18th Avenue (tel: 751-1950). Great flavors since 1959, always popular.
- *Sunset* — **Polly Ann Ice Cream**: 3142 Noriega, near 38th Avenue (tel: 664-2472). More than 400 tasty and exotic flavors in a tiny, cheerful shop.

— Chapter Twelve —
EATING OUT IN ASIA

AN ASIAN TOWN
If it's all just Chinese food to you, it won't be after you've lived in San Francisco a while. Differing aromas from the hundreds of Chinese, Vietnamese, Thai, Korean, and Japanese restaurants permeate the city, enticing an Asian population that numbers upwards of 175,000 and the rest of the city as well. Each neighborhood has its Asian restaurants, and some areas cater to particular nationalities: Japantown and Chinatown of course, but also Larkin Street for Vietnamese restaurants and provisions, Clement Street for a lively mix of Asian establishments, and Irving Street in the Outer Sunset for its own eclectic mix from the Far East.

Fortunately for San Francisco's discerning diners, there are simply too many Asian restaurants to describe here, so just a few representative samples are given, along with a description of their culinary approach. Become a true San Franciscan and make your own list of favorites.

FIRST, THE CHINESE

Chinese restaurants are in the majority in San Francisco. Both complex and subtle, Chinese food is almost always economical: a hearty lunch in a neighborhood Chinese restaurant may cost under $5.00, and a dinner not much more. In a society not rich enough to offer a slab of meat or a quarter-chicken to each person, Chinese cooks learned to base their dishes on the inexpensive rice or noodles, topped with the region's vegetables and a flavored sauce. To this might be added a few ounces of meat or poultry, or along the coast, fish. For thousands of years this method of cooking has provided a nutritious diet of carbohydrates, vegetables, and an adequate amount of protein.

Despite some similarity in philosophy, the cuisines of China differ widely, owing to differences in regional ingredients, soil and climatic conditions, and of course, ancient traditions. Here, although the ingredients come from this one fertile area, many Asian restaurants focus on one region's cuisine, and often this can be identified by their names, such as **The Hunan**, the **House of Nan King**, **Parc Hong Kong**, or **The Taiwan**. Even these, however, may include in their repertoire special dishes from other regions—Cantonese dishes in a Hakka restaurant, or Shanghai dishes in one that says it is Cantonese.

The restaurants differ in style, quality, popularity, and price, as do all others. In Chinatown especially, you cannot judge the quality of the food by how the place looks. Some unpretentious, basic-looking dives serve the best food in their class (although you might hesitate to take an out-of-town colleague there) and some of the most reputable-looking places may not be as good.

With Chinese food, price does not determine quality.

Chinese chefs, like others in the city, cater to Western tastes by cooking with low or no oil and some, such as **Brandy Ho**, **Sage,** and **The Hunan**, proudly advertise that they use no monosodium glutamate (MSG). Hearty, healthy, Chinese breakfasts are also gaining in popularity, especially the thick rice porridge known as *congee* (or *juk/jook*) from the south of China; it can come with meatballs, fish—even jellyfish. Or from northern China, try the dough dishes such as "Chinese donuts" and warm bowls of soybean milk, either salty or sweet.

Differing Cuisines

It was **Cantonese** immigrants who originally brought their cuisine to these shores during the mid-19th century. Canton specializes in a delicate cuisine, lightly flavored and sauced, thus preserving the character of the ingredients, especially the mild fish and chicken pieces that are added to the fresh vegetables. This also holds true of the cuisine from **Hong Kong**.

Slightly more piquant, with highly flavored, sometimes sweetened sauces are the seafood dishes from the city of **Chiu Chow**, which sits just at the northern edge of Canton. Even farther north, on the Pacific coast by the mouth of the Yangtze River, **Shanghai** developed a heavy and hearty cuisine, with strongly flavored dishes braised in dark soy sauces.

- **Fountain Court**: 354 Clement, at 5th Avenue (tel: 668-1100). Interesting Shanghai cuisine in a neighborhood eatery. Crowded on weekends for *dim sum*.
- **Harbor Village**: 4 Embarcadero Center (tel: 781-8833). Excellent *dim sum* at lunch and delicate seafood dishes. Overflows with families on weekends, but the food is worth the wait.
- **Oriental Pearl**: 760 Clay Street, near Kearny (tel: 433-1817). Cantonese and Chiu Chow seafood cuisine. *Dim sum* at lunch.

Daily menu outside a Chinese restaurant.

More expensive (and better appointed) than the majority of Chinese restaurants in the area, the menu is also more imaginative.

In the north, where rice does not grow plentifully, dough dishes provide the major starch. Noodles served with a variety of sauces and toppings, dough-wrapped dumplings, and dishes made with pancakes are standard. Because Peking (now Beijing) was the capital of the empire, some particularly delicate dishes were created for the Mandarins who ruled. **Peking/Mandarin** cuisine also offers some of China's more imaginative dishes.

- **San Tung**: 2240 Irving Street (tel: 661-4233); also at 1031 Irving (tel: 242-0828). Neighborhood restaurants in the Sunset, featuring excellent dumplings and noodles.
- **Firecracker**: 1007 Valencia Street (tel: 642-3470). Popular and noisy spot for imaginative Beijing cuisine, offering low oil and lots of garlic. Closed Monday.
- **Mandarin:** Ghirardelli Square (tel: 673-8812). Upscale Northern Chinese restaurant with beautiful views.

In the hot southern portion of China, **Hunan** and **Szechuan** have always been poor districts. Their cuisines were developed to keep people cool and to preserve perishable meats. Hot and spicy food, the Chinese believe, keeps people cool internally, so Hunan food especially is very salty and extremely spicy. Chilies and salt also encourage people to eat more rice and drink more tea, so that they eat only a little meat. Smoking preserves meats, and smoked hams and ducks and heavy, spicy sauces characterize this cuisine, which is very popular in San Francisco. Szechuan food does not approach the fire of the Hunan, although it too is quite spicy.

- **Hunan Restaurant**: 924 Sansome Street, off Broadway (tel: 956-7727). Small chain of excellent restaurants, often rated the best Hunan food outside of China. Extremely spicy dishes (that can be modified to your taste) and smoked meat dishes.

The Mandarin Restaurant in Ghirardelli Square.

Hakka means "guest." The Hakka were wanderers, nomads who adapted their own cuisine to the regions where they stopped, incorporating those regions' cuisines into their own. Try the creative dumplings, the hearty clay pot dishes, and the salt-baked chicken, all traditional Hakka favorites.

- **Ton Kiang**: 5821 Geary Boulevard, near 22nd Avenue (tel: 386-8530). Salt-cooked chicken, clay pot dishes, fermented, wine-flavored dishes, seafood, and some of the city's best *dim sum*, any time of day.
- **Dragon River**: 5045 Geary, at 14th Avenue (tel: 387-8512). Flavorful Hakka and Cantonese dishes in a neighborhood restaurant in the Richmond.

With some dishes emanating from the north of China and others from the island itself, **Taiwanese** cuisine tends to blend several Chinese cuisines and features dough-based staples such as dumplings and pancake dishes. Some also favor the "hot pot" **Mongolian** cuisine in which a pot of boiling broth is brought to the table along with raw vegetables and meats/fish, to be prepared by the patron.

- **Taiwan Restaurant**: 289 Columbus Avenue, at Broadway (tel: 989-6789); 445 Clement (tel: 387-1789). Noodle dishes and seafood.
- **Coriya**: 852 Clement, at 10th Avenue (tel: 387-7888). Hot pot and Taiwanese cuisine.
- **Happy Valley Chinese Seafood**: 1255 Battery Street, in Levi Plaza (tel: 399-9393). Mongolian hot pot and seafood dishes.

Dim Sum

Dim sum ("small bites") is popular for lunch and brunch. In *dim sum* restaurants, carts with stacks of little bamboo baskets containing steamed or fried dumplings (filled with seafood, chicken, pork, vegetables—or tasty combinations thereof) are wheeled by the tables for the diners to choose among. *Bow* (large steamed rolls with barbequed pork), *siu mai* (pork dumplings), *ha gow* (steamed shrimp dumplings), egg rolls, and pot stickers (fried dumplings) are standards. On the table are small carafes of soy sauce, vinegar, and hot sauce, to mix and use as you choose.

Dim sum is usually served at midday, although to cater to Western tastes, *dim sum* houses in San Francisco may offer it in the evening as well. A traditional *dim sum* house will usually open at about 10:00 am and close mid-afternoon. In San Francisco, however, these restaurants may also serve a regular menu at midday and stay open with their regular menu in the evenings. In some restaurants the little dishes and baskets left on the customers' tables are counted in order to determine the bill; in others, the waiter marks on the bill how many items have been chosen.

In the smaller eateries in Chinatown, the waiters may not speak English, so just point to dishes that look appealing. *Dim sum* is not expensive; if you don't like what you've chosen, you're not risking much. Of course, if you see chicken feet, you'll know right away what they are.

- *Financial District* — **Yank Sing**: 427 Battery Street (tel: 781-1111); 49 Stevenson Street (tel: 541-4949). The Rincon Center branch is open weekdays only (tel: 957-9300).
- *Chinatown* — **Gold Mountain**: 644 Broadway (tel: 296-7733)

JAPANESE CUISINE

Japanese food emphasizes harmony, and dishes are arranged to be as pleasing to the eye as to the palate. Japanese cuisine is delicate, featuring low-fat fish, gently sauced dishes, braised meats, tofu, fresh vegetables, several types of flavorful noodles, and, of course, the increasingly sought-after *sushi*. The lightly battered and fried *tempura* fish and vegetables are popular, as is *sukiyaki*, the meat and vegetable casserole cooked at the table. The many varieties of *sake* — a clear rice wine — may be consumed hot or cold; experiment with different sakes at some of the new sake bars that are opening up in conjunction with regular wine bars, in Japanese restaurants, or on their own.

Authentic and varied Japanese restaurants are clustered in and around the Japan Center but most neighborhoods have their own favorites, both for cooked dishes and for sushi, which is one of San Franciscans' favorite foods. Because sushi is so much in demand, it is fortunate that residents of different neighborhoods think the sushi bar in their own district is the best. This means delicious sushi is available throughout the city any day of the year.

If you are a beginner at sushi, consider **Isobune** at 1737 Post Street in the Japan Center (tel: 563-1030). Little boats carrying freshly made sushi dishes sail along an oval canal, displaying the preparations as they move along. Choose those that look appealing.

Prices are reasonable, so as with *dim sum*, if you select a dish you don't care for, you haven't risked very much. Isobune is a friendly place: sushi lovers sitting next to you will be happy to advise you on selections if you're not sure.

- *Cow Hollow* — **Ace Wasabi's Rock 'n' Roll Sushi**: 3339 Steiner Street, at Chestnut (tel: 567-4903). Great sushi in a loud, trendy, typical San Francisco atmosphere. Open only for dinner, and always crowded.
- *Inner Sunset* — **Ebisu**: 1283 9th Avenue (tel: 566-1770). Small, popular eatery with good sushi and other dishes.
- *Inner Sunset* — **Hotei**: 1290 9th Avenue (tel: 753-6045). Japanese noodle cuisine in a charming setting.
- *Japan Center* — **Mifune**: 1737 Post Street (tel: 922-0337). Soba and udon noodles with a variety of add-ins, to make a delicious, inexpensive meal.
- *Mission* — **Blowfish Sushi to Die For**: 2170 Bryant Street (tel: 285-3848). Some of the city's best sushi, plus an imaginative and well-created menu.
- *Mission* — **Tokyo Go Go**: 3174 16th Street, near Valencia (tel: 864-2288). Eclectic and trendy, serving interesting, fun sushi combinations at moderate prices. Closed Monday.
- *Richmond* — **Kabuto**: 5116 Geary Boulevard (tel: 752-5652). Full Japanese menu, excellent sushi, friendly service. Dinner only. Closed Sunday and Monday.

SOUTHEAST ASIAN CUISINES

Of course, in San Francisco there is always more to try, and dozens of Southeast Asian restaurants show off their differing cultural and historical traditions. Many use rice or noodles as a base, and most specialize in seafood dishes. Because the climate of these countries is generally hot, the food can be quite spicy; you can order "medium spicy" or "not spicy" if you think the fiery peppers will not suit your palate.

- *Thai* — **Thep Phenom**: 400 Waller Street (tel: 431-2526). Spicy seafood dishes, curries with coconut, duck curry, squid salad, catfish with lemongrass; dinner only. **Modern Thai**: 1247 Polk Street, near Bush (tel: 922-8424). Upscale Thai cuisine in a pleasant setting; closed Tuesday. Many other Thai restaurants in the city.
- *Vietnamese* — **Slanted Door**: 584 Valencia Street (tel: 861-8032). Trendy but authentic, serving five-spice roast chicken, clay pot dishes, papaya salad. **Pacific Restaurant-Thai-Binh-Duong #2**: 337 Jones Street, in the Tenderloin (tel: 928-4022). Excellent spring rolls and *pho*, the Vietnamese soup of noodles, meats, vegetables, and bean sprouts. Lunch only. **La Vie**: 5830 Geary (tel: 668-8080). Popular Richmond restaurant blends the Chinese influence from the north and the French from the south. Dishes are interesting and flavorful.
- *Korean* — **Seoul Garden**: 1702 Post Street, in Japantown (tel: 346-3486). Marinated fish, pork, or chicken *shabu shabu* (that you barbeque at your own table on charcoal braziers). Dishes accompanied by rice, pickles, and salads. *Kim chee*, a fiery hot cabbage accompaniment is not for the faint of heart. Others include **Heavenly Hot Restaurant**: 4627 Geary (tel: 750-1818); **Korea House**: 1620 Post Street (tel: 563-1388); **Brother's Restaurant**: 4128 Geary (tel: 387-7991).
- *Singaporean* — **Straits Cafe**: 3300 Geary Boulevard (tel: 668-1783). A melange of Pacific seafood cuisines, Indian curries, and other exotic aromas, with attractive dishes set out on banana leaves.
- *Cambodian* — **Angkor Wat**: 4217 Geary Boulevard (tel: 221-7887). A delicious mingling of Asian tropical flavors, of coconut milk and lemongrass, yet with overtones of France.
- *Burmese* — **Nirvana**: 544 Castro Street (tel: 861-2226). Melange of Indian, Chinese and other Southeast Asian aromas. Excellent noodle dishes, five-spice roast chicken, and fish. Substantial use of garlic and relishes.

Pan-Asian

As is to be expected in a city where differing cultures meet head on, the trend now is for Asian restaurants to meld their own differing cuisines to create a *Pan-Asian* flavor, a slightly more restrictive yet imaginative approach to *fusion cuisine*. Some offer full menus, others are mainly noodle houses.

- *Castro*—**Tin Pan**: 2251 Market Street (tel: 565-0733). Excellent and popular Asian bistro serving noodle dishes and other flavorful dishes in a friendly atmosphere.
- *Cow Hollow*—**Betelnut**: 2030 Union Street (tel: 929-8855). Crowded and fun, serving Pan-Asian cuisine with flavors of China, Indonesia, and Vietnam. Expensive. Walk-in traffic eats at the bar.
- *Embarcadero*—**Longlife Noodle Company & Jook Joint**: 139 Steuart Street (tel: 281-3818). Lively Pan-Asian establishment serving innovative noodle dishes and *jook*. Inexpensive. Also at Metreon, in Yerba Buena.
- *Haight*—**Citrus Club**: 1790 Haight Street, at Shrader (tel: 387-6366). Popular, inexpensive noodle house that avoids heavy oils, using citrus flavors instead. Closed Monday.
- *Marina*—**Zao Noodle Bar**: 2301 Chestnut Street (tel: 928-3088). Flavors from Southeast Asia: "health and wisdom in a bowl." Also at 2406 California Street (tel: 345-8088) and in Palo Alto.
- *SOMA*—**AsiaSF**: 201 9th Street, at Howard (tel: 255-2742). Crowded, noisy, and good-natured, this restaurant/cabaret catering to both straights and gays offers good food and a "gender illusion" show on the catwalk. Closed Monday and Tuesday. Nightclub downstairs on weekends.

— Chapter Thirteen —

EXPLORING THE MARKETS

OUTDOOR MARKETS

Outdoor markets, often called "farmers' markets," sell the region's freshest seasonal produce, usually of better quality and often at lower cost than that of supermarkets. In addition to these year-round markets in the city, there are farmers' markets in most of the towns of the Bay Area, including one that is exceptionally varied at the Marin Civic Center in San Rafael on Thursday and Sunday.

Look for produce that is certified "organic," meaning that it was not treated with chemical pesticides or fertilizers and that the soil is rotated according to healthful standards. Organic meats come from animals raised without growth hormones or antibiotics, and without pesticide-treated feed. Organic groceries tend to cost slightly more.

- *Wednesday and Sunday*: Market Street at United Nations Plaza. Large inexpensive market, with many stalls for Asian produce. Flowers, fish, herbs, etc.
- *Saturday:* Green Street at the Embarcadero. Upscale market, with the highest quality of produce, fresh breads, pastas, fish, meats, and several stalls that sell freshly cooked foods to eat at tables nearby.
- *Saturday*: Alemany Boulevard at Crescent, near Highway 280. Enormous international farmers' market. Go early before the crowds arrive. Or go late when some produce is reduced in price.
- *Tuesday*: Justin Hermann Plaza, at Market and Steuart Streets, during the clement months.

Market day in downtown San Francisco.

SUPERMARKETS

The **Safeway**, **Bell's**, **Albertson's**, and **Cala Foods** chains have stores throughout the city. All are open daily at least until 9:00 pm and are often open for some portion of the day on holidays; the Cala on Geary and the Marina Safeway are open 24 hours daily. In addition to their freshly cut meats, fish, produce, and staple goods, supermarkets carry alcoholic beverages, magazines, and over-the-counter medications. Some have prescription-filling pharmacies, either within or next door. All the large supermarkets accept major credit cards and bank debit cards. Many also have ATM machines on the premises if you need cash.

The merchandise at San Francisco supermarkets is usually guaranteed, so if there is something wrong with a product you have bought, most will take back the item provided you have a receipt. On perishable items, look on the package to make sure that the expiration date has not passed; if it has, supermarkets will generally exchange the item. (Foreigners should note that in the United States, dates are written with the month, day, and year, in that order.) Several supermarkets stand out for their particularly fine selections; prices match the quality.

- *Pacific Heights* — **Mollie Stone's**: 2435 California Street, near Fillmore (tel: 567-4902). Elegant market with excellent fresh and smoked fish counters, well-cut meats, beautifully prepared meals to take out, cheeses, organic produce. A small cafe. Parking lot.
- *Portola* — **Pommon's Tower Market**: 635 Portola Drive (tel: 664-1600). Well-stocked independent market, with an excellent meat and fish department, plus an interesting deli counter.
- *Presidio Heights* — **Cal-Mart**: 3585 California Street, in Laurel Village (tel: 751-3516). Extremely upscale and well-maintained supermarket. Interesting deli section and independently run meat department. Fresh breads, excellent produce.
- *Sunset* — **Andronico's**: 1200 Irving Street, at Funston (tel: 661-

3220). Upscale supermarket with a superior takeout department (hot and cold), a salad bar, and seating nearby. Excellent butcher and fish department, a table just for different olives, a wealth of cheeses and fresh breads, interesting produce. Other locations.

Health Food Supermarkets

In addition to their preservative- and chemical-free fresh and packaged food products, the shops below also carry vitamins, natural cosmetics, and brochures and books on natural living in the Bay Area. **Real Foods** is a chain that has locations throughout the Bay Area. All are open on Sunday.

- *Polk/Van Ness* — **Whole Foods Market**: 1765 California Street (tel: 674-0500). Large, well-stocked health food supermarket, with an extensive takeout section of prepared foods, artistically prepared meats to take home and cook, excellent fresh fish, bakery. Generally expensive, but extremely high quality. Parking available, but lot is crowded at peak shopping hours. Also in Mill Valley and Berkeley.
- *SOMA* — **Rainbow Grocery**: 1745 Folsom Street (tel: 863-0621). Cooperative, worker-owned health food market, with an excellent selection at good prices. Some parking available.

Discount Supermarkets

Discount supermarkets may not carry all the particular brands you like, but those that do are generally of good quality, and the price is right. Occasionally you have to buy in bulk, by the case.

- **Smart & Final**: Three locations. Packaged foods, cleaning items, janitorial supplies. Extra savings with Smart Advantage card. Ample parking. Others throughout the Bay Area.
- **Trader Joe's**: Two locations. Extensive selection of packaged and frozen goods, dairy products, snack foods, bakery items, and spirits. Other locations throughout Bay Area.

- **Foods Co**: Two locations. Warehouse supermarket with a well-rounded selection at good prices. Ample parking.
- *South of Market* — **Grocery Outlet**: 1717 Harrison Street (tel: 552-9680). Also known as "Canned Foods Warehouse." Excellent prices but inventory changes, so stock up on items you like. Ample parking.
- *South of Market* — **Costco**: 450 10th Street (tel: 626-4288). Warehouse selling all sorts of items, mostly in bulk. Packaged and fresh foods, frozen items, alcoholic beverages, and much more. Small membership fee.

SHOPPING FROM HOME

Inquire whether your supermarket has home delivery, for not all do. Some, such as Whole Foods Door to Door, offer telephone/fax/e-mail ordering (tel: 800/529-5761; fax: 972/774-0865; e-mail: iscom@aol.com). You can also order grocerices online (www.peapod.com; www.webvan.com). Www.planet-organics.com offers local organic produce grocery items.

SHOPPING IN ASIA

Shopping in Chinatown can be an other-world experience, especially on Saturday and Sunday. Crowds of people carrying overflowing bags push and shove as they walk down Stockton, Powell, or the side streets. They, however, will no doubt have found excellent prices and high quality fish and poultry, and produce of all sorts. Both produce and packaged goods are displayed outside the shops in boxes or on shelves, and this contributes to the traffic jam. Because signs are in Chinese and not all personnel speak English, sometimes shopping is a challenge. Nonetheless, Chinatown is a great place to shop if you're not faint of heart. Parking is impossible, and parking lots on the periphery can cost up to $2.00 for 20 minutes. Either hoof it or take public transportation. No matter how you get there, don't miss Chinatown on market days, quintessentially San Franciscan.

Fresh fish at a Chinese market.

Asian markets, however, are visible throughout the city, both in supermarkets and small shops. The specialty markets—fish markets and butchers—are listed within their categories; see below.

- *Chinatown*—**Happy Supermarket**: 1230 Stockton Street (tel: 677-9950). Large bustling supermarket. Live fish in tanks, meats, produce.
- *Japantown*—**Super Koyama**: 1790 Sutter Street, at Buchanan (tel: 921-6529). Modern Japanese grocery. Fresh ingredients for sushi, sukiyaki, soups, and most Japanese meals. Fish and meat freshly cut. Good produce.
- *Japantown*—**Uoki Market**: 1656 Post Street, between Buchanan and Laguna (tel: 921-0515). Busy Japanese grocery, with fish freshly prepared, produce, canned goods.
- *Mission*—**New Bombay Bazaar**: 548 Valencia, near 16th Street (tel: 621-1717). Large store for Indian packaged goods, spices, herbs. Audio-Video selections. Small eat-in/takeout place next door. Closed Monday.

EXPLORING THE MARKETS

A Chinese market.

- *Outer Sunset* — **Twenty-Second and Irving Market**: 2101 Irving Street (tel: 681-5212). A multicultural market with a little of everything from everywhere, and Asians, Russians, and Arabs come to find it here. Excellent produce.
- *Richmond* — **Richmond New May Wah Supermarket**: 547 Clement Street (tel: 668-2583). Two entrances to this large supermarket, one for fresh fish and meats, the other for produce and packaged goods.
- *Tenderloin* — **New Chiu Fong**: 724 Ellis Street, near Polk (tel: 776-7151). Vietnamese supermarket with an extensive selection: fresh meats and poultry, produce, herbs, packaged goods.

SMALL ETHNIC GROCERIES

In addition to the ubiquitous Asian shops, don't miss the small ethnic delicatessens with their international selections. Most have packaged goods as well as deli counters for fresh-made specialties. Of course the Mission will have more Latin American shops, Chinatown and Japantown their own shops, Outer Geary the Russian stores, and North Beach the Italian. Here are just a few.

- *Italian* — **Lucca Ravioli Company**: 1100 Valencia Street at 22nd Street (tel: 647-5581). Old-time deli offering ready-to-cook pasta dishes, homemade pizza, sausages, sauces, wines, cheeses, etc. Closed Sunday.
- *Italian* — **Molinari**: 373 Columbus Avenue, at Vallejo (tel: 421-2337). Freshly cut sandwiches, smoked meats, buffalo milk mozzarella and other cheeses, sausages; a selection of everything Italian. Closed Sunday.
- *Jewish* — **Moishe's Pippic**: 425-A Hayes Street, at Gough (tel: 431-2440). Chicago-style Jewish deli, open at breakfast and lunch. Good corned beef, Chicago hot dogs, etc.
- *Latin American* — **Casa Lucas**: 2934 24th Street (tel: 826-4334). Open-front store selling fresh produce, herbs, Mexican sausages and cheeses. Everything for Latin American cooking.

- *Mexican* — **La Palma Mexicatessen**: 2884 24th Street (tel: 647-1500). Excellent tortillas, fixings for burritos and tacos, freshly made chips. Ingredients for Mexican cooking.
- *Middle Eastern* — **Haig's**: 642 Clement, near 8th Avenue (tel: 752-6283). Haig's famous hummus and baba ganoush can now be found in some supermarkets, which is fortunate, for parking near Clement Street can be difficult. Packaged goods, tables to eat in. Closed Sunday.
- *Russian* — **Gastronom Deli & Bakery**: 5801 Geary Boulevard (tel: 387-4211). Excellent smoked meats and fish, Russian salads, and packaged goods. Also at 2801 Judah Street (tel: 664-1835).

BAKERIES

San Francisco is proud of its sourdough bread, crusty and flavorful, with a vaguely sour and slightly chewy interior. It originated here during the Gold Rush, when French baker Isadore Boudin melded sourdough yeast into a French baguette. Today, many restaurants bring sourdough loaves or rolls to the table, and supermarkets sell it sliced in loaves, as classic baguettes, and even as sourdough English muffins. **Boudin**, with outlets around the city, still sells sourdough breads and rolls, baguettes, other breads, sandwiches, etc, and has just celebrated its 150th anniversary.

Bakeries serve their neighborhood's ethnic populations: North Beach is known for its Italian pastry shops, the Mission along 24th Street for excellent Mexican baked goods. Supermarkets now stock locally baked breads, bagels, and pastries; look for fresh breads baked by **Acme**, **Metropolis**, **Parisian**, **Semifreddi**, and the **Noe Valley Bakery**. **Eppler's** is a full-line bakery that is popular and **Just Desserts** is renowned for its delicious cakes. Below are a few of the city's fine bakeries—ones you might miss if you don't know that neighborhood.

- *Bayview* — **Wendy's Cheesecake Bakery**: 4942 3rd Street (tel:

822-4959). Cheesecake, sweet potato pie, pecan pies, etc. Barbeques. Closed Sunday.
- *Chinatown* — **Eastern Bakery**: 720 Grant Avenue (tel: 392-4497). One of Chinatown's more extensive bakeries, offering prepared pork buns and pot stickers, other baked goods, plus mooncakes — pastry with a variety of sweet fillings.
- *Cow Hollow/Marina* — **Bepples Pies**: 1934 Union Street, at Laguna (tel: 931-6225) and 2142 Chestnut Street, at Steiner (tel: 931-6226). Delicious fruit pies, and meat and vegetable pies. Eat in or take out.
- *Hayes Valley* — **Citizens Cake**: 399 Grove Street at Gough (tel: 861-2228). Breads, pies, sticky buns, and wood-oven pizzas. Opens at 7:00 am weekdays, 9:00 am weekends.
- *Mission* — **Golden Crust Pies & Baker's Delight**: 3233 24th Street (tel: 824-7117). Delicious home-baked pies and breads in an unassuming shop. Don't miss it!
- *North Beach* — **Liguria**: 1700 Stockton Street (tel: 421-3786). Just Italian *focaccia* bread: plain, tomato, onion, raisin. Sometimes there's discounted *focaccia* in the freezer. Go early, for when they sell out, the shop closes.
- *North Beach* — **Italian French Baking Company**: 1501 Grant Avenue (tel: 421-3796). Excellent homemade breads, rolls and pastries.
- *North Beach* — **Victoria Pastry Co**: 1362 Stockton (tel: 781-2015). For more than 80 years, the ever-popular Victoria has been selling Italian pastries, cakes, pies, etc.
- *Pacific Heights* — **Bay Bread**: 2325 Pine Street (tel: 440-0356). Excellent hearth-baked artisan breads, made with organic flour, from the retail store of this restaurant supplier. Olive bread, herbed *fougasse*, *brioche*, and others. Closed Monday.
- *Pacific Heights* — **Pâtisserie Delanghe**: 1890 Fillmore Street, at Bush (tel: 923-0711). Homemade French pastries such as sweet rolls filled with fresh fruit and custard, eclairs, cream puffs. Closed Monday.

- *Richmond*—**Moscow and Tblisi Bakery**: 5540 Geary Boulevard (tel: 668-6959). Wonderful, always crowded, bakery selling excellent rye breads, filled *piroshkis*, and Russian pastries.

CHEESE

Cheese in the United States tends to be pasteurized, so there may be fewer of the delicate flavors and varieties found in other countries. Supermarkets generally have cut cheeses, and some of the better stores mentioned above (Andronico's, Whole Foods, etc) have superior selections. A few dedicated cheese shops carry an extensive stock, and most also carry interesting gourmet items and some wines.

- *Cole Valley*—**Say Cheese**: 856 Cole Street (tel: 665-5020)
- *Polk/Broadway*—**Leonard's 2001**: 2001 Polk Street (tel: 921-2001)
- *Twin Peaks*—**Creighton's Cheese and Fine Foods**: 673 Portola (tel: 753-0750)
- *Glen Park*—**Cheese Boutique**: 666 Chenery (tel: 333-3390)
- *Mission*—**24th Street Cheese Company**: 3893 24th Street, at Sanchez (tel: 821-6658)
- *Western Addition*—**Country Cheese**: 415 Divisadero Street (tel: 621-8130). Closed Sunday.
- *Pacific Heights*—**Artisan Cheese**: 2413 California Street (tel: 929-8610)

FISH

Living so close to the sea, there's no reason for you to settle for less than the freshest of seafood. All varieties of domestic fish are available according to the season, and with refrigeration standards so high, fish from other regions is also good. But local waters offer some fish you might not have heard of; once you've tasted local sand dabs, petrale, and rex sole, you'll be hooked. During Dungeness crab season, supermarkets sell crab already cooked and cleaned; fish markets may sell them whole, or cooked and cleaned.

Supermarkets carry many varieties of seafood already cut and packaged, and not relying on local weather conditions, may stock Atlantic salmon or other non-local fish. Whole Foods, Andronico's and other superior supermarkets, however, tend to use local suppliers; a few have sushi chefs cutting fresh sushi. Dedicated fish markets throughout the city are also excellent.

Although many of the old fishing piers have been taken over by tourist attractions, the fishing fleet still docks at "Fish Alley," on the Jefferson Street promenade, between Taylor and Jones. If you don't mind cleaning your own fish, try buying whole fish direct from the fishermen on Saturday morning; go early to have a better selection. Look also at the Ferry Plaza market on Saturdays, where the **Monterey Fish Company** — Berkeley's premier fish market — maintains a stall.

Asian fish stores are generally of high quality. Look especially around the Japan Center, where groceries sell sliced fish for sushi. In Chinatown, don't be taken aback seeing people selecting live turtles and frogs; before being taken out of the store, the staff prepares them. In Chinatown, however, you basically have to know your fish, because few people speak English, and the staff is so busy handling crowds they wouldn't have time to explain, in any case.

- *Chinatown*—**New Sang Sang Market**: 1143 Stockton Street (tel: 433-0403). One of the best fish stores in Chinatown. Excellent selection, good prices, the freshest of the fresh.
- *Inner Richmond*—**Wing Hing Seafood Market**: 633 Clement Street (tel: 668-1666). Freshly cut and live fish to choose among in this authentic Asian fish mart.
- *Inner Richmond*—**Seafood Center**: 831 Clement, near 10th Avenue (tel: 752-3496). Extremely wide, high-quality selection.
- *Outer Sunset*—**Irving Seafood Market**: 2130 Irving Street (tel: 681-8369). Small but excellent fish selection.

- *Outer Sunset* — **Yum Yum Fish**: 2181 Irving Street (tel: 566-6433). Small Japanese market with a good variety, plus a chef cutting fresh sushi to take home or to eat in at the few tables.
- *Polk/Van Ness* — **Swan Oyster Depot**: 1517 Polk Street, near California (tel: 673-1101). A San Francisco tradition for 75 years. Fresh fish to take out, but regulars sit at the counter for delicious oysters, Crab Louie, chowder. Closes 5:30 pm; closed Sunday.
- *Potrero Hill* — **Nikko Fish**: 699 Illinois, at 3rd and 18th Streets (tel: 864-5261). Fresh fish in a tiny open-front shop. Closed Sunday.

MEATS AND POULTRY

The better supermarkets listed above have excellent selections of ready-cut meats and some specially prepared items ready to take home and cook such as kabobs and marinated or stuffed meats. The selection at Whole Foods is impressive. But neighborhood butchers offer all of the above, plus personalized service and, often, home delivery. For holidays, place your order well in advance.

- *Bayshore* — **Polarica**: 107 Quint Street, near Third and Cesar Chavez (tel: 647-1300). Game and game birds, excellent chicken, imported lamb, wild mushrooms, berries, and smokehouse products.
- *Chinatown* — **New On Sang Poultry Co**: 1114 Grant Avenue (tel: 982-4694). Fresh fish and poultry, nicely displayed, plus prepared dishes to take out. Smaller shop at 617 Clement Street (tel: 752-4100).
- *Laurel Village* — **Bryan's Quality Meats**: 3473 California Street (tel: 752-3430). Respected grocer and butcher of exceptional quality. Fresh fish, artfully cut meats, prepared foods, salads. Parking in back. Closed Sunday.
- *Mission* — **Mission Market Meat Department**: 2590 Mission, at 22nd Street (tel: 282-1030). Excellent meats in a Latino

market building that also houses the Mission Market Fish and Poultry (tel: 282-3331).

- *Mission* — **Lucky Pork Store**: 2659 Mission, near 22nd Street (tel: 550-9016). A Chinese pork butcher popular with Latin Americans in the Mission district. All cuts, plus beef and goat.
- *North Beach* — **Little City**: 1400 Stockton, at Vallejo (tel: 986-2601). North Beach's premier butcher, with a good variety of high-quality, well-cut products.
- *Van Ness* — **Harris' Restaurant**: 2100 Van Ness (tel: 673-1888). Excellent steak house sells prime, aged meat at a retail counter during the dinner hours when the restaurant is open.

Kosher Meat

Most supermarkets carry standard packaged kosher products, and all carry kosher for Passover items in the spring. Unfortunately, there are only two designated kosher meat outlets in the city. Ask at the Jewish Community Federation for *Resource*, a comprehensive guide to Jewish life in the Bay Area.

- *Outer Richmond* — **Israel Kosher Meat and Poultry**: 5621 Geary Boulevard (tel: 752-3064). Kosher meats, Empire poultry, frozen selections, deli department with sliced meats, plus packaged goods, kosher wine.
- *Outer Sunset* — **Tel Aviv Kosher Meats, Deli & Liquor**: 2495 Irving Street (tel: 661-7588). A small market in the Outer Sunset with kosher meats, frozen and packaged goods.

COFFEE BEANS

Those same people who know exactly what kind of coffee they want in the coffeehouses also know exactly what kind of bean they want to grind at home or have the coffee roasters blend for them. Many supermarkets have their own selection of coffee beans and grinders, and **Peet's Coffee and Tea** and the **Spinelli Coffee Company** chains have several locations in the city. Try one of these specialty shops, especially those in North Beach.

- *Cole Valley*—**Bean There**: 201 Steiner Street (tel: 255-8855). Sip in or take out coffee and teas. Coffee is ground to order for your cup of coffee. Light meals.
- *Cow Hollow*—**Union Street Coffee Roastery**: 2191 Union Street (tel: 922-9559). Excellent coffee in this small roastery at the corner of Steiner Street.
- *North Beach*—**Graffeo Coffee Roasting Co**: 733 Columbus Avenue (tel: 986-2420). Since 1935, roasting dark and light Arabica beans. Offers decaffeinated Colombian, produced without chemicals. Also in San Rafael.
- *North Beach*—**Caffé Roma Coffee Roasting Company**: 526 Columbus Street (tel: 296-7662). Long-established North Beach coffee roaster.
- *North Beach*—**Caffe Trieste**: 609 Vallejo (tel: 982-2605). Next to the famous North Beach coffeehouse, this is a long-established coffee roaster, with its rich aromas wafting down the street.
- *Outer Sunset*—**House of Coffee**: 1618 Noriega Street (tel: 681-9363). Middle Eastern shop with good ground beans for Turkish coffee. Closed Sunday.

EATING OUT AT HOME

After all this, do you still not feel like cooking or even going out? Then pick up a catalogue at street-side boxes from **Waiters on Wheels** (tel: 252-1470; www.waitersonwheels.com). Fine restaurants of all categories and price ranges display facsimiles of their menus for order by telephone. Pay a small surcharge and tip the driver, and you can have hot, ready-cooked meals from the best restaurants delivered to your door. Solely on the Internet, try **food.com** (www.food.com).

However, many restaurants themselves—especially just about every Asian restaurant, including the sushi bars—have takeout. If you do have the energy just to pick up a ready-cooked meal, try one of these shops or restaurants that offer takeout of their specialties. As already noted, the better supermarkets also have extensive counters with prepared dishes, ready to reheat.

- *Bernal Heights* — **Hungarian Sausage Factory**: 419 Cortland Avenue (tel: 648-2847). Sausages, hams, sauerkraut, stuffed cabbage, all take home or eat in. Evenings only; closed Monday.
- *Chinatown* — **Janmae Guey**: 1222 Stockton Street, near Broadway (tel: 433-3981). Delicious Chinese barbequed duck, chicken, pork ribs, and noodles to take out or to eat in. Inexpensive.
- *Embarcadero* — **MacArthur Park**: 607 Front Street (takeout tel: 781-5560). Restaurant known especially for its barbequed ribs and chicken; has an extensive counter for full-meal takeout.
- *Marina* — **Lucca**: 2120 Chestnut Street (tel: 921-7873). Exceptional Italian delicatessen selling pastas, sauces, cheese, frittatas, focaccia, salads, imported packaged products. Delicious sandwiches, freshly cut.
- *North Beach* — **Florence Ravioli Factory**: 1412 Stockton Street, near Columbus (tel: 421-6170). Popular Italian deli, with imported products, cheeses, prosciutto, and homemade ravioli.
- *North Beach* — **GiraPolli**: 659 Union Street (tel: 434-4472). Among the best of the rotisserie chicken in San Francisco. Comes with potatoes, vegetable, and a roll. Extremely difficult to park. Dinner only.

— CHAPTER FOURTEEN —
WATERING HOLES

THE FRUIT OF THE VINE

California produces more than 90 percent of the wine made in the United States. The majority comes from the inland Central Valley, but the best comes from Northern California where the climate and soil are ideal. The cool breezes along the coastal strip of land that stretches from Mendocino in the north to Santa Barbara in the south encourage some of the most complex Chardonnays in the world, and some of the rich, red Pinot Noirs also prefer the foggy coasts. The vines that prefer the hot inland valleys produce the popular Merlot and the Sauvignon Blancs that range from the crisp to the creamy rich.

What people call the "wine country" comprises the Sonoma Valley, with its varying climates, and the Napa Valley, with its warm summer days and cool nights, so welcoming to the vines of the excellent, bold Cabernet Sauvignons, the ever-popular Chardonnay, and Zinfandel, a California favorite. But northern California offers much more. Just a bit farther north, the Alexander Valley and the land up toward Mendocino are also conducive to vines. Vineyards and wineries dot the map in the East Bay—in the Livermore Valley and Tri Valley, for example, heading up to the Sierra foothills toward Amador and El Dorado counties. And to the south, the Monterey, Salinas, and Carmel Valleys are all rich with vines.

Wine has been produced in the nearby valleys since the early 1800s, when Spanish priests first planted grapes for sacramental wines. In the late 1850s the Hungarian immigrant Agoston Haraszthy started producing and selling wine in Sonoma, at what is now the famous Buena Vista Winery. Just a few years later, Charles Krug brought German grapes into the Napa Valley; it is he who is credited with bringing grapes into the area although a few decades earlier Charles Yount had already planted vines for his family's use, near what is now Yountville.

Now, wine production is one of the area's most important industries, reaching ever more into new tastes and territories. The appreciation of the populace has kept up with the expansion, encouraging California winemakers to become among the most innovative in the world, willing to experiment with flavors and textures, with richer, fruitier combinations. If the French chateau methods were once the basic model for winemaking, California vintners—increasingly taking into consideration the area's climate and soil—are now adding a southern Mediterranean influence.

Exploring Wine Country

In the Napa and Sonoma valleys there are hundreds of wineries—both large with many brands, and "boutiques" that make just a few types of wine under one brand name. Napa alone has more than 150 wineries, many of which flank the bisecting Highway

29. Almost all wineries have tasting rooms, with opportunities not just to taste the wines, but to learn about the grapes, the winemaking process, and the differences that give the wines their own particular essence. Some of the wineries also have picnic tables and gift shops, and some offer full meals to show off the range of their wines. The tourist offices below should have detailed information about wineries in their areas.

- **Napa Valley Visitors Bureau**: 1310 Napa Town Center, off First Street, Napa (tel: 707/226-7459; www.napavalley.com)
- **Sonoma Valley Visitors Bureau**: 453 First Street East, Sonoma (tel: 707/996-1090; www.sonomavalley.com)

You can also enjoy an afternoon's ride on the **Napa Valley Wine Train**, which provides a formal meal and wine tastings while touring the area; it leaves from central Napa (tel: 800/427-4124).

The **Blue & Gold Fleet** offers a one-day Wine Country tour from San Francisco, starting with a catamaran ride across the bay (info tel: 773-1188; reservations tel: 705-5555). Also in the city, **Napa Valley Winery Exchange**, at 415 Taylor Street, specializes in California wines. The proprietor will discuss them with you, find wines to fit your taste, and can advise on places to visit in the wine country (tel: 771-2887); closed Sunday.

The longer you are in California, the more you can appreciate its wines. The more you learn about them, the more you will be able to distinguish each nuance and overtone in their wide range of tastes, colors, and textures. To begin, consider one of the wine appreciation seminars at the continuing education establishments in San Francisco mentioned in Chapter Seven, haunt the wine shops that have tastings on weekends, and make periodic ventures to the areas that produce different grapes. Look in the newspapers for tours, special wine-related outings, and wine festivals. For a handy reference, buy *A Companion to California Wine: An Encyclopedia of Wine and Winemaking from the Mission Period to the Present*, a detailed and well-presented description of the history, geography, grapes, and wineries of California. *Food and Wine Magazine's* annual *Official Wine Guide* has a section on California wines, and it is both basic and detailed in its descriptions.

Don't forget, though, that the whole point of drinking wine is to enjoy it. No matter the current popularity of certain wines, the superior attitude of certain wine snobs, and even the authoritative stance of shop proprietors—everybody has different tastes, so if you don't like a wine, it's not for you.

Trying Wines

In restaurants, wine is sold by the glass and by the bottle (generally 750 ml), and sometimes by the half-bottle. Depending on how much you drink, it can make economic sense to order a bottle of wine for two people, as there are four 6 oz. servings in a bottle, and the cost is perhaps 20 percent less than four single glasses.

Waiters in just about any restaurant are knowledgeable about the wines of that restaurant and will be glad to discuss the wine appropriate for your meal and for your taste. Some restaurants will allow you a small taste of a wine before you order a glass, and most will also allow you to exchange it for another if you do not like it. It is very rare for a wine to be sent back because it has "turned" and isn't good. Many restaurants have a "house wine," and these are often produced from famous wineries but labeled with the name of the restaurant.

The price of a bottle of wine in a restaurant is increasing, as establishments try to turn a larger profit any place they can. Generally, the price should be about double what the establishment paid for the bottle, but some restaurants are now charging triple. Once you have learned about wines and their prices, you can determine which varietals and vintages are worth the price.

Many bars hold special tastings from particular wineries (as do the wine shops mentioned below). Some offer "flights," samplings of similar wines, often in half-glass sizes. You can also try the wine bars, although in San Francisco, where interesting wines are so easily available in just about any eating establishment, there are fewer bars devoted solely to wines than in other cities.

- *Financial District*—**London Wine Bar**: 415 Sansome Street (tel: 788-4811)
- *Hayes Valley*—**Hayes and Vine**: 377 Hayes Street (tel: 626-5301)
- *Union Square*—**First Crush**: 101 Cyril Magnin (tel: 982-7874)

PURCHASING WINE

Prices run the gamut from the very cheap to the astronomical. The type of wine, the vineyard, the number of bottles produced, and the particular year the grapes were harvested all contribute to how a wine is priced. California wines have become popular worldwide and some recent harvests have been small, so the price of the better wines has increased. In general, the better the wine, the higher the cost. But good, drinkable wines are available at reasonable prices, often at under $10 per bottle, so it is not necessary to spend a fortune on wine. It all just takes know-how: knowing where and when to shop for wines, reading advertisements for sales, buying enough to create a cellar of wines to drink at future dates, and paying attention not only to the offerings of major wineries, but experimenting with "boutique" wineries that produce small amounts of good wines.

Shops have sales on particular items, and when they do, think about stocking your cellar. All the discount groceries mentioned in Chapter Thirteen sell well-known labels at good prices, plus interesting imported wines, not just from France or Italy, but from Chile and Australia as well; if you have found a wine you like, go back immediately and buy more, for inventory runs out quickly and that particular wine may not turn up again. Supermarkets sell a variety of wines, but these are not necessarily the best buys. Many of the wine shops have tastings of the wines they are currently featuring, and surprisingly, these are usually affordable.

- *Bayshore* — **Beverages & More**: 201 Bayshore Boulevard (tel: 648-1233). A large selection of wines and spirits, both domestic and imported. Good prices. Other stores in the area (info tel: 888/772-3866).
- *Cow Hollow* — **PlumpJack Wines**: 3201 Fillmore Street, near Union (tel: 346-9870). Popular neighborhood shop, offering more than one hundred California and Italian wines at reasonable prices.
- *North Beach* — **Coit Liquor**: 585 Columbus Avenue (tel: 986-4036). Small shop but extensive selection of domestic, French, and Italian wines. Good prices and knowledgeable personnel.
- *Polk/Van Ness* — **The Jug Shop**: 1567 Pacific Avenue, at Polk (tel: 885-2922). Large liquor shop with excellent prices, an extensive collection of wines and beers.
- *SOMA* — **Wine Club**: 953 Harrison Street (tel: 512-9086). Excellent prices on a large selection of domestic and imported wines; tastings, books, accessories. Entrance and parking on side, along Oak Grove Street.

The Wine Label

Labels say it all, front and back. The front carries specific information that is required by the U.S. Bureau of Alcohol, Tobacco and Firearms. The brand name of the wine is often most prominent, as wineries strive for customer recognition and loyalty. For small companies this may be the name of the winery itself; large companies may have several brand names. The type of wine is generally specified by the variety of grape, such as Pinot Noir, and these varietals must contain at least 75 percent of the named grape. Some lesser wines may use a semi-generic name such as Burgundy or even an overall name such as "red table wine," and some blends may bear the name *Meritage*. Nearby will be the "appellation of origin," indicating where the grapes were grown. Appellation is increasingly noticed by consumers, focusing on the soil and the site as much as the winemaker.

At the bottom, the name of the winery that bottled the wine usually appears. Although the winery may be in Napa, it doesn't mean the grapes are from there (that's the appellation of origin): if the label says "produced by," it means that at least 75 percent of the wine was made by the bottler; if it says "cellared by," or "vinted by," the wine was probably purchased from a different winery. The percentage of alcohol appears on the front label along with the date, known as the "vintage year," that the grapes were picked.

The back of the label often describes the wine in detail, and sometimes says which food it best accompanies. It also contains the required warnings about alcohol and health.

BREW PUBS

Beer appreciation is growing among San Franciscans. The city does not lack for pubs that offer a wide selection of draft and bottled domestic and imported beers and ales, plus interesting selections from regional micro-breweries. Taking on the character of the neighborhood they serve, pubs offer various kinds of entertainment, including large television screens for sports viewing. But it is the brew-pub—saloons that handcraft their own recipes for beers and ales on the premises—that offer the most innovative selections of brews. Some offer standard pub fare, some are elegant restaurants in themselves, and all provide a convivial atmosphere.

The micro-brewery trend may well have started here in San Francisco, when in 1965 the decision was made to preserve the bankrupt **Anchor Brewing Company**, at 1705 Mariposa Street. Now it is San Francisco's local pride, brewing the famous Anchor Steam Beer; the factory does not have a pub, but does give tours and tastings (tel: 863-8350).

- *Fisherman's Wharf*—**Steelhead Brewing Company**: 353 Jefferson Street, in Anchorage Plaza (tel: 775-1795). Good micro-brewery from this west coast chain. Gourmet pizza, pasta, burgers, and seafood.

- *Haight* — **Magnolia**: 1398 Haight Street, at Masonic (tel: 864-7468). A brew pub in the heart of the Haight, serving lunch, dinner, and weekend brunch.
- *Marina* — **Faultline Brewing Company**: 2001 Chestnut Street (tel: 922-7397). Good beers and a homemade root beer, pub food, and imaginative upscale entrees.
- *North Beach* — **San Francisco Brewing Company**: 155 Columbus Avenue, at Pacific (tel: 434-3344). Domestic and imported beers, plus those brewed on the premises. Tastings, good food, and live music most evenings.
- *Ocean Beach* — **Beach Chalet**: 1000 The Great Highway at John F. Kennedy Drive (tel: 386-8439). Fabulous views of the beach, an eclectic menu, plus sampler of beers brewed on the premises.
- *Pacific Heights* — **The B Spot**: 2301 Fillmore Street, at Clay (tel: 614-1111). Three handcrafted beers and upscale pub food.
- *Potrero Hill* — **Potrero Brewing Company**: 535 Florida Street (tel: 552-1967). Outdoor dining, pool tables, full bar, house-made beers and ales.
- *SOMA* — **Thirsty Bear**: 661 Howard Street (tel: 974-0905). Brewery and restaurant serving Spanish food.
- *South Embarcadero* — **Gordon Biersch**: 2 Harrison Street, at the Embarcadero (tel: 243-8246). German beers, extensive menu, plus pizza and snacks. Crowds often spill out onto the street.
- *Union Square* — **E & O Trading**: 314 Sutter (tel: 693-0303). Southeast Asian restaurant and brewery.

THE BAR

Bars come in many shapes and forms: the romantic bar with a spectacular view atop a tall hotel, the loud sports bar with television screens in every corner, the neighborhood bar where you can spend a comfortable evening chatting with your friends. Most restaurants have a bar in front, and these can seat people waiting for their table, diners without a reservation, or those just wanting to stop by for a drink. Some bars open by lunchtime, some in the late afternoon, and restaurant bars are generally open during the restaurant's business hours. Restaurant and other bars usually offer inexpensive cocktails, beers, and snacks in the early evening, during an often loosely defined "happy hour," to a regular clientele that gathers after work. Some bars have theme nights, others have live music; some are known for their particularly delicious concoctions (especially nowadays the martini and the cosmopolitan) — experimentation is what San Francisco is about. Whatever your choice, you'll find it somewhere in the city. No bar may serve alcoholic beverages between 2:00 am and 6:00 am, and most take their last call around 1:45 am.

Bars such as **The Cliff House**, **Top of the Mark** in the Mark Hopkins Hotel, **Harry Denton's Starlight Room** at the Sir Francis Drake, or **The Equinox** at the top of the Grand Hyatt have spectacular views and are fun to go to from time to time but are often crowded with tourists. Some bars, a few of which are listed below, also have great views, are directly on the waterfront, and have outdoor tables during good weather.

A host of Irish bars such as **The Plough and the Stars**, **The Front Room**, **Lefty O'Doul's**, **Pat O'Shea's Mad Hatter**, and **Martin Macks Bar** in the Haight offer Irish beers in addition to a full bar and decent bar food, dart competitions, and live music, and they celebrate all Ireland's holidays in grand style. Otherwise, here are few of the greats:

- *Cow Hollow* — **Perry's**: 1944 Union Street (tel: 922-9022). One of the original singles bars, this remains a lively place to gather, with good pub food and a friendly atmosphere.
- *Embarcadero* — **Bix**: 56 Gold Street, between Sansome and Montgomery (tel: 433-6300). Jazz piano, supper-club menu, great bar in an Art Deco ambience, splendid martinis. Often rated as San Francisco's best bar.

- *Embarcadero* — **Pier 23**: Pier 23 (tel: 362-5125). Right on the water, this bar is great all day long. Tables outside, live music in the evenings, a popular weekend brunch.
- *Mission* — **Blondie's Bar and No Grill**: 540 Valencia Street (tel: 864-2419). No ambience, no grill, nothing but what some people say are the best drinks in town, especially the oversized, delicious martini.
- *Mission* — **Dalva**: 3121 16th Street, at Albion (tel: 252-7740). A DJ spins music for a lively crowd in this bar that is rated among the best in the city.
- *North Beach* — **Tosca**: 242 Columbus Avenue (tel: 986-9651). Almost a landmark for everyone who comes to San Francisco and a loyal clientele of locals. The jukebox plays only opera. Try its brandy-laced cappuccino.
- *North Beach* — **BlueBar**: 501 Broadway (tel: 981-2230). Downstairs from the popular Black Cat restaurant, this beautiful, comfortable bar schedules jazz, performance art, poetry performances, and short plays.
- *South Embarcadero* — **The Ramp**: 855 China Basin, off Third Street (tel: 621-2378). Right on the water amid the working piers, with an outdoor bar and tables.
- *South Embarcadero* — **Mission Rock**: 817 China Basin Street, near Mariposa (tel: 626-5355). Great deck for sunning, listening to music. Inexpensive drinks and good food.
- *Union Square* — **Red Room**: 827 Sutter, in the Commodore Hotel (tel: 346-7666). Also a city favorite, this bar is glamorous in its all-red decor. Crowded by the fashionable.
- *Union Square* — **The Redwood Room**: Clift Hotel, 495 Geary (tel: 775-4700). Not to be confused with the Red Room, this is one of the city's classiest bars, good for a drink before or after the theater.

DRINKING AGE

In California, you must be 21 years of age in order to purchase or consume alcohol. Even if you are a young-looking 35-year-old, you may be "carded," that is, asked to show your identification. Take it as a compliment. As discussed in Chapter Ten, do not drink alcohol and drive; San Francisco's police are tough on drivers who have been drinking.

— CHAPTER FIFTEEN —
THE SPORTING LIFE

ALL YEAR 'ROUND
The Bay Area's moderate climate allows outdoor activity on just about any day of the year, from sailing on the Bay, to jogging along its shores, to bicycling on hilly trails, to playing tennis and rollerblading—almost anything that can be done outdoors. Access to outdoor sports, in fact, is a main draw for people moving to the Bay Area. San Francisco itself has more than 120 parks (many with miles of hiking trails), over 70 playgrounds, five golf courses, 100 tennis courts, nine swimming pools, almost six miles of ocean beach, several lakes, fishing piers, fly-casting pools, and a marina with a small craft harbor. Private facilities throughout the city offer gyms with aerobics programs, yoga, and martial arts. The

Bay Area also has famous national baseball and football teams. What more could one want?

RESOURCES

The daily newspapers report results of the previous day's important sporting events and announce the events of that day and those in the near future. For articles of seasonal interest and extensive ads for shops, gyms, resorts, vitamins, and more, look for *City Sports*, a tabloid handout found in sports shops and health clubs (10 issues annually). Other free sport-specific tabloids such as *Inside Tennis* or *Hockey and Skating* can be found in shops and fitness clubs.

SPECTATOR SPORTS

San Franciscans are avid sports spectators. Seats for the major games are often sold out long in advance, but the city's sports bars provide large-screen TVs for viewing of just about any match shown on cable or satellite. Tickets for all sporting events are available from the box office or from BASS (tels: 478-2277; 510/762-2277). The San Francisco Giants have several stores in San Francisco, where you can get information on games, get tickets, and buy souvenirs.

Baseball

The San Francisco team, **The San Francisco Giants**, belongs to the National League (ticket office tel: 800/442-6873). After many years of torturing fans at windy, cold Candlestick Park, the team plays in the new Pacific Bell Park in sunny, warm China Basin. Seating 41,000 people, this park may be reached by bus, train, streetcar, and ferry. It is within walking distance of the Financial District.

The Oakland team, **The Oakland Athletics (The A's)**, belongs to the American League (ticket office tel: 510/638-0500). It plays at the Oakland Coliseum, at Interstate 880 and Hegenberger Road. The BART Colosseum Station is close by.

Football
Overlapping the summer baseball season, the football season begins in late August. The **San Francisco 49ers ("The Niners")** is the home team (ticket office tel: 656-4900). And in Oakland, the team is **The Oakland Raiders** (tickets through BASS). Both are among the top teams in their respective "conferences," the rivalry between them (and their fans) is fierce, and fans are as partial to their football teams as they are to their baseball teams. The Raiders play in the Coliseum, and the Niners play at 3Com Park (formerly named Candlestick). Season ticket-holders account for most of the Niners seats, but tickets to the Raiders can sometimes be had.

Soccer
What the rest of the world calls football, Americans call soccer. Since the 1994 World Cup and the 1999 victory by the American women's team, soccer is gaining popularity in the United States. The Bay Area professional team **The San Jose Earthquakes** plays at Spartan Stadium at San Jose State University (ticket office tel: 408/985-4625). International soccer matches can be seen on the Spanish-language channels, selectively on the cable sports channels of ESPN and ESPN2 (plus regular "highlights of the week" programs), but only rarely on the national networks.

Basketball
The Bay Area team is the **Golden State Warriors**, which generally plays in the Oakland Coliseum Arena (ticket office tel: 510/986-2200). The season runs from November through April. Tickets are available at the box office or from BASS/Ticketmaster (tels: 421-8497, 421-2700).

Horse Racing
The two race tracks in the Bay Area alternate their schedules, so that racing takes place almost the entire year. **Golden Gate Fields**

is in Albany, on Gilman Street (off Interstate 80); races are held from January to the end of June (tel: 510/559-7300). **Bay Meadows** in San Mateo (off US 101, Hillsdale Exit) has thoroughbred and quarter horse tracks, and its season runs from August through January (tel: 650/574-7223).

WALKING

There's little to say about walking in San Francisco except that everyone does it. Walking is a favorite sport, and here in this moderate climate, many people walk 365 days a year. People walk to work whenever they can, wearing business suits and walking shoes (to be changed to dress shoes at work). For exercise, people walk up and down the hills, slowly or quickly, singly or in groups, along the Embarcadero, in the parks, at Crissy Field, along the $3^{1}/_{2}$-mile Golden Gate Promenade, across the Golden Gate Bridge. The best walking is where the views are breathtaking: the trails in the Presidio and Golden Gate Park certainly qualify, and Strybing Arboretum in Golden Gate Park is exceptional. So is Ocean Beach, even when the fog and wind are fierce.

RUNNING

Run anywhere you want in San Francisco, on city streets, up and down the hills, in the parks, along the waterfront. Joggers of all speeds run through the city streets before work and at lunchtime, and drivers are used to weaving around them. On weekends, runners prefer jogging where there is one of the city's famous views—all the places mentioned above, for walking. In the parks, women should stay on well-traveled paths, run during daylight hours, and perhaps run with a friend.

The **Dolphin South End Runners** is the largest running club in the area (infotel: 978-0837). The club sponsors friendly runs and competitive races, workouts and social events. There's a small membership fee and usually an entry fee for each race.

ENJOYING NATURE

You can appreciate the beautiful natural resources of the area without even leaving the city, by walking in **Golden Gate Park**, the **Presidio**, and along the shoreline at **Crissy Field**—but the entire Bay Area is a wealth of opportunities that can take many pleasant years to explore. For a description of the outdoor activities available, there's no book better than Peggy Wayburn's *Adventuring in the Bay Area*, which offers a region-by-region coverage of the nine Bay Area counties in terms of access, outings, weather, travel tips, natural history, and wildlife. An important reference to keep on your shelf. Also check the sports sections of the daily papers for their reports on "the outdoors."

Sierra Club, an environmental association, puts on a year-round schedule of hikes, backpacking trips, and other activities, plus social events. Contact the Bay Chapter office at 2530 San Pablo Avenue, Berkeley (tel: 510/848-0800), or its bookshop at 6014 College Avenue, Oakland (tel: 510/658-7470). For trail guides and environmental information, visit the Sierra Club Bookstore at 85 2nd Street (tel: 977-5600); closed Sunday. The **Golden Gate Audubon Society**, at 2530 San Pablo Avenue in Berkeley, hosts field trips, birdwatching walks, workshops, etc (tel: 510/843-2222).

To get involved in the parks, join **Friends of Recreation & Parks**, whose members enjoy the parks together, and who help parks by volunteering, sponsoring events, and raising money (tel: 750-5105; group walks info tel: 263-0991).

In addition to the natural areas described below, **McLaren Park**, **Glen Canyon Park**, **Bernal Park**, and others also have hiking trails. Consider especially the 100 acre Crissy Field, which is devoted to ecology and free recreation, and coastal areas such as **Golden Gate Promenade**, **Ocean Beach**, and the **Esplanade**, or the **Ridge Trail**, which stretches from Lake Merced to Golden Gate Park, and which will eventually circle the entire bay.

Golden Gate Park, dating from about 1865, is one of the country's major urban parks. Reclaimed from sand dunes and landscaped over about 25 years, the park now comprises some 1,017 diverse acres, offering respite and outdoor activities to hundreds of thousands of people each year. Its museums and concerts provide cultural and educational opportunities as well. The park begins at the Panhandle, between Oak and Fell Streets, which is lined by some of the oldest trees in the city. With rolling hills, fragrant forests, and seemingly endless variety, the park continues for some three miles out to the sandy beaches at the edge of the continent.

East of the 19th Avenue bisect, the park is the most civilized. Here are tennis courts, playgrounds, museums, the California Academy of Sciences, and the exquisite Strybing Arboretum and Botanical Gardens, as well as Stow Lake, the largest in the park. West of 19th Avenue, where the fog may hover for days, are the activities that take more space: golf, doggie runs and training, riding, soccer, polo, fly-casting, and model boat sailing. Especially beloved are the buffalos in the large paddock on John F. Kennedy Drive, at about 39th Avenue. Throughout the park there are hiking trails and bicycle paths, forested groves, and lawns and meadows for picnics or games of Frisbee, and there isn't a foggy or rainy day of the year that they're not enjoyed.

The Presidio: Larger than Golden Gate Park (almost twice as large as New York's Central Park), the Presidio's 1,410 acres were from 1776 a strategically placed military garrison. In 1994, however, the United States Army finally vacated this stunningly beautiful area that has been called "the jewel of the Pacific," turning it over to the Golden Gate National Recreation Area for an urban park. Fortunately it is now managed by the National Park Service, and is protected from development. The fragrant forests, unspoiled beaches, and coastal bluffs are open to the public, including many miles of paved roads and hiking trails, plus a golf course, bowling alley, and tennis courts for more structured recreation.

Golden Gate National Recreation Area (GGNRA): The GGNRA spans some 115 miles over a three-county area and is the largest urban national park in the world, encompassing parts of San Francisco itself as well as the wilder reaches outside the city. It includes the Presidio and the beaches mentioned below, Fort Mason and Fort Funston, and the Marin Headlands directly across the Golden Gate Bridge (which is also part of the GGNRA).

FARTHER AFIELD

Living in San Francisco means that within twenty minutes you can be walking the trails of the Marin Headlands in the GGNRA, or strolling among the spectacular redwood trees at Muir Woods. Just a few more minutes and you can be hiking the trails of Mt. Tamalpais, the highest mountain in the area. In fact, there are 43 state parks in the Bay Area, including the popular whale-watching spot **Sonoma Coast State Beach**, with ten miles of shoreline. Within three hours you can be on snowy slopes of the Sierra Nevada for a weekend of skiing or in a raft paddling down some of the fastest rivers in the west. For a day's outing, try these areas within easy reach from the city:

- *On the Bay* — **Angel Island**: A State Park, once the port of entry for Asian immigrants. With spectacular views and many miles of trails for hiking and bicycling, the 750 acre Angel Island is popular for camping and picnics. Daily ferries from Tiburon during the summer, weekends during the winter. Bikes are allowed and may be rented near the ferry and on the island. This is one of the first places the fog hits, so bring sweaters.
- *On the Ocean* — **Whale Watching**: During gray whales' migration season (December to May) the **Oceanic Society** leads whale-watching trips, plus cruises to the **Farallones National Wildlife Refuge**, a 950 square mile sanctuary off the coast that is a haven for marine mammals and sea birds (reservations tel: 474-3385). Dress warmly and bring binoculars.

- *Marin* — **Muir Woods National Monument**: Five hundred and sixty acres of towering redwoods (some 200 years old and 250 feet tall), six miles of footpaths, both hilly and flat, and beautiful light, filtering through the leafy bowers. Off Route 101, at Mill Valley exit, or off Route 1, Panoramic Highway.
- *Marin* — **Mt. Tamalpais State Park**: Fifty miles of hiking trails from the top of the mountain down to the ocean, campsites, horse trails, and exquisite views in this 6,300 acre park just a half-hour from downtown. Biking allowed on the fire roads. Mill Valley to Route 1, the Panoramic Highway.
- *East Bay* — **Tilden Regional Park**: Extremely popular East Bay park, its mountainous trails run past charming lakes, through a variety of nature areas.
- *East Bay* — **Mount Diablo State Park**: Challenging uphill (and then downhill) hikes with wonderful views in all directions.
- *Peninsula* — **San Bruno Mountain State Park**: One of the wildest of the parks in the area, with a 1,314-foot summit, 12 miles of trails, picnic tables, beautiful spring wildflowers on about 1,600 acres. At Brisbane. From Highway 101, take Sierra Point exit to Lagoon Road.
- *Peninsula* — **San Pedro Valley Park**: See charming Brooks Falls with their 175-foot drop; continue on to McNeil State Park and Montara Montain, with its gorgeous views of the coast. Off Linda Mar Boulevard in Pacifica.

BICYCLING

For sports cycling, the entire Bay Area has excellent trails on an extremely varied terrain, from mountainous to flat, and often with outstanding views. In the city, bikers head for Golden Gate Park, along the Great Highway, the Golden Gate Promenade, and around Lake Merced. There's a bicycle path on the Golden Gate Bridge, leading to some of Marin's most outstanding trails. For a complete resource, buy one of the guides to bicycling in the Bay Area; most rate the rides from gentle to challenging: try *Bay Area*

Bike Rides by Ray Hosler, or *Cycling the San Francisco Bay Area: 30 Rides to Historical and Scenic Places* by Carole O'Hare. For day rental in Golden Gate Park and nearby, try the stand at Stow Lake or one of the bike shops on Stanyan Street.

- *Cow Hollow* — **City Cycle**: 3001 Steiner Street (tel: 346-2242). Bicycles for the serious cyclist.
- *Fisherman's Wharf* — **Blazing Saddles**: 1095 Columbus Avenue and at Pier 41 (tel: 202-8888). Bikes come equipped with computers of tour routes of the Marin Headlands, down to Muir Woods, and up to Mt. Tamalpais.
- *Fisherman's Wharf* — **Adventure Bicycle Company**: 968 Columbus Avenue (tel: 771-8735). Tour suggestions detailed and displayed inside. Bikes, trailers for kids, etc.
- *Golden Gate Park* — **Surrey Bikes & Blades**: At Stow Lake (tel: 668-6699). Closed Wednesdays and in inclement weather.
- *Golden Gate Park* — **Golden Gate Park Bike and Skate**: 3038 Fulton, at 6th Avenue (tel: 668-1117). Bikes and inline skates for rent.
- *Haight* — **Avenue Cyclery**: 756 Stanyan Street (tel: 387-3155). Sales of upscale bicycling equipment, plus rentals for those who want to pedal in the park. Excellent repair shop.
- *Haight* — **American Cyclery**: 510 Frederick Street (tel: 664-4545) and 858 Stanyan (tel: 876-4545). Across from each other, two locations for this long-established, well-stocked shop.
- *Mission* — **Valencia Cyclery**: 1077 Valencia, at 22nd Street (tel: 550-6600; repair and parts shop tel: 550-6601). Large selection of equipment and accessories.

INLINE SKATING

For **inline skating**, many people take their rollerblades to Golden Gate Park, where a rollerblade hockey game can often be found near the tennis courts. The Marina Green or the Embarcadero are also popular for skaters. But people skate just about anyplace in the city, and sometimes you can find an inline game on the city's playgrounds. For indoor hockey in San Francisco, try **Bladium** at 1050 3rd Street, China Basin, which sponsors tournaments, leagues, and youth programs (tel: 442- 5060). In Oakland, try the **Sport Arena** at 210 Hegenberger Loop (tel: 510/562-9499). Look for the free *Hockey and Skating* tabloid that can be found in skate shops. Skate rentals can be found near Stow Lake in Golden Gate Park, on the park's periphery, and in various other locations around the city; see *Skates* in the Yellow Pages.

- *Fisherman's Wharf* — **New World Sports**: 1365 Columbus Avenue, at Beach (tel: 776-7801)
- *Haight* — **Skates on Haight**: 1818 Haight Street (tel: 752-8375)
- *Sunset* — **Skate Pro**: 3401 Irving (tel: 752-8776)

MULTI-SPORT FITNESS CLUBS

Urban San Francisco offers several extensive multi-sport fitness clubs, almost country clubs within the city. In addition to their standard facilities, most offer scheduled athletic events, tournaments, and social gatherings. Expect to pay an initiation fee, plus monthly dues.

- *City-wide* — **Embarcadero YMCA**: 169 Steuart Street, near Mission (tel: 957-9622). Popular facility with aerobics, yoga, and dance classes, Olympic-size pool, and racquetball/squash and basketball courts. The YMCA in the Presidio, at Lincoln and Funston Streets, also has an extensive fitness facility and pool (tel: 447-9622). The "Y" at 220 Golden Gate Avenue, close to the Civic Center, is similarly equipped (tel: 885-0460).
- *Embarcadero* — **Golden Gateway Tennis and Swim Club**: 370 Drumm Street (tel: 616-8800). Two outdoor swimming pools, nine tennis courts, a fitness center, aerobics classes, tournaments and special events — all in the heart of the city.
- *Masonic* — **Koret USF Health & Recreation Center**: Turk and Parker Streets (tel: 422-6820). Part of the University of San

Francisco, this facility with swimming pool, gym, and racquetball courts is open to non-students until 2:00 pm daily and all day weekends. Pay by the session or buy a pass for 15 sessions.
- *SOMA* — **San Francisco Tennis Club**: 645 5th Street (tel: 777-9000). An upscale club including indoor and outdoor tennis courts, a fitness facility, aerobics classes, sauna and hot tub, restaurant. In addition to the monthly dues, there is a court fee for using the indoor courts.
- *Telegraph Hill* — **San Francisco Bay Club**: 150 Greenwich Street (tel: 433-2200). Tennis, racquetball and squash, swimming pool, aerobics, sun deck, events and activities.

GYMS

In addition to the more extensive multi-sport clubs above, every neighborhood has its storefront gym, some just with workout machines, some more extensively equipped, offering aerobics classes, jacuzzi, and steam baths. You'll see these small clubs as you walk around your neighborhood; monthly dues are generally reasonable, and some clubs allow per-use payment. The downtown district has several chains of fitness clubs that open early and stay open late, and these, obviously, are most crowded before and after work, and at lunchtime. Facilities at these clubs vary; some have swimming pools and some do not, but they are all generally well-equipped for the activities they offer. These usually have short-term as well as regular membership, and if you belong to one, you may use the others in the chain.

- **Club One Fitness**: Locations in the Financial District, and others around the Bay Area.
- **24-Hour Fitness**: Seven locations throughout the city. Dozens of others throughout the Bay Area.
- **Pinnacle Fitness**: Six locations, two with indoor swimming pools.

TENNIS

More than 130 free public tennis courts dot the city's parks, and they are "first-come first-served." For the *Guide to Public Tennis Courts* ask at the **San Francisco Recreation and Parks Department** at McLaren Lodge, Fell and Stanyan Streets, in Golden Gate Park, or call the Tennis Department (tel: 753-7100). Golden Gate Park has 21 courts, which must be reserved in advance, and which cost a small fee (tel: 753-7001). The city also offers an extensive program of free tennis lessons. Below are some popular public courts; see also Multi-sport Fitness Clubs above.

- *Noe Valley* — **Dolores Park**: 18th Street and Dolores. Six courts. Daytime only.
- *Marina* — **Moscone Recreation Center**: Chestnut and Buchanan Streets. Four lighted courts.
- *Excelsior* — **McLaren Park**: Mansell Drive, near University Street. Six courts.
- *North Beach* — **North Beach Playground**: Lombard and Mason Streets. Three lighted courts.

SWIMMING

Yes, San Francisco is on the ocean, but swimming in the cold waters off the city's beaches can not only be chilling, it can definitely be risky: some of the most inviting-looking beaches have dangerous undertows and rip tides, so swimming, and wading — even in waters that appear calm — may be unsafe. It is best to sun yourself, jog, or walk along the beaches to enjoy the view, but to reserve your swimming for the city's pools. If you want a good swimming beach (despite the cold water) and pleasant amenities, go north to **Stinson Beach**, which on a good day is about 45 minutes from the city on the Panoramic Highway; on weekends, the lines of cars can seem endless.

If open water swimming in the Bay interests you, try the open water clubs: the **Dolphin Swim and Boat Club** is a group of hardy folk who swim in the Bay year round and row on the Bay and on Lake Merced. The clubhouse is at 502 Jefferson Street, at the foot of Hyde Street (tel: 441-9329). The Dolphins sponsor competitive swims and social events, announced in the quarterly newsletter. Meetings are the third Wednesday of the month. Try also the **South End Rowing Club**, next door at 500 Jefferson (tel: 776-7372).

- **Baker Beach**: In the Presidio. Popular for picnics, fishing and sunbathing (in various states of undress).
- **Aquatic Park**: Just beyond Ghirardelli Square at the foot of Van Ness, this is downtown's nearest swimming beach. Good sandy beach, but don't expect the water to be warm.
- **Land's End Beach**: Near Geary Boulevard and the Great Highway. Down a steep trail, a small picturesque beach popular with the gay crowd. Clothing optional. Swimming prohibited.
- **Ocean Beach**: Along the Great Highway. Always popular 4-mile strip of sand. Great for jogging, strolling, sunbathing. Often dangerous for swimming.
- **China Beach**: in Seacliff at 28th Avenue, off El Camino del Mar (tel: 558-3706). Down a steep trail to a swimming beach, protected from the tides. Swim in the summer months when a lifeguard is on duty. Call ahead to inquire about conditions, for weather changes quickly in San Francisco.

The best bet is to try a swimming pool. The multi-sport fitness clubs listed above have pools, and "Park and Rec" maintains eight municipal public pools. A full list, including opening hours for each pool, is available at McLaren Lodge, in Golden Gate Park. Prices are reasonable, especially if you buy a series. Swim lessons are also available.

- *Japantown* — **Hamilton Recreational Center**: Geary Boulevard at Steiner (tel: 292-2001)
- *Mission* — **Garfield Pool**: Harrison and 26th Streets (tel: 695-5001)

- *Mission* — **Mission Pool**: 19th Street at Valencia (tel: 695-5002)
- *North Beach* — **North Beach Pool**: Lombard Street at Mason (tel: 274-0200)
- *Panhandle* — **Angelo Rossi**: Arguello Boulevard at Anza (tel: 666-7014)
- *Parkside* — **Sava Pool**: 19th Avenue and Wawona (tel: 753-7000)
- *Sunset* — **Balboa Park**: Ocean Avenue and San Jose (tel: 337-4701)
- *Visitacion Valley* — **Coffman Pool**: Visitacion Avenue at Hahn (tel: 337-4702)

Other Water Sports

- *Sailing*: The opportunity to go sailing just about any time of the year is a distinct benefit of the San Francisco life. Opening Day on the Bay in May can be an awesome sight, and events over the Bay such as fireworks or the aerial displays of the Blue Angels see thousands of boats perched in the water waiting for the show. For people without boats, it's sometimes possible to sign on as crew. Try the **Saint Francis Yacht Club** (tel: 563-6363), or the **Golden Gate Yacht Club** (tel: 346-2628), both membership clubs located in The Marina, or one of the boat clubs toward the south at Pier 54. For sailing lessons, one of the best in the area is the **Cal Sailing Club**, at University Street at the Marina, in Berkeley (tel: 510/287-5905).
- *Surfing*: Surfing in wet suits is popular, but despite the surfers who brave the currents, remember that the undertows off Ocean Beach are dangerous. Beginners often surf at Pacifica's Linda Mar Beach, and experts go down to Half Moon Bay. Windsurfers tend to use Lake Merced and the more challenging area at Crissy Field, past the Marina. **San Francisco School of Windsurfing** offers courses in windsurfing on Lake Merced (tel: 753-3235); and **Boardsports**, which also has rentals of various types of water sports equipment, gives lessons near Alameda (tel: 929-7873).

THE SPORTING LIFE

Fishing off a municipal pier.

- *Rowing* — **Lake Merced Boathouse**: Rent a rowboat, canoe, or pedal boat, at Harding Road and Skyline Boulevard. **Stow Lake Boathouse** — Rent a rowboat or pedal boat in Golden Gate Park. Picnic on the island of Strawberry Hill. See also the swim and boat clubs mentioned above.
- *Fishing* — The city's municipal piers: at the end of Van Ness or at the end of Broadway — permit fishing in the heart of the city, and people occasionally reel in flounder, sand dabs, cod, bass, perch, or crabs. Unfortunately, cleanup programs to eliminate toxic substances and other contaminants in the Bay have been only partially successful. As of 1999 the California Office of Environmental Hazard Assessment suggests that adults should eat Bay fish no more than twice each month, and that striped bass more than 35 inches long not be consumed. Fortunately, people also fish from the banks or a boat on the 350 acre Lake Merced, which has been stocked with trout, rock cod, catfish and bass. Golden Gate Park has several fly-casting pools by the Anglers Lodge, just west of the Polo Fields.

GOLF

It may be surprising that there are five golf courses in a city as small as San Francisco. Some courses are nine-hole only, compact and full of twists and turns. Golf is a year-round sport, despite the winter rains and the summer fog, but San Franciscans are hardy, and swathed in sweaters and jackets, they wait patiently for their tee-off time. There are a few private membership clubs in the city, and many clubs around the Bay Area are open to the public. In the East Bay, **Tilden Park Golf Course** in Berkeley is particularly popular (tel: 510/848-7373), as is **Chuck Corica Golf Complex** in Alameda (tel: 510/522-4321). For a complete listing of the clubs in the Bay Area, purchase *The Golf Road Map* at golf shops (see Chapter Sixteen); see also the Yellow Pages for extensive listings.

For a covered practice range, putting green, and golf lessons in the heart of the city, try **Mission Bay Golf Center**, at 1200 6th

Street, off Fourth and Channel (tel: 431-7888). Although membership is not required, joining allows discounts on lessons and on buckets of balls, plus discounted play at the city's golf courses. The center hosts tournaments and social events.

- **Gleneagle's Golf Course**: In McLaren Park, at Sunnydale Avenue and Hahn Street (tel: 587-2425). A hilly nine-hole course, with wonderful views.
- **Golden Gate Park Golf Course**: 47th Avenue between Fulton and John F. Kennedy Drive (tel: 751-8987). Compact nine-hole course.
- **Harding Golf Course**: In Harding Park, at 99 Harding Road near Skyline Boulevard (tel: 664-4690). Both nine and eighteen challenging holes in a forested setting. Driving range.
- **Presidio Golf Course**: 300 Finley Road, at Arguello, in the Presidio (tel: 415-4653). Eighteen holes, practice center, Arnold Palmer Golf Academy.
- **Lincoln Park Golf Course**: In Lincoln Park, at 34th Avenue and Clement Street (tel: 221-9911). Eighteen difficult holes on beautiful terrain with spectaclar views. Practice area, putting green, etc.

SKIING

Some of the best skiing in the country takes place on the ski slopes of the Sierra Nevada, only three hours from San Francisco. In the winter, daily weather updates report the snow level and depth of snow pack of the major ski areas of the region: **Lake Tahoe**, **Incline**, **Alpine Meadows**, **Yosemite**, and **Bear Valley**. Be prepared to carry tire chains in your car and from time to time to be stuck in the mountains until the roads are cleared of snow. Sunday night traffic off the mountains can be slow. For highway conditions, call the California Department of Transportation's 24-hour automated information line; you will need to enter the number of the highway you are inquiring about (tel: 800/427-7623).

The **San Francisco Ski Club** (tel: 337-9333) is a club for single skiers and snowboarders, which also offers white-water rafting, bicycling outings and other events year-round. Sporting goods shops sell ski wear in the winter, some shops rent it, and most have information on ski areas: try these below:

- *Berkeley*—**REI Coop**: 1338 San Pablo Avenue, Berkeley (tel: 510/527-4140)
- *San Rafael*—**Swiss Ski Sports**: 821 E. Francisco Boulevard (tel: 721-2401)
- *San Francisco*—**Soma Sports**: 689 3rd Street (tel: 777-2165)

OTHER SPORTS

- *Basketball*—You can probably pick up a basketball game in the Golden Gate panhandle, Dolores Park, at some of the city's playgrounds, the Moscone Recreation Center in the Marina, or the Potrero Hill Recreation Center.
- *Bowling*—**Japantown Bowl**: 1790 Post Street, at Webster (tel: 921-6200). Large bowling complex with 40 lanes, a cafe, sports TV. Inquire about joining a league. **Presidio National Park Bowling**: Building 93, between Moraga and Montgomery Streets (tel: 561-2695). Yerba Buena Bowling Center: Metreon, 750 Folsom Street (tel: 777-3727). A San Francisco experience!
- *Dance*—**Academy of Ballet**: 2121 Market Street (tel: 552-1166). For all ages. Classes for toning and stretching, through classical ballet moves. **Renaissance Ballroom**: 285 Ellis Street (tel: 474-0920). Learn the cha cha or the waltz; most social dances are taught here. **Recreation and Parks Department Dance**: 50 Scott Street in the Harvey Milk Center (tel: 554-9523). Dance lessons in a variety of steps: square dancing, jazz, tap, etc. **Jewish Community Center**: 3200 California Street (tel: 292-1221). Dance lessons for all ages. Ballet, modern, jazz, swing, hip-hop, etc. See *Dancing* in the Yellow Pages and *Dance* in Chapter Seventeen.

Practicing tai chi in Washington Square.

- *Billiards* — **Chalkers Billiard Club**: 101 Spear Street, in Rincon Center (tel: 512-0450). Especially popular with the lunchtime office crowd; evening happy hour. **The Great Entertainer**: 975 Bryant Street (tel: 861-8833). Pool and billiard tables, snooker, shuffleboard, ping-pong, darts, video arcade, plus bar and restaurant. Open until 2:00 am weekdays, 3:00 am Saturday. **Hollywood Billiards**: 61 Golden Gate Avenue (tel: 252-9643). More than thirty antique pool tables, snooker and billiards. Open from 3:00 pm until 4:00 am on weekdays and 6:00 am on weekends. Happy hours weekdays 4:30–7:00 pm.
- *Horseback riding* — **Golden Gate Park Stables**: John F. Kennedy Jr. Drive and 36th Avenue (tel: 668-7360). Guided rides through the park and along the oceanfront, plus pony rides for children. Instruction available.
- *Ice-skating* — **Yerba Buena Gardens** sports a year-round, covered ice-skating rink. **Justin Herman Plaza**, at California Street and the Embarcadero, erects a small rink in the winter.

- *Martial Arts and Yoga* — As would be expected, San Francisco has many Asian exercise establishments. For any one of a dozen types of martial arts *dojos*, see the Yellow Pages under *Martial Arts Instruction*. Health clubs offer yoga classes for all levels of ability, and there are small studios in just about every neighborhood that specialize in a variety of yoga techniques and instruction. See *Yoga Instruction* in the Yellow Pages.
- *Rock Climbing* — **Mission Cliffs Rock Climbing Center**: 2295 Harrison, at 19th Street (tel: 550-0515). Indoor rock climbing on about 14,000 square feet of climbing terrain.

SPAS

What could be better after a long week at work than a relaxing couple of hours at a spa? Most health clubs have sauna and steam baths, and some offer massage; massage and beauty treatments are also available at some downtown salons. But locals are particularly fond of the **Kabuki Hot Springs** in the Japan Center, at 1750 Geary Boulevard, at Fillmore (info tel: 922-6000). Kabuki offers a full range of *shiatsu* massages, body treatments and Japanese baths. Try also:

- *Marina* — **Heaven Wellness Center**: 2215 Chestnut Street (tel: 749-6414). Salon and day spa offers hair services, plus massage and facials, steam, acupuncture, nutritional counseling and yoga classes.
- *Mission* — **Osento Baths**: 955 Valencia Street (tel: 282-6333). Gathering place for women. Peaceful bath house, with saunas, outdoor deck, massage.
- *Noe Valley* — **Elisa's Health Spa**: 4028A 24th Street (tel: 821-6727). Outdoor/indoor hot tubs, steam baths and sauna. Massage, skin peels, herbal body wraps.
- *Van Ness* — **The Hot Tubs**: 2200 Van Ness Avenue (tel: 441-8827). Hot tubs and saunas, shiatsu and Swedish massage. Also in Berkeley.

- *Union Square* — **Elizabeth Arden Red Door Salon & Spa**: 126 Post Street (tel: 989-4888). Luxurious spa. Hair and body treatments, cosmetics, makeovers, facials, aromatherapy massage, thermal wraps.
- *Union Square* — **77 Maiden Lane Salon & Spa**: 77 Maiden Lane (tel: 391-7777). Elegant downtown spa. Hair and makeup services, manicure, pedicure, hot mud treatments, and massage.

AND LAST... ABOUT DOGS

Brisk dog walking is good exercise and an excellent way to meet neighbors. While dogs are not allowed in most parks (signs are generally posted at entrances), some parks have areas designated "off leash" where dogs may run freely, and some neighborhood parks have dog runs. Golden Gate Park has several off-leash areas and Ocean Beach is off-leash until Stairway 21. Dolores Park between the Mission and Noe Valley is a dog and owner gathering place. Call "Park and Rec" for its brochure *Dog Running Areas in City Parks*.

Note that the city's "pooper-scooper" law requires that dog litter be picked up and disposed of properly, whether you are walking your dog in a park or on the street. People actually do obey the law, and the city is basically litter-free as a result. Carry a plastic bag with you and look for the nearest trash receptacle.

— Chapter Sixteen —

SHOPPING AT YOUR DOOR

ALL DAY, EVERY DAY

As small and compact as it is, San Francisco's stores sell everything you need for your home somewhere within the city's confines. Nothing is hard to find: consulting the Yellow Pages and understanding the commercial character of the different districts should allow you to make your way comfortably onto the shopping scene without trouble—and without much wait, for you can shop seven days a week, if the fancy strikes you.

Almost all stores are open by 10:00 am. Although service and repair shops are generally closed on Sunday, all large stores and chain stores are open on Sundays, and in fact, this is a popular shopping day. Sunday hours, however, may be shorter than on weekdays, so it is best to call ahead to check. Department stores may stay open until 9:00 pm and some of the national chains — **Tower Records**, **Virgin Megastore** — even later. Small shops generally close around dinnertime, although specialty boutiques and bookshops in areas where the evening is lively often stay open late. As mentioned in Chapter Thirteen, supermarket complexes open early and stay open late every day, and they often have hardware, pharmacy, stationery, and even a few clothing items — hosiery or underwear — you might want on a Sunday. Shops listed here are all open on Sunday, unless noted.

WHERE TO SHOP

A description of the city's shopping districts must begin directly on Union Square, where large multi-department shops rule the scene, selling goods from the utilitarian to the upscale and elegant. Macy's is the only true department store, stocking household goods, furniture, and linens, as well as clothing and accessories, and it has decent merchandise at good prices. **Saks Fifth Avenue** and **Neiman Marcus** are the most fashionable of the clothing chains. But the streets that surround Union Square house smaller, upmarket shops, and both local boutiques and branches of national chains. **Gump's**, the most elegant and prestigious of old San Francisco shops, has entrances on both Post and Maiden Lane. Just across Market Street, is **Nordstrom's**, a multi-story fashion mart atop the large City Centre Mall.

It would be your lucky day if you found a parking space around Union Square, so do not count on it. Most parking meters in this area are reserved during the day for commercial vehicles unloading their wares (so why trucks insist on double parking and blocking the streets remains a mystery). Other meters may be for a half-hour only and cost as much as 25 cents for 10 minutes. Fortunately, three city-run parking lots are located in the area (see Chapter Ten), and nearby Market Street offers public transportation to most parts of the city.

Union Square, the city's major theater and shopping district.

Although the department stores have their attractions, San Franciscans in general are partial to the districts for everyday shopping. Each neighborhood has its commercial character, and you will come to know what type of items and prices you will find on Union Street (high) as opposed to those you will find on Haight (low). On Union, for example (if you can find a parking space), starting at about Gough, you'll find lively upscale and interesting clothing and jewelry boutiques intermingled with crowded trendy restaurants and cafes, bars and nightspots. The same holds true on Chestnut Street and on Upper Fillmore, from about Washington to California, which includes some elegant resale shops. The Sacramento and Presidio intersection has artsy shops of all sorts, but also a large selection of children's items, reflecting its neighborhood's ambience (also true of Noe Valley). North Beach has fewer clothing shops than coffeehouses, but Chestnut and Union Streets are only a short drive away, and the four-building Embarcadero Center a short walk.

Some areas are known for a particular focus: art galleries downtown and around the Civic Center, antique shops on Jackson and on Sacramento near Presidio, modern furniture below Potrero Hill, appliances South of Market or in the Mission. South of Market also sees the huge discount chains—**Costco**, **Office Max**, **Bed, Bath and Beyond**—and small factory clothing outlets: some are so popular that tour buses from the suburbs bring people in on Saturdays for a day of discount shopping.

Check also commercial corridors such as Geary Boulevard, Lombard Street, and 19th Avenue. These arteries and their side streets all have stores and local services, and in these areas parking may well be easier. The malls and some large shops and chains, of course, have parking lots for their customers.

Nationwide stores in all merchandise categories are increasingly present in the city. These shops—**Borders** and **CompUSA**, for example—offer good prices and an extensive selection. But citizens' groups are fighting to exclude these megastores from their districts, trying to preserve both the character of the neighborhoods and the small independent merchant. As rents continue to rise in the city, forcing the small business out, they may have less success than at present. The above notwithstanding, chains and local businesses combine to make all shopping options available, and you should have no trouble finding what you want.

PRICES AND PAYING

The few stores and services mentioned below have been selected as representative examples of the types of shops in San Francisco that give good quality for the price—whatever the price. That does not mean that you won't find a bargain elsewhere, for you certainly will. Nor does it mean that a particular discount store will be inexpensive, but it certainly will offer a steep discount from the retail price and be worth the money for that particular item. People do not bargain on prices, as a rule, but if merchandise is damaged and you still want to buy it, you may be given a discount.

Except for some small shops, stores accept the major credit cards. Some will also take a personal check on a California bank (a few will take out-of-state checks) when you produce photo identification. It is illegal for a shop to ask that a credit card be used as identification. Stores do not charge extra for using a credit card, but a few will offer a discount for cash.

Ask about the store's refund policy. The large stores and chains generally make refunds with no questions asked if the merchandise is brought back within a reasonable length of time — a week or so — and will also exchange ill-fitting goods for a larger or smaller size, or even a different color. Some stores will exchange for other merchandise only. Stores are not required to make refunds, and each store sets its own policy. If there is an unusual policy, such as "all sales final," a notice is often displayed; this sign is also often displayed during a sale. If you have doubts, ask in advance.

The sales tax in San Francisco is 8.5 percent; in outlying areas it may be somewhat less. This is not a value added tax, and foreign visitors do not receive a refund upon leaving the United States. There are duty free shops in the Union Square area.

SHOPPING CENTERS

Small shopping malls that cater to locals — with markets, repair shops, pharmacies — cluster in the different neighborhoods. The larger malls are generally anchored by a large clothing store such as Macy's, surrounded by dozens of smaller specialty stores. **Stonestown Galleria** is the largest and most varied shopping mall in the city, rivaling those in the suburbs which sprawl across many acres; downtown, **City Centre** has some interesting shops, and, as mentioned above, it is anchored at the top by Nordstrom's.

Otherwise, for the best range of shops, think about the enormous suburban shopping malls that are close to the city, but which do require transportation by car.

A few minutes south of the city, try **Serramonte Center** and **Westlake Shopping Center** in Daly City, **Tanforan Park** in San Bruno, and, just a little bit farther, **Hillsdale Shopping Center** in San Mateo. Farther south, in Palo Alto, it's worth an afternoon just to explore the extremely upmarket **Stanford Shopping Center**, off Highway 280. About 15 minutes north of the city, at Corte Madera, two major shopping malls—**Town and Country** and **The Village**—flank the 101 Freeway. Nearby in the East Bay, try the **South Shore Center** in Alameda or the **Pacific East Mall** in Albany. In Oakland, **Jack London Square** offers shopping and restaurants on the edge of the bay. More extensive malls are farther east at Walnut Creek and Pleasanton, several anchored by large department stores; in Concord look for **The Willows** and **Sun Valley**.

In addition to the malls within the city listed below, **The Cannery**, **Pier 39**, **The Anchorage**, and **Ghirardelli Square**, although primarily tourist destinations, do hold some interesting and offbeat shops. And the **Canton Bazaar** and **China Trade Center** on the tourist path in Chinatown offer imported goods such as clothing, jewelry, some Oriental furniture, and table linens.

- *Downtown*—**San Francisco Centre**: 855 Market at 5th Street. A vertical shopping mall of small shops, anchored by the upscale Nordstrom clothing retailer.
- *Downtown*—**Crocker Galleria**: 50 Sutter Street, near Montgomery. Multi-story mall of elegant boutiques and little eateries; cafe-style tables and chairs under the skylight give the feeling of eating outdoors in any season.
- *Embarcadero*—**Embarcadero Center**: Battery and Sacramento Streets. A three-level shopping, dining, and cinema complex, spread across four buildings connected by walkways. Parking garage.

- *Pacific/Presidio Heights* — **Laurel Village**: 3500 California Street, past Presidio. Excellent local mall, with upscale supermarts, wine store, kitchenware store, children's clothing and toy stores, bookstore, cafes, etc. Metered parking in front and free in rear.
- *Sunset* — **Stonestown Galleria**: 19th Avenue at Winston Drive. Almost a city in itself, Stonestown contains a supermarket, dozens of shops, Nordstrom's and Macy's department stores, a multiplex cinema, a medical building, and small restaurants. Parking.
- *Wharf* — **Northpoint Centre**: 250 Bay Street, between Powell and Mason. Neighborhood convenience mall with Safeway, Walgreens, Blockbuster Video, Radio Shack, General Nutrition, and a few small shops. Parking.

CLOTHING

Shops throughout the city offer clothing of all styles, quality, and prices. Those near Union Square may sport designer labels and the highest prices, but even the outlying districts sell interesting clothes at prices that match the quality and design. Shopping is almost a game for many San Franciscans, however, who tend to brag about how little they paid for an item of clothing or an accessory. That one can shop adequately and inexpensively is not only owing to the frequent sales of those department stores and boutiques, but to the presence in the city and the entire Bay Area of a wide selection of designer discount shops, factory outlet stores, and nationwide discount clothing chains. These offer out-of-season clothes, discontinued styles, and overstocks. It isn't likely that you would find any damaged or inferior merchandise, but of course the quality reflects each manufacturer's approach.

Within the city, the South of Market area abounds with small discount shops, plus the family clothing chain **Burlington Coat Factory**, at 899 Howard Street (tel: 495-7234), and other inexpensive chains such as **Marshall's**, **Mervyn's**, and **Ross**.

Discount houses, of course, usually stock what happens to come in and may not replace an item once it is sold out. Sales assistance in the larger shops may not be as personal as in smaller stores, but customer service is generally good. And, although many have been in their locations for years, bargain shops may come and go. Call in advance to be certain the shop is still there and to ascertain its hours. For a complete guide, look for the often updated *Bargain Hunting in the Bay Area* by Sally Socolich. The shops directly below, which are well-established, are just a few examples of the range of merchandise available. For well-priced appliances, furniture, and household items, see below.

- *Family clothing*—**Esprit Factory Outlet**: 499 Illinois, at 16th Street (tel: 957-2540). Well-known designer selling casual clothes and shoes for the family. Sales make the prices even better.
- *Men's clothing*—**California Big and Tall**: 625 Howard Street (tel: 495-4484). Clothes for large and tall men. Closed Sunday and Monday.
- *Men's shirts*—**Van Heusen Factory Store**: 601 Mission Street (tel: 243-0750). Van Heusen shirts for men, casual sportswear for men and women.
- *Women's clothing*—**Georgiou Factory Outlet**: 925 Bryant Street (tel: 554-0150). Past season's designs and overstocks from this well-known chain of contemporary women's clothes. Good prices and a "club" card for extra discounts. Closed Sunday. Other shops in outlying areas.
- *Women's clothing*—**Loehmann's**: 222 Sutter Street (tel: 982-3215). Outpost of New York store selling designer clothes at excellent prices. Also in Westlake Mall in Daly City.
- *Bedclothes*—**Warm Things**: 3063 Fillmore Street, near Union (tel: 931-1660). Factory-direct prices on goose down comforters, shams, covers, robes, slippers, and down vests. Stores in other areas.

- *Jewelry* — **Cresalia Jewelers**: 111 Sutter Street (tel: 781-7371). Large shop with a wide selection of jewelry and watches, silver, and table accessories at excellent prices.
- *Luggage* — **Luggage Center**: 828 Mission Street (tel: 543-3771). Discounts on a variety of brand name luggage and accessories. Repairs. Closed Sunday. Also in Berkeley and Burlingame.
- *Music* — **Tower Outlet**: 660 3rd Street, near Townsend (tel: 957-9660). Overstocks and returns from the Tower Records chain. CDs, videos, cassettes, books. A changing but always interesting selection.
- *Perfumes* — **Perfumania**: 333 Jefferson Street (tel: 931-0815). Brand name perfumes for men and women at good prices. Special sales.
- *Sports gear* — **North Face Outlet**: 1325 Howard Street (tel: 626-6444). Huge warehouse of outdoor equipment: tents, clothing, sleeping bags, etc.

Beyond the City

Factory outlet malls offer good prices because the stores are run by the companies themselves, thereby bypassing the wholesaler and retailer whose prices must reflect their own profits. Several outlet malls are within an hour's drive of the city in all directions (except West, of course). Famous designers such as Liz Claiborne, Jones of New York, Donna Karan, and Tommy Hilfiger have stores in several of the malls offering out of season clothes and overstocks, and sometimes returns from other shops; clothing is generally of the same quality as found in retail stores.

Some of the malls have so many stores and are so spread out they have free shuttle buses. All are open on Sunday and have ample parking, but are crowded on weekends and before holidays.

- *Napa County* — **Napa Premium Outlets**: One of the newest and most popular, with about 50 stores. At Highway 29 and First Street in Napa.

- *Napa County* — **St Helena Premium Outlets**: Small upscale outlet mall. On Highway 29, just north of St. Helena.
- *Sonoma County* — **Petaluma Village Outlets**: About 50 stores of all types. Take 101 north; exit at old Redwood Highway.
- *South* — **Outlets at Gilroy**: Almost 200 factory stores, famous clothing labels, housewares, books, etc. Take Highway 101 south to the Leavesley exit. Shuttle bus between three different areas of shops.
- *South* — **Great Mall of the Bay Area**: Almost two hundred shops and several large anchor stores. At Milpitas, off Highways 680 and 880, at the Montague Expressway and Capitol Avenue.
- *Northeast* — **Factory Stores at Vacaville**: 321 Nut Tree Road, Vacaville. More than 125 stores with a convenient shuttle bus.

Children's Clothing and Equipment

Department stores, shopping centers, and some discount shops carry good quality children's clothing and furniture, and both the **Gap Kids** and **Gymboree** chains have several outlets. The most varied shops tend to be in family neighborhoods, especially in Presidio Heights and Noe Valley. For advertisements for children's shops and services (as well as articles of interest and schedules of child-oriented events), pick up *Bay Area Parent* or *Parents' Press*, which are free monthly tabloids. You can find them most often in children's shops.

- *Laurel Village* — **Junior Boot Shop**: 3555 California Street (tel: 751-5444). Longtime children's shoe shop.
- *Noe Valley* — **Little Bean Sprouts**: 3961A 24th Street (tel: 550-1668). Neighborhood shop with clothes and accessories for young children.
- *Noe Valley* — **Small Frys**: 4066 24th Street (tel: 648-3954). Comfortable, affordable clothing for children, newborn to size 7. Famous brands.

- *Noe Valley*—**Peek.a.bootique**: 1306 Castro Street (tel: 641-6192). New and used clothes, equipment, playthings for the smaller set.
- *Presidio Heights*—**Tuffy's Hopscotch**: 3307 Sacramento Street (tel: 440-7599). Good selection of children's shoes.
- *Presidio Heights*—**Jonathan Kaye**: 3615 Sacramento Street (tel: 922-3233). Children's furniture, clothes, knickknacks.
- *Presidio Heights*—**Kindersport**: 3566 Sacramento Street (tel: 563-7778). Junior ski and sports outfitters. Good selection.
- *Presidio Heights*—**Dottie Dolittle**: 3680 Sacramento Street (tel: 563-3244). Upscale, classic children's clothing for play or dress from infants to girls size 14.

... And Their Toys

The internationally known **Toys 'R' Us** has several locations in the city and suburbs, and **F.A.O. Schwarz** at 48 Stockton Street is an outpost of the elegant New York shop (tel: 394-8700). Local toy shops, however, are often learning-centered:

- *Laurel Village*—**Hearth Song**: 3505 California Street (tel: 379-9900). Thousands of toys, dolls, games, books and gifts. Also in East Bay.
- *Noe Valley*—**The Ark**: 3845 24th Street (tel: 821-1257). Well-stocked neighborhood toy shop.
- *Downtown*—**Jeffrey's Toys**: 7 3rd Street (tel: 243-8697). Excellent selection in a well-established toy shop.
- *West Portal/Cow Hollow*—**Ambassador Toys**: 186 W. Portal Avenue (tel: 759-8697). Handcrafted toys, and dolls from around the world, plus a good selection of books and games. Also at 1981 Union (tel: 345-8697).
- *Laurel Village*—**Imaginarium**: 3535 California Street (tel: 387-9885). Educational, imaginative toys, "where bright futures begin."

Sports Clothing and Gear

Most of the pro shops at sports clubs have clothing items and equipment, but these may be more expensive than the large chain stores or small shops dedicated to the sport you are interested in. Sporting tabloids carry ads for sporting goods, and the sports section of daily newspapers announce sales as well. For sporting gear, also try the **REI Coop** at 1338 San Pablo Avenue, in Berkeley (tel: 510/527-4140); and see the North Face, above.

- **Big 5**: Sporting equipment and clothing chain with several stores in the area; in San Francisco, at Lakeshore Plaza, 1533 Sloat Boulevard (tel: 681-4593).
- *Financial District* — **Don Sherwood Golf and Tennis World**: 320 Grant Avenue (tel: 989-5000). Long-established shop selling equipment, clothing, footwear. Also in Walnut Creek and San Jose.
- *Financial District* — **Tennis & Squash Shop of San Francisco**: 424 Clay Street (tel: 956-5666). A large selection of tennis and squash racquets and accessories. Stringing available.
- *Marina* — **MetroSport**: 2198 Filbert Street, at Fillmore (tel: 923-6453). Dedicated to the runner, selling footware, apparel and accessories. Also in Palo Alto and Cupertino.
- *Russian Hill* — **Lombardi Sports**: 1600 Jackson Street, at Polk (tel: 771-0600). Huge sporting goods shop selling equipment and clothes at good prices.
- *SOMA* — **Soma Sports**: 689 3rd Street, at Townsend (tel: 777-2165). Everything for the skier, and other sports as well.
- *Union Square* — **Copeland's Sports**: 901 Market Street (tel: 495-0928; golf tel: 512-7272). Large store with sporting equipment, athletic shoes, active wear, and a large golf selection. Good prices. Also at Stonestown Galleria (tel: 566-5521; golf tel: 566-5544).
- *Union Square* — **McCaffery's Golf Shop**: 80 Sutter Street, at Montgomery (tel: 989-4653). Golf equipment at good prices.

SETTING UP HOUSE

Kitchens and bathrooms in rental houses and apartments come fully equipped with appliances and cupboards, but you may need some smaller appliances, lamps, carpets, or housewares. Three suburban department stores offer reasonable prices on high-quality appliances and are only a short drive from the city center.

- **Sears**: Tanforan Mall, San Bruno (info tel: 650/553-8800)
- **JC Penney**: Westlake Shopping Center, Westlake (info tel: 650/756-3000)

Shops below also offer good prices and an extensive selection. Look, too, for some of the major chains such as **Home Depot**, which is at 2 Colma Boulevard, in Colma (tel: 650/755-9600), or at Costco, described in Chapter Thirteen, which also has kitchen appliances and houseware.

- *Bayshore*—**Goodman Lumber**: 445 Bayshore, between Alemany and Cesar Chavez (tel: 285-2800). Enormous store selling appliances, garden furniture, fixtures, hardware, tools, and housewares. Good prices.
- *Bayshore*—**Peer Light**: 301 Toland Street, near Cesar Chavez (tel: 543-8883). Electrical and lighting supplies, chandeliers, wall lamps, some table lamps. Good prices. Closed Sunday.
- *Civic Center*—**Circuit City**: 1200 Van Ness (tel: 441-1300). Home appliances, televisions, computers and printers, videos, music systems.
- *Mission*—**A&M Carpets**: 98 12th Street, at South Van Ness (tel: 863-1410). Wide variety of carpets on rolls, reproductions of Oriental rugs, discontinued smaller rugs, berbers, all at good prices. Closed Sunday.
- *Mission*—**Cherin's**: 727 Valencia Street (tel: 864-2111). Long-established shop selling kitchen equipment, washers and dryers, built-in appliances. Low prices. Closed Sunday.
- *Richmond*—**Lamps Plus**: 4700 Geary Boulevard (tel: 386-0933).

A vast assortment of lamps and electrical fixtures, at factory-direct prices. Other shops in Bay Area.

- *South of Market* — **House of Louie**: 1045 Bryant, at 9th Street (tel: 621-7100). Excellent prices on all kinds of home appliances, from kitchen and bathroom equipment to televisions, mattresses, and some furniture.
- *South of Market* — **City Lights**: 1585 Folsom, at 12th Street (tel: 863-2020). An extensive selection of lighting fixtures, lamps, bulbs, ceiling fans. Closed Sunday.
- *Sunset* — **ABC Appliances**: 2048 Taraval, at 31st Avenue (tel: 564-8166). Good prices on large appliances, kitchen and bathroom equipment. Open Sunday 10:00 am–2:00 pm.

For kitchen items, try Macy's, hardware stores such as **Cole Hardware** at any of its three locations, or a houseware specialty shop. The **Williams-Sonoma** chain sells expensive, elegant kitchen and diningware, gadgets, and cookbooks; the downtown shop is at 150 Post Street (tel: 362-6904), and there are several others in the city and suburbs. **Crate and Barrel**, the inexpensive homeware chain, also has addresses throughout the area; the San Francisco shop is at 125 Grant Avenue (tel: 986-4000).

- *Bayshore* — **Heritage House**: 2190 Palou Avenue (tel: 285-1331). Brand names on china, glasses, flatware. Good prices. Bridal registry. Closed Sunday.
- *Castro* — **Cliff's Variety**: 479 Castro, near 18th Street (tel: 431-5365). Housewares, hardware, gadgets, knickknacks in a large, friendly store.
- *Chinatown* — **Ginn Wall Hardware**: 1016 Grant Avenue (tel: 982-6307). Large shop selling hardware, plus woks, steam baskets, kitchen implements and everything else you'd want for Chinese cooking.
- *Cow Hollow* — **Fredericksen's Hardware**: 3029 Fillmore Street, near Union (tel: 292-2950). Much more than a hardware store,

Fredericksen's well-stocked shelves hold a good selection of kitchen implements and housewares.

- *Fisherman's Wharf* — **Cost Plus Imports**: 2552 Taylor Street (tel: 928-6200). Inexpensive, colorful housewares, some furniture, baskets of all shapes and sizes, and a packaged gourmet food and wine section.
- *Presidio Heights* — **Forrest Jones**: 3274 Sacramento Street, near Presidio (tel: 567-2483). Packed floor to ceiling with lamps, housewares, gadgets, baskets — wonderful to browse through.
- *South of Market* — **Bed, Bath and Beyond**: 555 9th Street (tel: 252-0490). Brand-names of bed and bath, kitchen equipment, housewares. Also in Oakland.
- *Union Square* — **Sur La Table**: 77 Maiden Lane (tel: 732-7900). Interesting kitchen implements you might not find elsewhere — for people who take cooking seriously. Cookbooks, dishware. Closed Sunday.

Furniture

Furniture stores run the gamut from tiny expensive boutiques to large showrooms in nearby suburbs, to discount clearance centers. Some of the smallest shops are the most interesting, and these often advertise in the Sunday *Examiner Magazine*. Several shops with eclectic collections are focused just below Potrero Hill. National furniture chains have showrooms outside the city center: **Levitz** is off Highway 101 in south San Francisco, **Ethan Allen** is off Highway 101, at the Tiburon exit, and **Breuners** and **Thomasville** have several outlets. **Scandinavian Designs** has outlets in the East, North and South Bay. Check also the three suburban department stores listed above. Within the city, Macy's has an extensive furniture showroom. Look also in the Yellow Pages.

- **Copenhagen**: 1835 Van Ness Avenue (tel: 775-4000). This "house of Danish furniture" has several levels of contemporary furnishings for the home and office.

- **Noriega Furniture**: 1455 Taraval, at 25th Avenue (tel: 564-4110). Upscale furniture outlet with downscale prices. Excellent designer pieces, lamps, wall decorations. What they don't have can be ordered. Open until 9:00 pm Thursday; closed Sunday.
- **Tiempo Interiors**: 383 Rhode Island, at 17th Street (tel: 626-3888). Interesting modern furniture and lighting. Also in San Rafael.

If you are confident of your ability to detect imperfections, or if you are willing to take a color someone else ordered and then returned, or a discontinued style, try a clearance center.

- **Sears Outlet Store**: 1936 West Avenue 140th, San Leandro (tel: 510/895-0546). Major appliances and furniture. One of a kind, out of carton, discontinued, used, scratched and dented merchandise.
- **Macy's Furniture Clearance Center**: 1208 Whipple Road, Union City, about 1 mile east of Highway 880 (tel: 510/441-8833). Enormous depot for canceled orders, floor samples, returned, damaged or slightly soiled merchandise, surplus inventory, etc. Call for days and times.
- **Busvan**: 900 Battery Street (tel: 981-1405). Funky but agreeable shop of basic, bargain furniture, new and used. Look hard and you'll find bargains. Also at 244 Clement, near 4th Avenue (tel: 752-5353).
- **Furniture Express Outlet**: 667 Folsom Street (tel: 495-2848). Scandinavian and contemporary furniture, some unpainted wooden items. Good prices.

Furniture Rental

If you are staying short-term or renting temporarily, you might try renting furniture. Both companies below offer high-quality, attractive furniture and appliances.

- **Cort Furniture Rental**: 447 Battery Street (tel: 982-1077).

Other locations, plus some furniture clearance centers in the suburbs.
- **Brook Furniture Rental**: 500 Washington Street, at Sansome (tel: 956-6008; fax: 956-9390)

House Plants
Flower stands dot the street corners of the city in every season of the year, and flowers and plants can be had at supermarkets and even some hardware stores. Large garden stores can be found in towns throughout the Bay Area. Also take a look at the bustling Flower Market at Sixth and Brannan Streets: some of the wholesalers sell their plants and flowers to retail customers, plus accessories and holiday decorations. The Flower Market is open weekdays from 2:00 am to 2:00 pm.

- **Plant Warehouse**: 1461 Pine Street, near Polk (tel: 885-1515). Good for house plants. Also at 3237 Pierce Street (tel: 345-1597).
- **Red Desert**: 1632 Market Street (tel: 552-2800). Cactus and succulents.
- **Plant'It Earth**: 2215 Market Street, at Sanchez (tel: 626-5082). House plants, orchids, grow light systems, organic soils and foods.
- **Sloat Garden Center**: 2700 Sloat Street (tel: 566-4415). Indoor and outdoor plants, soil, tools, etc.

FILLING YOUR BOOKCASE
Major chains—**Borders, B. Dalton, Walden Books**—offer books at excellent prices, sometimes at a discount with a membership card. But do not neglect the independent bookshops, each with its own character and approach, and all struggling to survive in a market increasingly infiltrated by the chains. Many shops have authors' events. Used book shops—**Green Apple, Acorn**, and **Carroll's**—offer bargains and some great finds.

The annual **San Francisco Book Festival** is held each fall at Fort Mason. The San Francisco Public Library maintains a full schedule of literary events: readings, slide presentations, exhibits, etc. In addition, The Friends of the San Francisco Public Library sponsor a season of prestigious literary events and readings each year; inquire at the library.

North of the city in Corte Madera, **Book Passage** at 51 Tamal Vista Boulevard (tel: 927-0960) is a well-known shop with an extensive travel collection, a cafe, and a regular schedule of author appearances. In Berkeley, **Cody's Books**, at 2454 Telegraph Avenue, is the place to find everything and everybody (tel: 510/845-7852). And south in Menlo Park, try the wonderful **Kepler's Books and Magazines** at 1010 El Camino Real (tel: 650/324-4321).

- *Castro*—**A Different Light Bookstore**: 489 Castro Street (tel: 431-0891). Center for gay and lesbian books, periodicals.
- *Civic Center*—**McDonald's Bookshop**: 48 Turk Street, at Market (tel: 673-2235). Since 1926, this large shop has been selling used books and periodicals—in all categories and languages. Closed Sunday.
- *Civic Center*—**A Clean Well Lighted Place for Books**: 601 Van Ness Avenue (tel: 441-6670). Extensive collection. Readings and authors' events.
- *Downtown*—**Alexander Book Co**: 50 2nd Street (tel: 495-2992). Excellent collection, plus an informative newsletter. Readings at lunchtime. Closed Sunday.
- *Downtown*—**Stacey's**: 581 Market Street (tel: 421-4687). Popular, well-stocked, multi-level bookshop.
- *Japantown*—**Marcus Book Store**: 1712 Fillmore Street (tel: 346-4222). Books, greeting cards, games, and posters of interest to the African American community. Also in Oakland.
- *Hayes Valley*—**Get Lost Travel Books**: 1825 Market Street (tel: 437-0529). Travel books, maps, and travel gear.

- *Mission* — **Modern Times**: 888 Valencia, at 20th Street (tel: 282-9246). Left-wing periodicals, general interest books, books for gays and lesbians, multicultural books for children, and some books in Spanish.
- *North Beach* — **City Lights**: 261 Columbus Avenue, at Broadway (tel: 362-8193). Owned by Lawrence Ferlinghetti, poet laureate of San Francisco. Open until midnight.

Foreign Language Bookstores

- *Chinese* — **Eastwind Books & Arts**: 1435 Stockton Street (tel: 772-5888). Extensive selection of Chinese-language books for adults and children. English-language section upstairs.
- *Chinese* — **China Books and Periodicals**: 2929 24th Street, between Alabama and Florida (tel: 282-2994). Chinese and American books about all facets of China.
- *Chinese* — **New China Books**: 642 Pacific Avenue (tel: 956-0752). General store and Chinese cultural center, with current periodicals, books, videos, and compact discs.
- *European* — **European Book Company**: 925 Larkin Street, near Geary (tel: 474-0626). French, German and Spanish books. Current foreign newspapers and magazines. Closed Sunday.
- *European* — **Café de la Presse**: 352 Grant Avenue at Bush (tel: 398-2680). French, Italian, and German newspapers, periodicals and books, and a cafe that is good for a leisurely cup of coffee.
- *Italian* — **A. Cavalli Italian Bookstore**: 1441 Stockton Street (tel: 421-4219). Italian books, periodicals, a few housewares and knickknacks, guidebooks to Italy, etc. Closed Sunday.
- *Japanese* — **Kinokuniya Bookstore**: 1581 Webster Street, in the Japan Center (tel: 567-7625). Major selection of books and current periodicals in Japanese, some in English.
- *Korean* — **Korean Book Center**: 5633 Geary Boulevard, near 20th Avenue (tel: 221-4250). Books in Korean, newspapers and magazines, cassettes, CDS, and gifts. Closed Sunday.

- *Spanish* — **Iaconi Books**: 970 Tennessee Street (tel: 821-1216). Excellent selection for children, young adults, and adults. Open weekdays.

Computers

Computers shops are everywhere. General electronics shops such as the **Good Guys** and **Circuit City** stock computers, as do the large office supply chains — **Office Depot**, **Office Max**, and **Staples**. The nationwide chains have excellent prices on both Apple and IBM-compatible products. Although local shops may have a smaller inventory, they can often order what you want and in general offer more personal service. See the Yellow Pages under *Computer Dealers* for addresses. For up-to-date information on technology and advertisements for computers and accessories, look for the free tabloids *Computer Currents* or *Micro Times*, both of which can be found in news boxes on city streets.

- **CompUSA**: 760 Market Street (tels: 800/266-7872, 391-9778). Large selection of hardware and software. Also at Tanforan Shopping Center in San Bruno.
- **ComputerWare**: 343 Sansome Street (tel: 362-3010). A dedicated Mac resource, selling hardware, software, peripherals and accessories.

— Chapter Seventeen —

THE ENTERTAINMENT SCENE

THE CITY THAT KNOWS HOW

From world-class opera, ballet, and symphony, to live theater, to American and international films, to rock concerts that draw thousands, to topless bars that draw mostly tourists, and to cabaret, dance and comedy clubs, San Francisco has something for everyone. Restaurants offer jazz, jazz clubs serve food, art galleries and museums serve wine and canapés at their exhibit openings, bookstores host readings by famous authors, and in general, you can find something interesting to do just about any time of day. In this city that celebrates its love of the outdoors, you'll also find lively neighborhood street fairs, outdoor concerts and theater, opera in the parks, and spectacular events on the Bay. And it seems as though there's always a parade or a race somewhere in the city on any given Sunday.

Each district has its own entertainment approach, and this reflects the mood of the area. North Beach, for instance, is known for its coffeehouses and topless bars, Nob Hill for its plush piano bars, and SOMA for its offbeat nightspots and dance clubs. The Castro, of course, is known for its gay hangouts, although gay-friendly bars can be found throughout the city. And the Mission, while remaining distinctly Latino, is beginning to reflect its new popularity with the cyberspace set.

Think also of options in nearby cities, for they are usually less than a half-hour away and often reachable by BART. The **Oakland Ballet**, for example, and the **Berkeley Symphony** both draw major performers on the classical music scene. **Ashkenaz** in Berkeley features Caribbean music, and in Oakland, **Yoshi's** currently performs the best jazz in the area (and offers good sushi as well). The popular **Pacific Film Archives**, also in Berkeley, screens everything from classics to cult favorites.

For outdoor events, pay attention to the weather of the particular area. Sunday afternoon concerts at Stern Grove, for example, may be foggy and windy, even as eastern portions of the city may bask in the sun. Be prepared to bring a jacket to any outdoor event, plus groundsheets for the damp grass.

San Francisco is an "early city," as people who work in the Financial District go to work before dawn. Most people eat dinner before their evening's entertainment, and afterwards head for home. Some clubs remain open after 2:00 am, not serving alcohol, and although the younger set might head to **The Endup** or to 24-hour **Sparky's** for a hamburger, most San Franciscans just go home.

INFINITE RESOURCES

The daily newspapers list that day's (and upcoming) events in their Arts/Datebook sections. On Friday, along with weekend listings, most of the reviews of films and other works that are opening appear; opera and concert reviews generally appear a day or two after the opening. On Sunday, when the San Francisco newspapers issue one combined paper, the *Pink Section* lists the events for the week to come. The free weekly tabloids, *The Bay Guardian* (www.sfbg.com) and *SF Weekly* (www.sfweekly.com), announce all the major events as well, and also more of the small offbeat and eclectic happenings. Advertisements for events project well into the future, sometimes several months. The publications below list and review events.

- *San Francisco*: monthly magazine listing events, public TV, and radio schedules
- *San Francisco Arts Monthly*: extensive calendar of arts and cultural events each month
- *East Bay Express*: an extensive free weekly tabloid covering events in the East Bay
- *Icon*: lesbian monthly, publishing articles and reviews, and listing some events
- *Pacific Sun:* covering events in Marin County
- *Poetry Flash*: a Berkeley publication, lists current literary events
- *Bay Area Reporter*: gay newspaper, listing and reviewing current events
- *San Francisco Bay Times*: gay and lesbian newspaper that lists and reviews events

You can also search on the Internet; as of this writing, these were the most popular sites:

- www.citysearch7.com
- www.sfstation.com
- www.digitalcity.com/sanfrancisco
- www.bayinsider.com
- www.sfgate.com

GETTING TICKETS

Tickets to the most popular events—classical concerts, theater, rock concerts, and sporting events—are snapped up quickly, so, although it's cheaper to buy them at the box office, it is often best to order them through a ticket agency, despite the service charge. Order well in advance. Phone orders are accepted with a credit card number, and tickets can be delivered, mailed, or held at "will-call" at the box office. You may also order tickets on the Internet, from **www.tickets.com**.

- **BASS Tickets**: Tickets for concerts, theater, sporting events, and just about anything else, throughout the Bay Area (tels: 478-2277, 776-1999, 510/762-2277). BASS has outlets at **Tower Records** at Bay and Columbus Streets and **Wherehouse Music** at 165 Kearny.
- **City Box Office**: 153 Kearny Street, at Sutter (tel: 392-4400). Open weekdays and Saturday until 4:00 pm.
- **Tix Bay Area**: A small booth nestled on the sidewalk on the east side of Union Square, along Stockton Street (tel: 433-7827). Half-price tickets for day-of-performance theater and musical events. Cash only. Open 11:00 am–6:00pm Tuesday–Thursday, until 7:00 pm weekends. Closed Sunday and Monday.
- **Mr. Ticket**: 2065 Van Ness Avenue (tel: 292-7238). Tickets for sports, concerts, theater, and all arena events.
- **Ticketmaster**: Phone orders for all tickets (tels: 421-8497, 421-2700).

In addition to Tix above, there are other opportunities for reduced-price or even free tickets. If you volunteer at a theater, for example, you can see the show for free. Students with valid identification can often get reduced-price tickets. Some smaller theaters also offer reduced-price tickets an hour before a performance starts, and a very few allow you to pay what you can at the door.

MUSEUMS

To learn about the city's museums, consult a tourist guidebook, for such guides offer the most extensive information about the collections in each museum. Also stop by the **San Francisco Visitors' Center** (see Calendar below). Many museums host traveling exhibits, and these may require ticket purchase in advance. The newspapers list these special exhibitions. Most museums have one day a month when admission is free.

If you are interested in volunteering your expertise at one of the city's many museums, libraries, or cultural institutions, call the San Francisco Volunteer Center, or the Volunteer Centers of the Bay Area, both mentioned in Chapter Nine.

- **Business Art Council**: 235 Montgomery Street (tel: 352-8832). Coordinates volunteers to use their professional expertise in museums, theaters, and other arts-related non-profits.
- **Contemporary Extension**: 151 3rd Street (tel: 357-4086). Member-run organization for the young professional who wants to expand knowledge and take an active role in supporting the **Museum of Modern Art (MOMA)**.
- **Friends of the San Francisco Public Library** (tel: 557-4256). Friends volunteer at the library, help operate the several bookshops, and support the library in other ways.

To get the most out of cultural activities, you might attend "preview" seminars and lectures focusing on upcoming performances and exhibits. Universities offer courses on the season's opera selections, and these are often listed in the opera program. In addition, the **Junior League of San Francisco** sponsors each year a series of free preview lectures concerning that evening's performance either at ACT (American Conservatory Theater) or the San Francisco Ballet. Lectures are given by the play's director or by people connected with the ballet. Call for a schedule (tel: 775-4100).

THEATER

As you would imagine, San Francisco's theater scene is wildly diverse, from Shakespeare in the Park to experimental efforts in tiny, offbeat venues, and to Broadway musicals that stay around for years. Some theaters offer readings of new works, which of course vary in style and quality. Look for *Callboard*, which is available at Tix and sometimes in bookstores.

Generally, live theater is performed Tuesday–Sunday, and Mondays are "dark." On Sundays, there are matinees at the important theaters, except at "Berkeley Rep," described below. Some touring companies come through with short runs, and their schedules may be different. Note that most theaters use volunteers in some capacity or other, often as ushers. If this interests you, call the theaters directly for information.

- **ACT (American Conservatory Theater)**, at 415 Geary Street, is the city's major local theater company (tel: 749-2228). Pronounced "ay-cee-tee," not "act", ACT offers both classics and new works, and features visiting artists along with the local cast. Generally the annual repertory performs eight plays, from fall through spring. Subscriptions and single performance tickets are available.
- **Berkeley Repertory Theatre**, at 2025 Addison Street, near the Berkeley BART station, is the East Bay's premier theater company, and many San Franciscans subscribe as well as to ACT (tel: 510/845-4700). "Berkeley Rep" performs both classic and contemporary works. The season is fall to spring, with special summer performances.

Three theaters—**The Curran, Golden Gate**, and **The Orpheum**—are known for "best of Broadway" plays and musicals that have either played in New York or are heading there. They also host some local performances. Tickets may be had from the joint ticket office (info tel: 551-2000; telephone orders tel: 512-7770) or from BASS. **Marines Memorial Theater** also hosts

Broadway musicals and some local productions (tel: 771-6900).

Fort Mason, the former military installation turned cultural center, with its three theaters, presents innovative drama, new music, unconventional plays, children's entertainment, imaginative dance, and more. Look for performances at the **Bayfront Theater** (tel: 392-4400), the **Cowell Theater** (tel: 441-3400), and the **Magic Theater** (tel: 441-8822). The **Young Performer Theater** highlights aspiring actors (tel: 346-5550).

Beach Blanket Babylon, at 678 Beach Blanket Babylon Boulevard (Green Street), is a rather zany musical spoof of pop culture (and local celebrities) which has been running for 25 years, changing its content to fit the times (tel: 421-4222). There are also a few theater festivals; check newspapers for dates.

- June — **In the Street Festival**: Street festival in the Tenderloin celebrates street theater and performance art.
- September — **California Shakespeare Festival**: Golden Gate Park and other venues around the Bay Area. Bring a sweater.
- September — **Fringe Festival**: Ten days of just about anything you can imagine, with local and visiting performers and companies. In various venues around the city.
- September–October — **Solo Mio Festival**: Held at theaters at Fort Mason, this festival features one-person shows.
- July–September — **Mime Troupe in the Park**: First show held at Dolores Park and other city parks.

CLASSICAL MUSIC

The San Francisco Symphony holds its concerts at Louise M. Davies Symphony Hall, at Van Ness Avenue, at Grove (ticket office tel: 864-6000; ticket fax: 554-0108). The regular season runs from September to June, with special events year-round. Long-time subscribers retain the best seats from year to year, but as the building dates only from 1982 (upgraded in 1992), the acoustics throughout the hall are very good. Occasionally tickets become available at the last minute, and some inexpensive Center Terrace seats (to the rear of the stage) are sold two hours before performances. The Symphony issues an annual schedule that details all ticket options, including dates for the open rehearsals, which take place on Wednesday mornings, about once a month; tickets cost $15 and there is no reserved seating. If you are interested in the symphony, consider joining the groups below:

- **San Francisco Symphony Volunteer Council**: Davies Symphony Hall (tel: 552-8000). Volunteer behind the scenes at the gift shop, in the office, with the Concerts for Kids Program, and more. **Symphonix** is the young professionals group. It offers meetings, musical programs, social events, discounts on dinner and concerts.

San Francisco Opera draws international stars for its lavish productions, which are staged at the War Memorial Opera House: 301 Van Ness Avenue (tel: 864-3330). The season usually begins in mid-September. Subscribers renew their seats from year to year, but single tickets can be had, and occasionally people stand outside at performance time trying to sell single tickets for that evening's performance or others in the future. Tickets can cost up to $145 for a box seat, yet cheaper alternatives exist and standing room is available. The box office is at 199 Grove Street. If you are interested in becoming involved in the opera, consider joining these groups:

- **San Francisco Opera Guild Volunteer Program**: 301 Van Ness Avenue (tel: 565-6433). Volunteer throughout the opera world: in the gift shop, administrative offices, costume shop, or in other ways behind the scenes. **Bravo!** is a young professionals' group that participates in a variety of events related to the opera: receptions, benefits, etc (tel: 565-3285).

San Francisco Ballet, the oldest ballet company in America, performs new works and classical ballet. Its regular season takes place at the Opera House, after the opera season closes, generally from February until June (tel: 865-2000). Special events include the ballet's annual performances of Tchaikovsky's *Nutcracker Suite* at Christmas. Subscriptions may be customized to only the performances you choose. Although tickets go quickly, sometimes there are single tickets available, and students with identification may buy discounted tickets on the afternoon of the performance.

- **Encore!** 455 Franklin Street (tel: 553-4634). Young professionals attend social and educational events, get discounted tickets to the ballet, etc.

San Francisco is also known for its locally based dance troupes. Look for performances of the **ODC Theater** and the **Margaret Jenkins Dance Company**, which performs at Yerba Buena and tours worldwide. **Smuin Ballets** performs at Fort Mason's Cowell Theater.

And More ...

Performing groups have their own seasons and specialties. **San Francisco Performances**, a major presenter of chamber music, has a fall-spring schedule. **The Women's Philharmonic** and students of the **San Francisco Conservatory of Music** have regular concerts. Look also for performances of San Francisco's own **Kronos Quartet**, which for more than 25 years has performed 20th century music from Bela Bartok to Duke Ellington.

Gay men might also want to audition or volunteer for the **San Francisco Gay Men's Chorus**: 400 Castro Street (tel: 863-4472). The chorus presents three major concerts each year, plus outreach concerts for community groups. Auditions for singers are held twice yearly; inquire at the SFGMC office. Volunteers are always needed to keep track of wardrobe, ticket sales, production, etc.

- **Stern Grove Midsummer Music Festival**: 44 Page Street, Suite 600 (tel: 252-6252). Eleven free outdoor concerts in a

lovely eucalyptus stand at Stern Grove, off 19th Avenue and Sloat. Popular with all San Franciscans—from the counterculture to the highly cultured. Be prepared for fog. Offerings range from classical to blues, from ballet to jazz. For children there's a nice playground, and for golfers, a putting green.
- **Midsummer Mozart Festival** held in Davies Hall and in Berkeley, at the Congregational Church (tel: 954-0850)
- **Classical Philharmonic**: 1155 East 14th Street, Suite 215 (tel: 989-6873, 510/352-3945, 925/484-9783). Varied repertoire for the chamber symphony performed December–May in San Francisco, Pleasanton, and Castro Valley.
- **Sunday Concerts in the Park**: Band shell in front of the California Academy of Sciences. Every Sunday in the summer, the Golden Gate Park Band gives a free concert at 1:00 pm. Great for a picnic.
- **Noontime Concerts**: International touring musicians play half-hour classical music programs on Tuesday and Thursday at 12:30 pm at Old Saint Mary's Cathedral at 600 California Street, and Wednesday at 12:30 pm at St. Patrick's Church, at 756 Mission.
- **Old First Concerts** are held year-round on Friday evenings and Sunday afternoons at the Old First Church, at 1751 Sacramento Street (tel: 864-3330). From jazz and world music to chamber and choral, this series is inexpensive and extremely popular.

DINNER WITH MUSIC

Dozens of restaurants play live music, and conversely dozens of live music venues serve good food. Newspapers usually have advertisements not only for supper clubs, but for popular brunch restaurants—**Pier 23** or **Scott's Embarcadero**, for example—that also have live music. Don't forget the East Bay, where **Yoshi's** serves the hottest jazz and coolest sushi. A few other suggestions:

The Entertainment Scene

- **Biscuits and Blues**: 401 Mason Street, at Geary (tel: 292-2583). Blues club serving Southern food—biscuits, shrimp, catfish, chicken, and corn fritters—and live music every night. Closed Monday and Tuesday.
- **Bix**: 56 Gold Street, between Sansome and Montgomery (tel: 433-6300). Excellent menu, cool piano and jazz.
- **Black Cat**: 501 Broadway, at Kearny (tel: 981-2233). Lunch, dinner and jazz until 2:00 nightly.
- **Bruno's**: 2389 Mission Street (tel: 648-7701). Old Italian restaurant reborn by adding live music and a dance floor. Closed Sunday.
- **Café Claude**: 7 Claude Lane, off Bush at Kearny (tel: 392-3505). French food in a casual atmosphere. Live jazz evenings except Wednesday and Sunday.
- **Enrico's**: 504 Broadway (tel: 982-6223). Sidewalk cafe in North Beach serving good food and live jazz.
- **Piaf's**: 1686 Market Street (tel: 864-3700). French cuisine and a lively cabaret performance.

ROCK CONCERTS

When touring rock groups and performers come to the area, they perform at large concert halls and arenas. Events are publicized well in advance and tickets sell quickly, so check ticket agencies as soon as you see the ad for a concert that appeals to you. On the Internet, try www.sfbayconcerts.com or the **Be-At-Line** after 2:00 pm for up-to-the-minute information (tel: 626-4087).

- **The Fillmore**: 1805 Geary Boulevard
- **Bill Graham Civic Auditorium**: 99 Grove Street
- **The Warfield**: 982 Market Street
- **Great American Music Hall**: 859 O'Farrell Street

Most concert sites around the Bay Area are accessible by public transportation, and most have extensive parking facilities.

- **Concord Pavillion**: 200 Kirker Pass Road, Concord
- **Oakland Coliseum**: Hegenberger Road and I-880, Oakland
- **Cow Palace**: Geneva Avenue and Santos Street, Daly City
- **Shoreline Amphitheater**: 1 Amphitheater Parkway, Mountain View
- **Zellerbach Hall**: University of California, Berkeley
- **Greek Theater**: Outdoors at the University of California, Berkeley

To hear music at the clubs in the city, check the listings above or *SF Weekly* or the *Bay Guardian*, both of which publish lists of venues. Many of the best rock clubs—**Slim's**, **Maritime Hall**, **Bottom of the Hill**, **Chameleon**, and **Paradise Lounge**—are South of Market. **Bimbo's**, which presents live jazz and blues, is in North Beach, on Columbus. Most of the clubs charge admission, ranging from $3 to $40, and a few require the purchase of two drinks. Not all take credit cards.

BLUES

The weekend-long **San Francisco Blues Festival** takes place late in September on the Great Meadow at Fort Mason. In addition to Biscuit and Blues and Pier 23 mentioned above, blues clubs such as **Blues Stop** and **Boom Boom Room** are extremely popular.

JAZZ

Jazz can be found just about anywhere, at any time, especially South of Market or in the Mission. Elsewhere, check the clubs such as **Bimbo's**, **Elbo Room**, **Storyville**, **Hotel Utah**, and **El Rio**, mentioned below. **Rasselas**, near staid Pacific Heights, swings until 1:30 am. Don't neglect jazz in the East Bay, however—**Yoshi's**, mentioned above, and **Kimball's East**, in Emeryville. In addition, jazz festivals play an important part of the musical year.

- July—**San Francisco Summer Jazz Festival**: Free noontime concerts

THE ENTERTAINMENT SCENE

- July—**Fillmore Street Fair**: Jazz and All that Art on Fillmore
- Mid-September—**San Francisco Jazz Festival**: Two weeks of jazz, in venues around the city

DANCE

From salsa to swing, you can find dance opportunities in dozens of venues around the city, whether live to a band, with a disc jockey, or in places where there's just a jukebox and an empty space in front of it. When you check out dance clubs, find out hours of opening and cover charges.

- **1015 Folsom** (recorded information tel: 431-1200). Three rooms of loud danceable music, often voted the best dance spot in the city.
- **Broadway Studios**: 435 Broadway (tel: 291-0333). Dance or take dance lessons. Three bars, large wooden ballroom-style dance floors.
- **Café du Nord**: 2170 Market Street (tel: 296-8696). Old speakeasy now offering salsa, swing, cabaret, and theme nights.
- **DNA Lounge**: 374 11th Street (tel: 626-1409). Trendy locale, cutting-edge live music, DJ spinners on Fridays.
- **Metronome Ballroom**: 1830 17th Street (tel: 252-9000). Dance lessons and general dancing in a real ballroom below Potrero Hill.
- **Roccapulco**: 3140 Mission Street, near Cesar Chavez (tel: 648-6611). Salsa is the beat in this two-story club, performed by visiting international groups.
- **Six**: 60 6th Street (tel: 863-1221). Not a great neighborhood, but a great dance venue. Two levels, a comfortable lounge, and always interesting music.
- **Sound Factory**: 525 Harrison, at 1st Street (tel: 339-8686). In a warehouse-type space, a variety of music type and a party atmosphere.

FILMS

Films play a major part in the entertainment life of San Franciscans: first-run American movies, major foreign films, independent art films, and revivals of some of those that have been overlooked or almost forgotten. Almost all the newly released films can be found in different venues at different times, making it convenient to see one where and when you want. At the most popular films, however, lines can be long, so be prepared to go early and to wait. Often there are two lines: the "ticket holders" line for people who have already bought their tickets, and the line for those waiting to purchase them.

Most of the major movie theaters are multi-screen. The largest (so far) is the **Sony Metreon** at Yerba Buena Gardens, with 15 screens, a giant IMAX screen, eight restaurants, theme and game areas, and retail stores. **AMC Van Ness** has 10 screens; the **AMC Kabuki-8** has eight. Even some of the oldest cinemas have split their space to allow two screens. In a very few — **Opera Plaza** and the **Lumiere** — some of the screening rooms (and screens) are quite small, so there, too, if you think a film will be crowded, go early to get a seat.

New films open on Friday. Film schedules are printed in every daily newspaper, and on Friday there are film reviews. The *San Francisco Chronicle* prints pictures of a little man in a chair next to each review: if he's shown dozing, you might want to skip the picture, but if he's shown applauding wildly or jumping out of his chair, you can expect the film to be a success. San Franciscans often talk about movie reviews in terms of the "little man." The free weekly newspapers — *The Bay Guardian* and *SF Weekly* — also review films according to their newspapers' slants, as do the gay newspapers, *The Bay Area Reporter* and the *Bay Times*.

Interesting and Unusual

Some cinemas are known for their particular mix. **The Castro** hosts revivals and many of the film festivals during the year.

The extensive Landmark chain—**Bridge**, **Clay**, **Embarcadero**, **Lumiere**, and **Opera Plaza**—shows the best of the foreign films, as well as first-run American movies. (At Opera Plaza, you can often find films that were at other theaters for a while; catch them here before they disappear altogether.) And some small "cult" moviehouses—**Roxie** and **Red Vic**—show unusual foreign films, "art" films, and other independent films that might not be commercial enough to hit the bigger houses.

Films are also sometimes screened at museums such as the **Museum of Modern Art** or at the **Yerba Buena Gardens Center for the Arts**, generally in conjunction with a current exhibit. Yerba Buena also shows the avant-garde and experimental films of the **San Francisco Cinematheque** on Thursday nights; on Sundays their films are shown at the **San Francisco Art Institute** on Chestnut Street.

Foreign Films

Foreign films are shown with subtitles, not dubbed. In addition to the cinemas (including the World Theater on Broadway, which shows films in English and Chinese), check the foreign language institutes, which schedule regular showings of films, which may or may not have subtitles: **Goethe Institute, Alliance Française,** and the **Istituto Italiano di Cultura.** A new phenomenon, **Foreign Cinema** at 2534 Mission, near 21st Street, is a French bistro that shows foreign movie classics on a large white wall overlooking the dining area (tel: 648-7600). Reserve in advance; closed Monday.

Prices and Bargains

Most theaters offer a "bargain matinee" for the first performance of the day. The Landmark chain offers a multi-ticket discount coupon, and AMC theaters have a card that offers a free film after 20 visits. A regular seat currently costs $7–8 for adults. Seniors are allowed discounts at any showing. AMC theaters consider people 55 and over to be seniors, but at other theaters people are considered seniors at either 62 or 65.

You can buy tickets in advance for major shows. AMC theaters have a ticket machine in the lobbies. Otherwise, you can either go to the box office and purchase your ticket for a screening later that day or you can call **Movie Phone** and order tickets to films and festivals by credit card (tel: 777-3456). There is a $1 surcharge on each ticket.

Film Festivals

Almost every month there are film festivals, some lasting one week and others two weeks. Some draw the entire city to major movie houses, some are revivals shown in smaller venues. Look for festivals that celebrate local film and video makers, of which there are many. Films to be shown have their dates and venues announced well in advance, and often they are screened in more than one theater around the Bay Area. Film festivals are eagerly awaited, so buy your tickets well in advance.

Outside the city, the October **Mill Valley Film Festival** shows dozens of independent and international films, in addition to hosting a "videofest" of interactive media programs. Other well-regarded festivals in the area are the **Bay Area Women's Film Festival** in Berkeley in March and the **Black Filmworks Festival** in Oakland in September.

- Mid-March—**Asian-American Film Festival**, at the Kabuki and Castro theaters
- Mid-April—**San Francisco International Film Festival**: Two weeks of films, held mainly at the Kabuki, and also at other venues
- Sometime in April—**Italian Film Festival**: Various venues around the city
- Late in June—**International Lesbian and Gay Film Festival**, coinciding with Gay Pride celebration. Generally at the Castro, Victoria and Roxie theaters.

- Sometime in July—**San Francisco Jewish Film Festival**: International films with a Jewish theme, generally at the Castro, in Berkeley, and in Mill Valley.
- Sometime in September—**Festival Cine Latino**, usually held at the Victoria and at Yerba Buena Gardens.
- Mid-November—**American Indian Film Festival**, held at the Palace of Fine Arts Theater.
- Sometime in November—The **Film Arts Festival of Independent Cinema** shows works from Bay Area filmmakers. At several venues, including the Castro and the Roxie, plus the Main Library and Asian Art Museum.

COMEDY CLUBS

In addition to the several comedy clubs, each August San Francisco hosts a **Comedy Celebration Day**, which takes place in Sharon Meadow of Golden Gate Park.

- **Cobb's Comedy Club**: 2801 Leavenworth Street, in the Cannery (tel: 928-4320)
- **The Punch Line**: 444 Battery Street, at Washington (tel: 397-7573)

GAY AND LESBIAN RESOURCES

For a comprehensive look at gay and lesbian San Francisco, visit A Different Light Bookshop or Modern Times (see Chapter Sixteen), or **Bernal Books,** the well-stocked general bookstore for the Bernal Heights community, at 401 Cortland Avenue (tel: 550-0293). Look for a gay/lesbian guidebook, such as *Fodor's Gay Guide to San Francisco and the Bay Area* by Andrew Collins. Some others, such as *Time Out: San Francisco*, have sections on gay- and lesbian-friendly venues.

To find out what's going on currently, refer to the daily newspapers and the well-known publications listed at the beginning of this chapter; look also for *Frontiers*, *Creampuff*, *Odyssey*, and *Q San*

Francisco, all of which have news, articles, ads, and information about events. In addition to the general websites also listed above, you can search gay-specific sites for information (www.webcastro.com; www.qsanfrancisco.com).

- **Pacific Center** acts as a resource for gay/lesbian information throughout the entire Bay Area (tel: 510/548-8283). Open 4–10 pm weekdays, and 11 am–5 pm Saturdays.
- **James C. Hormel Gay and Lesbian Center**, at the San Francisco Main Public Library (tel: 557-4566). Books, periodicals and articles of interest for the gay/lesbian life.
- **Women's Building**: 3543 18th Street (tel: 431-1180). Community center offering meeting space to several lesbian and feminist groups, plus hosting its own events, meetings and seminars for women. Free publications are generally found in the lobby.
- **Lesbian/Gay/Bisexual/Transgender Community Center**: 1800 Market Street. Not yet open as of this writing, the center is planned as the community's central information point.
- **Lesbian & Gay Historical Society of Northern California**: 973 Market Street (tel: 777-5455). Historical archives.
- **Eureka Valley-Harvey Milk Library**: 3555 16th Street (tel: 554-9445). This branch of the Public Library has a good collection of gay/lesbian materials, including the current local and national gay newspapers.

For the Men ...

In terms of gay venues, there are hundreds of gyms, bars, shops, and restaurants that are either completely gay or gay-friendly. Although the Castro now seems to be permanently the heart of the community, the Polk Gulch area is becoming popular once again (**Tango Tango**, **The Giraffe**, and **1100 Polk Club**). In 1999, the *San Francisco Chronicle's* "Readers' Choice Poll" rated **The Cafe** at 2367 Market Street and the nearby **Café Flore** at 2298 Market as the city's best gay hangouts. The *Bay Guardian* rated **The Stud** at 399 9th Street as the best gay bar.

For the Women ...
Although two women together have always been accepted more readily than two men together, since the feminist movement of the seventies, lesbians have felt more at home in Berkeley and in Oakland. Currently, the lesbian presence in San Francisco is increasing, especially in the Inner Mission and Bernal Heights. In recent *Chronicle* and *Bay Guardian* surveys, **The Lexington Club** at 3464 19th Street, between Mission and Valencia, was rated as the "best lesbian hangout." **The Cafe** was rated second, and the **Wild Side West** at 424 Cortland Avenue, in Bernal Heights, was rated third. **El Rio**, at 3158 Mission Street, is popular for dancing to live music with a distinctly Latin rhythm; it sports a mixed clientele. The bookshops with lesbian sections and the gay/lesbian tabloids should have some information about what's currently hot; watch also for information on events, especially in the *Icon* and *Bay Times*; *Girlfriends* is issued monthly. You can also access www.qsanfrancisco.com.

CALENDAR OF NATIONAL HOLIDAYS AND LOCAL EVENTS

An international city, San Francisco celebrates the festivals of many countries. Some festival dates may vary from year to year, depending on the calendar. As for local events, do not forget that San Franciscans love to party, and that tourists expect—and get—a lively scene. You can find a parade, race, or walk in honor of a charitable cause almost every weekend of the year. Look for each neighborhood's weekend street fair, for each one reflects the ambience of that district. It would be impossible to list them all here, but some of the major events are listed below, and the film and theater festivals above. Look also in the daily newspapers, the *Bay Guardian* and the *SF Weekly* for festivals and fairs in towns throughout the Bay Area, especially the county fairs in summer. And, you can get cultural event information from the Visitors' Information Center on the lower level of Hallidie Plaza, at Market Street and Powell, or if you have the patience to sit through a long recorded message, by phone (tel: 391-2000; 24-hour recorded info tel: 391-2001; www.sfvisitor.org).

Many national holidays are celebrated on Monday, no matter the actual date they commemorate, in order to give workers a long weekend break. On national holidays, all government offices are closed, including the Post Office, but except for Christmas and Easter, the largest stores and supermarkets may be open for at least part of the day. Banks are closed on national holidays but by law may not be closed more than three days in a row, and on any day cash can be had from the ubiquitous ATM machines. National holidays are printed in boldface type.

January
- **1: New Year's Day**
- **Third Monday: Martin Luther King Jr Day**. In honor of the civil rights leader slain in 1968.
- Late month or early February: Tet Festival. Near the Civic Center. Multicultural event, with Asian, Latino and African American groups celebrating Vietnamese New Year.

February
- **Third Monday: President's Day**
- Dates vary: Chinese New Year. A long parade, marching bands, dragons, and lots of firecrackers.
- San Francisco Ballet season begins.

March
- Sunday closest to March 17: St. Patrick's Day Parade. All the Irish bars celebrate well into the night.
- Late month: Tulip Festival at the tourist attraction Pier 39.

April
- Mid-month: Cherry Blossom Festival at the Japan Center. Parade, arts and crafts, tea ceremonies, performances, all held on two successive weekends.
- Baseball season begins: Opening games for San Francisco Giants and Oakland A's.

May
- 5: Cinco de Mayo: Latin American festival and parade at the Civic Center and at 24th and Mission.
- Third Sunday: Bay to Breakers Race. A San Francisco "happening," drawing 100,000 runners, would-be runners, people in outrageous costumes, people in no costumes at all. A 12 km course from the Bay to the Ocean.
- Opening day on the Bay: Official sailing season begins, although people sail all year, weather permitting.
- Odd-numbered years only: Black and White Ball. The whole city comes to this charity benefit held in various venues. Wear only black or white, dance, and listen to the music.
- **Last Monday: Memorial Day**
- Memorial Day Weekend: Carnaval. Lively festival in the Mission district.

June
- First weekend: Union Street Festival. Extremely upscale arts and crafts fair, plus entertainment, food, etc.
- Second weekend: Haight Street Fair. Typically Haight, but with excellent food stalls of all sorts.
- Fourth Sunday: Lesbian, Gay, Bisexual, Transgender Pride Celebration. Second largest annual event in the State (after the Rose Bowl Parade), with 200 floats, people strolling alone or as couples, celebration until all hours.
- Dates vary: San Francisco Ethnic Dance Festival. Dozens of ethnic dance troupes and soloists perform at the Palace of Fine Arts.

- All summer: Stern Grove Midsummer Music Festival. Free Sunday concerts in Stern Grove.
- June and July: Midsummer Mozart Festival, held at Davies Hall and in Berkeley.

July
- **4: Independence Day**
- Midmonth: San Francisco Marathon. Twenty-six mile course from Golden Gate Park to the Civic Center.
- Dates vary: *Nihonmachi* Street Fair in Japantown. Entertainment, food, crafts.

August
- Date varies: Football season begins. San Francisco 49ers opening game.

September
- **First Monday: Labor Day**
- Labor Day Weekend: A La Carte, à la Park — Sharon Meadow, Golden Gate Park. Huge food fair, with offerings from some of San Francisco's popular restaurants. Tastings of California's best wines, as well.
- Latino Summer Fiesta: 24th Street and Mission; formerly celebrating Mexican Independence Day, it's now a general patriotic Latino festival. Crafts, booths, food, entertainment.
- Mid-month: San Francisco Jazz Festival.
- September–October: San Francisco Shakespeare Festival. Free Shakespeare plays outdoors at Liberty Tree Meadow in Golden Gate Park. Dress warmly.
- San Francisco Opera and Symphony season begins; also Opera in Golden Gate Park on the first Sunday of the season.
- Third weekend: San Francisco Blues Festival at the Great Meadow at Fort Mason.
- San Francisco Fair: Check date by calling 391-200.
- End of month: Folsom Street Fair. Certainly one of the city's

more colorful and eccentric neighborhood fairs. Can draw more than 100,000 people.

October
- Early in month: Blessing of the Animals at St. Boniface Church, near the Civic Center. On the Feast Day of St. Francis of Assisi, the patron saint of animals, the annual pet-blessing event.
- Early in month: Immigrant Pride Day. Since 1995, a threefold event celebrating Immigrant Pride Day, Dia de la Raza, and Indigenous People's Day, at 24th Street, from Mission Street to Bryant.
- First Sunday in October: Castro Street Fair. Gay and lesbian festival, drawing all of San Francisco.
- **Second Monday: Columbus Day**. Celebrates the Italian heritage in San Francisco. Parade on Columbus Avenue, festivities, a fair at Fisherman's Wharf, and a blessing of the fishing fleet. Usually the U.S. Navy comes to town for Fleet Week, and The Blue Angels, precision Navy flyers, take to the skies over San Francisco.
- Closest to full moon: Chinese Moon Festival, annual harvest event in Chinatown.
- Mid-month: Open Studios. Artists all over town open their studios to the public.
- Toward the end of the month. San Francisco Book Festival. San Francisco Bay Area Book Council sponsors a major independent bookseller event at Fort Mason. Books on display and some at bargain prices, book signings, readings, etc.
- 31: Halloween. Celebrated around the Civic Center, but also in the Castro, with outrageous costumes. This is one of the major events of the year.

November
- 2: *Dia de los Muertos*: Mexican fiesta, exhibits, and lively parade to honor the dead. In the Mission.

- **11: Veterans Day**. Parade along Market Street to the Ferry Building.
- **Fourth Thursday: Thanksgiving Day**
- Late in month: Run to the Far Side. Walk or run, dressed in a costume depicting your favorite cartoon character from Gary Larson's *Far Side* cartoons. Benefit for the California Academy of Sciences.

December

- Dates vary: Christmas Tree and Chanukah Menorah lighting in various venues around the city—Union Square, Ghirardelli Square, Fell and Stanyan Streets.
- Mid-month: Sing-it-yourself-Messiah, at Louise M. Davies Symphony Hall. The San Francisco Conservatory of Music gives people the chance to sing Handel's *Messiah*.
- Mid-month: Nutcracker Suite performed by San Francisco Ballet.
- **25: Christmas Day**

THE AUTHOR

Frances Gendlin has held leadership positions in magazine and book publishing. She was editor and publisher of *Sierra*, the magazine of the Sierra Club, a worldwide environmental organization, and was the association's director of public affairs. As executive director of the Association of American University Presses, she represented the 100-member publishing houses to the public and fostered scholarly publishing interests. In 1997, she wrote *Rome At Your Door* (also published as *Living & Working Abroad: Rome*), a widely read guide to living in that city. In 1998, using the same format, she wrote *Paris At Your Door* (*Living & Working Abroad: Paris*).

While she was growing up, her family moved several times to different areas of the United States, each with its own characteristics and culture, climate, and cuisine. This has led her to appreciate many new cultures, to wonder about their differences and similarities to her own, and to try and understand them. All her life she has enjoyed travel and new adventures, meeting interesting people and making new friends.

After having lived in San Francisco for twenty years, Frances Gendlin now has moved to New York. She owns a freelance editorial business. She evaluates manuscripts and guides, helps writers with their projects, and teaches English and business writing to foreign professionals, both in the United States and abroad. Thanks to the advent of the modem and fax, she can work virtually anywhere in the world. She has thus been able to arrange her professional life to accommodate her love of travel. Currently, she spends part of each year in Rome and Paris.

INDEX

African Americans 12, 41, 56, 117
airports: Oakland International 61
apartments 72, 74, 77–79
avenues 53–55

banking 90–91
bars 239–41
bicycling 164, 250–51
books, recommended:
   bargain-hunting 271
   Bay Area guide 247
   food guides 182
   gay-friendly entertainment venues 300–2
   history 21
   tourist guide 21
   wine reference guides 234–35
bookshops 94
business:
   networking 156–58
   office space 158–59
   start-up guidance organizations 156
   tourism 154–55
   U.S. Small Business Administration (SBA) 155
cars 110–11; *see* driving
child care 128–29
children: enrichment programs 129–30; *see also* schools, shopping
Chinese 15, 32–33, 35, 54, 117, 133
citizenship, US 107
climate 22–23, 60
coffeehouses 202–203
counties 59, 61, 63–66
credit cards 91, 187

dance classes 260, 296
Davis, Gray 115
dentists 147
districts and neighborhoods:
   Alamo Square 41, 81
   Bayview 57
   Bernal Heights 26, 49–50, 83
   Buena Vista 52
   Castro 25, 26, 47–49, 83
   Central Waterfront 43
   Chinatown 26, 31–34, 133
   Civic Center 29
   Cole Valley 52, 81
   Cow Hollow 25, 38–39, 81
   Crocker Amazon 56, 57
   Diamond Heights 25, 51, 81
   Embarcadero 34
   Excelsior 56
   Financial District 29–30
   Forest Knolls 52
   Glen Park 51
   Haight 26, 52–53, 72
   Hayes Valley 42, 83
   Hunters Point 57, 72
   Japantown 40–41
   Lakeshore 55
   Marina 38–39, 81, 83
   Miraloma Park 51
   Mission 25, 26, 44–46, 71, 72, 81, 133
   Multimedia Gulch 43, 47
   Nob Hill 25, 30–31
   Noe Valley 49, 83
   North Beach 35–36
   Ocean Beach 54
   Oceanview Merced Ingleside (OMI) 55–56
   Pacific Heights 25, 26, 39, 81, 83
   Parkside 55
   Parnassus Heights 52
   Pine Lake Park 55
   Portola 56
   Potrero Hill 26, 46–47, 83
   Presidio Heights 39–40
   Richmond 54
   Russian Hill 25, 36, 38, 83
   Sherwood Forest 51, 81
   SOMA (South of Market Area) 29, 42, 43, 83
   South Beach 42
   South Park 43
   St. Francis Wood 51

Sunset 53, 54, 133
Sutro Heights 52
Telegraph Hill 36–37
Tenderloin 29, 72, 133
Twin Peaks 50–51
Union Square 27, 43
Visitacion Valley 56
West Portal 51
Western Addition 25, 26, 40–41, 72
Westwood Highlands 51
Westwood Park 51
Diversity Immigrant lottery 105–106
dogs 263
drinking age 242
driving 170–72
    buying a car 174
    car registration 173
    DMV (California Department of Motor Vehicles) 174
    DUI, DWI (drink driving) 173
    license 174
    seat belt rules 171–72

earthquakes 23–24, 26, 27, 29, 30, 38, 42
education: extended courses and workshops 137–38; *see also* schools
electricity 86–87
embassies and consulates 108–109
employment:
    agencies 153–54
    career guidance 152–53
    illegal 102
    job advertisements 152
    résumé 151
entertainment:
    ballet 291–92
    blues 295
    classical music 290–93
    comedy clubs 300
    dancing 296
    films 297–300
    foreign films 298
    Internet sites 286
    jazz 295–96
    movie reviews 297
    newspaper listings 286
    rock concerts 294–95
    theaters 289–90
    tickets 287, 299
environmental associations 247

fitness clubs 252–53
flat: definition, compared with apartment 74

garbage disposal 90
gays 12, 13–15, 48, 292
    entertainment resources 300–302
    Harvey Milk 48
    religious centers for 97
Gold Rush 15, 25, 33
Golden Gate Bridge 10
green card 107
gyms 253; *see also* fitness clubs, sports

hair salons 92–93
Haraszthy, Agoston 233
health:
    alternative medicine 145–46
    emergency services 142
    free clinics 146–47
    see insurance
hippies 52, 53
HIV/AIDS 148
holidays 302–307
hospitals 142–43
housing:
    buying 79–83
    Brown Shingles 81
    California Bungalow 81
    Craftsman bungalows 67, 81
    Queen Anne 48, 50, 81
    retirement complexes 85
    statistics 68
    student 84
    Victorians 41, 45, 48, 49, 51, 53, 81–82

ice cream 204
identification cards: International Student Identity Card (ISIC) 105
immigration 99–100
    past immigration policies 33
Immigration and Naturalization Service (INS) 100–101, 108
import tax 109, 111
insurance:
    automobile 175–76
    earthquake 90
    health 104, 140–41
Internet 89
Italians 12, 35

Japanese 41, 133

INDEX

Koreans 133
Krug, Charles 233

Latinos 12, 26, 44–45, 50, 56, 117
laundromats 91–92
Levi Strauss & Company 13, 21
libraries 138–39

maps:
    California State Automobile Association (AAA/Triple A) 162, 172
    counties 58
    districts 28
    San Francisco streets 160
medicine 111–12, 143–44
Mexicans 100
Mission Dolores 20
movie theaters 297–98
museums 288

nature rambles 247–50
newspapers 93–94
North American Free Trade Agreement (NAFTA) 103

parking 74, 172–74
    Department of Parking 173
parks 20, 27, 34, 40, 51, 53–54, 247–49
    dog running areas 263
    see also environmental associations, Recreation and Parks Department
pets 111
pharmacies 143–44
population statistics 12, 21, 22
    education 117
postal service 89
pubs and breweries 238–39

radio 88
real estate agents 73, 79–80
Recreation and Parks Department 130–31
    Latchkey Program 128
religious centers 95–97
rent/rental:
    control 70–71
    listings 72–74
    procedure 74–75
    rates: *see* apartment complexes, districts and neighborhoods
    short-term 75–76
    residential hotels 77

restaurants:
    breakfasts 201–202
    California Cuisine 181, 189–93
    Chinese 206–12
    dim sum 211–12
    dress code 184
    Italian and pizza 197–99
    Japanese 212–13
    Latin American 196–97
    live music 29394
    making reservations 183–84
    newspaper surveys 182
    opening times 185
    ordering wine 235
    Pan-Asian 215
    prices 186–87
    San Francisco cuisine 188–89
    seafood 193–94
    Southeast Asian 213–14
    takeouts 200–201, 230–31
    vegetarian and kosher 194–95
    see also coffeehouses
roommate services 84–85
Russians 12, 54, 133

schools 114–27
    bilingual education 117
    charter schools 119–20
    Child Development Program 123, 127
    English-as-a-Second Language (ESL) 117
    English-language proficiency 119
    English-language schools 133–34
    Gifted and Talented Education (GATE) 117
    Open Enrollment Request (OER) 118, 121
    Parent Information Center, Educational Placement Center 118
    placement process 118–19, 121
    preschools 122–24
    private schools 116, 124–27
    public schools 115, 117, 121–22
    San Francisco Unified School District (SFUSD) 115, 116
    School Match 116
    specialized and technical 136–37
shopping:
    Asian food 220–23
    bakeries 224–26
    bookshops 280–83

INDEX

    cheese 226
    children's clothing, toys, etc. 273–74
    clothing 270–72
    coffee beans 229–30
    computers 283
    discount stores 44, 219–20, 272–73
    districts 265–67
    ethnic delicatessens 223–24
    factory outlets
    fish 226–28
    hardware and other household items 276–80
    health food 219
    kosher meat 229
    malls 268–70
    meat and poultry 228–29
    outdoor markets 216–17
    plants 280
    sports clothing and gear 275
    supermarkets 218–20
    wine 236–38
Silicon Valley 9, 66, 150
smoking 187
Spanish 19–20, 44, 233
spas 262–63
sports:
    baseball 244
    basketball 245, 260
    billiards 261
    bowling 260
    football 245
    golf 258–59
    horse racing 245–46
    horseback riding 261
    ice-skating 261
    inline skating 251–52
    martial arts and yoga 262
    news 244
    rock climbing 262
    running 246
    skiing 259–60
    soccer 245
    swimming and water sports 254–56, 258
    tennis 254

Stonestown Galleria 55
storage lockers 97–98
streets 161–62
    "diamond lanes" 171
    one-way 171
    street cleaning 173
student housing 84
suburbs 61–67

telephone service 87–88
television 88
tipping 187
TOEFL (Test of English as a Foreign Language) 104, 133
toilets, public 177
tourist information:
    Napa Valley Visitors Bureau 234
    San Francisco Convention & Visitors Bureau 18
    Sonoma Valley Visitors Bureau 234
transportation:
    BART 60, 166
    buses and ferries 168–69
    cable car 24–25, 165–66
    handicapped access 177
    MUNI (Municipal Railway) 164–65
    taxis 169–70
travel agents 105

United States Information Agency (USIA/USIS) 103
universities 43, 55, 57, 61, 67, 134, 135–36

visas 101–104
voting 97

walking 163–64, 246
whale watching 249
wine bars 235–36
wine country 232–35
women: health care 144–45
Women's Initiative for Self Employment (WISE) 155